America's Counter-Revolution

AMERICA'S COUNTER-REVOLUTION
The Constitution Revisited

SHELDON RICHMAN

Griffin & Lash
Ann Arbor, Michigan

Published by
Griffin & Lash
Ann Arbor, Michigan

This book was printed in the United States of America
on acid-free paper.

This is the third, corrected, printing of this book.

ISBN 978-0692687918

Sheldon Richman.
America's Counter-Revolution: The Constitution Revisited
1. Constitutional history—United States 2. Constitutional law—United States 3. Anarchism I. Title

To the constitutionalists of all parties

"A nation which makes greatness its polestar can never be free; beneath national greatness sink individual greatness, honor, wealth and freedom. But though history, experience and reasoning confirm these ideas; yet all-powerful delusion has been able to make the people of every nation lend a helping hand in putting on their own fetters and rivetting their own chains, and in this service delusion always employs men too great to speak the truth, and yet too powerful to be doubted. Their statements are believed—their projects adopted—their ends answered and the deluded subjects of all this artifice are left to passive obedience through life, and to entail a condition of unqualified non-resistance to a ruined posterity."

—ABRAHAM BISHOP (1800)

Contents

Foreword

This much I can assure the reader: after reading this book, you will never think about the U.S. Constitution and America's founding the same way again. Sheldon Richman's revealing and remarkably well-argued narrative will permanently change your outlook.

Richman, one of this country's most treasured thinkers and writers, digs through a period of American history that manages to be almost invisible to most people. He brings the whole period to life in ways that upset core tenets of the American civic religion.

If you ask the average American to summarize the founding in a few minutes, you will hear a story about a bad foreign king, a tea party, a defiant declaration, a war, and then the immaculate conception of the glorious U.S. Constitution that has guarded our liberty ever since. The entire period called "the founding" is smashed together into one short span, from conception to birth to the greatest document in the history of humankind. At best, the short period between the war and the Constitution is dismissed as merely transitional.

As it turns out, there's a missing 12 years in this conventional account: the time between when the Articles of Confederation were sent to the states for ratification and its replacement in 1789 by the new Constitution. What were the Articles? Why were they replaced? Who replaced them? Was there a debate, and did opponents make valuable points? These are the questions that Richman addresses here. In doing so, he draws on the most contemporary and important scholarly research, while putting the evidence in prose that is accessible and compelling.

His argument at first appears shocking. The small elite who won the day didn't actually share the values and ideals that drove the war for independence from Britain. These "founders" plotted and schemed to impose a new government that dramatically enhanced and centralized government power. Their stroke of genius in pulling off this coup d'etat was selling the Constitution as a means of guaranteeing freedom and limiting government. In fact, it was the opposite: the imposition of a new statist yoke to replace the one just cast off; the complete reversal of a hard-won freedom.

Provocative, isn't it? Yet it's all true. Also striking is Richman's thorough documentation of the arguments of the Constitution's opponents, the Anti-Federalists. (These terms can become very confusing. The so-called Federalists were actually the centralists, while the anti-federalists were dedicated to the decentralist ideals of the federalist tradition.) As it turns out, the Anti-Federalists warned about the provisions of the Constitution that they believed would eventually erode rights and liberties. They went further to explain that the structure of the Constitution itself was designed to achieve this very result, benefitting a ruling class at the expense of the people.

While today's conservatives are routinely shocked at how government violates the Constitution, Richman has a different take: the intrusive and parasitical government we have today was baked into the original design, which is precisely why Richman argues that the Anti-Federalists were right all along. As for the protection of rights and liberties that comes from the most famous section of the Constitution, the Bill of Rights, it wasn't even part of the original draft sent to the states for ratification.

To reduce the argument here to its essence: the Constitution, far from limiting government, was actually designed to bring about a new one that betrayed the ideals of the Declaration of Independence itself. The ratification of the Constitution was a counter-revolution. There is a reason it has done a poor job in protecting freedom: it was never intended to do so.

Finishing his detailed and exciting argument, Richman turns to the alternative. Must we reject constitutions completely? Not at all. We just need to dispense with the myth that a state can be restrained by a document. What actually restrains power in society is freedom itself, and that includes freedom over the choice of rules we adopt in regulating our lives. Under freedom, these rules are emergent and evolutionary, subject to a market test of trial and error and unending exploration of better ways of living and getting along.

The careful reader will detect in Richman's conclusion the emergence of a highly sophisticated and distinctly 21st century form of libertarianism. For him liberty is not an alternative set of central plans, pre-packaged laws, and visions of justice and truth that are imposed from above by wise intellectuals who know what's what. Richman's libertarian anarchism defers to the wisdom of social processes themselves.

In all my years of thinking about these topics, I've wondered if there was a way forward that could blend the best of the insights of Albert Jay Nock, F.A. Hayek, Ayn Rand, Murray Rothbard, and contemporary polycentric legal theorists. Must we follow some one thinker to the end or can we extract their best insights to improve our conception of what freedom looks like? In so many ways Richman has provided that answer. He has done it, and it's a breath of fresh air.

On a personal note, Richman has been a mentor to me since I first started really thinking, and I know this because he is the person who taught me how. For longer than a year I was privileged to spend time with him talking about ideas. In this period he taught me to avoid dismissive slogans and preset dogmas. He taught me how to be at once open to new ideas and committed to permanent principles. Time and again I saw him as a model of how to think through issues carefully, drawing on logic, experience, and evidence. As the years have gone by I've seen how he has maintained this intellectual discipline, never becoming lazy about his thinking but rather finding delight in the process of coming to ever greater understanding. He never ceases to challenge us to new heights of intellectual integrity and rigor.

It was sometime in the last year or two that I had dinner with him and a few friends. Around the table he dazzled us all with his insight and erudition. As usual he was as interested in what we were thinking as he was eager to express his own thoughts. His powerful mind was on display as I had never seen it. Everyone felt enlightened and delighted. We paid the bill and left.

Outside the restaurant we said goodbye, and I walked one way while he went the other. I stopped and watched him walk away and briefly teared up with the full realization of the treasure we have in our midst. He seemed at the moment to be a living representative of a great tradition. In my imagination I saw Nock, Thomas Paine, Frank Chodorov, Murray Rothbard. I blinked and saw something even more wonderful:

my own friend, as unique and brilliant an exemplar of the ideas of liberty as we could ever hope to have among us.

I can't fully express just how honored I am to have been invited to write the foreword to this powerful book. I am deeply in Sheldon's debt. After you read this book, you too will join the ranks of his many intellectual proteges.

—JEFFREY A. TUCKER
Liberty.me and Foundation for Economic Education

Introduction

But whether the Constitution really be one thing, or another, this much is
certain—that it has either authorized such a government as we have had, or
has been powerless to prevent it.
      —Lysander Spooner, "The Constitution of No Authority"

This is not a history of the U.S. Constitution or the founding of the
American republic. Rather, it is a brief against the proposition that
the Constitution was a landmark in the long and continuing struggle
for liberty. Sadly, it was not. Instead, it was a counter-revolution, in many
ways a reversal of the radical achievement represented by America's break
with the British empire. The constitutional counter-revolution was the
work not of radicals, but of *conservatives* who sought, in the words of
Robert Morris, the ambitious nationalist Superintendent of Finance
under the Articles of Confederation, a nation of "power, consequence,
and grandeur." These men understood that the government of such a
nation-state must have the unlimited power to tax, to maintain a permanent debt through a central bank, to regulate and promote trade, and
to keep a standing army—all of which was secured, extra-legally and
duplicitously, through the process that delivered the U.S. Constitution.
Of course, the power to tax, which the Confederation government
lacked, was the key, for without it, none of the rest could be accomplished. As historian E. James Ferguson put it, "Proceeding rigidly by
the axiom that related sovereignty with revenue power, the founding
fathers crowned the new government with unlimited powers of taxation" (*The Power of the Purse*, 1961).

That the nationalists were motivated in part by an exaggerated fear
of democracy in the states should be no excuse in the eyes of libertarians
for their maneuvering to create a new central government, far from the
people's watchful eyes, with vast and broad powers. The nationalists
would have sought those same powers regardless of how the state legis-

latures had conducted their business, because a loose federation of states under the Articles of Confederation could never have given the nationalists what a unified, essentially de-federalized state could provide.

How can libertarians look on this conservative, even reactionary achievement with fondness? This book will attempt to show that they should not.

Like most Americans and libertarians, I started out with a favorable attitude toward the Constitution, believing that it indeed was a landmark in the struggle for liberty and that it served well as a protector of our rights until, intentionally or not, it was misinterpreted and twisted into a weapon against liberty. My embrace of the libertarian philosophy in the late 1960s did not change this attitude. For quite a while after that moment, I maintained my respect for what the framers had done in Philadelphia from May to September 1787 and for what the state ratifiers did thereafter.

But slowly, over time, my view changed, and I began to see the Constitution as the product of a counter-revolution. My revisionism was fueled by my exposure to political theory, much of it anarchist, including that of Murray Rothbard and Lysander Spooner, but also by my reading of history, as the following pages will show.

I hasten to note that one's view of the Constitution need not depend on whether one rejects all government, as an anarchist does. After all, the opponents of the Constitution were not, to our knowledge, anarchists. They opposed vague and concentrated government power far from the people over a large territory, but not, alas, power per se. They accepted the states' exercise of power—that is, the initiation of force—including the power of taxation, perhaps believing with Thomas Paine that government is "a necessary evil." Contrary to James Madison's famous and then-novel view that liberty could be best safeguarded in a large republic, many Anti-Federalists, the dubious term given to all critics of the centralist scheme embodied in the Constitution, stood with Montesquieu, in believing that a free republic had to be a small republic, in which a homogeneous people could know their governors personally and keep a close watch on them. (They would have rejected as a false alternative the Tory clergyman Mather Byles's question: "Which is better—to be ruled by one tyrant three thousand miles away or by three thousand tyrants one mile away?"—a question made famous by Mel Gibson in *The Patriot*.)

The critics were not even consistent limited-government advocates of laissez faire, according to which the state did nothing more than keep the peace so the marketplace could operate for the benefit of all. Revealingly, Anti-Federalist Patrick Henry complained that the new Constitution would leave the states little to do but "take care of the poor—repair and make high-ways—erect bridges, and so on, and so on." This reveals that taking care of the poor, as well as administering the infrastructure, was a normal function of state and local government. So much for the proposition that welfare-state measures were something new in 1933. They may have been new at the national level, but not at the state level. (For more on this, see Jonathan Hughes's *The Governmental Habit Redux: Economic Controls from Colonial Times to the Present* [1991].)

Nevertheless, in my view, the men called Anti-Federalists were closer to libertarianism than their nationalist adversaries, who called themselves (with some disingenuousness) Federalists. (Elbridge Gerry, who wanted the Constitution amended before it was adopted, thought that better terms for the opposing sides were *ratificationists* and *anti-ratificationists*, or, for short, *rats* and *anti-rats*.) The Anti-Federalists would have endorsed what Jeffersonian Republican Abraham Bishop of Connecticut would say a dozen years later: "A nation which makes greatness its polestar can never be free." As Max M. Edling wrote in *A Revolution in Favor of Government: Origins of the U.S. Constitution and the Making of the American State* (2003): "It makes sense to see Antifederalism as an anti-statist argument against the formation of a 'fiscal-military state' in America." In general, these were men who distrusted men with power, especially elites at a distance. As proto-Public Choice theorists, they understood that under-determinate constitutional language would tend to be interpreted and wielded by those with the greatest interest in enlarging government power, while the rest of the population was busy making a living and raising families. This was less of a problem (though still a problem) when government was simple and close, but they thought it was intolerable with a complicated governmental system far away, in which "representatives" from large districts would most likely be drawn from society's aristocracy.

Yet we must be careful. As Pauline Maier shows in *Ratification: The People Debate the Constitution, 1787-1788* (2010), this was no simple contest pitting two distinct teams against each other. Each side consisted of men holding a range of views; the range was clearly larger on the Anti-Federalist side. The advocates of ratification had their differences, but they all wanted the special state ratifying conventions to approve the plan for the new government, even if some hoped for amendments. But the Anti-Federalists held diverse views. Some wanted an outright rejection of the Constitution, favoring instead modest amendments to the Articles of Confederation to strengthen the national government with a limited power to tax and to regulate and promote trade. Others called for amendments to the Constitution before ratification. Still others favored ratification with amendments to follow in the first Congress. Some believed that blocking ratification was hopeless—the convention and the Constitution had the blessing of the most popular man in the country and the presumptive first president, George Washington—so they worked for second-best solutions.

Despite the differences, everyone in the critical camp favored the union (contrary to Federalist charges that the Anti-Federalists were foreign agents seeking to divide the United States into several confederations) and supported strengthening the central government to some extent. In other words, they conceded that there were problems with the existing system that needed addressing at the national level, a major concession that probably guaranteed their defeat.

Yet they had something even more important in common: their suspicion of concentrated power and their consequent view that the confederation of states should not be scrapped for a "consolidated" system in which, as Federalist Papers coauthor John Jay put it, the states would be equivalent to counties in the states, subordinate to the national government.

This was no melodrama, with Dudley Do-Right on one side and Snidely Whiplash on the other. History is rarely so black and white. Federalists had valid concerns about the future of liberty, including property rights, at the hands of state legislatures, which exercised the power to grant debt relief, emit paper money, and enact other forms of wealth transfers. But these concerns were likely exaggerated. (Also see chapter 1 for how a successful grassroots tax rebellion spurred the nationalists.) It's hard to know how frequently the states tampered with loan contracts or violated property rights, although it occurred to some extent. But it's reasonable to expect that a state known for interfering with property and contracts would lose vital and entrepreneurial individuals to those states that abstained from or minimized interfering. Who would continue to lend money in a state where the legislature would without warning grant relief to borrowers or stay court judgments on behalf of creditors? In other words, such problems would tend to work themselves out as long as states respected freedom of exit and people could vote with their feet. Creating a central government with virtually unlimited powers (despite what its backers said) seems a strange way to prevent abuses by state legislatures.

If outright confiscations of property were routinely perpetrated, we can ask the same question we asked about debt relief. Competition among states for investment, in time, should have discouraged flagrant violations of property rights. But we cannot rule out that the confiscations that occurred had something to do with the acquisition of property that did not meet Lockean standards. "Much loyalist property," Arthur A. Ekirch Jr. wrote in *The Decline of American Liberalism* (1955), "found its way into the hands of a new group of wealthy landed proprietors." Government-based land speculation was common. War, Randolph Bourne counseled, is the health of the state. It's also the health of war profiteers. That goes for revolutionary wars too.

As for paper money, which at the time few people objected to, the story is more complicated. Several states used moderately depreciating fiat currency to keep tax rates low or in lieu of taxation altogether. In other words, the transfer of purchasing power from the people to the state via paper money substituted for the armed taxman, who could show up at the door and confiscate property for nonpayment. This is no endorsement of government fiat money or taxation, but since those were the only feasible options, paper money worked reasonably well in many, but not all, places. After all, times were different then: most working people were farmers who could avoid the money economy without much inconvenience. This aspect of the story does teach one lesson: fiat money and war are a dangerous combination.

(Before the Revolution, Americans at all socioeconomic levels got angry when the Parliament passed prohibitions on legal-tender laws in regard to state-issued paper money in the colonies. Contrary to libertarian assumption, Americans liked their paper money. The Constitution later barred the states from issuing it because of the bad experience with the wartime Continental currency, but it did not stop the states from chartering banks that could print notes, which they commonly did. As a result, growing America was awash in paper money after the Constitution took effect: "By 1819," Gordon S. Wood wrote in *The Radicalism of the American Revolution* (1991), "Alexander Baring, the head of the great British financial family, could tell a committee of the British House of Commons that 'the system of a paper currency has been carried to a greater extent in America than in any other part of the world.'")

Just as some Federalists had (in part) good motives for favoring the Constitution, so some Anti-Federalists no doubt had bad motives for opposing it. For example, Southern patrician opponents might have feared that a strong national government would limit or abolish slavery. And Anti-Federalists who were prominent in their state governments might not have liked their positions downgraded as the states became less important in a consolidated political system. (Federalists unjustly made this charge against particular Anti-Federalists.)

The upshot is that there could have been honorable and dishonorable reasons to take either side. Similar people—such as creditors and debtors, planters, and merchants—could be found in both camps. The Federalist side may well have been an example of Bruce Yandle's "Baptists and bootleggers" phenomenon harkening back to Prohibition, that is, an alliance of those who believed (or publicly emphasized) a moral case for the Constitution and those who expected to benefit materially from it. We should not rule out that a given individual was both a "Baptist" and a "bootlegger."

As usual, this history is complicated. But that should not overshadow the fact that leading Federalists, those most responsible for the Constitution as written, were looking for more in a fortified central government than mere protection of life and property from hyperactive state legislators. The leading Federalists wanted a strong central government and a consolidated system because they understood those things were necessary for a continental and even hemispheric market-empire (Indians, Britons, Spaniards, French, and Russians had to be removed one way or another) and a commercial world power reaching to Asia. They sought national greatness, a new empire (to be sure, with elements of liberal republicanism) to replace the exhausted empires of the Old World.

And the leading Anti-Federalists were no mere radical democratic defenders of provincialism trying to thwart the inevitable flow toward cosmopolitanism. Contrary to common impression, they embraced commerce and world trade—albeit as mercantilists, like their Federalist counterparts. (Adam Smith's *The Wealth of Nations* was just a decade old and not widely read.) They distrusted political power per se, which they associated with aristocracy, even if they could not imagine a society without it at all. If there had to be power, they thought, let it be limited and exercised over a small area through many representatives watched closely by the people—for large districts and small legislatures would mean ersatz representation, that is, rule by an elite wielding vague and effectively unlimited power. Contrary to what some historians (Charles Beard and Jackson Turner Main, for example) have believed, Herbert J. Storing wrote in *What the Anti-Federalists Were For* (1981),

> There were very few "democrats" among the Anti-Federalist writers (or probably among Americans of any kind), if by that is meant those who believe simply that the will of the majority of the people is law and that will ought to be exercised as directly and with as little restraint as possible. However, the Anti-Federalists *were* typically more democratic than the Federalists in the specific sense that they were less likely to see majority faction as the most dangerous and likely evil of popular government. They were inclined to think, with Patrick Henry, that harm is more often done by the tyranny of the rulers than by the licentiousness of the people. Moreover, so far as there may be a threat of licentiousness, it is to be met in the same way, fundamentally as the threat to [sic] tyranny: by the alert public-spiritedness of the small, homogeneous, self-governing community.

Likewise, historian Cecelia Kenyon earlier wrote ("Men of Little Faith: The Anti-Federalists on the Nature of Representative Government," *William and Mary Quarterly*, January 1955),

> The Anti-Federalists were not latter-day democrats....They were not confident that the people would always make wise and correct choices in either their constituent or electoral capacity, and many of them feared the oppression of one section in the community by a majority reflecting the interests of another. Above all, they consistently refused to accept legislative majorities as expressive either of justice or of the people's will. In short, they distrusted majority rule, at its source and through the only possible means of expression in governmental action over a large and populous nation, that is to say, through representation.... Their philosophy was primarily one of limitations on power....

Indeed, the Anti-Federalist using the name Agrippa (James Winthrop) spoke for many when he said that a bill of rights, which the Constitution as written lacked, would "serve to secure the minority against the usurpation and tyranny of the majority." These were no majoritarians.

But were they nevertheless "men of little faith," as Kenyon dubbed them? If vast, virtually unlimited power on a national scale was what they were being asked to have faith in, then yes, and proudly so. The Federalists repeatedly argued that since the needs of the new nation were unlimited, power too must be so. "The means, the Federalists argued again and again, must be proportioned to the end, and the end in the case of the general government is not capable of being limited in advance," Storing wrote. "As bounds cannot be set to a nation's wants, so bounds ought not to be set to its resources." As Alexander Hamilton, the staunchest of nationalists, wrote in Federalist 23:

> For the absurdity must continually stare us in the face of confiding to a government the direction of the most essential national interests, without daring to trust it to the authorities which are indispensable to their proper and efficient management. Let us not attempt to reconcile contradictions, but firmly embrace a rational alternative.

This was one of the Federalists' favorite arguments in favor of a standing army. (See chapter 3.) These men were not for limited government except in the most abstract way. To be sure, they favored due process in a constrained republican system ("the rule of law") over arbitrariness, but that is not the same as strict limits on power and scope. When Madison wrote in Federalist 51, "You must first enable the government to control the governed; and in the next place oblige it to control itself," it was as if he were saying the genie had to be let out of the bottle in order to restrain it.

The Anti-Federalists were skeptical, as they should have been. One would expect any libertarian to be sympathetic to those who had little faith in such an argument. Unfortunately, the Anti-Federalists shared too many Federalist premises to adequately meet the argument, although they tried valiantly to expose what the nationalists were up to: "They charged that the Federalists were more or less deliberately using an argument about means to enlarge the ends of government," Storing wrote, "shifting their gaze from individual liberty to visions of national empire and glory." Indeed, they were. They essentially said that the time had come to end the preoccupation with liberty, which was useful in the striving for independence, and turn to more important things now: nation-building.

At the New York ratifying convention, Hamilton said:

In the commencement of a revolution which received its birth from the usurpations of tyranny, nothing was more natural than that the public mind should be influenced by an extreme spirit of jealousy. To resist these encroachments, and to nourish this spirit, was the great object of all our public and private institutions. The zeal for liberty became predominant and *excessive*. In forming our Confederation, this passion alone seemed to actuate us, and we appear to have had no other view than to secure ourselves from despotism. The object certainly was a valuable one, and deserved our utmost attention; but, sir, there is another object, equally important, and which our enthusiasm rendered us little capable of regarding: I mean a principle of *strength* and *stability* in the organization of our government, and *vigor* in its operations. [Emphasis added.]

Benjamin Rush, a signer of the Declaration of Independence, member of the Pennsylvania ratifying convention, and the father of American psychiatry, took this a step further: he diagnosed "the excess of the passion for liberty" as a mental illness. "The extensive influence which these opinions [excited by the excess passion for liberty] had upon the understandings, passions and morals of many of the citizens of the United States," Rush said, "constituted a species of insanity, which I shall take the liberty of distinguishing by the name of Anarchia." To tamp down the potential for this disease, Rush advised that pupils be taught that they were "public property."

Storing emphasized the Federalists' subtleness in changing the agenda:

Indeed, the stress placed by Federalists on national defense and a vigorous commercial policy often seemed to mask a radical shift in the direction from the protection of individual liberty to the pursuit of national riches and glory. When the Anti-Federalists saw the new Constitution defended as having the "noble purposes" to make us "respectable as a nation abroad, and rich as individuals at home' and as calculated to promote "the grandeur and importance of America, until time shall be no more," they feared for the principles of the American governments. "You are not to inquire how your trade may be increased," Patrick Henry warned, "nor how you are to become a great and powerful people, but how your liberties can be secured; for liberty ought to be the direct end of your Government.'"

Henry, who worked overtime to keep things on track, went on:

Shall we imitate the example of those nations who have gone from a simple to a splendid Government? Are those nations more worthy of our imitation? What can make an adequate satisfaction to them for the loss they have suffered in attaining such a Government—for the loss of their liberty? If we admit this Consolidated Government, it will be because we like a great splendid one. Some way or other we must be a great and mighty empire; we must

have an army, a navy, a number of things: When the American spirit was in its
youth [This was in 1788!], the language of America was different: Liberty, Sir,
was the primary object. [These words would be more inspiring had Henry,
like other southern Anti-Federalists, not owned slaves.]

When Federalists admonished Anti-Federalists about lacking confidence in the virtuous men who would govern, the Anti-Federalists
scoffed. Anticipating Thomas Jefferson's language in the Kentucky Resolution protesting the Federalists' Alien and Sedition Acts 10 years later,
they responded that confidence was not the appropriate disposition for
free people toward the government. What is? Jealousy. "They ought to
be so [jealous]," an Anti-Federalist said. "It was just they should be so;
for jealousy was one of the greatest securities of the people in a republic." Moreover, Agrippa added for good measure, "let us not flatter ourselves that we shall always have good men to govern us."

The Anti-Federalists could not discuss power without expressing
their distaste for aristocracy. If they seem like radical democrats, it may
be because they opposed rule by aristocrats. The Revolution (as we'll
see) was as much an internal struggle against a conservative elite as an
external struggle against the British. Aristocracy in the new nation was
no imaginary nemesis. The Federalists complained that with the break-
down in social distinctions achieved through the Revolution (apparel
no longer indicated who was well-born and who was not), the wrong
sort of people were populating the state legislatures, people who actually
worked for a living. The remedy was a national government, which for
various reasons would favor prominent wealthier men. In Wood's words,
the new system would "act as a kind of sieve" to exclude those who
were "unfit" to govern wisely and dispassionately with an eye to the
general welfare. To be sure, America's aristocracy was seen as a "natural
aristocracy," one based not on heredity, but on education, virtue, and
merit, which was all the more reason to have a proper vetting process.
The Anti-Federalists were unimpressed.

In retrospect, the Anti-Federalists seemed destined to lose because
they conceded too much. (They were also handicapped, as Maier and
Wood documented, by newspaper bias toward the Federalists, who were
concentrated in the cities and towns.) Anti-Federalists objected to
power, but only up to a point. They were willing to accept a stronger
national government, and they accepted taxation, regulation, and other
government activism at the state and local level. This reduced the force

of their case against the Federalists. They were arguing not about power per se, but about which level of government should have the upper hand. That made the difference a matter of degree not kind, which gave the advantage to the nationalists. "In any conflict between two men (or two groups) who hold the same basic principles," Ayn Rand wrote in "The Anatomy of Compromise, "it is the more consistent one who wins." Unfortunately, the Federalists were the more consistent.

The Anti-Federalists also were plagued by (at least apparent) contradictions. Some complained that the proposed new government would be too complicated to be monitored by average people, enabling the rulers to escape responsibility; others said it was not complicated enough—that it lacked sufficient checks and balances. This conflict could perhaps be reconciled by the belief (Storing suggests) that if simple government was out of the question, the second-best position was a government of effective checks and balances—which this new government would not be. Moreover, many Anti-Federalists made the dubious argument that small republics were better protectors of liberty because their populations were homogeneous: that is, a wide harmony of interests would avert battles for political advantage. But as the Federalists point out, small territories don't necessarily have homogenous interests; farmers, merchants, and manufacturers, for example, have different interests that clash in a political arena that permits wealth transfers. The existing states already demonstrated this truth.

The dispute about levels of government, however, introduces a topic worth considering briefly. James Madison, an author of the Federalist Papers, said the states and other local authorities should be tolerated "so far as they can be subordinately useful." He and other leading nationalists wanted the Constitution to include a congressional power to veto state laws; and they did not like that states were to be equally represented in the Senate, the members of which were to be elected by the state legislatures. In other words, they did indeed favor a consolidated system with a centralized government, and not a federation of states. This is confirmed by the absence in the Constitution of anything like Article II of the Articles of Confederation, which affirmed that "each state retains its sovereignty, freedom, and independence, and every power, jurisdiction, and right, which is not by this Confederation expressly delegated to the United States, in Congress assembled." Only the need to compromise at the Philadelphia convention kept Madison and his colleagues from getting all they wanted in these matters. But they were under no illusions: they knew that the boundary between the states and national government, like the boundaries between the three branches of the national government, had not been clearly drawn and would be determined politically in the years to come. Libertarian and conservative constitutional sentimentalists, or "fetishists," as Jeffrey Rogers Hummel calls them, display a naïveté on this score when they demand that the Constitution be interpreted either as the framers intended or as people understood it at the time.

For their part, Anti-Federalists were shocked, on seeing the preamble's first words, "We the People," that the Constitution was written not as though the union were a federation of sovereign states, but rather a single population to be ruled directly by a central government in an extended republic. "The question turns, sir on that poor little thing—the expression, We, the *people*, instead of the *states*, of America," Patrick Henry said. "States are the characteristics and soul of a confederation. If the states be not the agents of this compact, it must be one great, consolidated, national government, of the people of all states."

Samuel Adams made the same point more colorfully: "I confess, as I enter the Building I stumble at the threshold. I meet with a National Government instead of a Federal Union of Sovereign States."

This was not knee-jerk parochialism, for as Jacob T. Levy showed in *Rationalism, Pluralism, and Freedom* (2015), liberalism (broadly defined) has always had two conflicting approaches to protecting individual liberty and autonomy. One, the rationalist approach, stands for the proposition that liberty could best be protected by a central government applying a single liberal legal code directly to individuals over a large territory. Such a system would check potentially oppressive associations, both private and political. This is the approach of Voltaire, Thomas Paine, and John Stuart Mill, among others.

The other, pluralist, approach insists that liberty is best protected by a layered system in which a variety of associations stand between the individual and the central government to check its power. State and local governments were counted in this buffer of intermediate entities. We find this view espoused by Montesquieu, Tocqueville, and Lord Acton.

As Levy pointed out, on paper both approaches have virtues with respect to protecting the individual. But in reality (leaving aside obvious problems for libertarians like taxation), things work out differently, and each side has generally ignored the risks its own position presented. States are never disinterested justice-dispensing machines, for reasons, among others, captured by terms like *public choice*, *regulatory capture*, and *knowledge problem*. And private associations, including families, fraternal entities, and religious groups, can be oppressive and costly to escape, even when not outright aggressive. Unlike private groups, state and local governments, of course, can legally use aggressive force and hence were an even bigger danger.

So neither rationalism nor pluralism can guarantee the individual his or her liberty.

It's easy to see that the Federalists tended toward the rationalist camp and the Anti-Federalists toward the pluralist camp, though few individuals have ever been pure rationalists or pure pluralists. Some Federalists praised the move from the Articles of Confederation to the Constitution on the explicit grounds that the new national government would relate directly to the individual citizen. (This enthusiasm, however, was not necessarily out of a love of liberty; an independent power to tax people directly was understood to be the key to national greatness.) A direct central-state-to-citizen relationship is precisely what the Anti-Federalists feared; they saw the states, among other associations, as buffers between the individual and a distant ruling aristocracy. (Madison is a complicated case; as we've seen, he was not fond of the states, but he famously thought an extended republic would, in Levy's words, "multiply factions to make it difficult to assemble a majority coalition in favor of any particular partial interest." Charitably put, his was a horizontal rather than vertical pluralism. The reader may judge for himself or herself how that's worked out.)

Levy argued that these two approaches cannot be reconciled or transcended and that the risk to liberty comes from all directions. As long as governments exist, pluralism seems the better of the two approaches, primarily because the smaller the jurisdiction the cheaper the exit. The potential to vote with one's feet at least has some chance to exert pressure on state and local governments to minimize their burdens. The resulting competition ought somewhat to serve the cause of liberty. (Of course we today are in a different position from the Americans of 1787-88. Our political system has both rationalist and pluralist elements with no radical change in the offing. So our best hope, for now, is for each component to block the usurpations of the other.)

What was missing from the debate in the late 18th century was the anarchist perspective. By this I mean that neither side could imagine how order and prosperity could be achieved and sustained without government, state or national, without the initiation of force. Lacking this perspective, the Anti-Federalists handicapped themselves because, as noted, it meant they shared many premises about the necessity of government with the Federalists. When they were accused of favoring anarchy, they could only react defensively. No one could respond in effect: "Anarchy, yes. Chaos, no." The Anti-Federalists needed to assimilate fully the truth that Paine (who failed to assimilate it fully himself) would formulate a few years later *Rights of Man* (1792):

> Great part of that order which reigns among mankind is not the effect of government. It has its origin in the principles of society and the natural constitution of man. It existed prior to government, and would exist if the formality of government was abolished. The mutual dependence and reciprocal interest which man has upon man, and all the parts of civilised community upon each other, create that great chain of connection which holds it together. The landholder, the farmer, the manufacturer, the merchant, the tradesman, and every occupation, prospers by the aid which each receives from the other, and from the whole. Common interest regulates their concerns, and forms their law; and the laws which common usage ordains, have a greater influence than the laws of government. In fine, society performs for itself almost everything which is ascribed to government."

Government, Paine went on to say, "purloins from the general character of man, the merits that appertain to him as a social being."

Being a political document and hence the product of compromise, the Constitution contains enough ambiguity that at times it has furnished grounds for limiting government power. The subsequently appended Bill of Rights has helped in this regard, although it has not been an unmixed blessing, since it has also shifted the burden from justifying a claimed power to justifying an asserted right. (The Ninth Amendment's acknowledgement of unenumerated rights has not done the work some hoped it would do.) Nevertheless, we can be thankful that occasionally government-limiting interpretations have prevailed. Let's hope that becomes more common. But we should not overlook all the outrages that have been defended—and upheld by the Supreme Court—on the basis of one constitutional provision or another. There's simply no gainsaying Lysander Spooner's observation, quoted above: "But whether the Constitution really be one thing, or another, this much is certain—that it has either authorized such a government as we have had, or has been powerless to prevent it."

★★★

Most of the chapters of this book originated as TGIF (The Goal Is Freedom) columns I wrote over nearly 10 years for the websites of the Foundation for Economic Education and the Future of Freedom Foundation. Others were first published on my blog, *Free Association* (sheldonrichman.com), after the TGIF column moved there. In preparing the book I have added material, amplified points, and, I hope, removed unnecessary repetition. I hope the reader will forgive whatever overlap remains.

While I was turning out these articles, I was urged to be cautious because "people need their fairy tales." I took this to mean that most Americans grow up learning American history with a fairly libertarian slant, and we libertarians ought not undercut that narrative. If people believe that the Constitution is an extension of the Declaration of Independence, then all well and good. Keep your revisionism to private meetings.

That has long struck me as short-sighted and self-defeating. We do no one, especially young libertarians, any favors by leaving historical misconceptions intact. Nothing sets up budding libertarians for disillusionment more effectively than to send them into intellectual battle on campus armed with false history. It's like sending sheep to the slaughter, because sooner or later they will encounter professors and students who know better. The results won't be pretty. I speak from experience.

My interest in constitutional revisionism was sparked most directly by my friend and mentor Walter E. Grinder, after I wrote an article about the unconstitutionality of trade protectionism. He's been a source of encouragement and reading suggestions for a long time. I could not have written this book without the inspiring example set by one of my oldest friends, Jeffrey Rogers Hummel, a first-rate historian and economist. It was he who clued me in to the importance of the public-finance aspects of early American history, something I was inclined to underestimate. For many years I've benefited from conversations and email exchanges with him. In many respects this book would have never been produced without the help and concern of my friend Gary Chartier. Not only did he take on the task of laying out the book, designing the cover, and arranging for its publication, he contributed to the content through our near-daily discussions, his probing questions, and his gentle but constant imploring that I get the book done. Thanks, I needed that. And thanks, also, to Less Antman, whose friendship and generosity are beyond words. I'm especially grateful for the pleasant environment in which I was able to complete this book.

Over the years I had able copy-editing assistance and helpful suggestions from Michael Nolan, Mike Reid, and Chad Nelson. This printing, in particular, reflects the careful scrutiny of Beth Cody.

Finally, thanks to all who have supported my work through Patreon and PayPal.

Of course, any errors herein are my responsibility.

Writers get themselves into trouble when they set out to write the last word on a subject. I have no doubt that there's much more to be said on this subject, so let the conversation proceed!

1

Conceived in Tyranny

If the American Revolution was in some large measure a tax rebellion, we should appreciate the bitter irony that the U.S. Constitution was in some large measure a *reaction to* a tax rebellion. It's another reason we can reasonably view the move toward the Constitution—toward, that is, the concentration of power in a national government—as a counter-revolution and something for libertarians to abhor.

Shays's Rebellion was the mass tax resistance that lit a fire under conservative nationalists who were already looking for ways to concentrate power in the central government. They had long been frustrated with the weak quasi-government of the Articles of Confederation (1781-89), which amounted to a one-house congress with no power to tax or regulate trade, and no executive or judicial branches. (This is not to say it had no powers worth objecting to.) To be sure, Americans of the day had various economic and social problems—many caused or aggravated by active state governments—but collapse and chaos were not at hand, whatever the nationalists said. They assumed that only a strong central government could promote trade and cure the fiscal and monetary woes, but that's because they saw the European states as their only model. They also wanted a standing army ready to advance, if necessary, what they saw as America's commercial and geopolitical interests. They knew they would not get that from the states.

The nationalists started making progress toward their objectives in the early 1780s, when the war wasn't going well and foreign loans were needed. But as the war wound down to a successful conclusion, the nationalists, who hoped the conflict would go on long enough for them to achieve their centralist goals, lost their primary case for government expansion—especially the power to tax—and by 1783 they were in retreat. The wealthy merchant Robert Morris, whom Congress had named Superintendent of Finance, could not manage even to persuade all the states to allow the confederation government a 5 percent tariff. He had hoped for a general federal power to tax, and was willing to go to great lengths to secure it—even to solicit pressure from the government's creditors and, to nationalist George Washington's mind at least, disgruntled, unpaid military officers and troops at their Newburgh, New York, encampment. "He was convinced," E. James Ferguson wrote, "that the outburst at camp was hatched in Philadelphia and gave credence to rumors that Robert and Gouverneur Morris were at the bottom of it…. [Nationalist Alexander Hamilton] did not contradict the allegations against Robert and Gouverneur Morris, except to say that he himself might be accused of playing a deep game. It was no secret that he had tried to align the army with the public creditors." (See Ferguson's *The Power of the Purse* [1961].)

But the nationalists did not give up their dream of creating a European-style fiscal-military state—complete with aristocratic and monarchical elements—albeit one tailored to the American suspicion of centralized government power. As John Jay, coauthor of the Federalist Papers and America's first chief justice, put it, "Men will not adopt & carry into execution, measures the best calculated for their own good without the intervention of a coercive power. I do not conceive we can exist long as a nation, without having lodged somewhere a power which will pervade the whole Union in as energetic a manner, as the authority of the different state governments extends over the several States." (Quoted in Pauline Maier's *Ratification: The People Debate the Constitution, 1787-1788* [2010].)

Then along came Capt. Daniel Shays. In 1786 a controlling faction of the Massachusetts legislature got the bright idea to retire its Revolutionary War debt in a mere 10 years. The legislators thought that they could copy their quick payoff program that followed the Seven Years' War, but they failed to take into account that the new per capita debt was far larger and that therefore the consequences of paying it off quickly would be devastating for the taxpayers. The policymakers "were rigid, unrealistic, and uncompromising in their effort to retire the public debt too rapidly given the magnitude of the state's obligations," Edwin J. Perkins wrote in *American Public Finance and Financial Services: 1700-1815* (1994).

While other states showed mercy to the taxpayers by spreading out debt retirement, thereby keeping tax rates in check, or by implicitly taxing the people by issuing paper money instead of imposing direct taxes, Massachusetts was tone deaf to the people's circumstances. Its burdensome poll and property assessments drove western Massachusetts farmers, many of whom got foreclosure notices when they couldn't pay their mortgages after paying their taxes, to revolt. Shays's Rebellion used to be described as a class revolt of debtors against mortgage lenders, a leveler movement, but the case that it was essentially a tax revolt has been solidly made by eminent historians of the period, as well as by contemporary observers.

Perkins wrote: "Despite the resolve of the urgency faction to coerce citizens into meeting the state's financial obligations in short order, signals of impending difficulties emerged in the mid-1780s. Tax arrearages grew year after year. Of the $930,000 assessed against persons and property between 1780 and 1782, nearly half was past due as late as December 1785. Between 1782 and 1786 additional taxes of $3.3 million were scheduled for collection, yet by October 1787 more than $1.4 million, or 40 percent, were past due. Under the state's internal revenue system, the locally elected tax collector in each town was held personally liable for the quota assigned by the state treasurer; and after July 1786 county sheriffs became liable for arrearages as well. To escape governmental claims against their own assets, collectors and sheriffs were forced to file suit against tax delinquents and to seize farms, crops, livestock, and other property when payments were not forthcoming."

As a result, "bands of rioters closed the courthouses in several inland towns during the second half of 1786 in a sustained effort to prevent evictions and forced sales of properties," Perkins wrote. "Under the leadership of Daniel Shays, a disgruntled and embittered farmer, armed civilians numbering perhaps two thousand, marched on the federal arsenal at Springfield in January 1787. In the brief battle, cannon fire killed three rebels and drove off the rest, but they soon regrouped."

When similar trouble had brewed in other states, the governments made conciliatory offers and the trouble subsided. Not in Massachusetts. Governor James Bowdoin called up over 4,000 troops and quashed the uprising within two months.

But that wasn't the end of it. "The elections of 1787 sent new blood to the legislature and a new governor, John Hancock.... Shaken by the threat to popular government, Hancock and legislative leaders belatedly abandoned the program of accelerated debt retirement and suspended the tax collections associated with that program. They sponsored tax reductions and private debt relief laws that gave middling citizens some breathing room. Tax assessments on persons and property dropped significantly from 1787 through 1790." (Massachusetts would later benefit from Treasury Secretary Alexander Hamilton's 1790 federal debt-assumption program.)

Thus the rebels won.

Shays's Rebellion might not look so earth-shaking in retrospect, but it scared the hell out of the nationalists—or at least they pretended it did—and they saw in the popular uprising an opportunity to press their centralist agenda. "The adherence to an irresponsible, impractical, and ultimately unnecessary program of fiscal policy in this solitary, critical state," Perkins wrote, "contributed to the renewed movement for a more permanent and more centralized national government with enhanced taxing power." According to Gordon S. Wood, "Shays's uprising in 1786 was only the climactic episode in one long insurrection, where the dissolution of government and the state of nature became an everyday fact of life. Indeed, it was as if all the imaginings of political philosophers for centuries were being lived out in a matter of years in the hills of New England" (*The Creation of the American Republic, 1776-1787* [1998]).

Wood also reported that "So relieved by the rebellion were many social conservatives that some observers believed the Shaysites were fomented by those who wanted to demonstrate the absurdity of republicanism. Nothing so insidious has been proved, but many social conservatives did see the rebellion as encouraging the move for constitutional reform," i.e., centralization.

Since the conservative nationalists favored aristocratic republican rule over the liberal democracy favored by the radicals, the conservatives would have been understandably alarmed at what had happened in Massachusetts. "Not only the fact of the rebellion itself," Wood wrote, "but the eventual victory of the rebels at the polls brought the contradiction of American politics to a head, dramatically clarifying what was taking place in all the states."

Sincere or not, this alarm was communicated to George Washington at his home in Mount Vernon. By this time Washington had been named by the Virginia assembly as a delegate to the coming federal convention in Philadelphia, but he was unsure whether he would go. Those reporting to him about Shays's Rebellion would have had reason to hope that by exaggerating the turmoil, they could motivate Washington, a nation-alist who favored a strong central government, to go to Philadelphia, giving the convention and resulting constitution a prestige no one else could have bestowed.

"Everything [is] in a state of confusion," David Humphreys wrote Washington. "Discontent was 'not confined to one state or to one part of a state' in the northeast, Henry Lee told Washington in September 1786 but pervaded 'the whole,'" Maier wrote. "...Washington's corre-spondents—above all Humphreys, [Henry] Knox, and General Benjamin Lincoln [who put down the rebellion], all old army officers—sent Wash-ington detailed reports slanted against the insurgents in Massachusetts." But, Maier added, "the problem was hardly as serious or as intractable as Knox had claimed. Washington, however, believed the frenzied reports he received." (By contrast, Rufus King calmly advised John Adams that the rebellion was a response to onerous taxes: "You will see this business greatly magnified and tories may rejoice, but all will be well.")

Wood noted, citing an observer, that "these rioters were not rabble.... They were country farmers under strong economic pressures, prompted by 'a certain jealousy of government, first imbibed in the beginning of our controversy with Britain, fed by our publications against the British government, and now by length of time became in a manner habitual and ready to rise whenever burthens press, at once concluding, that *bur-thens* must be *grievances*.'"

In other words, since the revolution had been in large part a tax re-bellion, Americans were in no mood to substitute a Yankee taxman for a British taxman. In several states before 1789, controlled emissions of paper money functioned as a satisfactory alternative to direct taxation; that is, the currency depreciation was moderate and undisruptive. The resulting implicit transfer of purchasing power from the people to state governments had advantages (assuming government exists)—for exam-ple, no taxman visited people's homes or seized property from delin-quent taxpayers.

Much of the Anti-Federalist case against the proposed Constitution focused on the new national government's virtually unlimited power to tax. For a host of reasons, however, Americans' abhorrence of taxation was not enough to thwart ratification. Thus the United States that emerged in 1789 was born in reaction to a tax rebellion, which is not exactly a libertarian pedigree.

2

The Constitution Revisited

W hy do so many people, including many libertarians, see the U.S. Constitution as a landmark achievement in the struggle for liberty? On principle alone, consistent advocates of liberty should have become wary in time. A document that is adored at virtually every position in the political firmament should arouse suspicion among libertarians.

Moreover a smattering of historical knowledge should have been enough to turn suspicion into outright skepticism. The Constitution was not the first constitution of the United States. Under the Articles of Confederation (for all its faults) the central quasi-government had *no power to tax* (hence my calling it a quasi-government), *regulate trade, or raise an army*. Money and soldiers had to be requisitioned from the states, which were often reluctant to comply. Under the second constitution the new government assumed those powers and more, including the express power to grant patents and copyrights (which necessarily interfere with rights in physical property) and unspecified or implied powers, such as the power of eminent domain. You'll not find this power to appropriate private property enumerated in the document proper, but thanks to the takings clause of the subsequently added Fifth Amendment (part of the "Bill of Rights"), which feebly limits the implied power with requirements regarding "public use" (now, under *Kelo* interpreted to include private use) and "just compensation," we know it is there (perhaps tucked into the necessary-and-proper clause). Considering this historical context alone, how could a libertarian adore such a document?

In practice the U.S. Constitution was a *tax, trade-regulation/promotion, and military project*. In furtherance of that objective, the machinery of government had to be constructed so that the right sort of people, virtuous and nationally minded, would get into power, unobstructed by the radical plebeians emboldened and liberated by the American Revolution. Hence the Federal Convention in Philadelphia in 1787.

The push for a new constitution came from conservative men who openly complained that America's problem lay in too little, not too much, central government. "The evils suffered and feared from weakness in Government have turned the attention more toward the means of strengthening the [government] than of narrowing [it]," James Madison, father of the second constitution, wrote to Thomas Jefferson. "It has never been a complaint agst. Congs. that they governed overmuch. The complaint has been that they have governed too little," James Wilson, an important but largely ignored nationalist, added. Earlier, John Jay, who along with Madison and Alexander Hamilton wrote, under the name "Publius," the series of pro-Constitution newspaper articles that came to be known as the Federalist Papers, said about central government power: "the more the better." Hamilton himself said, "The fundamental principle of the old Confederation [viz., sovereignty of the member states] is defective; we must totally eradicate and discard this principle before we can expect an efficient government." And Fisher Ames, an influential nationalist and participant at the Philadelphia convention, added, "Everyman of sense must be convinced that our disturbances have arisen more from the want of power than the abuse of it."

Further historical investigation reveals that the Constitution was put over on the American people by dubious means. After nationalists in some state legislatures began choosing delegates for a meeting in Philadelphia to address problems of government finance and trade, the Confederation Congress resolved that a convention should be held for the express purpose of amending the Articles. Under the Articles of Confederation, any amendment would have to be approved by the Congress and *all* 13 state legislatures. But once assembled, the convention, after locking the doors to the public, dispensed with an official record (though Madison and others kept notes), tossed out the Articles, and started from scratch, working from Madison's centralist Virginia Plan. Moreover new rules for ratification were included in the proposed Constitution: only nine states would need to ratify for it to take effect (for those states), and, crucially, the proposed constitution would be submitted not to the state legislatures but rather to specially elected conventions—driving home the point, later argued by the Anti-Federalists, that the new country was no longer a confederation of sovereign states but a "consolidated government." This prompted Patrick Henry to ask, "Who authorised them to speak the language of, *We, the People,* instead of *We, the States?*"

Little wonder Albert Jay Nock, in *Our Enemy the State* (1935), called the Philadelphia convention a coup d'etat.

If changing the rules was not bad enough, the misnamed Federalists handicapped the equally misnamed Anti-Federalists during the ratification debates with their control of the mail and influence over the newspapers. As Pauline Maier notes in *Ratification: The People Debate the Constitution, 1787-1788* (2010), most newspapers were in the cities, where merchants, who tended to favor the Constitution for its trade-promotion power, were concentrated. They did not look kindly on editors who published anti-Constitution articles. Editors who prided themselves on presenting a range of opinion "suffered verbal attacks, canceled subscriptions, and threats of mob violence." Anti-Federalist authors, who also risked reprisal, wanted to write under pennames, but some editors would not allow it, although Federalists were able to do this. Maier reports that "only twelve out of over ninety newspapers and magazines published substantial numbers of essays critical of the Constitution during the ratification controversy."

Speaking of the ratification debate, isn't it strange that libertarian constitutionalists ignore the most libertarian activists and commentators of the day—the Anti-Federalists—to keep their narrative intact? "The Antifederalists' opposition to the Constitution was an opposition to the creation of a central government, which they feared would become as heavy and as powerful as the governments of contemporary European states," Max M. Edling wrote in *A Revolution in Favor of Government: Origins of the U.S. Constitution and the Marking of the American State* (2003). "...The Antifederalist fear was that the Constitution would create a state that would bring about a growth of armies, taxes, and [permanent] public debt, as well as the concomitant strengthening of centralized power." And why did the Anti-Federalists fear these things? Because they would rob the people of their liberty, their individual rights.

This opposition sheds light on an important controversy. While it would be naïve to suggest that particular influential nationalists were oblivious to how a strong central government with unlimited taxing powers would serve their personal financial interests (say, by maximizing the value of their wartime government securities or western land claims), the presence of this incentive, however important, was hardly decisive or necessary. Even without an existing personal financial stake, the nationalists would have pushed for the Constitution and the centralization of power. They wanted a different nation from the one they had. (We should not overlook the self-regarding motive, however. "To eliminate entirely the role of economic motive in the political affairs of the time is as doctrinaire and as unnecessary as [Charles] Beard's overstatement of it," E. James Ferguson wrote. (See *The Power of the Purse* [1961]. On the controversy of financial motivation, see along with Ferguson, Charles Beard's *An Economic Interpretation of the Constitution of the United States*; Forrest McDonald's *We the People* [1992]; Robert A. McGuire's *To Form a More Perfect Union*; Edling's *A Revolution in Favor of Government*; and *Our Enemy the State*. Let us note that Federalists like James Wilson accused Anti-Federalists of having financial motives for opposing the Constitution.)

The nationalists sought a strong state with the power to tax, regulate and promote trade, and raise and maintain a standing army because in their eyes that is what "a great and respectable nation" (as one nationalist put it) required to deal with other world-class countries in pursuit of security and commerce. (This point is easily overlooked if Federalism is identified exclusively with Madison's aspiration to rein in the states.) "The Federalists ... argued that it was crucial that Congress was granted powers similar to those of European governments," Edling wrote. "The Antifederalists claimed that such a development would mean the end to popular liberty in America." Moreover, as Anti-Federalist Arthur Lee wrote to Samuel Adams, "Every engine is at work here to obtain permanent taxes."

This Anti-Federalist opposition alone, which was a well-articulated critique both of concentrated power and aristocracy, should make any champion of liberty suspicious of the Constitution. (The Bill of Rights came nowhere near addressing the Anti-Federalists' objections; see chapter four.)

The historian Gordon S. Wood shed even more unflattering light on the Constitution in his in his Pulitzer Prize-winning book, *The Radicalism of the American Revolution* (1993). Wood showed that as the 1780s wore on, the revolutionary leaders, Hamiltonian and Jeffersonian alike, were unhappy with how things were turning out in the new country. Both sides had hoped that the people would embody classical republican values and put the general welfare over their particular financial interests. To their dismay, people were more interested in improving their economic well-being than in contributing to the new nation's good. The Hamiltonians were especially upset that the public was taking its egalitarian, anti-aristocratic attitudes to such great lengths. They had not expected the common people to govern themselves directly. Rather, they (that is, propertied white males) were supposed to elect as their representatives detached wise, virtuous, and educated men who were immune to the vicissitudes of the marketplace. Democratic participation by common people was more acceptable to the Jeffersonians, but like the Hamiltonians, they lamented the preoccupation with commercial self-interest and the use of state legislatures to secure it. "By the 1780s," Wood wrote, quoting Yale College President Ezra Stiles, "it was obvious that 'a spirit of *locality*' was destroying 'the aggregate interests of the community.'" Government had been envisioned as an above-the-fray enlightened referee that balanced competing particular interests and served the general welfare. Instead it had become, to some extent, an auction house.

What to do? Convene a federal convention and try again. And that's what they did.

Those who wanted a new constitution reconciled themselves to the fact that people would inevitably put their own "narrow" interests first. According to Wood,

> Madison and others were now willing to allow these diverse competing interests free play in the continent-sized national republic created by the new Constitution of 1787. But Madison and the Federalists ... were not modern-day pluralists. They still clung to the republican ideal of an autonomous public authority that was different from the many private interests of the society.... They now knew that [quoting Madison's Federalist 10] "the regulation of these various interfering interests forms the principal task of modern Legislation," but they also hoped that by shifting this regulation to the national level these private local interests would not be able to dominate legislation as they had in the states and become judges in their own causes.

The advocates of the new constitution believed that a central government could play the umpire's role, Wood added, "because the men holding office ... would by their fewness of numbers be more apt to be disinterested gentry who were supported by proprietary wealth and not involved in the interest-mongering of the marketplace."

This point was critical. Common people were preoccupied with making a living. But those who were suited to govern did not have to work and therefore only they could be counted on, first, to ascertain the general interest and, second, to work unfailingly to achieve it. Hamilton made this argument even though he had to earn his living as a lawyer. When this was pointed out, he replied that lawyers were different from self-interested merchants, mechanics, and farmers. According to Hamilton, Wood wrote, "being a lawyer was not an occupation and was different from other profit-making activities." Lawyers and other professionals, Hamilton said, "truly form no distinct interest in society" and thus can be "an impartial arbiter" of everyone else's claims. Anti-Federalists scoffed at this, understanding that no ruling class could be expected to be disinterested.

The Federalists painted lurid pictures of legislative majorities representing the common people in the states running roughshod over the propertied minority. But wouldn't a national legislature be subject to the same problem? The Federalists thought that in an extended republic, particular interests would offset one another, mitigating the problem. But as Wood wrote in another book (*The Creation of the American Republic, 1776-1787* [1998]), "The Federalists were not as much opposed to governmental power in the states as to the character of the people who were wielding it."

This too should be enough to make libertarians wary about the second constitution. But there's more. Madison and other centralizers, Wood wrote in *The Radicalism of the American Revolution*, believed that what was missing in American government was a *monarchical* element. The revolutionary leaders were happy to be rid of the British monarchy, but they came to believe, in light of what I've described above, that perhaps they had thrown the baby out with the bathwater.

> Madison expected the new national government to play the same suprapolitical neutral role that the British king had been supposed to play in the empire. In fact, Madison hoped that the new federal government might restore some aspect of monarchy that had been lost in the Revolution.... That someone as moderate and as committed to republicanism as Madison should speak even privately of the benefits of monarchy adhering in the Constitution of 1787 is a measure of how disillusioned many of the revolutionary gentry had become with the democratic consequences of the Revolution.

The Madisonians later saw the judiciary as playing this neutral role, but the radicals feared that this meant rule by an unelected elite.

"In place of the impotent confederation of separate states that had existed in the 1780s," Wood wrote, the Federalists aimed to build a strong, consolidated, and prosperous 'fiscal-military' state in emulation of eighteenth-century England, united 'for the accomplishment of great purposes' by an energetic government composed of the best men in the society."

Thus the prime movers of the second constitution sought to reintroduce *hierarchy, aristocracy, and even elements of monarchy* in order to rein in the radical social and political egalitarianism that had made the American Revolution unique in world history. Why? We've already dealt with the question of personal interest, which is relevant but misleadingly narrow and determinist. However, the Revolutionary War debt played another role in motivating the move to centralization. Both the nationalists and decentralists understood that if the central government, rather than the state governments, assumed responsibility for the debt, loyalty and hence power would necessarily shift away from the states. This shift was indispensable to creating a new and enduring nation, indeed, an empire throughout North America if not the entire the Western Hemisphere. This was the goal of men such as Robert Morris, a member of the confederation Congress, a wealthy Philadelphia merchant, and a staunch nationalist, who as Superintendent of Finance worked under the Articles of Confederation to put in place a program that included a separate executive, congressional taxing power, a central bank, and a permanent debt. He mostly failed, but much of his scheme was enacted in the Constitution and subsequent measures. Treasury Secretary Alexander Hamilton carried out a federal debt-assumption program in 1790.

In "The Constitution as Counter-Revolution: A Tribute to the Anti-Federalists" (Libertarian Alliance, online at http://www.la-articles.org.uk /FL-5-4-3.pdf), Jeffrey Hummel summed up the situation:

> The nationalists ... vigorously opposed state assumption [of the war debt]; it was a method of paying off the debt that would diminish the prestige of the central government relative to the states and thereby threatened the nationalists' overriding objective. Morris effectively forestalled repudiation and, for the most part, state assumption. Lingering on, the national debt provided both a continuing rationale for national taxation and another special interest supporting such taxation.

It is revealing that the nationalists had tried to use the war to beef up the confederation government, for example with the power to tax. However, the war ended too soon for Morris's purposes: a "continuance of the war," he said, "is necessary until we shall acquire the habit of paying taxes." War is indeed the health of the state.

Libertarians of course would have rejected the nationalists without *fully* embracing the decentralist democrats, if indeed that's what they were. As noted, Cecelia M. Kenyon and other historians document that the leading Anti-Federalists were not majoritarians, but advocates of individual liberty. (This does not mean that people did not seek to use their state legislators for economic gain at the expense of others, of course.) At any rate, aristocracy versus economic democracy is a false alternative. The missing option is Adam Smith's "simple system of natural liberty": individual freedom rooted in natural rights and natural law. Both the nationalists and democrats would have claimed the ideal of self-government. However, neither construed this as literally *self*-government. The self is an attribute of individual human beings not of groups. In the political realm groups do not govern themselves. Some govern others.

The nationalists prevailed in that they secured their Constitution (albeit with compromises). However, Wood emphasized that things could have turned out worse.

> The Anti-Federalists lost the battle over the Constitution. But they did not lose the war over the kind of national government the United States would have for a good part, at least, of the next century. Their popular understanding of American society and politics in the early Republic was too accurate and too powerful to be put down—as the Federalists themselves soon came to appreciate. Even the elections for the First Congress in 1788 revealed the practical realities of American democratic life that contradicted the Federalists' classical republican dreams of establishing a government led by disinterested educated gentlemen.

But in time, despite setbacks here and there, the Federalists and their successors prevailed as the 19th century wore on. In many respects the second constitution fulfilled its unlibertarian purpose. It even delivered a standing army, despite Americans' distrust of the military. We turn to that matter next.

3
The Constitution and the Standing Army

The U.S. Constitution can reasonably be seen as a massive tax and mercantilist trade-promotion program. However, there's a third leg to this stool. It was a national-security program as well—almost a proto-PATRIOT Act. As historian Walter Millis wrote, "Though the point has not often been noticed, the Constitution was as much a military as a political and economic charter" (*Arms and Men: A Study in American Military History* [1956]). Indeed, these three elements formed an integrated project: it gave the new central government independent power to raise revenue by taxing individuals directly and to establish an army and navy in order to advance, by force if necessary, American trade. This, I submit, was not exactly a libertarian project.

While the nationalists saw military power as essential to the development of American commerce, the ability to raise an army and navy was intended to accomplish more than that; it was aimed at continental hegemony and national security in what was regarded as a hostile world. As Madison told the Virginia ratifying convention, America was surrounded by countries "whose interest is incompatible with an extension of our power and who are jealous of our resources to become powerful and wealthy. [They] must naturally be inclined to exert every means to prevent our becoming formidable." Thus the nationalists sought a permanent military establishment—albeit initially small—powerful enough that no nation would challenge the nation's interests (as interpreted by its rulers).

Whom did the Federalists fear? "The hostile nations the Federalists were talking about [Spain and England]," Max M. Edling wrote in *A Revolution in Favor of Government: Origins of the U.S. Constitution and the Making of the American State* (2003), "had dominions to the north and south of the union, while in the west they fuelled the animosity of the Indian nations."

It's odd, then, that many libertarians think an obsession with national security dates back only to the end of World War II and Harry Truman's National Security Act of 1947. In fact it goes back to the very beginning of the republic, when Americans who sought to expand the power of the central state warned that because America was exceptional, it faced constant danger from the old colonial powers and the Indian nations, whose lands Americans coveted. Security, the nationalists explained, required consolidation (rather than the loose "league of friendship" under the Articles of Confederation) and a ready peacetime military. Yes, a standing army was potentially dangerous, they said, and so need not be large; but America, as a unified extended republic secure between two oceans, would not have to fear a permanent military establishment.

Some libertarians believe that since Americans opposed a standing army, as the vocal Anti-Federalists did, the Constitution forbade it. That is not the case. No prohibition is to be found. On the contrary, the Third Amendment, which prohibits the quartering of troops in private homes without consent in peacetime, assumes the existence of a peacetime standing army. (Thanks to Gary Chartier for pointing out this connection.)

But that's the least that can be said. Congress was empowered virtually without qualification to raise an army and navy, the only restriction being that the military budget can be for no more than two years at a time: "Congress shall have the power to …To raise and support Armies [and] To provide and maintain a Navy." Moreover, control of the state militias was taken from the states and nationalized. (See Article I, Section 8. In 1783 the Confederation Congress created a committee, chaired by Alexander Hamilton, to plan for a peacetime army and navy. Committee member Madison was unconvinced that Congress had the power under the Articles of Confederation to carry out such a plan.)

These powers in the proposed Constitution outraged the Anti-Federalists. They pointed out that this shift in responsibility for defense to the national government would reduce the states to mere administrative districts. They also warned that a professional military could enforce federal tax and other laws, suppressing the liberty of Americans, who would be unable to resist because the militias would be gutted through federal neglect. Herbert Storing cautioned against reading the Anti-Federalists too literally on this point, suggesting that we "subsitut[e] 'bureaucracy' for 'standing army' [in their statements]. The Anti-Federalists were not so much worried about military coups or about 'militarism' in the popular sense, as about rigid rule of a large and varied republic by the force of government, of which the standing army is the ultimate expression" (*What the Anti-Federalists Were For* [1981]). Oddly, the Federalists responded that the Constitution would preclude federal coercion of the states because the new central government would "act directly upon citizens as individuals," as Arthur A. Ekirch Jr. explained in *The Civilian and the Military: A History of the American Antimilitarist Tradition* (1972). Small comfort for those citizens, of course.

The Federalists understood that most Americans were suspicious of a professional military, so the Federalists gave assurances that the armed forces would be small and stationed at the frontiers, where few people would see them. But the Anti-Federalists were not pacified. "My great objection to this Government is, that it does not leave us the means of defending our rights; or, of waging war against tyrants," Patrick Henry said. "Have we the means of resisting disciplined armies, when our only defence, the militia, is put into the hands of Congress?" Edling commented that "the argument that the Constitution would allow the national government to create a standing army in order to expropriate the people's property [through arbitrary taxation] shows that the Antifederalist objections to the Constitution were grounded in traditional Anglo-American individuals rights."

Another concern of the Anti-Federalists was that the Constitution could authorize conscription. Anti-Federalist writer "Brutus" (Robert Yates) warned of a coming "Prussian militia": If "the general legislature deem it for the general welfare to raise a body of troops, and they cannot be procured by voluntary enlistments, it seems evident, that it will be proper and necessary to effect it, that men be impressed from the militia to make up the deficiency." The Anti-Federalists saw the necessary-and-proper clause as a blank check for the central government.

And that wasn't all that worried the Anti-Federalists. As Edling explained: "By law the American militia consisted of all men between the age of sixteen and sixty. Congress's unlimited power over the militia therefore gave it power over the vast majority of adult men, which meant that the entire political nation was within reach of the government's command." The especially radical Anti-Federalist Luther Martin pointed out that members of the nationalized militia "from the *lowest* to the *greatest* [could] be *subjected* to *military* law, and *tied up* and *whipped* at the *halbert* like the *meanest* of *slaves*."

Anti-Federalists, perhaps seeing the writing on the wall but also re-alizing that many Americans did not like being called away from their homes for militia duty, were willing to concede power to the national government to raise an army in wartime—but not in peacetime. How-ever, the Federalists, as one of them, James Wilson, put it, wanted "the appearance of strength in a season of the most profound tranquility," that is, a peacetime standing army.

That the proposed Constitution put the military under civilian con-trol pleased the critics, who were also relieved that although the presi-dent would be commander-in-chief, the Congress controlled the purse and held power to declare war. (We know what became of that power.) However, with the ominous rise of the Society of the Cincinnati and with retired Gen. George Washington as the likely first president of the United States under the Constitution, how comforted should they have been about all this? ("Almost at once," Ekirch wrote, "the Society was criticized as an attempt to establish the former Revolutionary officers as a hereditary aristocracy, and the volume of protest soon reached im-pressive proportions.")

The Anti-Federalist case against unlimited central control of the mil-itary obviously did not prevent ratification of the Constitution, but it did yield proposed amendments to limit Congress's power, such as re-quiring a two-thirds majority of voting House members to approve the raising or keeping of troops in peacetime. That proposal was ignored, however, when Madison assembled what would become the Bill of Rights. Earlier, Luther Martin and Elbridge Gerry's amendment at the federal Convention to cap the number of troops failed, prompting Gerry, Edmund Randolph (an ambivalent Federalist), and George Mason to refuse to sign the Constitution.

The Federalist Papers, newspaper columns written to sell the Con-stitution to the public, were stunningly frank in their defense of the vast military powers enumerated in the Constitution. In Federalist 41 Madi-son wrote:

> Security against foreign danger is one of the primitive objects of civil society. It is an avowed and essential object of the American Union. The pow-ers requisite for attaining it must be effectually confided to the federal coun-cils....
>
> Is the power of declaring war necessary? No man will answer this ques-tion in the negative. It would be superfluous, therefore, to enter into a proof

of the affirmative. The existing Confederation establishes this power in the most ample form.

Is the power of raising armies and equipping fleets necessary? This is involved in the foregoing power. It is involved in the power of self-defense.

But was it necessary to give an INDEFINITE POWER of raising TROOPS, as well as providing fleets; and of maintaining both in PEACE, as well as in WAR?

...The answer indeed seems to be so obvious and conclusive as scarcely to justify such a discussion in any place. With what color of propriety could the force necessary for defense be limited by those who cannot limit the force of offense?...

How could a readiness for war in time of peace be safely prohibited, unless we could prohibit, in like manner, the preparations and establishments of every hostile nation?

Answer these questions as you may, but don't think for a minute that the Constitution did or was intended to limit the national government's power to raise and keep a peacetime standing army, or what Madison and his allies euphemistically called a "peace establishment." At the Federal Convention Madison had acknowledged that "according to the views of every member, the Gen[era]l. Govt will have powers far beyond those exercised by the British Parliament."

As indicated, Madison tried to allay fears of a standing army by arguing that a unified country would preclude the dangers experienced in Europe. "The Union itself, which it [the Constitution] cements and secures, destroys every pretext for a military establishment which could be dangerous," he wrote. "America united, with a handful of troops, or without a single soldier, exhibits a more forbidding posture to foreign ambition than America disunited, with a hundred thousand veterans ready for combat.... A dangerous establishment can never be necessary or plausible, so long as they continue a united people." (But note: he did not favor only a handful of troops or none at all.)

Indeed, he wrote, investigation into the matter

must terminate in a thorough and universal conviction, not only that the constitution has provided the most effectual guards against danger from that quarter [i.e., standing armies], but that nothing short of a Constitution fully adequate to the national defense and the preservation of the Union, can save America from as many standing armies as it may be split into States or Confederacies, and from such a progressive augmentation, of these establishments in each, as will render them as burdensome to the properties and ominous to the liberties of the people, as any establishment that can become necessary, under a united and efficient government, must be tolerable to the former and safe to the latter.

In other words, it's not the central government's peacetime standing army that would be dangerous. It's the standing armies of small sovereign states that were to be feared. Of course the states had citizens militias, not standing armies.

In Federalist 23 Alexander Hamilton declared:

The principal purposes to be answered by union [and hence the powers to raise taxes and military forces] are these—the common defense of the members; the preservation of the public peace as well against internal convulsions as external attacks; the regulation of commerce with other nations and between the States; the superintendence of our intercourse, political and commercial, with foreign countries.

The authorities essential to the common defense are these: to raise armies; to build and equip fleets; to prescribe rules for the government of both; to direct their operations; to provide for their support. *These powers ought to exist without limitation* [italics added], BECAUSE IT IS IMPOSSIBLE TO FORESEE OR DEFINE THE EXTENT AND VARIETY OF NATIONAL EXIGENCIES, OR THE CORRESPONDENT EXTENT AND VARIETY OF THE MEANS WHICH MAY BE NECESSARY TO SATISFY THEM.

What was that about powers "few and defined," as Madison promised?

In case anyone missed it the first time, Hamilton repeated:

Whether there ought to be a federal government intrusted with the care of the common defense, is a question in the first instance, open for discussion; but the moment it is decided in the affirmative, it will follow, that that government ought to be clothed with all the powers requisite to complete execution of its trust. And unless it can be shown that the circumstances which may affect the public safety are reducible within certain determinate limits; unless the contrary of this position can be fairly and rationally disputed, it must be admitted, as a necessary consequence, that there can be no limitation of that authority which is to provide for the defense and protection of the community, in any matter essential to its efficacy that is, in any matter essential to the FORMATION, DIRECTION, or SUPPORT of the NATIONAL FORCES.

This is reminiscent of young William F. Buckley's declaration that "we have got to accept Big Government for the duration [of the Cold War]—for neither an offensive nor a defensive war can be waged ... except through the instrumentality of a totalitarian bureaucracy within our shores."

In Federalist 25 Hamilton wrote that defense cannot remain the province of the states because "the territories of Britain, Spain, and of the Indian nations in our neighborhood do not border on particular States, but encircle the Union from Maine to Georgia. The danger, though in different degrees, is therefore common."

In other words, the new central state was first and foremost to be a national-security state, or a "fiscal-military state," European-like but superficially tailored to Americans' distrust of centralized power and elites. Like Madison, Hamilton tried to turn this distrust on its head. "As far as an army may be considered as a dangerous weapon of power," he wrote, "it had better be in those hands of which the people are most likely to be jealous than in those of which they are least likely to be jealous. For it is a truth, which the experience of ages has attested, that the people are always most in danger when the means of injuring their rights are in the possession of those of whom they entertain the least suspicion." Or: better to give the power to distant strangers than to nearby acquaintances.

The Anti-Federalist argument was that the nearby government of a small republic was one the people could more easily watch. The Federalists' government, they said, would be dominated by an elite, which would have an advantage over working- and middle-class people in gaining seats from the proposed large congressional districts in which one man would represent up to 30,000 people. The Anti-Federalists also invoked a version of the dispersed costs/concentrated benefits argument in claiming that the unorganized masses, unlike the well-organized special interests, would find it impractical to keep an eye on the new government.

Admittedly, the Anti-Federalists' worst fears did not come to pass, but that happy outcome had much to do with the resistance mounted by their successors, the congressional Republicans, to the Federalists' proposed military buildup. (Later, the Republicans became militarists. See chapter 19 on the War of 1812.) While in the early decades, the professional army was occasionally used domestically by both Federalists and Republicans (legislation permitting this was passed in the Jefferson administration), federal laws by and large did not require such heavy-handed enforcement, though it became more common later. As Edling wrote, "According to one estimate, the army was employed in more than three hundred labor disputes in this period [1867-1957]." The domestic use of the army to enforce law domestically was banned under the Posse Comitatus Act of 1878 "except in such cases and under such circumstances as such employment of said force may be expressly authorized by the Constitution or by act of Congress."

The military establishment was of course essential in building the bloody and costly American empire, starting with the conquest of much of North America. The people may not have wanted a standing army, but they wanted things that could only be acquired with it. (See chapter 15.)

4
The Bill of Rights Revisited

In *Empire of Liberty: A History of the Early Republic: 1789-1815* (2009), Gordon S. Wood wrote, "Benjamin Rush [a signer of the Declaration of Independence who voted to ratify the Constitution in Pennsylvania] described the new government in 1790 as one 'which unites with the vigor of monarchy and the stability of aristocracy all the freedom of a simple republic.'" But is that union coherent?

Was Rush's invocation of "the freedom of a simple republic" mere lip service to satisfy ordinary Americans? In his case, perhaps so. As noted, the physician diagnosed the "excessive" passion for liberty a mental illness, which he named "anarchia." But at the risk of being too charitable, we can say that the new country's patricians valued personal liberty, at least to an extent. They did not want the arbitrary rule of an absolute monarchy, and they realized that the new government had to be popularly accepted or the people might rebel. But it is important to understand that the framers of the second U.S. constitution did not intend for the complex governmental structure devised at the Federal Convention to protect Americans' liberty directly. Rather, the ultimate protector was to be the wise and virtuous ruling elite, the gentlemen of leisure (along with working lawyers and other professionals) who, free of the daily cares of laboring in the marketplace, could referee clashing particular interests and thereby effect the *general* welfare. The purpose of the political process established in 1789 was to assure that the right sort of people would be selected to govern and the wrong sort would be weeded out, as alas they had not been in the several states since the Revolution.

"What actually bothered the Federalists," Wood wrote in *The Creation of the American Republic, 1776-1787* (1998), "was the sort of people who had been able to gain positions of authority in the state governments, particularly in the state legislatures." Wood quoted Anti-Federalist

Patrick Henry: "The Constitution reflects in the most degrading and mortifying manner on the virtue, integrity, and wisdom of the state legislatures; it presupposes that the chosen few who go to Congress will have more upright hearts, and more enlightened minds, than those who are members of the individual legislatures." Thus, "The federal government would act as a kind of sieve," Wood added, quoting James Madison, "extracting 'from the mass of the society the purest and noblest characters which it contains.'" As one critic of the Constitution noted, the plan was "dangerously adapted to the purposes of an immediate *aristocratic tyranny.*" And, Wood noted, "even young John Quincy Adams" saw the Constitution as (in Adams's words) "calculated to increase the influence, power and wealth of those who have it already."

In light of this insight into constitutional history, we may now inquire into the nature and purpose of the Bill of Rights, the 10 amendments adopted immediately after the new government went into operation.

As Wood noted in *Empire of Liberty*, Americans were surprised that the proposed Constitution had no bill of rights. Furthermore, most of those who had participated in the convention were apparently surprised that everyone else was surprised. In fact, no one even mentioned a bill of rights during the convention until the closing days, when George Mason raised the matter. "It was voted down by every state delegation," Wood wrote. Bear in mind that some state constitutions had bills of rights, so including one would have blazed no new ground. (The lack of interest in a bill of rights reminds me that when Alexander Hamilton was asked why God was not mentioned in the Constitution, he reportedly said, "We forgot.")

Anti-Federalists like Mason made the lack of a bill of rights the top talking point against the Constitution (a fatal strategic error, as we'll see), and the issue came up repeatedly in state ratifying conventions. While no state convention conditioned ratification on the addition of a bill of rights (states had to vote up or down), Wood wrote, "many of the states had ratified the Constitution on the understanding that some changes would be made in order to protect people's rights, and popular expectation was high that amendments would be added as soon as possible."

This made the Federalists unhappy. The last thing they wanted was to tamper with their handiwork before it had a chance to go into effect. Besides, they said, no bill was needed. In the Federalists' eyes, "the Constitution had been drafted in part to protect the rights of Americans," Wood wrote. "But the Constitution was designed to protect the Americans' rights from the abusive power of the state legislatures." Hamilton and others argued further that if the national government, unlike state governments, could exercise only enumerated powers, then the document *itself* was a bill of rights. Why declare a right to freedom of the press, they asked, if government had no express power to regulate the press?

Because of the Constitution's necessary-and-proper clause, the Anti-Federalists did not believe this talking point about enumerated powers, nor should they have believed it. As noted, the power of eminent domain was not enumerated, but we know from the Fifth Amendment's "takings clause" that the framers viewed the power either as an inherent possession of government or as necessary and proper for the exercise of other powers. The Anti-Federalists also pointed out that the government should be limited in *how* it exercised enumerated powers.

After enough states ratified the Constitution, all but one Federalist was willing to ignore their promise to add a bill of rights: James Madison. At first he was also willing to let the matter go, but his sense of honor (and pressure from Thomas Jefferson) prevailed, and he strove to keep his promise when he was elected to the first Congress as a member of the House of Representatives. (He had lost out on the Senate when the Virginia state legislature selected two Anti-Federalists.), "As he [Madison] told a friend," Wood wrote, "a bill of rights would 'kill the opposition everywhere, and by putting an end to the disaffection to the Govt. itself, enable the administration to venture on measures not otherwise safe.'"

Thus did Madison make a virtue of expediency.

Nearly 200 amendments had been recommended by the state ratifying conventions, and so Madison sorted through them. "Yet Madison was determined that his bill of rights would be mainly limited to the protection of personal rights," Wood wrote, "and would not harm 'the structure & stamina of the Government.'" In other words, most of the proposed amendments and the Anti-Federalists' most serious objections—among them, Congress's unrestricted power to maintain a peacetime standing army—would be ignored. Revealingly, Madison favored an amendment, in Wood's words, "to protect certain rights from the states," which shows that the Federalists were truly nationalists. It failed, just as Madison's proposal at the Federal Convention to empower Congress to veto state legislation failed.

By the time Madison got through all the amendments, Wood added, "many Federalists had come to see that a bill of rights might be a good thing after all. Not only was it the best way of undercutting the strength of Anti-Federalism in the country, but the Bill of Rights that emerged, as Hamilton pointed out, left 'the structure of the government and the mass and distribution of its powers where they were.'"

In the end, Americans got a government with nearly a comprehensive power to tax and regulate/promote trade, as well as potential blank checks in the form of the general-welfare, necessary-and-proper, supremacy clauses, the lack of a prohibition on a standing army, and more. (They had other concerns: the powerful executive, the Senate, and the judiciary.)

But what of the Bill of Rights?

"Madison's amendments, as opponents of the Constitution angrily came to realize, were 'good for nothing' and were 'calculated merely to amuse, or rather to deceive,'" Wood wrote, quoting critics. "They affected 'personal liberty alone, leaving the great points of the Judiciary & direct taxation & c. to stand as they are.'"

Aedanus Burke, a Representative from South Carolina, said Madison's amendments "are little better than whip-syllabub, frothy and full of wind, formed only to please the palate.... I think it will be found that we have done nothing but lose our time, and that it will be better to drop the subject now and proceed to the organization of the government."

But since some Anti-Federalists had put a great deal of emphasis on the lack of a bill of rights, once the amendments were ratified, the critics appeared to be unwilling to take yes for an answer. They had far deeper grievances, but further complaints now looked obstructionist. "Anti-Federalists in the Congress," Wood wrote, "began to realize that Madison's rights-based amendments weakened the desire for a second convention and thus actually worked against their cause of fundamentally altering the Constitution." They had been bested in this historic game of chess.

Actually, the Bill of Rights largely embodied uncontroversial traditional rights of Englishmen. Indeed, in sorting through the amendments, Wood wrote, "Madison ... extracted mainly those concerned with personal rights that he thought no one could argue with."

Wood continued: "Unlike the French Declaration of Rights of Man and Citizen issued by the National Assembly in 1789, the American Bill of Rights of 1791 was less a creative document than a defensive one. It made no universal claims but was rooted solely in the Americans' particular history. It did not invent human rights that had not existed before, but mainly reiterated long-standing English common law rights."

To see this point clearly, recall that in 1798 the Federalist Congress passed the Sedition Act, which prohibited one to "write, print, utter or publish … any false, scandalous, and malicious writing or writings against the Government of the United States, or either House of the Congress of the United States, with intent to defame the said government, or either house of the said Congress, or the President, or to bring them … into contempt or disrepute, or to excite against them, or either or any of them, the hatred of the good people of the United States." Little good the First Amendment did to stop it. Wood explained:

> Americans believed in freedom of the press and had written that freedom into their Bill of Rights. *But they believed in it as Englishmen did.* Indeed, the English had celebrated freedom of the press since the seventeenth century, but they meant by it, in contrast with the French, no prior restraint or censorship of what was published. Under English law, people were nevertheless held responsible for what they published. If a person's publications were slanderous and calumnious enough to bring public officials into disrespect, then under the common law the publisher could be prosecuted for seditious libel. The truth of what was published was no defense; indeed, it even aggravated the offense. [Emphasis added.]

Bad as it was, the Sedition Act was more liberal than the common law because it permitted truth as a defense.

Wood summed up the story of the Bill of Rights thus: "Under the circumstances the states ratified the first ten amendments slowly and without much enthusiasm between 1789 and 1791; several of the original states—Massachusetts, Connecticut, and Georgia—did not even bother. After ratification, most Americans promptly forgot about the first ten amendments to the Constitution. The Bill of Rights remained judicially dormant until the twentieth century."

This does not mean the Bill of Rights has been worthless. To the extent it has worked to restrain government power, we should be grateful. (That also goes for the 14th Amendment, which applied the Bill of Rights to the states.) But its presence eventually shifted attention from asking where in the Constitution a claimed power was enumerated to asking where in the Bill of Rights a claimed right was enumerated. And the effort to procure the Bill of Rights distracted from weightier matters, leaving the national government with its frighteningly broad powers intact.

$$5$$

Lost Articles

The Constitution says that to be elected to the U.S. Senate, a person has to be 30 or older, a citizen for at least nine years, and a resident of the state from which the candidate is elected.

Alas, it says nothing about knowing American history.

Good thing for Sen. Lindsey Graham, the South Carolina Republican. He'd have to find honest work.

Interviewed after the State of the Union address in 2007, Graham was asked about the continuing violence in Iraq, nearly three years after the U.S. invasion. Trying to put the difficulties in perspective, he said the United States did not get its constitution until 1789, years after achieving independence from Great Britain.

Buzz! Wrong answer, Sen. Graham. But as a consolation prize you get to take home a copy of Merrill Jensen's book *The New Nation: A History of the United States During the Confederation, 1781-1789* (1950). And we'll also throw in a copy of Herbert Storing's *What the Anti-Federalists Were For* (1981). And thanks for playing our game.

Seriously, I realize that children learn virtually nothing about the eight years before 1789 during which the United States existed under the Articles of Confederation. But shouldn't someone who holds himself qualified to be a U.S. senator know that what we call the Constitution was really America's *second* constitution?

The Articles were adopted by the Second Continental Congress on November 15, 1777, and took effect after ratification on March 1, 1781. That was seven months before Cornwallis surrendered at Yorktown on October 19, 1781, and two and a half years before the Treaty of Paris was signed on September 3, 1783.

Under the Articles the government of the United States, which was essentially confined to external affairs, consisted of a one-chamber Congress, with legislature, executive, and limited judicial functions. As noted, the new quasi-government had no power to tax, regulate trade (except with the Indians), or raise an army directly. If it needed money or soldiers, it had to requisition them from the states.

The states were represented in Congress by delegations of two to seven members, selected by a method chosen by each state legislature, but each state had only one vote. No person could be a member of Congress for more than three years in any six-year period.

The government had no separate executive branch or judiciary. The Congress selected a member to preside while it was in session; this person, who could hold the office no more than one out of three years, was known as the president of the United States. Why no independent executive? Because the recent unpleasant experience with the king of England made many members of the Continental Congress wary of untrammeled executive power. Ten men held the position of president, including John Hancock and Richard Henry Lee. John Hanson of Maryland, the third person to hold the office but the first person to hold it for a full one-year term after the Articles were ratified, was strictly speaking the first president of the United States.

The Articles remained in effect until the Constitution displaced them in 1789. The process by which the Articles were scrapped—rather than amended—in favor of an entirely new blueprint was dubious. As the pseudonymous Anti-Federalist "Federal Farmer" (most likely Melancton Smith of New York) wrote on October 8, 1787,

> A general convention for mere commercial purposes was moved for—the authors of this measure saw that the people's attention was turned solely to the amendment of the federal system; and that, had the idea of a total change been started [sic], probably *no state would have appointed members to the convention*. The idea of destroying, ultimately, the state government, and forming one consolidated system, could not have been admitted—a convention, therefore, merely for vesting in congress power to regulate trade was proposed. [Emphasis added.]

Eight years is a significant period for a nascent country to endure after breaking away from an empire. Graham's remarks were meant to suggest that what took place in the United States during that time was similar to what was taking place in Iraq in 2007. (Not much had changed in 2016.) But that is ridiculous. The 13 states did not embroil themselves in civil war or sectarian violence—neither internally nor with one another. Quite the contrary.

How was life under the Articles of Confederation? As Merrill Jensen wrote,

> Americans fought against and freed themselves from ... coercive and increasingly centralized power....They did not create such a government when the Articles of Confederation were written, although there were Americans who wished to do so....Thus the American Revolution made possible the democratization of American society by the destruction of the coercive authority of Great Britain and the establishment of actual local self-government within the separate states under the Articles of Confederation.

People in the new states, Jensen wrote, were full of optimism about the possibilities ahead. Criminal codes were made more humane, with the death penalty removed for all crimes but murder and, in some cases, treason. Property qualifications for voting were abolished over time. Charities and mutual-aid societies were formed, along with library, scientific, and medical associations. Schools were founded. The union of church and state was increasingly opposed. The steps in the direction of religious freedom and the complete separation of church and state were thus halting, but the direction was sure and the purpose was clear, Jensen wrote.

Of course, there was slavery, which contradicted the philosophy espoused in the Declaration of Independence. But some states moved against it. Within a few years after 1775, either in constitutions or in legislation, many of the new states acted against slavery. Within a decade all states except Georgia and South Carolina had passed some form of legislation to stop the slave trade, Jensen wrote. The New England states and Pennsylvania took steps toward abolition, and antislavery societies flourished.

What about the economies of the states? We can infer much from the fact that those who wanted to overthrow the Articles for a new constitution warned of *coming* economic turmoil if the central government were not fortified. Hence turmoil was a prediction *not* a description. The states were certainly no models of laissez faire, although some individuals—namely, white males—were free economically to a perhaps hitherto unknown extent. But then neither was the consolidated national system a practitioner of laissez faire after 1789. The first economic action of the first Congress under the Constitution was imposition of a broad protective tariff, which one newspaper described as "the second Declaration of Independence."

Rent-seeking (political entrepreneurship in pursuit of profits beyond what could be earned in the market) was seen in the states, as it has been in every real-world system. Subsidies, loans, monopoly charters, and land giveaways were common. In this largely agrarian society, Jensen wrote,

> the dominant note was sounded by American merchants and business men who lived mostly in the seaport towns....Their power was born of place, position, and fortune. They were located at or near the seats of government and they were in direct contact with legislatures and government officers. They influenced and often dominated the local newspapers which voiced the ideas and interests of commerce and identified them with the good of the whole people, the state, and the nation. [Hence, the bad name *capitalism* has had for many people since.]

Merchants and manufacturers disagreed on *what kind* of government intervention should exist, but not on *whether* it should exist. That's because they had different competitors. Merchants liked imports but wanted barriers to foreign (especially British) shipping, while manufacturers wanted barriers to foreign goods and didn't care about shipping. Part of the impetus toward a strong central government was businessmen's desire for a uniform national economic policy, since individual states, acting alone, could hurt themselves by having more stringent restrictions than their neighbors and one state could capture the lion's share of trade by competitively lowering its barriers. In other words, the constitutional consolidation of 1789 was part regulatory cartel.

There were also regional differences. Most manufacturing was in the North, so protectionist sentiment was concentrated there. The South had little manufacturing and wanted access to cheap foreign goods. Thus high protective tariffs found little support. Northerners who coveted the Southern market realized that only a nationwide trade policy would serve their interests. On the other hand, Southern farmers wanted as many shipping options as possible and had little interest in restrictions on foreign carriers.

Some state economies, but not all, suffered booms and busts—a depression in 1784-85—due to badly managed paper money (which nevertheless remained popular) and other government ineptitude. But the crises were not extraordinary. As Jensen summarized, "There is nothing in the knowable facts to support the ancient myth of idle ships, stagnant commerce, and bankrupt merchants in the new nation. As long ago as 1912, Edward Channing demonstrated with adequate evidence that despite the commercial depression, American commerce expanded rapidly after 1783, and that by 1790 the United States had far outstripped the colonies of a few short years before."

Despite intervention, white men still had a virtually unprecedented degree of economic freedom. A man could easily get a plot of land and take care of his family by farming. (Some states operated land banks to extend mortgages to individuals through the emission of paper money.) There was no distant overbearing central bureaucracy to worry about. Contact with government was minimal.

Thus contrary to Sen. Graham, pre-1789 America had a constitution, almost no central government, relative prosperity, and peace. (Of course it also had slavery, wars on Indians, and the oppression of women, but that continued for a long time under the Constitution, fortified by a broad power to tax.)

As Jensen said, the men who wrote the Constitution of 1787 were quite a different set of men from those who signed the Declaration of Independence in 1776. Let's further explore those early years of the republic.

6

History Lesson Lost

Call me nostalgic, but I still have a thing for the Articles of Confederation. Admittedly, it's a tempered nostalgia, for as Murray Rothbard reminded us, even the Articles represented an intolerable centralization of power, a triumph of conservatism over radicalism. (See volume four of Rothbard's *Conceived in Liberty* [1979/2011].)

Maybe it's the enticement of forbidden fruit. In the government schools I attended, little if anything was said about the eight years during which the United States of America were governed under the Articles. The curriculum writers must have had a good reason for not devoting class time to that period. What didn't they want us to know?

If we heard anything about those eight years, it would have been that the period was a mess: provincialism, mobocracy, depression, trade barriers at state borders, and an impotent national government that had to beg the states for money and militiamen. Thank goodness—the teacher probably said—that wiser heads prevailed and the impractical decentralization of the Articles was replaced by the Constitution, which gave the national government badly needed potency while simultaneously restraining it from violating our liberties. Remember James Madison, Federalist 51: "You must first enable the government to control the governed; and in the next place oblige it to control itself."

Maybe what the schools didn't want us to know was that life under the Articles, as pointed out in the last chapter, wasn't so bad after all—at least for white males with property. America got along without a central taxing authority and distant impersonal bureaucracy; obviously it wasn't so good for African Americans, Indians, and white women, but their fate did not change in 1789. Under the Articles, that narrow slice of the population enjoyed economic growth, and the transition from a collection of colonies to a confederation of sovereign states was reasonably smooth. As already noted, it certainly wasn't a period of laissez faire, and many of the problems experienced, such as periodic inflation and depression, were attributable to grants of privilege and government mismanagement of paper money. Contrary to common libertarian assumption, fiat paper money was popular in the colonies and states. Thus British Parliament's 1764 attempt to restrict colonies' enactment of legal-tender laws was resented across the socioeconomic spectrum. According to historian E. James Ferguson, Benjamin Franklin said such outside monetary restrictions helped drive a wedge between the colonies and the British Empire. "In North America [unlike in England] pragmatism won out over theoretical abstractions and moralistic pronouncements," historian Edwin J. Perkins wrote. (See Ferguson's *The Power of the Purse: A History of American Public Finance, 1776-1790* [1961] and Perkins's *American Public Finance and Financial Services: 1700-1815* [1994].)

Even interstate protectionism is more legend than fact. Economic historian Jeffrey Rogers Hummel handily disposes of that myth in "The Constitution as Counter-Revolution: A Tribute to the Anti-Federalists (online at http://www.la-articles.org.uk/FL-5-4-3.pdf)":

> Indeed, subsequent accounts have blown this rationale [for strengthening the central government] up into an utterly fanciful picture of competing trade barriers between the various states disrupting the American economy. The two factual instances on which this overblown picture is largely based involve New York and Connecticut, which taxed foreign goods entering from neighboring states—an economically insignificant restriction. *The prevailing rule prior to the Constitution was complete free trade among the states.* [Emphasis added.]

In fact, in the Federalist Papers Alexander Hamilton said he favored the Constitution in part because it would enable American to triple its tariff against Europe. Competition among the states tended to lower barriers to foreign products. The Constitution can be seen as constructing a protectionist cartel. (More on this in chapter 12.)

If life under the Articles was reasonably good (again, for white males, especially those with property), why was the first constitution scrapped in favor of a plan for a more powerful central government? Merrill Jensen, the respected historian of the period, offered an explanation in his book *The Articles of Confederation: An Interpretation of the Social-Constitutional History of the American Revolution, 1774-1781* (1940). Jensen explained that the negative impression of the confederation period was fostered at the time by those who favored nationalism (over true federalism) and centralized power. Those forces prevailed, and as we know, the victors largely write the history. "Posterity has seldom questioned their partisan interpretation," Jensen wrote.

> The Articles of Confederation have been assigned one of the most inglorious roles in American history. They have been treated as the product of ignorance and inexperience and the parent of chaos; hence the necessity for a new constitution in 1787 to save the country from ruin. In so interpreting the first constitution of the United States and the history of the country during its existence, historians have accepted a tradition established by the Federalist Party. They have not stopped to consider that the Federalist Party was organized to destroy a constitution embodying ideals of self-government and economic practice that were naturally abhorrent to those elements in American society of which that party was the political expression.

This bias toward the Federalist narrative is discussed at length by Pauline Maier in *Ratification: The People Debate the Constitution* (2011). "We tend to believe everything [the Federalists] said…," Maier wrote. "But the Federalists … controlled the documents on which historians depend. They owned most of the newspapers. They sometimes paid those who took notes on the convention debates or subsidized the publication of their transcripts. In some places, above all Connecticut, Federalists forcibly blocked the circulation of literature critical of the Constitution."

Jensen went on to describe the deep division that existed in the British North American colonies and, after the Revolution, in the states. Groups of people are rarely of one mind, and the colonies and states were no exception. As to be expected, a privileged elite came to dominate the government of each colony; power and land were handed out as royal favors, and the recipients became entrenched. In the Northern and Middle colonies, merchants constituted the most powerful group. In the South that rank was held by the large planters. These people came to think of themselves as the wise and disinterested aristocracy destined to govern, and they were not eager to give up power to the radical democrats who were the first to push for independence from Britain. When possible, merchants and planters secured their positions by denying the vote to men who held no or too little property or by denying farmers in outlying areas full representation in the legislatures or sometimes any representation at all. Taxation without representation was thus practiced by one group of colonists against another. The victims of this policy were not happy about it and were determined to change the system.

Holding political power was the key to retaining wealth and economic influence against upstart rivals. Jensen noted that in Pennsylvania, for example, "the merchants had tried by various means to overthrow the system of markets and auctions in order to get a monopoly of the retail trade….The merchants likewise tried to check the activity of wandering peddlers." Then as now, businessmen preferred cartels and monopoly privileges (the exclusive corporate charters of old) to free and unpredictable competition. When one recognizes the politically powered land speculation that was rampant, one can see how economic interest could have had a hand in shaping political visions. The holders of political power were not invincible, however, and in some colonies democratic and agrarian challengers succeeded in winning control.

The upshot is that the contending groups—the "radicals" and the "conservatives"—had different economic and political interests and thus different views about independence from Great Britain. When British usurpations made independence an imperative even for many conservatives, these groups disagreed about how the new nation should be governed. The mercantile interests tended to favor nationalist centralization, which was seen as the best way to maintain power and to hold back the radical democrats. The mass of people who felt themselves imposed on by those interests tended to favor decentralization because they believed they had a better chance for justice with local self-government. Thus what Jensen called the "internal revolution" was at least as important as the external one against the British. Indeed, the revolution against Britain was seen by the radicals as a means to success in the revolution against domestic aristocracy. The conservatives understood this too. Jensen wrote,

> The interpretation of the Revolution is often confused by the insistence that all revolutionists were radicals. Probably most radicals were revolutionists, but a large number of revolutionists were not radicals. The conservatives were those who—whether they desired independence or not—wanted to maintain the aristocratic order in the American colonies and states. The radicals were those who wanted changes in the existing order, changes which can be best described as democratic, though the term is necessarily relative.

The Articles of Confederation, Jensen noted, were the radicals' triumph over the conservatives in the Second Continental Congress, "a constitutional expression of the philosophy of the Declaration of Independence." But the conservatives did not give up their nationalist aspirations. After years of denigrating the confederation and attempting to amend the Articles, they finally got their way in 1787 and used the Federal Convention to scrap them in favor of a strong central government. The Antifederalists warned about its dangers, but to no avail.

The framers' anti-democratic tenor is often taken as a sign of their liberalism. However, Jensen's approach sheds a different light on the matter. Whether democratization is good or bad depends on the context. When it is an assault on individual sovereignty, it is bad. But when it is a move against aristocracy and mercantilism, it is good. According to Jensen, the proponents of democracy and local self-government were disfranchised, overtaxed small farmers trying to resist the entrenched mercantilist elite. They may not have been consistent libertarians, but they were more libertarian than their adversaries. Thus the attack on democracy can be seen as a defense of aristocracy. It doesn't look so good in that light.

Dispersed power is a pillar of liberalism. (Although it must be acknowledged that liberalism also contains a strain in favor of centralization. See Jacob T. Levy's *Rationalism, Pluralism, and Freedom* [2015] and my discussion of his book in the introduction to this volume.) Decentralization entails smaller jurisdictions, competition, and relative ease of exit. The Articles of Confederation, though hardly perfect, embraced those principles. The plan that took its place exchanged those principles for the promise of horizontal checks and balances within a strong central government over a large geographical area. It's fascinating to ponder how things would have turned out had that exchange not taken place.

7

The Decline of American Liberalism

A good description of the early years of America is to be found in Arthur A. Ekirch Jr.'s classic, *The Decline of American Liberalism* (1955/1967). By *liberalism*, Ekirch meant classical liberalism, or something closely resembling libertarianism. In his foreword, Ekirch wrote: "Since the time of the American Revolution the major trend in our history has been in the direction of ever-greater centralization and concentration of control—politically, economically, and socially. As part of this drift toward 'state capitalism' or 'socialism,' the liberal values associated with the eighteenth-century Enlightenment—and especially that of individual freedom—have slowly lost their primary importance in American life and thought."

But he added, "Despite the pessimism implied in such a stand, I wish to disclaim any intent to essay the role of a Jeremiah or a Cassandra. My purpose is rather that of an historian and social scientist. I desire to examine the history of liberalism because I think that evidence of a decline would tell of an important facet of our history, deserving more consideration than it has hitherto received.... I believe the weakening of the liberal tradition should be of sufficient concern to cause us to reassess that easy assumption of continual progress which has so frequently characterized American historical writing."

In chapter 2, "The Hope of America," Ekirch wrote,

It is not far from correct to say that liberalism and colonial America grew up together.... Probably the majority of the settlers who came to America did so because of their longing to break away from the rigid class society and restraints of Europe. In one way or another the average settler was fleeing absolutism.... An abundance of free land ensured the widespread diffusion of property, higher wages, and greater social equality. Feudal customs of restricted land tenure proved impossible of general application in the New World. No hereditary aristocracy of lords and ladies owned exclusive title to the land, and the Old World customs of primogeniture and entailed estates were never popular in the colonies. Prosperity bred economic individualism and, in a land of seemingly boundless wealth, mercantilist notions of political economy began to yield the economic stage to a rising laissez-faire capitalism....

In large part therefore the American colonial economy fulfilled liberal expectations, approximating closely the agrarian dream of a society in which property was widely diffused and divided on fairly equal terms. Only the presence of the lower class of Negro slaves and indentured white servants intervened to mar the picture of a free and liberal social system.... Almost as unfortunate as the Negro slave was the American Indian, who, though not enslaved, was often warred upon and divested of his lands and hunting grounds.

While Ekirch wrote glowingly of the rise of liberalism in colonial America (without ignoring the contradictions of chattel slavery and the oppression and extermination of Indians) he, like historian Vernon L. Parrington, underscored a shift in emphasis that occurred during the Revolution with its "encroachment of a new spirit of nationalism and Americanism upon the older, local frontiers of colonial days." He quoted Parrington, who wrote that the Revolution "marked the turning point in American development; the checking of the long movement of decentralization and the beginning of a counter movement of centralization....The history of the rise of the coercive state in America, with the ultimate arrest of all centrifugal tendencies, was implicit in that momentous counter movement."

Ekirch himself went on to note that "in the process of fighting the Revolution, economic advantage and social privilege were by no means eliminated. Much loyalist property, for example, found its way into the hands of a new group of wealthy landed proprietors. Such transfers sometimes did more to advance speculation in land prices than to further the achievement of an agrarian diffusion of property. Army contracting also resulted in the creation of new wartime fortunes.... [M]ost governmental regulation of the period was favorable to business."

Ekirch described the illiberal movement that occurred after the Revolution in a chapter he titled "Federalist Centralization and Consolidation." He and Parrington differed with other historians not in their seeing a conservative counterrevolution, but rather in seeing it as something permanent. The Jeffersonian and Jacksonian periods revived the declining liberalism to some extent, "but the shift in American thought in the period between the Declaration of Independence and the adoption of the Constitution represented more than a temporary reaction. It was rather, as Parrington insisted, a turning point of American history and a direct challenge to the liberal tradition." Specifically, in part the shift was characterized by business's "look[ing] to government for economic support." He pointed out, "In a variety of ways therefore the war had an educational effect upon American business thinking and practice, especially teaching businessmen to identify themselves with the policies and operations of government. After the return of peace, it was only natural that the new generation of businessmen should strive to enlist the aid of the government in preserving and increasing their wartime gains."

This attitude and other things, such as the government-debt speculators' wish to protect their investments, intensified the conservatives' discontent with the Articles of Confederation, which (as we've seen) set up a weak central government without authority to levy taxes or regulate trade. This discontent was increased by rebellious farmers and mechanics who "were beginning to unite in their opposition to strong government and higher taxes." (Shays's Rebellion in 1786 is the best-known example.) Even greater centralization of power was the conservatives' answer. Ekirch quoted James Madison, a nationalist, who explained the move to centralization as a way "to protect the minority of the opulent against the majority."

The conservative reaction resulted in the 1787 Federal Convention at Philadelphia. "[A]ll fifty-five of the delegates were men of considerable and varied property holdings, ranging from the possession of slaves and lands to investments in government securities and far-flung business enterprises," Ekirch wrote. His discussion of this period sheds valuable light on constitutional matters still relevant today, for example, the allegedly clear distinction between strict constructionism and living-constitutionalism. Here's what he said:

> Fundamental to an understanding of the Constitution adopted at Philadelphia is the realization that it represented a compromise made possible by the large areas of essential agreement among the delegates. Between the two poles of a colonial and Revolutionary radicalism—which favored democratic individualism and state rights—and a lingering British conservatism—which frankly preferred a constitutional monarchy and the rule of a propertied aristocracy—compromise was relatively easy to achieve. The delegates to the Philadelphia Convention were overwhelmingly agreed upon the necessity of a government that was national, yet republican, and there was little sentiment

in behalf of either a monarchy or the kind of decentralized government illustrated by the Articles of Confederation. In accord therefore on the basic theory of the new government, the delegates fashioned *a document whose meaning depended to a considerable extent upon how it was interpreted. The very vagueness and silences of the Constitution left much to be inferred and decided in the future.* [Emphasis added.]

This undercuts the claim of constitutional sentimentalists that the framers intended to create a government that was limited to "few and defined" powers by a constitution that was not open to interpretation.

In the document Ekirch perceived homage to liberalism in the tacit acknowledgement of natural rights (later made explicit in the Bill of Rights), the (appearance of) limited powers, and the separation of branches. Yet he also saw an illiberal delegation of economic powers to the central government: "The men at Philadelphia were convinced that the economic powers hitherto wielded by the states would be safer in the hands of a centralized national government. To this end, Congress was given exclusive authority to coin money and to regulate both foreign and interstate commerce. Thus the stage was set for the abandonment of laissez-faire liberalism and the substitution of economic nationalism or government paternalism."

The so-called Federalists, epitomized by Alexander Hamilton, were the first to rule under the Constitution and thus were able to establish important precedents under which we still labor. For example, Ekirch noted, when Hamilton asked Congress to charter a national bank—"a significant example of government paternalism," in Ekirch's words—and Jefferson protested on constitutional grounds, "Hamilton answered with his famous doctrine of implied or resulting powers—that certain powers are implied, or are the result of other powers specifically enumerated in the Constitution." (The Anti-Federalists had warned of the danger of implied powers.) That doctrine has stood the advocates of robust central government in good stead ever since. (Madison appears to have been the author of the implied-powers doctrine, as shown in this volume.)

Ekirch summed up the period thus:

The Federalists were correct in pointing out the necessity of the rule of law, rather than of revolution, for the preservation of liberalism, but they erred in the way they interpreted the laws at home. Using the checks and balances of the Constitution to thwart popular control, they went on to violate their own concept of a balanced government, adopting *a broad and elastic interpretation of the Constitution* and using expanded power of government and *the vague concept of the general welfare* for the benefit of a particular class—the commercial, propertied aristocracy. But, though overthrown in 1800, the remnants of the defeated Federalists later had the grim satisfaction of seeing their Jeffersonian opponents embrace many of the same consolidating principles that they had earlier so bitterly denied. [Emphasis added.]

In other words, the conservatives gave birth to the living constitution.

8

Where Is the Constitution?

The title question is not like "Who's buried in Grant's tomb?" And the answer isn't "the National Archives." I mean the *real* constitution—the set of dispositions that influence what most Americans will accept as legitimate actions by the politicians and bureaucrats who make up the government—not a mere piece of parchment behind glass or a booklet in someone's pocket. This real constitution more or less makes the written Constitution what it is at any given time. When Peter Finley Dunne's Mr. Dooley said that "th' Supreme Court follows th' illiction returns," he was exaggerating only a bit.

The U.S. Constitution has changed over the years, without being formally amended, in response to changes in the real constitution. *Plessy v. Ferguson* became *Brown v. Board of Education*, for example. The commerce clause came to be interpreted in ways that would have astounded some (but not all) earlier Americans. Same with the general-welfare clause. This presents a problem for constitutionalists: constitutions (rules) can neither interpret nor apply themselves. *People* interpret and apply them. As legal scholar John Hasnas points out, the rule of law under a monopoly government legal system inevitably is a rule of men and women. (See his "The Myth of the Rule of Law," *Wisconsin Law Review,* 1995, online at http://faculty.msb.edu/hasnasj/GTWebSite/MythWeb.htm). So how can a constitution do the work that the constitutionalists expect it to do?

Conservatives scoff at the idea of a living Constitution, the proposition that its meaning should change with the times. The economist Thomas Sowell, like the late Justice Antonin Scalia, quips that a living Constitution is really a dead Constitution. By that he means that unless the Constitution's content is fixed and timeless, it no longer qualifies as a constitution.

This argument has a plausible ring. But it runs up against the problem I've cited. No set of rules interprets or applies itself, and no guide to interpretation can interpret itself. In that sense all constitutions are living. It is too glibly asserted that we know what the Constitution "really means: means to whom? The framers? The ratifiers? The people of 1788? Us? The Constitution is a historical and political document, and people divine its meaning from their changing views of the epoch that produced it, which is in turn influenced by their moral and political values. As the historian Merrill Jensen wrote in *The New Nation: A History of the United States During the Confederation, 1781-1789* (1950),

> Since the founding fathers themselves disagreed as to the nature of the history of the period and as to the best kind of government for a new nation, it is possible to find arguments to support almost any interpretation one chooses. It is not surprising therefore that conflicting interpretations have filled thousands of pages and that all this effort has never produced any final answers and probably never will, for men have ever interpreted the two constitutions of the United States in terms of their hopes, interests, and beliefs rather than in terms of knowable facts.... When the Constitution was submitted to the public in October 1787 the controversy rose to new heights. Men talked in public meetings and wrote private letters and public essays in an effort to explain, justify, or denounce what the Convention had done.... Some said there would be chaos without the new Constitution; others said that there would be chaos if it were adopted.

And the framers were alive during this debate! What chance do we have?

Jensen went on:

> Once it was adopted Thomas Jefferson and Alexander Hamilton, with two opposed ideas of what the United States should be, laid down two classic and contradictory opinions of the nature of the Constitution. The two basic interpretations may be simply stated. Jefferson held that the central government was sharply limited by the letter of the Constitution; that in effect the states retained their sovereign powers except where they were specifically delegated. Hamilton argued in effect that the central government was a national government which could not be restrained by a strict interpretation of the Constitution or by ideas of state sovereignty.

Who was right? Jefferson or Hamilton? What does *right* signify here?

The Auburn University philosopher Roderick T. Long has touched on this subject in "Rule-following, Praxeology, and Anarchy" (*New Perspectives on Political Economy*, 2006, online at http://pcpe.libinst.cz/nppe/ 2_1/nppe2_1_3.pdf). Long's purpose was to explore the political and other implications of what the philosopher Ludwig Wittgenstein called the "rule-following paradox." We know rule-following when we see it and engage in it, Wittgenstein observed, but what *is* it? It is neither words in one's mind or on paper (or parchment) that *compel* certain behavior, nor a sequence of physical motions, which could be consistent with many different rules. Rather, it's a kind of *purposeful human action* (à la Ludwig von Mises) in a particular context that cannot be reduced to either a mental state nor a series of bodily motions. Long quoted Wittgenstein: "[A] move in chess doesn't consist simply in moving a piece in such-and-such a way on the board—nor yet in one's thoughts and feelings as one makes the move: but in the circumstances that we call 'playing a game of chess', 'solving a chess problem', and so on."

Thus, Long continued, "One moral of the paradox is that action is an indivisible whole, of which thoughts and movements are aspects but not separable ingredients; *action* is more than the sum of its parts. The identity of my thoughts depends on how I translate them into action—not bodily movement, but action."

This may not seem to shed light on the problem at hand: seeing to it that a particular interpretation of the Constitution is followed. But Long continued:

> If I think that following a rule *must* somehow be anchored by the rule's having its application already built into it, then a close look at rule-following is bound to turn vertiginous, because there's no such thing to be found. As Wittgenstein puts it, "any interpretation still hangs in the air along with what it interprets, and cannot give it any support." But what he infers from this is not that grasping a rule is impossible, but rather that "there is a way of grasping a rule which is *not* an *interpretation*, but which is exhibited in what we call 'obeying the rule'."

This isn't just esoteric abstract philosophizing. As Long writes,

> Just as it's tempting to think that my grasp of a rule is something independent of my actions, something that *makes* me behave in a certain way, so it's equally tempting to think that a society's legal system is something external to that society that *makes* it orderly. But as the rule-following paradox shows, there couldn't be any such self-applying entity....

To return to the Constitution, it's not as if the proper interpretation (whatever that may be) can be hardwired and somehow imposed to guarantee that legislators, presidents, and judges will act in certain ways, or that the public will demand such. At every point *people* will be making decisions, including decisions over which interpretation of the rules is right. "Government is not some sort of automatic robot standing outside the social order it serves," Long wrote. "Its existence ... depends on ongoing cooperation, both from the members of the government and from the populace it governs."

In other words, a particular interpretation of the Constitution in reality means that people act in particular ways to achieve particular values in particular situations, and they expect others to act in particular ways. There's no automatic pilot, no impersonal mechanism, and no mere declaration or constitution that can get society to where you want it to go.

Long added:

> Presumably a mere written document is not sufficient to limit the government's power; what's needed are actual institutional structures. But these sorts of constitutional restraints, such as checks and balances and divided powers, do not exist in their own right, as external limitations on society as a whole; on the contrary, they exist only insofar as they are maintained in existence by human beings acting in systematic ways....
>
> Just as it's tempting to think that my grasp of a rule is something independent of my actions, something that makes me behave in a certain way, so it's equally tempting to think that a society's legal system is something external to that society that makes it orderly. But as the rule-following paradox shows, there couldn't be any such self-applying entity; and since individuals do manage to follow rules pretty well most of the time—and since societies do likewise manage to maintain order pretty well most of the time—the absence of such a self-applying entity is no problem at all.

This is something like what Thomas Paine had in mind (without fully appreciating it), as noted previously, when he wrote in *Rights of Man* (1792), "Great part of that order which reigns among mankind is not the effect of government. It has its origin in the principles of society and the natural constitution of man. It existed prior to government, and would exist if the formality of government was abolished. In fine, society performs for itself almost everything which is ascribed to government."

Long concludes from this that the challenges of bringing about a free society under the principle of market anarchism, or statelessness, are similar to those faced by advocates of limited government: the latter gain no advantage from their written constitution or court of final jurisdiction. Those things provide no greater guarantee of freedom than a competitive, polycentric legal order because rules are not the external constraints they think they are.

As Jeffrey Rogers Hummel explained in the "The Constitution as Counter-Revolution" (online at http://www.la-articles.org.uk/FL-5-4-3.pdf), the Federal Convention of 1787 was dominated by nationalist Hamiltonians rather than (anti-)federalist Jeffersonians. In drafting the document the centralists largely got their way (despite some compromises), and that Constitution was ratified by state conventions. Then at Anti-Federalist insistence the Bill of Rights (which, as we saw in chapter 4, did not change the structure of the government) was added. Yet, Hummel writes, "The Anti-Federalists … won on the question of how the Constitution would operate in practice…. To oversimplify only slightly, the Federalists got their Constitution, but the Anti-Federalists determined how it would be interpreted." The Federalists' words didn't deliver what they hoped—at least for a while.

Thus words faithfully recited or carefully inscribed on parchment will never assure liberty. If you doubt this, look around. If liberty is to be made full, government power must be rolled back (on the way eventually to being abolished). And if government power is to be rolled back, the real constitution—the one embedded in people's own actions and expectations about the actions of others—must be pro-liberty. That's why there's no substitute for education and an intellectual–moral revolution.

9

James Madison: Father of the Implied-Powers Doctrine

A free society depends ultimately on people having a disposition favoring justice, which includes respect for other people's rights. As I discussed in the last chapter, this requires more than the words they recite or put on paper. Most crucial is how they *act* and expect others to act—the rules they follow. For this reason it is futile to put undue emphasis on written constitutions as the key to liberty. The real constitution is within each of us. If the freedom philosophy is not inscribed in the actions of people, no constitution will help.

The 1977 Soviet Constitution proclaimed, "In accordance with the interests of the people and in order to strengthen and develop the socialist system, citizens of the USSR are guaranteed freedom of speech, of the press, and of assembly, meetings, street processions and demonstrations.... Citizens of the USSR are guaranteed freedom of conscience, that is, the right to profess or not to profess any religion, and to conduct religious worship or atheistic propaganda." The 1936 Constitution contained some of the same guarantees.

How much were those words worth?

I am reminded of the weak protection afforded liberty through mere words by Richard Labunski's book *James Madison and the Struggle for the Bill of Rights* (2006). Labunski provides a well-written account of how James Madison kept his promise to have the first U.S. Congress amend the new Constitution in order to add a bill of rights. As I've already pointed out, the resulting Bill of Rights did not address the deepest concerns of the most libertarian activists at the time, the Anti-Federalists. But the behind-the-scenes story sheds light on the thinking of the man regarded at the father of the Constitution.

Before we get to that story, however, we should take a closer look at Madison's pre-Constitution record. Madison was a member of Congress under the Articles of Confederation. As already described, the relatively bare-bones Articles left little for ambitious nationalist politicians seeking to expand the power of the central government to work with. But that did not stop them from trying. For example, the Congress's Superintendent of Finance, Robert Morris, argued that Congress, which could not impose taxes, had an *implied* power to force the states to finance the federal war debt. Less than two weeks after the Articles took effect, Congressman Madison thought he found a way to increase the national government's power. He introduced an amendment that stated: "A general and implied power is vested in the United States in Congress assembled to enforce and carry into effect all the articles of the said Confederation against any of the States which shall refuse or neglect to abide by such determinations."

Note the phrase "general and implied power." Constitutionalists, including libertarian constitutionalists, despise the implied-powers doctrine because it contains the potential for unlimited power. Yet here was Madison seeking to incorporate the doctrine into the Articles.

As Ralph Ketcham wrote in *James Madison: A Biography* (1971), "Madison sought as well to make the mode of enforcement explicit: Congress was authorized 'to employ the force of the United States as well by sea as by land' to compel obedience to its resolves." Once again we see Madison's nationalism and centralism.

The amendment, along with others that would have bulked up the central government, failed. Ketcham noted that Madison then became "more devious" in his attempts to enlarge its powers. In the end he gave up; hence, the move toward a convention, the scrapping of the Articles, and the formulation of a new constitution in order to create a government with far more sweeping powers.

Ketcham also noted that Madison again revealed his constitutional philosophy when, before the Federal Convention, he "opposed a strict definition of 'the extent of Legislative power'" in advising Kentuckians who were contemplating a state constitution.

As described in chapter 4, Madison entered the first Congress under the new Constitution determined to add a modest bill of rights, one that would leave the government's structure and powers intact while invoking traditional, uncontroversial rights of Englishmen. (The one amendment Madison apparently really wanted—a prohibition on *state* violations of freedom of speech, press, and religion and the right to a jury trial—was removed by the Senate, whose members were chosen by state legislatures.)

Madison revealed an important element of his constitutional philosophy during the debate on what would become the 10th Amendment to the Constitution. As introduced, it read: "The powers not delegated to the United States by the Constitution, nor prohibited by it to the states, are reserved to the states respectively, or to the people."

Congressman Thomas Tudor Tucker of South Carolina proposed the addition of a single word: *expressly*. It thus would read: "The powers not *expressly* delegated to the United States by the Constitution, nor prohibited by it to the states, are reserved to the states respectively, or to the people." Here Tucker was making a last-ditch attempt to salvage language from the Articles of Confederation, Article II of which declared, "Each state retains its sovereignty, freedom, and independence, and every power, jurisdiction, and right, which is not by this Confederation expressly delegated to the United States, in Congress assembled." (More on this in the next chapter.)

Madison opposed Tucker's amendment, however, arguing that "it was impossible to confine a government to the exercise of express powers; there must necessarily be admitted *powers by implication*, unless the constitution descended to recount every minutiae." (Emphasis added.) Here, again, Madison invoked the need for implied powers, the Anti-Federalists' nightmare.

Tucker's amendment failed twice, first in the committee of the whole and then in the full House, by a 32-17 vote.

As Labunski noted, the change would have had dramatic consequences: "The Tucker amendment would have greatly diminished congressional authority under the 'necessary and proper' clause, which had granted Congress substantial discretion to carry out responsibilities assigned by the Constitution." At least it would have created tension within the document, undercutting those who sought to interpret the government's powers in the broadest possible way. The necessary-and-proper clause was a source of great concern to the Anti-Federalists. "Brutus" had warned that "no terms can be more indefinite than these, and it is obvious, that the legislature alone must be the judge what laws are proper and necessary for the purpose." And in Federalist 44 Madison had responded that "no axiom is more clearly established in law or in reason than that wherever the end is required, the means are authorized; wherever a general power to do a thing is given, every particular power necessary for doing it is included." That is exactly worried the Anti-Federalists.

This episode raises interesting questions. In light of Madison's plea that there must necessarily be admitted powers by implication, what are we to make of his famous line in Federalist 45 that "the powers delegated by the proposed Constitution to the Federal Government, are few and defined"? When constitutionalists, libertarian or otherwise, appeal to original meaning, intent, or understanding, which one have they in mind? And which counts more: what was said during deliberations over the text (according to Madison's notes); what was said in the Federalist Papers, which were polemical newspaper columns written to win public support for the Constitution; or what was said by Madison in the debate over the Bill of Rights? Is Madison a reliable ally to be cited with confidence?

Moreover, when the Constitution says, "Congress has the power To make all laws which shall be necessary and proper for carrying into execution the foregoing powers, and all other powers vested by this Constitution in the government of the United States, or in any department or officer thereof," where is the bright line that limits the scope of the national government?

Most important, how is something as malleable as the language of a political document borne of compromise to protect our freedom from those who would read its phrases broadly?

Madison was right, of course. No constitution could expressly enumerate all powers without appending an endless list of minutiae. There must be implied powers. But that's the danger of a constitution and a monopoly constitutional government. Implied powers must be inferred, and inference requires interpretation. Who is likely to have the inside track in that process: those who seek to restrict government power or those who seek to expand it? We know the answer to that question.

The Constitution or Liberty

"Each state retains its sovereignty, freedom, and independence, and every power, jurisdiction, and right, which is not by this Confederation expressly delegated to the United States, in Congress assembled."

We might think those words—or words to the same effect—are in the U.S. Constitution. But they are not. They are from Article II of the Articles of Confederation, America's first constitution. They could have been placed in the U.S. Constitution but were deliberately left out in 1787 and again in 1789.

As we saw in the last chapter, after the Constitution was ratified, something vaguely like Article II was added to the Constitution as the 10th Amendment. Unfortunately it is like Article II in the same sense that a whale is like a fish—superficially.

As noted in the last chapter, the 10th Amendment says: "The powers not delegated to the United States by the Constitution, nor prohibited by it to the States, are reserved to the States respectively, or to the people."

One significant difference, as we've already seen, is that Article II qualifies the word *delegated* with *expressly*. The 10th Amendment does not, due to James Madison's opposition. The difference was no oversight. Thus while the Articles of Confederation really was a document of explicitly enumerated congressional powers, or an honest attempt at such, the Constitution, contrary to widespread belief, was not.

The two clauses had another significant difference, as William Crosskey noted in *Politics and the Constitution in the History of the United States* (1953). Article II says expressly undelegated powers are *retained* by the states. But in the 10th Amendment, such powers are *reserved*. To *retain* is to keep what one already possesses. To *reserve* something to someone does not imply it was previously possessed. Thus the 10th Amendment diminishes the states compared to Article II. Crosskey also offers persuasive evidence that virtually no one—neither the Federalists nor Anti-

Federalists—thought the 10th Amendment changed the nature of the Constitution. On the contrary, it was taken as a reaffirmation.

In a 2005 research paper titled "The Dubious Enumerated Power Doctrine" (online at https://law.utexas.edu/faculty/calvinjohnson/DubiousEnum.pdf) Professor Calvin H. Johnson of the University of Texas Law School presented formidable evidence that the framers had no intention of limiting the national government's powers to the 16 items listed in Article I, Section 8, of the Constitution.

"In carrying over the Articles' wording and structure, they removed old Article II's limitation that Congress would have only powers 'expressly delegated' to it," Johnson wrote. "When challenged about the removal, the Framers explained that the expressly delegated limitation had proved 'destructive to the Union'.... Proponents of the Constitution defended the deletion of 'expressly' through to the passage of the Tenth Amendment. That history implies that not everything about federal power needs to be written down."

The Federal Convention of course operated on the assumption that more, not fewer, powers were needed for the national government than were allowed under the Articles. Johnson quotes some of the framers to indicate this attitude. As already noted, Madison wrote to Jefferson that "the evils suffered and feared from weakness in Government have turned the attention more toward the means of strengthening the [government] than of narrowing [it]."

When the convention began its work the delegates passed resolutions to guide the committees that were drafting particular sections of the document. Johnson explained that one such binding resolution specified that the new government would have every power enumerated in the Articles and an additional power (quoting the resolution) "to legislate in all Cases for the general Interests of the Union."

This conflicts with the common view that Article I, Section 8, of the Constitution exhausts the national government's powers. That view is undermined by several inconvenient facts. For example, the first clause of Article I, Section 8, states, "The Congress shall have Power To lay and collect Taxes, Duties, Imposts and Excises, to pay the Debts and provide for the common Defence and general Welfare of the United States...." That's a hefty grant of power that does not appear to be further restricted by any subsequent language. (Jefferson and Madison disagreed. See Madison's Federalist 41, keeping in mind, again, that the Federalist Papers were essentially ad copy for the Constitution and against the Anti-Federalist opposition.) The 16 specific powers that follow don't appear to limit the taxation clause but rather coequal provisions. (See chapter 11, "Was the Constitution Really Meant to Constrain the Government?")

But then why include a list of powers if it was not meant to be exhaustive? Johnson responded: "Reading the Constitution as giving a general power to provide for the general welfare means that the enumerated powers of clauses 2 through 17 are *illustrative* of what Congress may do within an appropriately national sphere, but are not exhaustive." (Emphasis added.)

In other words, Congress can't do whatever it wants: it can only act for the common defense and general welfare. But that's a lot and it's not all spelled out, especially since words don't interpret themselves. Thus in the eyes of the framers, the government would be limited, but not in the way that today's constitutionalists believe. The view among the framers was that Congress's jurisdiction covered all matters national in scope, leaving local matters to the states. But importantly, as Johnson wrote, "both Madison and Hamilton argued that the division between the federal and state governments was a legislative or political question that would be set in the future by competition between those governments for the loyalty of the people."

We know that the Constitution must have contained implied powers from the beginning. Article I, Section 9, expressly prohibits Congress from doing certain things, such as passing ex post facto laws and bills of attainder and granting titles of nobility. Why would such prohibitions have been thought necessary if Congress could exercise only enumerated powers? (We've already noted another example: the implied power of eminent domain, later limited, for a while, by the Fifth Amendment.)

Johnson's argument would not be news to the Anti-Federalists. (It should be noted that Southern Anti-Federalists like Patrick Henry objected to an expanded national government in part because they feared the taxing power might be used to free their slaves. Thus was a good cause, decentralization of power, perhaps permanently stained by a link to the abomination of slavery. Samuel Johnson had it right: "How is it that we hear the loudest yelps for liberty among the drivers of negroes?")

Moreover, when advocates of the proposed Constitution advertised the document as containing express, enumerated powers, the Anti-Federalists and fellow travelers such as Thomas Jefferson scoffed. For example, Federalist James Wilson said: "The congressional authority is to be collected, not from tacit implication but from the positive grant expressed in the [Constitution].... [E]verything which is not given [to the national government], is reserved [to the states]."

To which Jefferson replied: "To say, as Mr. Wilson does that ... all is reserved in the case of the general government which is not given ... might do for the Audience to whom it was addressed, but is surely gratis dictim, opposed by strong inferences from the body of the instrument, as well as from the omission of the clause of our present confederation [Article II], which declared that in express terms."

Calvin Johnson is happy the Constitution has expansive and implied powers. No libertarian would be. But we must separate what the Constitution appears to say and how we evaluate it, and resist the temptation to let our political-moral views warp our reading.

11

Was the Constitution Really Meant to Constrain the Government?

There's no shortcut to a free society. But that hasn't prevented some libertarians from looking for one. A shortcut favored by many advocates of limited government is the imagined restoration of the "lost" Constitution. If only we could get back to the Constitution as it was written and understood in its time, they say. It's a sincere wish, but as a path to a free society, it's riddled with potholes. Not that I don't want the Constitution interpreted in the most restrictive way in order to prevent violations of liberty. The problem is how we can get there from here. Many advocates of liberty think they just have to appeal to the "original meaning or understanding" and things would more or less take care of themselves. But if that were so, why are we in the mess we're in now? I presume that earlier generations interpreted the Constitution in a way more to the liking of today's constitutionalists. What happened? Since that time, the Constitution has never been suspended; the government wasn't replaced by a nonconstitutional regime. The formal Constitution has been in force continuously since 1789. Everything that happened was justified constitutionally.

So Lysander Spooner, the 19th natural-law individualist anarchist and constitutional scholar, was right. To quote him again: "the Constitution has either authorized such a government as we have had, or has been powerless to prevent it," he wrote in "The Constitution of No Authority" (online at http://praxeology.net/LS-NT-6.htm.). The "parchment barrier" against power (James Madison's term for the Bill of Rights) wasn't much of a barrier. (Where it appears to have worked, it's because the liberty in question is deeply rooted in people's values independent of any document. Why is the First Amendment more honored than the Fourth?)

This suggests that understanding the Constitution—and constitutional government itself—is not the straightforward project it's made out to be. The reason is not hard to discern. Controversies over the meaning of rules—especially rules about justice, freedom, and force, which must be applied in unforeseeable circumstances—are inevitable. As already discussed, constitutions do not speak for or interpret themselves. People interpret them. There is no way to avoid moral and political discourse. And there's always the chance that someone else's interpretation will prevail. What then?

The Constitution, let us not forget, was the product of compromise, crafted so as to be acceptable both to Federalists, who wanted a strong central government, and people who distrusted concentrated power. The proof is that Alexander Hamilton and Thomas Jefferson, whose political philosophies could hardly have been more different, both looked on the Constitution with favor (less so in Jefferson's case).

Can't we resolve the differences over meaning by appealing to the writings of the framers, such as the Federalist Papers or James Madison's letters and notes on the Federal Convention? We can try. But where does that get us? Anything the framers said or wrote about the Constitution was necessarily expressed in language—which inevitably will be subject to the same controversies regarding its application as the Constitution itself. The problem is merely moved back a step. Instead of arguing about the Constitution, we'd be arguing about what Madison, Hamilton, and John Jay *wrote* about the Constitution. But if a given interpretation of a constitutional clause is controversial, wouldn't the framers' statements about the clause be controversial also? How do we resolve any controversy? By resort to other statements? The process would have no end.

We've already seen Ludwig Wittgenstein's insight in this regard, "Any interpretation still hangs in the air along with what it interprets, and cannot give it any support. Interpretations by themselves do not determine meaning."

Take the pesky general-welfare Clause. The term *general welfare* appears in the preamble to the Constitution as well as in Clause 1 of Article I, Section 8, which sets out the powers of Congress. Contrary to what many constitutionalists believe, the clause looks like a general grant of power: "Congress shall have the Power *To* lay and collect Taxes, Duties, Imposts and Excises, to . . . provide for the common Defense and general

Welfare of the United States. . . ." (Emphasis added.) Following Clause 1 are 17 more clauses, each beginning with the capitalized word *To* like the one above. This suggests that all 18 clauses are coequal, independent items in a list. Clause 1, then, does not look like a preamble introducing an exhaustive list of 17 powers.

Madison rejected this interpretation, which had been voiced by the Antifederalists. In Federalist 41 he wrote:

> It has been urged and echoed, that the power to lay and collect taxes, duties, imposts, and excises, to pay the debts, and provide for the common defense and general welfare of the United States, amounts to an unlimited commission to exercise every power which may be alleged to be necessary for the common defense or general welfare. No stronger proof could be given of the distress under which these writers labor for objections, than their stooping to such a misconstruction.
>
> Had no other enumeration or definition of the powers of the Congress been found in the Constitution, than the general expressions just cited, the authors of the objection might have had some color for it; though it would have been difficult to find a reason for so awkward a form of describing an authority to legislate in all possible cases....
>
> But what color can the objection have, when a specification of the objects alluded to by these general terms immediately follows, and is not even separated by a longer pause than a semicolon?

Does this dispose of the matter? Hardly. First, the Constitution does not direct us to consult Madison for definitive interpretations of possibly vague clauses. (Must we also find out what Hamilton thought? Who else?) In the Federalist Madison was *selling* the Constitution to a partly skeptical population. It is plausible that the Federalists who dominated the state ratifying conventions were aware of this and didn't take Madison's pitch seriously. At any rate, we can't know what was in their minds when they voted yea. We only know what language they assented to.

Second, the construction of Article I, Section 8, is, alas, patently inconsistent with Madison's description. (I'm reminded of Chico Marx's line, "Who are you going to believe, me or your own eyes?") Madison's point about the semicolon is ironic, since it supports my view not his. Madison's case would have been stronger if the punctuation mark were a colon, since that's how we introduce lists. Semicolons suggest elements at the same level.

Some might say that we must judge Article I, Section 8, by the entire Constitution and specifically the purposes enumerated in the Preamble. Fine. Here's the Preamble:

We the People of the United States, in Order to form a more perfect Union, establish Justice, insure domestic Tranquility, provide for the common defence, promote the general Welfare, and secure the Blessings of Liberty to ourselves and our Posterity, do ordain and establish this Constitution for the United States of America.

Conspicuously missing from this list is: *to constrain the powers of government.* How did we overlook this? One comeback is that restraining government is implicit in the references to justice and liberty. In my view, justice and liberty certainly impose limits on anyone's power to use force, namely, limitation to defensive and restitutive purposes. But there are other notions of justice and liberty (which I would regard as mistaken). Advocates of expansive government power also see themselves as champions of justice and liberty—just ask them. How do we know that the language in the Constitution doesn't mirror those other notions? There was a good deal of government intervention in the states back then, including poor relief and regulation of commerce.

We could answer that question by pointing to the Declaration of Independence, which embraces the rights to life, liberty, and the pursuit of happiness. But does that really get us out of the woods? Someone who believes the Preamble authorizes the welfare state will similarly believe the rights to life, liberty, and the pursuit of happiness *entail* the welfare state. But even if the Declaration resists that interpretation, we must note, as historian Merrill Jensen did, that the authors of the Constitution of 1787 were quite a different set of men from those who signed the Declaration of Independence in 1776.

My message is not one of despair. But we will not promote the freedom philosophy merely by invoking a political document written by men who thought the main problem with America was too little, not too much, national government. Rather, we must cut to the chase and convince people directly that our concepts of freedom and justice best accord with their own deepest moral sense.

12

That Mercantilist Commerce Clause

The commerce clause in Article I, Section 8, of the Constitution has been used to justify a wide expansion of government power, from antidiscrimination laws to drug prohibition to a ban on guns near schools. In objecting to use of the commerce clause for such seemingly remote purposes, some constitutionalists, including many libertarians, rely on a particular historical interpretation of both the clause and the Constitution as a whole. Roger Pilon of the Cato Institute, for instance, writes,

> The Commerce Clause, through which so much modern drug law has been enacted, was written to enable Congress to regulate, or 'make regular,' commerce among the states—and, in particular, to enable Congress to override or address the state and foreign protectionism that was frustrating free trade when the clause was written.... It is all but a commonplace, however, that that was the principal rationale for the clause—indeed, for the new Constitution—in the first place. It was out of a pressing need to regularize the domestic and foreign commerce of the nation that was breaking down under government measures the Articles of Confederation permitted.

There certainly seems to be support for that position. As Pilon notes, Justice William Johnson wrote in *Gibbons v. Ogden*, the first major commerce-clause case: "If there was any one object riding over every other in the adoption of the constitution, it was to keep the commercial intercourse among the States free from all invidious and partial restraints."

But there is to be more to the story, and it goes against Pilon's argument. In 2004 a revealing paper appeared in the *William & Mary Bill of Rights Journal* with the curious title, "The Panda's Thumb: The Modest and Mercantilist Original Meaning of the Commerce Clause," by Calvin Johnson, whom we encountered in chapter 10 (online at https://tinyurl.com/htgezb4). I came across this paper for the first time while reading Richard Epstein's book *How the Progressives Rewrote the Constitution* (2007).

Let's start with the text. Article I, Section 8, Clause 3, of the Constitution delegates to Congress the power "to regulate commerce with foreign nations, and among the several states, and with the Indian tribes."

What does "regulate commerce" mean? Does it mean only to "make regular"? Johnson took a promising route to finding out. He wrote, "To determine what was meant by 'regulation of commerce,' this review collects and categorizes 161 uses of the phrase 'regulation of commerce' or the word 'commerce' in the debates over the adoption of the Constitution. One hundred thirty-nine of those uses are associated with a specific goal or program....The samples come from both sides of the debate and the sampling was intended to be omnivorous."

Here is Johnson's summary of his findings:

> In the original debates over adoption of the Constitution, regulation of commerce was used, *almost exclusively*, as a cover of words for specific *mercantilist* proposals related to deep-water shipping and foreign trade. The Constitution was written *before* Adam Smith, laissez faire and free trade came to dominate economic thinking and the Commerce Clause draws its original meaning from the preceding *mercantilist* tradition. All of the concrete programs intended to be forwarded by giving Congress the power to regulate commerce were *restrictions on international trade giving subsidy or protection to favored domestic merchants or punishing imports or foreign producers*. [Emphasis added.]

He added, "Neither trade with the Indians nor interstate commerce shows up as a significant issue in the original debates." And to drive the point home, he wrote, "It is often now stated that the major purpose of the Constitution was to prevent protectionist economic policies among the states and to establish a common market with free trade across state borders. *Barriers on interstate commerce, however, were not a notable issue in the original debates.*" (Emphasis added.)

This is consistent with the fact that the first economic bill passed by the first Congress under the Constitution—on July 4, 1789—was a comprehensive protectionist tariff. Moreover, as we've seen, the mercantilist Alexander Hamilton believed a strong national government was necessary precisely to keep the tariff against European goods higher than the states could have kept it. States competing for trade would drive it down to low levels, Hamilton feared. As he wrote in Federalist 12:

> It is therefore, evident, that one national government would be able, at much less expence, to extend the duties on imports, beyond comparison further, than would be practicable to the States separately, or to any partial confederacies: Hitherto I believe it may safely be asserted, that these duties have not

upon an average exceeded in any State three per cent. . . . There seems to be nothing to hinder their being increased in this country, to at least treble their present amount.

Treble what the states had imposed! But only if trade policy was cartelized under a central government. This was an important reason for replacing the Articles of Confederation with the Constitution. One can look at it as a document intended to stifle competition among the states.

Johnson reinforces this point: "Hamilton argued that imposts by the individual states would be difficult to enforce because the bays, rivers and long borders between the states made smuggling too easy. On the federal level, however, there was only one side to guard—the Atlantic. The general government would regulate commerce with a uniform impost and so make commerce productive of general revenue."

Revenue was one of the big attractions for the advocates of a strong central government. James Madison asked, "Was it not an acknowledged object of the Convention, and the universal expectation of the people, that the regulation of trade should be submitted to the general government in such a form as would render it an immediate source of general revenue?"

Unfortunately, Johnson adds, the Anti-Federalists did not oppose giving the national government the power to tax imports. They too were mercantilists. (*The Wealth of Nations* was barely a decade old.) However, as he points out, the national government didn't need the commerce clause to tax imports or to stop the states from doing so. Those things are handled elsewhere in Article I.

Johnson continued:

Commerce in the constitutional debates primarily referred, at 83% of the program-associated quotes, to Atlantic Ocean shipping. The most important issues within regulation of commerce were tax issues: *to regulate commerce meant to tax it* (27% of program-associated quotes). The remainder of the actively-proposed programs under regulation of commerce … were restrictions on foreign trade. Proponents of the Constitution advocated retaliatory tariffs against the British as punishment for excluding American ships from the British West Indies (28%) and they advocated giving American ships a monopoly on the export of American commodities (22%). [Emphasis added.]

As this shows, revenue was not the only concern. Johnson documents that Federalists and Anti-Federalists alike feared trade imbalances, the loss of gold and silver, and the importation of luxury goods. They were, at bottom, mercantilists. So too did they favor subsidies under the rubric "regulation of commerce." Johnson writes, "Hamilton had argued as early as 1781 that the Congress needed the 'power of regulating trade, comprehending a right of granting bounties and premiums by way of encouragement.'" He was joined in this mercantilist effort by George Washington and Madison, who, lamenting what he called "the present anarchy of our commerce," "joined [Johnson writes] in the enthusiasm, denouncing those who were 'decoying the people into a belief that trade ought in all cases to be left to regulate itself.'" It's unclear who thought that trade should regulate itself.

Johnson commented: "Indeed, given that Madison had condemned those who advocated free trade and had traced most of our political and moral errors to the imports that drained us of our precious metals, the insincere part of Madison's 1789 address to the House was the opening claim that he was 'the friend to a very free system of commerce.'"

The upshot of Johnson's thesis is that the commerce clause, contrary to common belief, was mercantilist in intent, although most of the protectionist program was never adopted because of popular resistance. As a result, Johnson doesn't believe the clause was the main impetus for the Constitution: "Clause 1, the first power listed, gives the federal government the power to tax to provide for the common defense and general welfare. The tax power gave effect and consequence to the federal government. The explanation for the constitutional revolution thus plausibly resides in Clause 1 … rather than in Clause 3, the Commerce Clause."

But what about Justice Johnson's quote above, claiming that the chief purpose of the Constitution was to keep interstate trade open? Professor Johnson responded: "Justice Johnson's comments are not a fair description of the effect of the Constitution, but they are a fair description of a movement for nationalization and against balkanization of the states, which includes the adoption of the Articles [of Confederation]. He continued:

> Reducing barriers on interstate trade, however, was not an important part of the constitutional debates. The major reason for this was that the goal had already been mostly achieved and not challenged. The Articles of Confederation had already prohibited any state from imposing a duty, imposition or restriction on any out-of-state citizens that it did not impose on its own inhabitants. The states seem to have followed the norm well enough that the issue did not make it among the issues the debaters were most concerned about.

Nevertheless, many people believe that interstate trade barriers were *the* concern of the framers and ratifiers. How can that be? It might have something to do with the fact, Johnson writes, that "The Federalists did use the specter of trade barriers to scare voters toward ratification of the Constitution.... [But] Hamilton's example of interstate barriers came from the German empire, not from the United States."

Two more brief points: First, the commerce clause is usually regarded as pertaining only to interstate commerce, but this is not self-evident. William Crosskey in *Politics and the Constitution in the History of the United States* (1953) argued plausibly that at the time, "among the several states" meant "among *the people* of the several states" and that an exclusively *interstate* meaning was almost certainly not intended. For example, he provided quotations from literate people at the time who referred to the duty of government to promote peace or tranquility or happiness "among the several states." The contexts of these quotations indicate that these could not have been meant to exclude *intrastate* peace or tranquility or happiness. In fact, in one example a delegate to the Federal Convention lamented that although Congress in the Confederation period "was intended to be a body to preserve peace among the states," it was not authorized to suppress Shays's Rebellion, an entirely intrastate affair.

Moreover, Crosskey provides many quotations showing that the word *state* itself more often than not meant *the people* of a state. This was apparently the default meaning; other senses of the word seemed to require specification. Had the framers meant "trade between people of different states," they were perfectly capable of saying that, as they did in Article III: "The judicial Power shall extend to all Cases ... between Citizens of different States."

Second, self-described strict constructionists insist that *commerce* means only trade, not manufacturing and other economic activities. But some historians who have examined how the word was used in 1787 say the word was more general. The upshot is that the commerce clause may not have been intended as a limit on the power of Congress to regulate trade, but more of a general grant of power. At the very least, this "original meaning" cannot be dismissed out of hand.

This brings us to Johnson's title, "The Panda's Thumb." Fans of Stephen Jay Gould will recognize that phrase. It's the title essay of one of his books and refers to the evolution of a panda's "thumb" from a wrist bone. Johnson's point is that from mercantilist beginnings, the commerce clause evolved into something very different: "That the power to regulate commerce was once a mercantilist clause, regulating commerce by restricting it, should not bother us very much. We are no longer mercantilists."

Considering the daily panic of pundits and politicians about the "trade deficit," one has to wonder what Johnson is talking about here.

13
The All-Embracing Power to Tax

Despite warnings from the Anti-Federalists, some people today refuse to believe that the Constitution gave Congress a virtually limitless power to tax. The vastness of this power can be seen in America's experience with the income tax. For many opponents of the income tax the name *Brushaber* is magical. It comes from *Frank R. Brushaber v. Union Pacific Railroad Co.*, the 1916 U.S. Supreme Court case that upheld the 1913 income-tax law passed under the 16th Amendment to the U.S. Constitution. That income-tax opponents would look with favor on a Supreme Court opinion that affirmed, in the most sweeping language, Congress's power to tax incomes "from whatever source derived" seems incomprehensible. But according to their reading of the case, *Brushaber* is salvation.

That reading, I'm sorry to say, is wrong—in the extreme. After close study of the case, its context, predecessors, and successors, I am compelled to conclude that *Brushaber* offers neither aid nor comfort to those looking for a legal escape from the hated income tax. If we are ever to get this monster off our backs, it will not be through casuistry and pettifoggery. We will have to pull off a far tougher feat: convincing a critical mass of the American people that taxation is theft.

A cautionary note: do not conclude from what I will demonstrate in this series of articles that I approve of the income tax. My book on that subject, *Your Money or Your Life: Why We Must Abolish the Income Tax,* makes my position clear. The tax (like all taxes) entails the threat of physical force against nonaggressors and is thus indistinguishable from robbery or extortion. In the most fundamental terms, the income tax is objectionable not because it's an *income* tax, but because it is an income *tax*. In other words, Frank Chodorov, one of my heroes, was wrong. It's not the income tax that is "the root of all evil." It's taxation per se—the transfer of purchasing power from the people to the state—that is the ultimate power without which government could not operate.

The gulf between morality and the edicts of governments is vast. To say that something is legal (in the narrow sense) or constitutional is not to say it is moral or proper. When I say the income-tax laws satisfy the requirements of the U.S. Constitution, I hope I will not be taken to say that the income tax is legitimate in the moral sense.

I know libertarians and others who insist that *Brushaber* shows beyond doubt that the federal government has no constitutional power to tax the wages of ordinary Americans and that the income-tax laws passed over the years were never intended to tax that form of income. In this view, the only income targeted for taxation was that which is derived from federal privilege: government employment, government contracts, corporate income, trade across national boundaries, business done in the federal possessions, etc. One looks at *Brushaber* in vain for such a statement. (If "privilege" is broad enough to include trade with foreigners, the concept is very broad indeed—broad enough to cover almost all people under the jurisdiction of the U.S. government and hence all forms of income.)

But according to *Brushaber* fans, the link between taxable income and federal privilege is indirect. The emptiness of this claim will be clear by the end of this chapter.

To understand *Brushaber* we have to understand why the 16th Amendment was passed. And to do that, we have to reach back to 1894, when Congress passed the Wilson-Gorman Tariff, which included an income tax. (The first U.S. income tax was passed during the War Between the States.)

But first we must pause to consider the matter of direct and indirect taxes, an important distinction in the Constitution. Article I, Section 8, Clause 1 of the Constitution states, "The Congress shall have Power To lay and collect Taxes, Duties, Imposts and Excises . . . ; but all Duties, Imposts and Excises shall be uniform throughout the United States." Article I, Section 9, Clause 4, states, "No capitation, or other direct, Tax shall be laid, unless in Proportion to the Census or Enumeration herein before directed to be taken."

This has been interpreted as a simple distinction: direct taxes must be apportioned among the states according to population; indirect taxes must be uniform throughout the states.

What seems simple on its face is not simple at all. It is far from clear what a direct tax is and what an indirect tax is. The Framers provided one example of a direct tax, the head tax, and used several terms for presumed indirect taxes: duties, imposts, and excises. But as we'll see, that doesn't tell us whether a given tax is, say, an excise tax or not.

In 1794, during George Washington's administration, Congress passed a tax on "carriages for the conveyance of persons," whether for hire or for personal use. This was not a sales tax, but a $16 assessment on every carriage owned, including those possessed at the time the tax was passed. Since the tax was not apportioned among the states, the courts were asked to declare it unconstitutional.

Was that a tax on the ownership of property, making it direct and in need of apportionment? Or was it on the *use* of property, presumably making it an excise and thus an indirect tax not in need of apportionment (but in need of uniformity)?

No less an authority on the Constitution than James Madison, a member of Congress, said it was a direct tax and hence unconstitutional as written. His friend Fisher Ames, a respected Federalist member of Congress, said it was an indirect tax and hence perfectly constitutional because "the duty falls not on the possession, but on the use." Arch-Federalist and Treasury Secretary Alexander Hamilton filed a brief in the case, in which he said, "If the meaning of the word 'excise' is to be sought in a British statute, it will be found to include the duty on carriages, which is there considered as an 'excise.'"

These men who attended the Federal Convention did not agree on whether this tax was direct or indirect.

Although each of the six Supreme Court justices had a different rationale, the Supreme Court, in *Hylton v. United States* (1796), sided with Hamilton and Ames. The tax was declared indirect and not in need of apportionment.

Here was an early clue that the distinction between direct and indirect was by no means straightforward. If Madison on one hand and Hamilton and Ames on the other couldn't agree on what seemed to be a simple matter, what lay ahead? In fact, efforts to decide what is direct and what is indirect have something of the feel of a coin toss. Earlier Hamilton had confessed confusion about the terms: "It is a matter of regret that terms so uncertain and vague in so important a point are to be found in the Constitution." No less an authority on the Constitution than Fisher Ames, who like Hamilton and Madison attended the Federal Convention, said, "It was difficult to define whether a tax is direct or not." Indeed, when someone at the Convention asked for a clarification of the term *direct taxation*, Madison recorded in his notes, "No one answered."

To add to the confusion, I will point out that while American legal authorities have regarded taxation of income generally as an indirect (excise) tax not requiring apportionment, the British have long regarded it as a direct tax.

The United States got its first income tax during the Civil war, again demonstrating that war harms ordinary people in more ways than one. In any war government becomes an especially voracious consumer of the people's resources, so it is no surprise that the first income tax came when it did.

Several successive wartime bills enacting progressive income taxes were passed by Congress, and when the war ended, the income tax did not. Changes to the law got rid of the progressive rate structure, but the tax continued. A flat rate of 5 percent was levied on incomes over $1,000. Out of a population of 39.5 million, no more than 250,000 people paid it. The tax, however, was set to expire in 1870, but it would not end. The pro-income-tax forces rallied, and Congress passed a 2.5 percent tax with a $2,000 exemption. Then, two years later, that tax was allowed to expire. For the first time since the war, (wealthy) Americans did not see their incomes taxed.

The big budget surplus was a major reason the tax was permitted to die. Meanwhile, the pro-tax lobby kept at work, prompting the introduction of 68 bills from 1874 to 1894. A big selling point for populists was that the income tax would permit large reductions in tariffs, which, they correctly argued, harmed working people for the benefit of wealthy manufacturers. Their wish to relieve workers of the burden of protectionism was admirable, but their strategy was flawed. Eventually, Americans would have an income tax and high tariffs. There's a lesson in that for all would-be tax reformers.

Congress next passed an income tax in 1894, during a depression that ate up the budget surplus. President Grover Cleveland, who said he opposed the tax, let it become law without his signature. The law imposed a 2 percent tax on "gains, profits and incomes" over $4,000 during a five-year period. Few people would have paid it—and it had a short life, because it was successfully challenged by a bank stockholder, Charles Pollock, who objected that taxation of dividend income as written in the law was unconstitutional because it was not apportioned among the states. His landmark U.S. Supreme Court case, *Pollock v. Farmers' Loan & Trust Co.* (1895), paved the way for the 16th Amendment.

To cut to the chase, the Supreme Court struck down the unapportioned tax. This has led people to conclude that the Court held income taxation itself unconstitutional. But, as we have seen, the Court did not say that.

The case had to be argued twice. In the first instance, the Court declared most of the bill unconstitutional, but split 4-4 on the question of whether a tax on general income was also unconstitutional. (One justice was ill.) On rehearing, the Court voted 5-4 to affirm its earlier decision and to add that income taxation per se was not barred by the Constitution.

The majority opinion, written by Chief Justice Melville Fuller, who has a classical-liberal reputation, is instructive. Recall that the Constitution distinguishes between direct taxes, such as a head, or poll, tax, and "Duties, Imposts and Excises," presumably indirect taxes. Direct taxes must be apportioned among the states according to the census. Indirect taxes do not require apportionment, but must be uniform throughout the country. Recall also that from the beginning, there was no general agreement on precisely which taxes were direct and which were indirect.

The 1894 tax was comprehensive, which led the Court to consider the nature of the tax as it affected different sources of income. Taking its two *Pollock* rulings together, the Court concluded that a general tax on income, being indirect, was constitutional without apportionment, but that a tax on income from real and personal property, being indistinguishable from a tax on the property itself, was direct taxation and thus required apportionment. Regarding the second point, the Court held,

> [Can] it be properly held that the constitution, taken in its plain and obvious sense, and with due regard to the circumstances attending the formation of the government, authorizes a general unapportioned tax on the products of the farm and the rents of real estate, although imposed merely because of ownership, and with no possible means of escape from payment, as belonging to a totally different class from that which includes the property from whence the income proceeds?

> ... Nor can we perceive any ground why the same reasoning does not apply to capital in personalty held for the purpose of income, or ordinarily yielding income, and to the income therefrom.

Thus the Court said that some taxes on income, depending on the source from which it derives, are direct taxes requiring apportionment. This did not mean that all income taxes were in that category. Determining whether a given tax is direct requires an examination of the income's source.

As to taxation of other income, the Court said it had "not commented on so much of it [the law] as bears on gains or profits from business, privileges, or employments, in view of the instances in which taxation on business, privileges, or employments has assumed the guise of an excise tax and been sustained as such."

In other words, a general income tax is an excise (indirect) tax and does not require apportionment. "[There] is no question as to the validity of this act," the Court ruled, "except [the sections on real and personal property]." Thus the tax on wages, salaries, and profits was held to be constitutional. But this created a problem. If the provisions that taxed income from real estate and securities were stricken, the Court said, "this would leave the burden of the tax to be borne by professions, trades, employments, or vocations; and in that way what was intended as a tax on capital would remain, in substance, a tax on occupations and labor. We cannot believe that such was the intention of congress." The Court concluded, "[The] scheme must be considered as a whole." So the entire act was stricken. This is what leads people to believe that income taxation in general was voided, but as we've seen, that is not the case.

The Court stressed that it was not its job to say whether an income tax was desirable. Nevertheless, it reminded the county that "the instrument [Constitution] defines the way for its amendment."

Champions of income taxation suffered a big setback. But they had one hope: a constitutional amendment. In 1913 the 16th Amendment was added to the U.S. Constitution. I leave aside the claims that the amendment was ratified improperly by the states. No court accepts this argument, which is based on trivialities. Besides, as we've seen, the case against the procedural integrity of the original Constitution's ratification is far stronger.

The 16th Amendment states: "The Congress shall have power to lay and collect taxes on incomes, from whatever source derived, without apportionment among the several States, and without regard to any census or enumeration."

In light of *Pollock* one can see the significance of the phrase "from whatever source derived." The amendment removed a restriction, one of the few, from Congress's power to tax, namely, by relieving it of the need to apportion a tax on income from property. As we shall see, it did not grant Congress the general power to tax incomes *because Congress needed no amendment to exercise a power the court said it already had.*

The same year that the 16th Amendment was ratified Congress passed a graduated income tax during a special session called by President Woodrow Wilson. As usual, the income tax began as a tax on the wealthy. (World War II turned it into a truly mass tax. That's war for you.) Shortly after passage, the tax law was challenged in federal court. The case culminated in a revealing Supreme Court decision, *Brushaber v. Union Pacific Railroad,* which was handed down in 1916. Frank Brushaber, a stockholder in the railroad, contended that the tax on the company violated due process. The Court rejected Brushaber's claims, arguing that it is "well settled" that the due-process provision is not a limit on the power to tax: "in other words, that the Constitution does not conflict with itself by conferring, upon the one hand, a taxing power, and taking the same power away, on the other, by the limitations of the due process clause."

For anyone looking for protection from taxation this is an ominous statement. The tax-protest movement attaches great weight to this opinion—for reasons that mystify me. The language of *Brushaber* should make any advocate of liberty cringe.

The Court laid the groundwork for its opinion by rehearsing the ruling in *Pollock*. It noted that the *Pollock* Court did not rule that income taxes in general were direct taxes requiring apportionment—only certain income taxes, namely, those on land and securities. The *Brushaber* Court commented,

> Nothing could serve to make this clearer than to recall that in the Pollock Case, in so far as the law taxed incomes from other classes of property than real estate and invested personal property, that is, income from "professions, trades, employments, or vocations," *its validity was recognized;* indeed, it was expressly declared that *no dispute was made upon that subject,* and attention was called to the fact that taxes on such income had been sustained as excise taxes in the past. [Emphasis added.]

In other words, Congress always had the constitutional power to tax incomes. (Tax-protest activists make much of the fact that the income tax is held to be an excise tax, but it's not clear what this gets them.)

The Court went on to say that the purpose of the 16th Amendment was to relieve the government of what the *Pollock* Court had to engage in, namely, an examination of the *sources* of income. In other words, future courts would no longer have to inquire whether a tax on a particular kind of income was in its effect a direct tax. Contrary to Frank Brushaber's argument, it said, no limitations on the power to tax incomes can be divined in the 16th Amendment. Indeed, all such contentions are "in irreconcilable conflict with the very purpose which the Amendment was adopted to accomplish."

If the opinion had stopped there, it would have been enough to depress opponents of income taxation. But the Court did not stop there. It went on to describe Congress's power to tax in the most sweeping terms possible, stressing that this power predated the 16th Amendment and was present from the beginning of the government. For example, the Court said that "the authority conferred upon Congress by § 8 of article 1 'to lay and collect taxes, duties, imposts and excises' is *exhaustive and embraces every conceivable power of taxation*" [emphasis added]. This is followed by: "[There] was authority given, as the part was included in the whole, to lay and collect income taxes," "the conceded complete and all-embracing taxing power," "the complete and perfect delegation of the power to tax," "the complete and all-embracing authority to tax"; and the "plenary power [to tax]."

In case someone missed the point, the Court also referred to "the all-embracing taxing authority possessed by Congress, including necessarily therein the power to impose income taxes."

Could that be any more clear?

No Court has contradicted the holding in *Brushaber*. One can quibble with the Court's opinion that the Amendment did not create a new class of taxation, namely, a direct tax that needed no apportionment. It seems to me that is what the Amendment did. But that is a side issue. The undeniable upshot of *Brushaber* is that *under the U.S. Constitution* Congress always had the power to tax anything, including incomes.

Thus the income tax is and has always been constitutional. The manufactured argument that the income tax was intended to, and constitutionally *could,* tax only incomes derived from some federal privilege is entirely lacking in foundation. If you ask proponents of this position to prove their case, they become evasive, or they make ludicrous arguments, along the lines that the word *includes* is a term of limitation rather than "a term of enlargement," as a court put it. (One writer argues that only government employees are subject to withholding because the code says, "[The] term 'employee' *includes* an officer, employee, or elected official of the United States, a State, or any political subdivision thereof, or the District of Columbia…." (Emphasis added.)

Like it or not (*Not!*) the U.S. Constitution empowers the Congress to levy any tax it wants. You may read the Constitution otherwise, but the constitutionally empowered courts have spoken. Reading one's libertarian values into the Constitution in defiance of the text and court holdings is futile. It can land you in prison—for life.

As we've seen, the Constitution's clauses are often vague, purposely so; it is a political document and the product of compromise. For better or worse the Constitution means what the occupants of the relevant constitutional offices say it means.

The battle over the taxing power took place long ago—in 1787— between the Federalists and Anti-Federalists, before the Constitution was ratified. Under the Articles of Confederation, Congress had no power to tax; it could only ask the states to raise money. When the Federal Convention (after violating its mandate merely to revise the Articles) proposed to give the central government that fearsome virtually unlimited power, the Anti-Federalists objected, predicting terrible things would happen. One Anti-Federalist warned, "By virtue of their power of taxation, Congress may command the whole, or any part of the property of the people." They should have been listened to, but the Anti-Federalists lost. We can't pretend the battle never occurred.

If we want to be free of income taxation (and all the rest) we will have to effect an intellectual revolution that will convince people that no one, no government, has the right to deprive peaceful people of their lives, liberty, or property. There is no shortcut to freedom.

14
The Constitution and Congressional Generosity

Every now and then we get a glimpse into what government officials, acting under the Constitution, really think about our rights to life, liberty, and property.

The U.S. Justice Department a decade ago provided such a glimpse in a controversial tax case, *Murphy v. IRS* (2007). How revealing it is! For it teaches us that if the government abstains from taxing all your income, you should be grateful for this "congressional generosity." The Anti-Federalists warned us.

To recap the case, Marrita Murphy was awarded $70,000 in compensatory damages for the mental distress and loss of reputation she claimed to have suffered after she acted as a whistleblower against her employer, the New York Air National Guard. She paid about $20,000 in federal income taxes on that money, but later asked for a refund on grounds that the damage award should have been excluded from her gross income under §104(a)(2) of the Internal Revenue Code (Title 26 of the U.S. Code). That section states: "gross income does not include— ... (2) the amount of any damages (other than punitive damages) received (whether by suit or agreement and whether as lump sums or as periodic payments) on account of personal physical injuries or physical sickness ...."

The IRS rejected the request because her injuries were nonphysical and the section specifies "physical injuries." She sued in federal district court and lost.

Murphy then appealed to the U.S. Court of Appeals for the District of Columbia Circuit. She argued that the compensation was covered by §104(a)(2), but if not, then the section is unconstitutional because it would permit the taxation of money that is not included in the constitutional and statutory meaning of "income."

The Justice Department rebutted that Murphy's injuries were nonphysical—and hence not included in §104(a)(2)—and that IRS policy was consistent with the concept of "income" as used since the 16th Amendment was ratified in 1913.

A three-judge panel stunned the government by ruling in Murphy's favor that §104(a)(2) is unconstitutional: "The framers of the Sixteenth Amendment would not have understood compensation for a personal injury—including a nonphysical injury—to be income." (Point of historical fact: the Amendment did not delegate to the government the power to tax income. Under the Constitution, it always had that power.)

Next, the Justice Department petitioned to have the case heard by the entire circuit court (en banc). However, before the court could rule on the petition, the original three judges announced they would rehear the case themselves. After doing so, they reversed their earlier ruling. If Congress wants to exclude from income damage awards for physical injuries but not for nonphysical injuries, that was Congress's prerogative, the judges said. As the Supreme Court put it in 1996, "exclusions from gross income were matters *not of right but rather of congressional generosity.*" (Emphasis added.) Taxpayers apparently should be grateful for what they are allowed to keep and should not ask for more.

Murphy asked the Supreme Court to take the case, but the Court said no. The decision stands.

The Justice Department's petition for rehearing is revealing—and chilling. The Department's task in the petition was to convince the court that the judges had defined "income" too narrowly, allowing them to exclude compensation for nonphysical injury from gross income. They had ruled that compensatory damages for injuries are intended to make a victim whole—that is, to restore something that is not taxable. Since the damage award was not a replacement for something taxable, such as wages, the judges initially said, the award itself should not be taxable.

What is ominous about the petition is how broadly the Justice Department views the government's power to tax. Unfortunately, the Department has the Constitution and a long line of cases to back up its position.

Here's a sample of what the Justice Department argued (internal quotes are from previous court opinions, citations are excised, and all emphasis is added):

Congress's power to tax income, like its power to levy non-direct taxes generally, is indeed "expansive." In Brushaber, the Supreme Court emphasized that Congress's taxing power is "exhaustive and embraces every conceivable power of taxation." It referred to the constitutional limitations as "not so much a limitation upon the complete and all-embracing authority to tax, but in their essence [ ] simply regulations concerning the mode in which the plenary power was to be exerted."…

In [Commissioner v.] Glenshaw Glass [1955], the Court reviewed the "sweeping scope" of the predecessor to §61(a) [the beginning of the section of the law defining "gross income"] and observed that it had "given a liberal construction to this broad phraseology in recognition of the intent of Congress to tax all gains except those specifically exempted." The Court held that income includes "undeniable accessions to wealth, clearly realized, and over which the taxpayers have complete dominion."

The Department's petition proceeded to quote earlier court opinions on the broad range of the government's power to tax, for example, "We have repeatedly emphasized the 'sweeping scope' of [§61, the code section that defines gross income] and its statutory predecessors" and "[Income] extends broadly to all economic gain not otherwise exempted."

The government's petition also emphasized that the decision not to tax something belongs to Congress—and Congress alone:

Any determination to exclude such damages from income is not required by the Constitution or driven by tax considerations, but is one of policy based upon value judgments…. Such determinations are the sole province of Congress, and … Congress established its clear intent to tax the type of award (for nonphysical damages) taxpayer here received.

In this connection, the petition quoted a 1996 Supreme Court case, *O'Gilvie v. U.S.*, which attributed the exclusion from gross income of compensatory damages for personal injury to—"congressional generosity"!

The petition closed with the claim that even if the damage award is not construed to be income "within the meaning of the Sixteenth Amendment," the government may still tax it:

The constitutional restrictions on Congress's taxing power deal only with how to tax, not what to tax. To conclude that the tax here is unconstitutional, the panel had to determine that it is either a direct tax requiring apportionment, or an indirect excise that is not uniform…. The panel wholly failed to perform this critical part of the analysis.

To boil the petition down to the fewest words: Congress has the constitutional power to tax whatever it darn well pleases, thank you. If it abstains from taxing a type of revenue (be it income or not), just be thankful for its generosity. But don't go thinking you have a right not to have it taxed.

Political officials may talk a limited-government game, but let a judge suggest there's something they can't tax and they show their true colors.

To be sure, Murphy's attorney, David Colapinto, responded to the petition, and he too cited Supreme Court cases. As philosopher John Hasnas wrote, "Because the legal world is comprised of contradictory rules, there will be sound legal arguments available not only for the hypothesis one is investigating, but for other, competing hypotheses as well." As noted, the Supreme Court declined to hear the case. But it would be mistake to think there is an objectively "right" answer. In the Constitution game, "right" (in the sense of what gets enforced) is whatever the courts decide. Constitutions and laws don't interpret themselves. People interpret them, and only some people's opinions count.

We really have no reason to be shocked by the government's extravagant claims because we were warned over 200 years ago. In 1787 the Anti-Federalist Robert Yates ("Brutus"), objecting to Congress's unlimited power to tax under the proposed Constitution, wrote, "This power therefore is neither more nor less, than a power to lay and collect taxes, imposts, and excises at their pleasure; not only the power to lay taxes unlimited, as to the amount they may require, but it is perfect and absolute to raise them in any mode they please."

15
Empire on Their Minds

The U.S. government's unceasing effort to control events around the globe is a topic of much discussion these days. Unfortunately, even many critics of the American empire think it is relatively new. Some do understand that its origins preceded the 20th century and that the empire did not begin with the Cold War or U.S. entry into the world wars. They would likely see the Spanish-American War in 1898 as the beginning, when America acquired territory as far away at the Philippines. But I would look even further back than that. How far back? The second half of the 18th century. The earliest days of American empire-building shed light on how America's earliest rulers perceived their constitutional powers and hence on the Constitution itself. The next two chapters are presented for that purpose.

Even the government's schools teach, or at least taught during my 12-year sentence, that America's founders had—let us say—an expansive vision for the country they were establishing. The historian William Appleman Williams's extended essay, *Empire as a Way of Life* (1980), provides many details. Clearly, these men had empire on their minds.

Before he became an evangelical for independence from Great Britain, Benjamin Franklin proposed a partnership between Great Britain and the American colonists to help spread enlightened empire throughout the Americas. His proposal was rejected as impractical, so he embraced independence from Britain—without giving up the dream of empire in the New World. George Washington would have shared the vision; he spoke of the "rising American empire" and described himself as living in an "infant empire."

Thomas Jefferson—"the most expansion-minded president in American history," (writes Gordon S. Wood in *Empire of Liberty: A History of the Early Republic: 1789-1815* (2009)—set out a vision of an "Empire of Liberty," later revised as an "Empire *for* Liberty," and left the presidency believing that "no constitution was ever before as well calculated as ours for extensive empire and self-government." Before leaving office, of course, he acquired the gigantic Louisiana territory from France (828,000 square miles) without constitutional authority, a violation he was fully aware of.

As Jefferson, who favored a U.S. shield showing a pillar of light shining down from heaven on the children of Israel, wrote James Monroe in 1801, after assuming the presidency, "However our present interests may restrain us within our own limits, it is impossible not to look forward to distant times, when our rapid multiplication will expand itself beyond those limits, & cover the whole northern, if not the southern continent, with a people speaking the same language, governed in similar forms, & by similar laws.

Indeed, in the eyes of the founders, the American Revolution was largely a war between a mature, exhausted empire and a nascent one. Many—but assuredly not all—Americans of the time would have cheerily agreed. The founders' goal was to bring civilization (which was still identified with England and many of its institutions) to the New World's benighted. As Jefferson indicated, this vision was more than continental, because South America was never regarded as permanently off limits. If expansion required conflict with the French and Spanish also, so be it, when the United States was prepared.

The Indian Wars were among the first steps in empire building. The unspeakable brutality and duplicity—the acts of ethnic cleansing and genocide, as we say today—were crimes, not merely against individuals, but also against whole societies and nations. "Imperialism" was not yet a word in use, but that's what this was, as were the designs and moves on Canada (one of the objects of James Madison's War of 1812), Mexico, Cuba, Florida, the Mississippi and New Orleans, Louisiana, the Northwest, and the Pacific coast (the gateway to Asia). The wishes of the inhabitants—who were "as yet incapable of self-government as children," as Jefferson said of Louisiana's residents—didn't count. (Lincoln's war is thus understood as an exercise in empire preservation.)

A good deal of this program was tied up with trade. For libertarians, trade far and wide is a good thing, but one must keep in mind that the expansion of trade in those days (as in these) depended on how strong the government, that is, its military, was. By hook and crook, a constitution—the Articles of Confederation—that denied the national government the powers to regulate and promote trade, to tax, and to raise an army and navy had been exchanged for one—the U.S. Constitution—that authorized those powers. Trade was a *policy*, not a recognition of individual freedom, and that meant government activism, which included selective embargoes, such as those imposed by Jefferson's program of "peaceful coercion," and even war if deemed necessary.

America's founders did not share of the view of a true liberal, Richard Cobden, who said several decade later, "They who propose to influence by force the traffic of the world, forget that affairs of trade, like matters of conscience, change their very nature if touched by the hand of violence; for as faith, if forced, would no longer be religion, but hypocrisy, so commerce becomes robbery if coerced by warlike armaments."

Obviously, the Articles of Confederation were a poor platform for empire building; not so the Constitution. "Both in the mind of Madison and in its nature," Williams wrote, "the Constitution was an instrument of imperial government at home and abroad."

I don't mean to say that the liberty of Americans was of no import to their rulers. In light of the Revolution, they understood that a government without broad acceptance would be doomed. I do mean, however, that liberty was to be subordinated (only to the extent necessary, of course) to national greatness, which was America's destiny. (I first heard the words "Manifest Destiny" in a government school. Do students hear it today?)

Americans sensed that something exceptional was happening. And indeed it was, as Wood explained in *The Radicalism of the American Revolution* (1991). To the dismay of the dominant Federalists, average Americans, exemplified by those whom Wood calls "plebeian Anti-Federalists," saw the revolution as having overturned hierarchical and aristocratic colonial society in favor of a democracy that facilitated personal and commercial self-interest. (This did not sit well with those who wanted America to be, per Wood, "either a hierarchy of ranks or a homogeneous republican whole.")

But even well-grounded exceptionalism can quickly turn dark by the belief in one's duty to enlighten—or , if necessary, exterminate—the benighted. And that's what happened. The Indian Wars were popular (the land was coveted), and so were the other imperial exploits. (This is not to say there were no dissenters.)

Williams notes that with exceptionalism came aloneness and thus danger. Thus the quest for security and tranquility for the new nation—invoked in precisely those words—fueled these imperial exploits. The national-security state is nothing new; only the technology and the wealth to make empire feasible have changed.

Some American figures glimpsed that empire and liberty might not so easily fit together. (The unabashed empire builders were convinced that freedom at home *required* empire.) The problem was that even many who opposed empire, sometimes quite eloquently, wanted ends that only an empire could procure. Williams puts John Quincy Adams in this small camp. Secretary of State Adams's July 4, 1821, speech, declaring that America "goes not abroad in search of monsters to destroy," was "thoughtful, powerful, and subversive," Williams writes. "But for the time Adams remained enfolded in the spirit of empire and was unable to control the urge to extend America's power and influence." (As secretary of state, he supported Maj. Gen. Andrew Jackson's seizure of Florida from the Spanish, although Congress had not declared war. In 1819, backed by a veiled military threat, Adams negotiated the Transcontinental Treaty under which Spain ceded the Florida territories over to the Mississippi River and defined a boundary between U.S. and Spanish territory that stretched to the west coast. This treaty along with the Treaty of 1818 with Britain, negotiated by Albert Gallatin, paved the way to America's status as a Pacific power. Adams's famous "monster" speech may be seen as a rationalization for not recognizing revolutionary governments in South America, when nonrecognition had other, less lofty reasons.)

Adams was the main author of the Monroe Doctrine, which announced not only that the United States would stand aloof from Europe's quarrels, but also that the Western Hemisphere was exclusively the U.S. government's sphere of influence: "The American continents, by the free and independent condition which they have assumed and maintain, are henceforth not to be considered as subjects for future colonization by any European powers," for any such extension would be taken as "dangerous to our peace and safety [i.e., our national security]."

So keep out of our backyard, Europe, and we'll keep out of yours. Nearly 100 years later, America would be at war in Europe.

16

The War of 1812 Was the Health of the State

In 1918, having watched in horror as his Progressive friends gleefully jumped onto Woodrow Wilson's war wagon, Randolph Bourne penned the immortal words: "War is the health of the state." As he saw things,

> The republican State has almost no trappings to appeal to the common man's emotions. What it has are of military origin, and in an unmilitary era such as we have passed through since the Civil War, even military trappings have been scarcely seen. In such an era the sense of the State almost fades out of the consciousness of men.
>
> With the shock of war, however, the State comes into its own again,...
>
> In general, the nation in wartime attains a uniformity of feeling, a hierarchy of values culminating at the undisputed apex of the State ideal, which could not possibly be produced through any other agency than war. Loyalty—or mystic devotion to the State—becomes the major imagined human value.

An earlier group of Americans would have agreed, although they would not have shared Bourne's horror. These are the men who sought war with England in 1812. As Wikipedia notes,

> The United States declared war on June 18, 1812 [after close party votes in Congress] for several reasons, including trade restrictions brought about by the British war with France, the impressment of American merchant sailors into the Royal Navy, British support of Indian tribes against American expansion, outrage over insults to national honor after humiliations on the high seas, and possible American interest in annexing British territory in modern-day Canada.

Here I will explore neither the justifications for the war nor the terms of the Treaty of Ghent. Suffice it to say that Britain ceased its impressment policy before the war started and sought to reconcile with America after the war, opening up opportunities for westward U.S. expansion at the expense of Spain and the Indians. Instead I'll focus on how the war eroded liberalism in the United States by concentrating power and interest in the national government. There's a lesson here: even a war that appears justifiable—Britain conscripted Americans into its navy and interfered with commerce—had enduring illiberal domestic consequences beyond the immediate transgressions of taxes, debt, and trade embargoes—dangerous precedents were set.

While I don't wish to overstate the liberalism of prewar America—slavery and the war on Indians were only the most egregious violations of the principles of liberty—it would be wrong to think that America did not become *less* liberal with the war, that Bourne's maxim was suspended in this case. It was not.

Prewar, there were still eminent voices favoring small government and decentralized power. Postwar, this was hardly the case. Indeed, the idea of a "living constitution" seems to have been born in this era. The War of 1812 should bring to mind the French saying "The more it changes, the more it's the same thing."

In the final chapter of *The Radicalism of the American Revolution* (1991), the historian Gordon S. Wood noted that as the 19th century unfolded, the survivors of the founding generation were unhappy with what they saw in America. "It was increasingly clear," Wood wrote, "that no one was really in charge of this gigantic, enterprising, restless nation … the most thoroughly commercialized society in the world." He continued: "The founding fathers, of course, had thought that eminent men and imaginative minds were in control of events and caused things to happen. But the heroic conception of society was now relegated to a more primitive stage of development." Thus,

> This democratic society was not the society the revolutionary leaders had wanted or expected. No wonder, then, that those of them who lived on into the early decades of the nineteenth century expressed anxiety over what they had wrought….
>
> Indeed, a pervasive pessimism, a fear that their revolutionary experiment in republicanism was not working out as they had expected, runs through the later writings of the founding fathers. All the major revolutionary leaders died less than happy with the results of the Revolution. The numbers of old revolutionaries who lost faith in what the Revolution had done is startling.

To their dismay, people were more concerned with their personal economic affairs than with the new nation. "White males had taken only too seriously the belief that they were free and equal with the right to pursue their happiness," Wood wrote. Thus commercial success outweighed republican virtue, disappointing Hamiltonians and Jeffersonians alike. "A new generation of democratic Americans was no longer interested in the revolutionaries' dream of building a classical republic of elitist virtue out of the inherited materials of the Old World."

As a result, "the founding fathers were unsettled and fearful not because the American Revolution had failed but because it had succeeded, and succeeded only too well."

The retired founders were not the only ones who worried. They were joined by the men who still exercised power, especially Republicans James Madison and James Monroe, and such influential men of the next generation as John Quincy Adams, Henry Clay, and John C. Calhoun. As war with England approached, Republicans (as opposed to the Federalists) had no problem finding silver linings. War would not only inject government with a new dynamism—with important implications for trade policy, money and banking, and internal improvements—it would also give the people a shot of badly needed national spirit.

Thus the War of 1812 is an underrated turning point in American history, rivaling the Civil War, the Spanish-American War, and the two world wars. Indeed, the War of 1812 helped to launch the empire that manifested itself in those later conflicts. In its aftermath, America's rulers could believe that their continental and global ambitions, backed by the army and navy, were fully realizable. They just needed a government equal to the task.

It's not too much to say that modern America was born in 1812–1815. While it was a Republican war—Federalists in the northeast opposed and even threatened secession over it—the postwar Republican Party took on most of the fading Federalist Party's program with respect to the role of government in the American economy. Advocates of smaller, decentralized government (Andrew Jackson and Martin Van Buren, among others) rallied in the decades before the Civil War, but in the end the mercantilists and militarists—advocates of Henry Clay's Hamiltonian American System—triumphed to the point that Grover Cleveland, outraged by the rampant privileges for business insiders, railed against what he called the "communism of combined wealth and capital" that had given rise to communism in its ordinary sense.

Before open hostilities with England broke out, Wood wrote in another book, *Empire of Liberty: A History of the Early Republic, 1789-1815* (2009), "America had been engaged in a kind of warfare—commercial warfare—with both Britain and France since 1806." As president (1801–1809), Thomas Jefferson had pushed Congress to impose a general trade embargo—a ban on *all* American exports—during the Napoleonic wars, when American merchant ships (and a warship) were interfered with, American neutrality violated, and merchant seamen impressed into the Royal Navy. Jefferson called this response, which was highly divisive because it disrupted so many Americans' means of earning a living, "peaceful coercion" and an alternative to war. Wood added, "The actual fighting of 1812 was only the inevitable consequence of the failure of 'peaceful coercion.'"

As the War of 1812 approached during the Republican administration of James Madison, the War Hawks saw silver linings everywhere. "Republicans even came to see the war as a necessary regenerative act—as a means of purging Americans of their pecuniary greed and their seemingly insatiable love of commerce and money-making," Wood wrote. "They hoped that war with England might refresh the national character, lessen the overweening selfishness of people, and revitalize republicanism." The money cost of war was dismissed as insignificant compared to national honor and sovereignty. Indeed, the war was called the "Second War of Independence." "Forget self and think of America," the *Richmond Enquirer* editorialized (quoted in Wood).

Republicans, of course, had previously warned of the dangers of war, including high taxes, debt, corruption, a big military, and centralized power. Madison himself famously said that war contained the "germ [of] all the enemies to public liberty." So now the party set out to prosecute a war while trying to avoid the evils they held were intrinsic to it. Republicans in Congress talked about cutting military spending even as war loomed. But it didn't quite work out that way. In early 1812 Congress built up the army, though it—initially—decided a navy was not needed against the greatest naval power on earth. (The strengthened U.S. navy later did very well against Britain.)

The Republican Congress also raised taxes, including dreaded internal taxes, conditioned on war actually breaking out. Madison, Wood wrote, "was relieved that at last the Republicans in Congress had 'got down the dose of taxes.'" Still, the government would have to borrow money to finance the war. The proliferation of government securities and new note-issuing banks followed, of course. (On the connections among the war, public debt, Madison's Second Bank of the United

States, inflation, government-sanctioned suspension of specie payments, government bankruptcy, and subsequent economic turmoil, see Murray Rothbard's *A History of Money and Banking in the United States* and his earlier *The Panic of 1819*.)

Wood noted that Americans hoped the war would deal a blow to the Indians in the Northwest, who had the support of Britain and whose land was much coveted. Indian removal (extermination) was a popular government program. Moreover, "with the development of Canada freeing the British Empire from its vulnerability to American economic restrictions, President Madison was bound to be concerned about Canada."

> Although Madison's government always denied that it intended to annex Canada, it had no doubt, as Secretary of State [James] Monroe told the British government in June 1812, that once the United States forces occupied the British provinces, it would be "difficult to relinquish territory which had been conquered."

Interest in Canada was not just material. A belief in "Manifest Destiny," though the term would not be coined until 1845, was a driving force. (Acquisition of Spain's Florida territories was also on the agenda.) America was the rising "Empire of Liberty," fated by providence to rule North America (at least) and displace the worn-out empires of the Old World.

Even though the war had no formal victor and produced no boundary adjustments (U.S. forces were repulsed in Canada after burning its capital, for which Britain retaliated by burning Washington, D.C.), Americans were generally delighted with the outcome, mistakenly thinking that Madison had dictated terms at Ghent. (Wood noted that a record 57 towns and counties bear Madison's name.) Wood wrote that a group calling itself the "republican citizens of Baltimore" expressed "a common refrain throughout much of the country" in April 1815 when it declared that the war

> has revived, with added luster the renown which brightened the morning of our independence: it has called forth and organized the dormant resources of the empire: it has tried and vindicated our republican institutions: it has given us that moral strength, which consists in the well earned respect of the world, and in a just respect for ourselves. It has raised up and consolidated a national character, dear to the hearts of the people, as an object of honest pride and a pledge of future union, tranquility, and greatness.

The anti-Hamiltonian Albert Gallatin, secretary of the Treasury from 1801 to 1814, said that because of the war, the people "are more American; they feel and act more as a nation." Arthur A. Ekirch Jr. reported in *The Decline of American Liberalism* (1955) that Gallatin admitted that (Gallatin's words) "the war has laid the foundation of permanent taxes and military establishments, which the Republicans had deemed unfavorable to the happiness and free institutions of the country."

Madison's restraint, however it is to be explained, ought to be acknowledged. As we have seen, he was an advocate of centralized government and implied powers, yet "he knew that a republican leader should not become a Napoleon or even a Hamilton," the sympathetic Wood wrote. He quoted an earlier admirer of Madison who said that the president conducted the war "without one trial for treason, or even one prosecution for libel." (Some Republicans viewed Federalists who were openly sympathetic to the British as traitors.) A more ambitious politician might have not have kept the "sword of war" "within its proper restraints." However, imperial chickens eventually come home to roost, and Madison indisputably reinforced the imperial course of his predecessors. Moreover, Jeffrey Rogers Hummel wrote in *War Is the Health of the State: The Impact of Military Defense on the History of the United States* (2012, online at http://papers.ssrn.com/sol3/papers.cfm?abstract_id= 2151041), Madison asked Congress for conscription—only the war's end kept Congress from acting—and later a peacetime standing army.

How the war dramatically changed America, the people, and the government is discussed at length in *Dangerous Nation* (2007) by Robert Kagan—the historian and prominent neoconservative thinker—and *John Quincy Adams and American Global Empire* (1992) by William Earl Weeks. (Unlike Weeks, Kagan approves of the war's effects and the American empire in general.)

Kagan noted that the war boosted efforts to expand America westward. "Indian tribes north of the Ohio River, deprived of British support, gave up vast stretches of land in the years immediately following the war," Kagan writes, "permitting a huge westward migration of the American population.... Trying to contain American continental aspirations after the war with Great Britain, John Quincy Adams observed, would be like 'opposing a feather to a torrent.'"

Kagan noted that

The requirements of fighting the war expanded the role of the federal government and exposed deficiencies in the operation of federal power under the old Jeffersonian Republican scheme—much as the Revolutionary War had pointed up the deficiencies of the Articles of Confederation. The end of the war in 1815 brought calls for augmented national powers even from Republicans....

Madison, Jefferson's staunch colleague in the struggle against Hamiltonian policies in the 1790s, now all but embraced the Hamiltonian system.

Attitudes toward the military also changed for reasons of national and economic security. When Monroe succeeded Madison as president, Weeks wrote, a

guiding principle ... in [his] effort to expand American foreign trade concerned the construction and maintenance of a formidable military force. Republicans traditionally had mistrusted large military establishments as subversive of republican institutions. Yet once again, the War of 1812 led to a reevaluation of a basic tenet of the Republican faith.

Indeed, future President John Quincy Adams, Monroe's secretary of state and a champion of Clay's American System, said, "The most painful, perhaps the most profitable, lesson of the war was the primary duty of the nation to place itself in *a state of permanent preparation for self-defense.*" (Emphasis added.)

"Along with support for a national bank," Weeks added, the Republicans' new imperial principles "stood as a dramatic break with the traditional philosophy of the Republican party. The vision of a decentralized inward looking agrarian republic had been replaced by an imperial vision which reflected many of the basic tenets of the disgraced Federalist party."

It's important to realize, Weeks wrote, that "after the Treaty of Ghent the search for new markets became the explicit aim of American foreign policy."

Kagan agreed: "the War of 1812 spurred the federal government to redouble efforts to open access to foreign markets." Previously, Republicans like Jefferson, while reconciled to the new commercial world, hoped that commerce would not dominate America or its politics since that preoccupation would inevitably draw the country into perpetual international turmoil. But with the war, many now saw things differently. "Active promotion of commerce required further expansion of American military strength, especially the navy," Kagan wrote.

In other words, America would not promote free trade by unilaterally setting a good example, as libertarians call for today. Instead, the government would aggressively open foreign markets, particularly the colonial possessions of the European powers, threatening retaliation against uncooperative regimes and displaying the military card rather prominently. But such "free trade" soon gave way to an explicit mercantilism, that is, special-interest economic protectionism. Weeks wrote that

> changing economic conditions had inspired a new vision of American empire based not on free trade but on protection of certain sectors of the economy. The shortages caused by embargo and war had led to the growth of an extensive manufacturing sector in the United States and a sizable constituency that wanted it protected from foreign competition, once peace was restored.

Revealingly, Weeks wrote, the postwar American Society of the Encouragement of American Manufactures, a pro-tariff group, boasted as members Thomas Jefferson and James Madison along with the old Federalist John Adams.

A remnant of small-government, decentralist, free-trading "Old Republicans" objected to this embrace of centralized power, mercantilism, and militarism, but their voices were fading. Against them, the rising generation of politicians saw the need for new principles. The Old Republicans' narrow interpretation of the Constitution, the new Republicans said, should not be treated as engraved in stone. "A new world has come into being since the Constitution was adopted," Henry Clay said. "Are the narrow, limited necessities of the old thirteen states … as they existed at the formation of the present Constitution, forever to remain a rule of its interpretation? Are we to forget the wants of our country?… I trust not, sir. I hope for better and nobler things."

Apparently the idea of a living constitution was born much earlier than the 1930s.

The new vision pervaded Monroe's administration, which the continental expansionist and militarist John Quincy Adams dominated as secretary of state, and then Adams's own term as president. (Opposition to the spread of slavery would check, temporarily, the drive for southwestern expansion, an ironic turn on Madison's principle that "ambition must be made to counteract ambition.") As for domestic policy, Kagan reported, in 1825, Adams's first year in power, he called for "a national university, government-sponsored scientific explorations, the creation of new government departments, the fostering of internal improvements, and even the building of a national astronomical observatory."

The "great object of the institution of government is the improvement of the condition of those who are parties to the social compact," Adams said. The government should not only provide internal improvement, such as canals and roads, but should also see to the people's "moral, political, intellectual improvement."

Adams's program, however, proved too much too fast for most Americans. So he, like his father, became a one-term president. But eventually the American System, often propelled by foreign policy and war, would return—for good.

The lesson here is that even a superficially justifiable war can be counted on to produce bad consequences and precedents. The Republicans could not fight a war unaccompanied by what Gallatin called "the evils inseparable from it[:] debt, perpetual taxation, military establishments, and other corrupting or anti-republican habits or institutions." They would sooner have squared the circle.

Moreover, the War of 1812 reinforced the executive branch's de facto monopoly over foreign policy. Within a few years the Monroe administration—and no one more staunchly than John Quincy Adams—would defend Gen. Andrew Jackson's invasion of Spanish Florida and undeclared war on the Seminoles, after which dissenting members of Congress could do nothing but gripe.

Randolph Bourne was right: war is indeed the health of the state.

17

Of Bumblebees and Competitive Courts

Considering that what liberty we continue to enjoy in the West is a product in large part of competition hundreds of years ago among legal institutions operating within the same territory, it's curious that so many libertarians still believe such an order—an essential feature of free-market, or natural-law, anarchism—would be inimical to liberty. Why wouldn't that which produced liberty be up to preserving it?

When I say that competition produced liberty, I of course do not mean that liberty was necessarily anyone's objective. Yet liberty emerged all the same, as if by an "invisible hand." That's how things often work. Good (and bad) consequences can be the result of human action but not of human design (to use a favorite phrase of F. A. Hayek's, which he borrowed from the Scottish Enlightenment thinker Adam Ferguson).

We should be delighted to know that something so wonderful as liberty can emerge unintentionally. It ought to give us hope for the future; if the libertarian movement is deficient, we need not assume that liberty has no chance.

Many authors from the 18th century onward have written about the unintended good consequences of competition, that is, the absence of monopolistic central control. They emphasized that in the West the rivalries between church and state, between nobles or parliament and crown, and between nation-states yielded zones of liberty that endure to this day, however diminished in particular matters. Competition among legal institutions—courts and bodies of law—within overlapping jurisdictions played a large role in this centuries-long beneficent process. These of course are not examples of anarchism; on the contrary, states existed. But competitive overlapping legal regimes are an element of market anarchism. So where a state coexisted with a polycentric legal order, we may say, with Bryan Caplan, that there existed "less than the minimum" state, that is, something that fell short of the night-watchman state favored by limited-government libertarians.

A good place to read about competition in law and dispute resolution is Todd J. Zywicki's highly accessible 2003 *Northwestern University Law Review* article "The Rise and Fall of Efficiency in the Common Law: A Supply-Side Analysis." An important feature that "influenced the common law's evolution," Zywicki wrote, "was the competitive, or 'polycentric,' legal order in which the common law developed. During the era that the common law developed, there were multiple English courts with overlapping jurisdictions over most of the issues that made up the common law. As a result, parties potentially could bring a particular lawsuit in a variety of different courts. In turn this created competition among these various courts for business."

The idea of courts competing for "business" sounds strange to modern ears, but it was commonplace before the 20th century. (The extent of private arbitration in international commerce today is largely unappreciated.) Zywicki's paper shows that the common law, which featured this competition, was efficient in the eyes of those who used its services. Monopoly is inefficient even (especially?) in matters of security, dispute resolution, and justice. Moreover, it's a mistake, as F. A. Hayek explained in *Law, Legislation, and Liberty* (volume 1, *Rules and Order* [1978]) to assume that government is the source of law.

Moves away from competition and the common law, then, aren't adequately explained by shortcomings in services to its consumers. Political ambition provides a more satisfactory explanation.

Zywicki draws on the legal historian Harold Berman, who wrote in *Law and Revolution: The Formation of the Western Legal Tradition* (1983), "Perhaps the most distinctive characteristic of the Western legal tradition is the coexistence and competition within the same community of diverse jurisdictions and diverse legal systems."

The legal philosopher Lon L. Fuller, in *Anatomy of the Law* (1968), went further, Zywicki shows: "A possible ... objection to the view [of law] taken here is that it permits the existence of more than one legal system governing the same population. The answer is, of course, that such multiple systems do exist and have in history been *more common* than unitary systems." (Emphasis added.)

The limited-government libertarian who insists that market anarchism cannot work because it lacks a monopoly court of final jurisdiction is like the apocryphal aerodynamicist who calculated that a bumblebee couldn't possibly fly. One needed only to point out the window, saying, "Behold!" Likewise, the natural-law market anarchist need only point to history.

Berman also wrote (quoted by Zywicki), "The same person might be subject to the ecclesiastical courts in one type of case, the king's courts in another, his lord's courts in a third, the manorial court in a fourth, a town court in a fifth, [and] a merchants' court in a sixth." This sounds as though the courts were not really competitive, but rather that the variety of courts constituted specialization and a division of labor. That inference would be wrong. To see this we may turn to a keen contemporaneous observer, Adam Smith. In *The Wealth of Nations* Smith noted that despite a de jure division of labor, courts in fact competed with one another, even to the point of entrepreneurially finding ways—indeed, creatively manufacturing reasons—to justify luring cases from other courts. Why do this? Because the courts obtained their revenues from fees paid by parties to cases. The more cases a court heard, the more money it earned, a state of affairs that Smith, no anarchist of course, approved of: "Public services are never better performed than when their reward comes only in consequence of their being performed, and is proportioned to the diligence employed in performing them."

Smith described the legal environment of his day,

> The fees of court seem originally to have been the principal support of the different courts of justice in England. Each court endeavoured to draw to itself as much business as it could, and was, upon that account, willing to take cognisance of many suits which were not originally intended to fall under its jurisdiction. The court of king's bench, instituted for the trial of criminal causes only, took cognisance of civil suits; the plaintiff pretending that the defendant, in not doing him justice, had been guilty of some trespass or misdemeanour. The court of exchequer, instituted for the levying of the king's revenue, and for enforcing the payment of such debts only as were due to the king, took cognisance of all other contract debts; the plaintiff alleging that he could not pay the king because the defendant would not pay him. In consequence of such fictions it came, in many cases, to depend altogether upon the parties before what court they would choose to have their cause tried; and each court endeavoured, by superior dispatch and impartiality, to draw to itself as many causes as it could. The present admirable constitution of the courts of justice in England was, perhaps, originally in a great measure formed by this emulation which anciently took place between their respective judges; each judge endeavouring to give, in his own court, the speediest and most

effectual remedy which the law would admit for every sort of injustice. [Emphasis added.]

Zywicki also quoted from Smith's *Lectures on Jurisprudence*: "Another thing which tended to support the liberty of the people and render the proceedings in the courts very exact, was the rivalship which arose betwixt them."

It may be argued that the state provided a backdrop to the competitive legal order, meaning that a forum of last resort was always available. This argument loses its force, however, when one realizes, as Edward P. Stringham shows in *Private Governance: Creating Order in Economic and Social Life* (2015), that private dispute-resolution procedures arose in matters where states abstained from involvement, such as the nascent stock markets.

"In short," Zywicki summed up, "a market for law prevailed, with numerous court systems competing for market share in order to increase their fees. This competitive process generated rules that satisfied the demand of consumers (here litigants) for fairness, consistency, and reasonableness."

Bumblebees fly and reasonably pro-freedom dispute resolution emerges without the state, no matter what a cloistered theoretician may think.

18
Looking Back at Magna Carta

June 15, 2015, was the 800th anniversary of the day in 1215 that rotten King John put his seal to the sheet of parchment called the Articles of the Barons—later to be known as Magna Carta—at Runnymede in England. It wasn't the first charter issued by an English monarch pledging to subordinate his power to the law (custom), yet it has had a staying power like no other in the imagination of people worldwide. Indeed, it is seen as a precursor to the U.S. Constitution. Magna Carta's endurance is especially ironic when you consider that at John's request, Pope Innocent III nullified the charter just 11 days later and excommunicated the rebellious barons who forced it on him. (Further ironies: the charter had been drafted by the learned archbishop of Canterbury, Stephen Langton, whom the Pope had selected over John's objection, and it affirmed the autonomy of the church.)

With the nullification, the civil war resumed between king and landholders who had grown tired of his taxes for wars in France (which he lost along with vast properties) and other impositions. In the end, however, they more or less triumphed, as John's successors, starting with his 9-year-old son, reissued the charter, albeit in revised editions. The principle that an English king was not a law unto himself would stand. While Magna Carta did not raise the curtain on a libertarian, or even classical-liberal, future, it may be said to have gotten the ball rolling, even if that was no part of anyone's intention.

The story of Magna Carta is instructive precisely because of its unintended consequences. This has long been noted, for example, by John Millar (1735-1801), a student of Adam Smith, a figure of the Scottish Enlightenment in his own right, and author of the multivolume *An Historical View of the English Government, From the Settlement of the Saxons in Britain to the Revolution in 1688* (1787). The judge and literary critic Francis Jeffrey wrote of Millar in 1804:

To some of our readers, perhaps, it may afford a clearer conception of his intellectual character, to say that it corresponded pretty nearly with the abstract idea that the learned of England entertain of a *Scotish* [sic] *philosopher;* a personage, that is, with little or no deference to the authority of great names, and not very apt to be startled at conclusions that seem to run counter to received opinions or existing institutions; acute, sagacious, and systematical; irreverent towards classical literature; rather indefatigable in argument, than patient in investigation; vigilant in the observation of facts, but not so strong in their number, as skilful in their application.

Jeffrey wrote that Millar's "leading principle" was that institutions evolve "spontaneously from the situation of the society." "Instead of gazing, therefore, with stupid amazement, on the singular and diversified appearances of human manners and institutions," Jeffrey wrote, "Mr. Millar taught his pupils to refer them all to one simple principle, and to consider them as necessary links in the great chain which connects civilized with barbarous society."

(I found Jeffrey's quotes in Mark Salber Phillips's introduction to Liberty Fund's 2006 edition of Millar's book. Phillips notes that one of Millar's objectives was "a rebuttal of what Millar took to be the royalist and authoritarian politics of Hume's *History [of England]*, though Millar salutes Hume as 'the great historian of England, to whom the reader is indebted for the complete union of history with philosophy.'")

Regarding Magna Carta, in book 2, chapter 1 of his *Historical View*, Millar wrote,

> The character of John ... is universally known, as a compound of cowardice, tyranny, sloth, and imprudence. This infatuated king was involved in three great struggles, from which it would have required the abilities of his father [Henry II], or of his great grandfather [Henry I, son of William the Conqueror], to extricate himself with honour; but which, under his management, could hardly fail to terminate in ruin and disgrace.

The struggles were against the challengers to his land holdings in France, Pope Innocent III, and the rebellious barons. After his humiliating losses in France, John made peace with the pope—accepting Langton at Canterbury and, in Millar's words, "surrendering his kingdom to the pope, and submitting to hold it as a feudatory of the church of Rome."

But his troubles were only beginning. Millar wrote:

> The contempt which this abject submission of their sovereign could not fail to excite in the breast of his subjects, together with the indignation raised by various acts of tyranny and oppression of which he was guilty, produced at

length a combination of his barons, who demanded a redress of grievances, and the restoration of their ancient laws. As this appeared the most favourable conjuncture which had occurred, since the Norman conquest, for limiting the encroachments of prerogative; the nobility and principal gentry were desirous of improving it to the utmost; and their measures were planned and conducted with equal moderation and firmness.

John would have none of it, and he moved to quash the rebellion of the barons. "He endeavoured by menaces to intimidate them; and, by delusive promises, to lull them asleep, in order to gain time for breaking their confederacy." When that failed, "he made application to the pope as his liege lord; and called upon his holiness to protect the rights of his vassal."

War broke out, and the king, "deserted by almost all his followers," saw the ranks of the rebels grow.

All further opposition, therefore, became impracticable. At Runnemede, a large meadow between Windsor and Staines; a place which has been rendered immortal in the page of the historian and in the song of the poet; was held that famous conference, when the barons presented, in writing, the articles of agreement upon which they insisted; and the king gave an explicit consent to their demands. The articles were then reduced into the form of a charter; to which the king affixed his great seal; and which, though it was of the same nature with the charters obtained from the preceding monarchs, yet, as it was obtained with difficulties which created more attention, and as it is extended to a greater variety of particulars, has been called, by way of distinction, *the great charter of our liberties.*

Millar claims that "feudal superiority of the crown, over the nobles" had been the rule since William the Conqueror (1066), so "it would probably have been a vain project to attempt the abolition of it." Then what was the point of the gathering at Runnymede on June 15, 1215?

The chief aim of the nobility, therefore, in the present charter, was to prevent the sovereign from harassing and oppressing them by the undue exercise of those powers, the effects of their feudal subordination, with which he was understood to be fully invested....

The jurisdiction exercised by the king, as a feudal superior, was another source of oppression, for which a remedy was thought requisite; and several regulations were introduced, in order to facilitate the distribution of justice, to prevent the negligence, as well as to restrain the corruption, of judges: in particular, it was declared, that no count or baron should be fined unless by the *judgment of his peers,* and according to the quality of the offence.

Millar then made an intriguing point about Magna Carta's application beyond the barons.

While the barons were thus labouring to secure themselves against the usurpations of the prerogative, they could not decently refuse a similar security to
their own vassals; and it was no less the interest of the king to insist upon limiting the arbitrary power of the nobles, than it was their interest to insist upon
limiting that of the crown. The privileges inserted in this great transaction
were, upon this account, rendered more extensive, and communicated to persons of a lower rank, than might otherwise have been expected. Thus it was
provided that justice should not be *sold,* nor unreasonably *delayed, to any person.*
That no freeman should be imprisoned, nor his goods be distrained, unless
by the *judgment of his peers,* or by the law of the land; and that even a villein
should not, by any fine, be deprived of his carts and implements of husbandry.

King and barons were aware of the fact, articulated by Étienne de
La Boétie, that since the few rule the many, the ruled have it in their
power to overthrow their rulers. Therefore, "liberal" measures are sometimes necessary to pacify the many to keep them from having revolutionary thoughts or to keep particular groups (such as the rising
merchant class) from shifting allegiance to another contender for power.
More often than not, acts of political kindness are the result of such a
motive.

Thus,

> It is worthy of notice, however, that though this great charter was procured
> by the power and influence of the nobility and dignified clergy, who, it is nat-
> ural to suppose, would be chiefly attentive to their own privileges; the interest
> of another class of people, much inferior in rank, was not entirely overlooked:
> I mean the inhabitants of the trading towns. It was declared, that no aid [trib-
> ute] should be imposed upon the city of London, unless with consent of the
> national council; and that the liberties and immunities of this, and of all the
> other cities and boroughs of the kingdom, should be maintained.... The in-
> sertion of such clauses must be considered as a proof that the mercantile peo-
> ple were beginning to have some attention paid to them; while the shortness
> of these articles, and the vague manner in which they are conceived, afford
> an evidence equally satisfactory, that this order of men had not yet risen to
> great importance.

With the Great Seal of the king affixed, copies of Magna Carta were
distributed throughout the country. But, Millar wrote, "nothing could
be farther from [John's] intentions, than to fulfil the conditions of the
charter."

> No sooner had he obtained a bull from the pope annulling that deed, and
> prohibiting both the king and his subjects from paying any regard to it, than,
> having secretly procured a powerful supply of foreign troops, he took the
> field, and began without mercy to kill and destroy, and to carry devastation
> throughout the estates of all those who had any share in the confederacy. The

barons, trusting to the promises of the king, had rashly disbanded their followers; and being in no condition to oppose the royal army, were driven to the desperate measure of applying to Lewis, the son of the French monarch, and making him an offer of the crown. The death of John, in a short time after, happened opportunely to quiet these disorders, by transmitting the sovereignty to his son Henry the third, who was then only nine years of age.

Under the prudent administration of the earl of Pembroke, the regent, the young king, in the first year of his reign, granted a new charter of liberties, at the same time that the confederated barons were promised a perpetual oblivion for the past, in case they should now return to their allegiance.

There is much more to this story, of course. Suffice it to say here that Millar draws three broad conclusions from his account.

First, he saw significance in the fact that Magna Carta was not the only charter issued by a king; as noted, others were issued before and afterward.

Taking those charters, therefore, in connexion with one another, they seem to declare, in a clear and unequivocal manner, the general and permanent sense of the nation, with respect to the rights of the crown; and they ascertain, by express and positive agreement between the king and his subjects, those terms of submission to the chief magistrate, which, in most other governments, are [not] otherwise explained than by long usage, and which have therefore remained in a state of uncertainty and fluctuation.

Second, contrary to "common opinion," Millar wrote, "from the Norman conquest to the time of Edward the first [reign, 1272-1307]; while the barons were exerting themselves with so much vigour, and with so much apparent success, in restraining the powers of the crown, those powers were, notwithstanding, continually advancing."

The repeated concessions made by the sovereign, had no farther effect than to prevent his authority from increasing so rapidly as it might otherwise have done. For a proof of this we can appeal to no better authority than that of the charters themselves; from which, if examined according to their dates, it will appear, that the nobility were daily becoming more moderate in their claims; and that they submitted, in reality, to a gradual extension of the prerogative; though, by more numerous regulations, they endeavoured to avoid the wanton abuses of it. Thus, by the great charter of Henry the third, the powers of the crown are less limited than by the charter of king John; and by this last the crown vassals abandoned some important privileges with which they were invested by the charter of Henry the first.

If Magna Carta was a key moment in the West's advancement toward liberalism, the trajectory was neither straight nor smooth.

Finally, we come to the law of unintended consequences. Millar said students of history "will easily see that the parties concerned in [the procurement of "these great charters"] were not actuated by the most liberal principles; and that it was not so much their intention to secure the liberties of the people at large, as to establish the privileges of a few individuals."

He summed up:

A great tyrant on the one side, and a set of petty tyrants on the other, seem to have divided the kingdom; and the great body of the people, disregarded and oppressed on all hands, were beholden for any privileges bestowed upon them, to the jealousy of their masters; who, by limiting the authority of each other over their dependants, produced a reciprocal diminution of their power. But though the freedom of the common people was not intended in those charters, it was eventually secured to them; for when the peasantry, and other persons of low rank, were afterwards enabled, by their industry, and by the progress of arts, to emerge from their inferior and servile condition, and to acquire opulence, they were gradually admitted to the exercise of the same privileges which had been claimed by men of independent fortunes; and found themselves entitled, of course, to the benefit of that free government which was already established. The limitations of arbitrary power, which had been calculated chiefly to promote the interest of the nobles, were thus, by a change of circumstances, rendered equally advantageous to the whole community as if they had originally proceeded from the most exalted spirit of patriotism.

The power of apparent precedent worked in the common people's favor; a small measure of liberty was parlayed into a larger measure, despite the efforts of the privileged classes.

When the commons, in a later period, were disposed to make farther exertions, for securing their natural rights, and for extending the blessings of civil liberty, they found it a singular advantage to have an ancient written record, which had received the sanction of past ages, and to which they could appeal for ascertaining the boundaries of the prerogative. This gave weight and authority to their measures; afforded a clue to direct them in the mazes of political speculation; and encouraged them to proceed with boldness in completing a plan, the utility of which had already been put to the test of experience. The regulations, indeed, of this old canon, agreeable to the simplicity of the times, were often too vague and general to answer the purposes of regular government; but, as their aim and tendency were sufficiently apparent, it was not difficult, by a proper commentary, to bestow upon them such expansion and accommodation as might render them applicable to the circumstances of an opulent and polished nation.

Can we libertarians do something similar today?

19
Magna Carta and Libertarian Strategy

Magna Carta is one of those things that virtually everyone across the political spectrum (however defined) has invoked in support of his or her cause. It's been enlisted in a variety of missions. Dissidents of all stripes have held it up as a shield against tyrants, while kings have used it to defend the legitimacy of their rule. Advocates of slavery took refuge in Magna Carta, but so did the proto-libertarian Levellers.

It's tempting to think of Magna Carta as a declaration of the limits of state power and therefore as an early charter of liberty. But the arguments against this perspective are persuasive. It contains little if any political philosophy. As the historian Nicholas Vincent said in an interview, the barons would be appalled by modern conceptions of liberty. It's also important to note that the barons, who appealed to English tradition, were not interested in *everyone's* liberty but only the liberty of a small minority of free men. The language imposing limits on the king's power was vague at best. Bringing the king under the rule of law sounds promising, but it leaves open the question of what the law should be. That was the king's province. The much-lauded clause 39 in the 1215 Magna Carta (there were several versions) stated:

> No free man shall be seized or imprisoned, or stripped of his rights or possessions, or outlawed or exiled, or deprived of his standing in any way, nor will we proceed with force against him, or send others to do so, except by the *lawful judgment of his equals or by the law of the land*. [Emphasis added.]

The italicized words are hardly crystal clear. Trial by jury in criminal matters did not exist at that time, according to the historian Richard Helmholz.

Those words are followed by: "To no one will we sell, to no one deny or delay right or justice."

Again, this sounds promising, but what is right or justice when the king owns his realm?

The principle "no taxation without baronial consent" also appears, though not in those exact words, of course. Nevertheless, the barons were not proto-libertarians. Defending the liberties of "free men" left a lot of people out of the class of beneficiaries. What the barons sought to minimize were John's arbitrary diktats over them. They didn't want it to be so "good to be the king."

Regardless, as we've seen, neither side abided by the agreement, and war between king and barons ensued. King John appealed for help from Pope Innocent III, who excommunicated the barons and declared Magna Carta null and void because the king had signed under duress. However, it was reissued by subsequent kings, albeit with important changes from the original, such as elimination of clause 61, which called for the creation of a council of barons that could sanction the king for wrongdoing. Why would any king reissue a charter that appeared to limit his power? Because having power doesn't mean never having to bargain with those who would oppose you—bargaining may be the least costly way to maintain *some* power. (This point is made clear in the excellent British television series *Monarchy*.)

As Magna Carta scholars point out, the interpretation (mythology) and impact of the charter over the last eight centuries are as important as—maybe more important than—the document and the authors' intentions themselves. Even if it wasn't actually a charter of liberty, it is regarded as such—by people, as I've already noted, who have widely differing views on liberty.

This has implications for libertarian strategy today.

That genuine liberty—in the sense of what Roderick T. Long calls "equality of authority"—can grow out of efforts intended to achieve something less is worth keeping in mind. (Lord Acton and John Millar had important things to say on this score.) I claim no profound insights in the matter of strategy, but I do know that social processes, like the people who actuate them, are complex, and therefore unintended consequences—good and bad—are ubiquitous and to be expected. This makes devising *a* strategy for social change complicated and more likely impossible. There's no algorithm for changing a society from unlibertarian to libertarian. We have no script. That's an argument for the "let a thousand flowers bloom" strategy.

If troublesome barons in the 13th century helped to promote future general liberty without its being part of their intention, the case for libertarian optimism may be buoyed. Things may look bleak on a variety of fronts, but we can never know what might turn the tide. Magna Carta is not the only example of such unintended consequences. In *Lust for Liberty: The Politics of Social Revolt in Medieval Europe, 1200-1425* (2006), Samuel K. Cohn Jr. described many peaceful and violent acts of resistance against local tyranny, some of which won significant concessions from rulers. It is unlikely the rebels carried a treatise on political philosophy under their arms or a theory of rights in their heads. They didn't gather in the village square to hear a political philosopher read from his latest treatise. The rebels simply reacted against particular burdens that had become intolerable; they did not set out to make a libertarian society. Yet they created facts on the ground, not always permanent, and set precedents for their descendents.

It's more than likely that theorists developed their ideas after studying local revolts. In those days, theory and history weren't compartmentalized. So it's a mistake to think that libertarian theory must precede libertarian social action or that inchoate resistance unguided by "pure" libertarianism can't make real progress toward liberty. Couldn't a thinker spin out a theory of individual rights without prompting from history? It's possible, but it seems more likely that historical episodes jump-started the intellectual process and that theory and action (history) will mutually determine each other. This certainly seems to have been the case with John Locke, Adam Smith, and many other thinkers.

If you want more a modern example to go with Cohn's, I recommend Thaddeus Russell's *A Renegade History of the United States* (2010), which chronicles how liberty was won in the streets through the misbehavior of riffraff who probably never read Locke or Paine or even Jefferson.

There is no *one right strategy*. If anything proves successful, it will be a loose web of complementary strategies (perhaps too loose to call a "web"), with a good measure of improvisation. Theories will prompt action; and action will prompt theories. Some approaches will consist in what will be labeled "compromise." (Oh horror!) That is, individuals and organizations will advance liberty through partial measures to reduce state power. Savvy libertarians will capitalize on such measures to push for more progress toward liberty. ("If you liked Measure X, you'll love Measure Y.") They won't let the perfect be the enemy of the good.

In truth, no compromise is involved if an incremental step is regarded *as such* and not as an end in itself.

I need not point out—or need I?—that merely because one incremental measure meets the libertarian standard as a genuine short-run step toward liberty, not all measures represented as such must do so. Each proposal is to be judged on its own merits, and good-faith disagreements are to be expected. That's the nature of the endeavor. I see no reason for libertarians, in the name of purity, to withhold support for steps that make real progress toward liberty and pave the way for more.

The libertarian movement needs individuals and organizations that devote their efforts to sound incrementalism, just as it needs those that do nothing more than teach pure libertarian philosophy. These approaches need not be at odds. In fact, they are complementary. One without the other is unlikely to succeed because society is unlikely to turn libertarian or dismantle the state all at once. Incrementalism without a guiding philosophy probably won't get us all the way to where we want to go, while merely issuing declarations about libertarianism is unlikely to bring about change. How do we get from here to there if it won't happen in a single bound?

It's important not to conflate philosophy and strategy. An uncompromising market anarchist can coherently embrace incrementalism, understanding that because of most people's conservatism, the state will not be abolished overnight. Murray Rothbard used to say that libertarians should take any rollback of state power they can get. In today's environment, we won't be setting the priorities.

What strikes me as futile is a "strategy" that consists in little more than boldly announcing that—if one could—one would push a button to make the government (or most of it) go away. That approach tells the uninitiated something about the speaker, but it says little about why a free society is worth achieving and why the state is our enemy. *That* requires something more than moralizing shock therapy.

20

The Constitution of Anarchy

This book has been a sustained attack on the idea that the U.S. Constitution is essentially a pro-freedom document. I have contended that, contrary to most people's—and many libertarians'—belief, the framers were not motivated by a love for individual liberty (though it had a place in their political vision) and that the Constitution has done a poor job of preserving individual liberty since it contains language suitable for justifying broad government power. But, admittedly, we in the United States have a good deal of personal freedom, despite the erosion of civil liberty, especially since 9/11, and substantial violations of freedom through taxation, regulation, monetary manipulation, subsidies, and other forms of privilege. If the Constitution is so bad, why do we have any freedom at all? That's what this chapter seeks to answer.

Let's start with with something that will surprise many readers: rejecting the U.S. Constitution does not require one to reject the very idea of a constitution. A free society needs a constitution; in fact, a free society would necessarily have a constitution. There is no choice in the matter. Every society has a constitution. The only question is whether it promotes liberty or violates it.

Here's the real shocker: this is true even of an anarchist society. How can that be?

Let's start by understanding (as I suggested in chapter 8) that a constitution need not be written. In "Market Anarchism as Constitutionalism," Roderick T. Long reminded us that England has an unwritten constitution. (*Anarchism/Minarchism: Is a Government Part of a Free Country?*, edited by Long and Tibor R. Machan, 2008.) Furthermore, a written one may or may not accord with how things are actually done. The Soviet constitution appeared to guarantee freedoms that in fact were routinely denied. Many other examples could be cited, including from the United States. James C. Scott, in *Seeing Like a State: How Certain*

Schemes to Improve the Human Condition Have Failed (1999), has much to say about how the real rules of a society, the ones displayed in common behavior, can differ vastly from the written rules, which are irrelevant to the life of the people. (This phenomenon often leads researchers to misunderstand the cultures they study.)

Clearly, Long wrote, "what matters is a nation's 'constitution' in the original sense of the actual institutions, practices, and incentive structures that are in place."

Since this is the case, we need to explore this matter more closely. What is a constitution typically thought to be? Aside from a blueprint of the government, it is thought to be a set of *restraints* on the conduct of government officials. Remember, Alexander Hamilton and other Federalists said the proposed Constitution was *by nature* a bill of rights, or a set of restraints on the government. Officials, they argued, may not do what they were not authorized to do by the Constitution. (Why that argument was illegitimate is a big part of this book.)

Think about that word *restraint*. Can a document restrain a government official? Obviously not. James Madison understood this when he called the Bill of Rights a "parchment barrier." So if government officials *are* restrained, something other than the written constitution must be doing the restraining. What could that be?

When a government official gives an order to another government official—say, a president orders generals to fight a war, a majority of Supreme Court justices strike down a law (ordering the executive branch not to enforce it), or a judge orders a sheriff to take a convicted defendant to prison—what gives rise to the broad social expectation that the order will be obeyed? One might think that those who carry out the order understand that they will be forced to do it—or fired—if they disobey. But this answer is of no help because we can just as easily ask why another official would follow an order to force the first one to carry out the order, or to fire that person. More likely, however, the first official carries out the order because he believes it's the right thing to do or that it is not his job to determine whether the order is right or wrong as long as it's deemed "lawful." This doesn't mean that no official would ever refuse an order, as the Kentucky county clerk Kim Davis did when she refused to issue marriage licenses to same-sex couples. And Long reminded us that "when the U.S. Supreme Court declared President Andrew Jackson's "Trail of Tears" policy unconstitutional, Jackson proceeded with the policy anyway, quipping '[Chief Justice] Marshall has made his decision; now let him enforce it!'"

So there's no guarantee that government officials will always act as they are "supposed" to act; as I said, no constitution, legal system, or statute forces them to do so. Yet they do so almost all the time. Why? Because routine conduct of a particular kind in such circumstances is part of what we mean by society's "actual institutions, practices, and incentive structures that are in place." What restrains government officials—and individuals in general—is something internal rather than external, contrary to what constitutionalists of all parties seem to believe. And, Long added, "those structures exist only insofar as they are continually maintained in existence by human agents acting in certain systematic ways. A constitution is not some impersonal, miraculously self-enforcing robot. It's an ongoing pattern of behavior, and it persists only so long as human agents continue to conform to that pattern in their actions." (On the role of ideology in restraining government, see Jeffrey Rogers Hummel's "The Will to Be Free: The Role of Ideology in National Defense," *The Independent Review*, Spring 2001, online at tinyurl.com/jxm6j38.)

Here's the key point: this feature is no less present in a stateless society than it is in a society with a government. How people, including people who run private defense and dispute-resolution firms, generally conduct themselves *constitutes* the society's incentive structures, that is, its institutions and expectations. Anarchy has a constitution fully as much as a society with a state.

Just as a society with government can have a better or worse constitution (in this real sense), so can an anarchist society. Any limited-government libertarian can point to governments he or she would not want to live under. Yet this does not lead such a libertarian to reject government per se. Similarly, any natural-law market anarchist could identify undesirable stateless circumstances without rejecting statelessness altogether. The difference lies in the (internal) constitution.

The natural question to ask is how we can assure that a stateless society has a good incentive structure, that is, one that promotes justice and liberty. It's an important question, but it's not a question for anarchists alone. It must also be directed to the advocates of government because they face the same challenge. They may not merely assume a proper constitution, for that would beg the question. Once this is understood, the limited-government criticism of market anarchism loses its force.

It is sheer myth that *government* creates the incentive structure it then operates within, and libertarians don't believe this is the case in areas other than law and security. (That is, they acknowledge the incentives inherent in the market process.) Imagine a government that would pass limited-government-libertarian (minarchist) muster. Where did it come from? If it was the product of a social agreement (which is not how governments arose historically), wouldn't the right incentive structure— that is, people's general expectations of themselves and others—have had to predate the government? The term *government* indicates a set of relationships among people, both rulers and ruled (who would likely outnumber their rulers). Ultimately, all those people have to cooperate generally, that is, assume their expected roles voluntarily, with a minimum of coercion. (This is baked into the terms *government* and *society*.) Again, a constitution and government are not outside society imposing rules of conduct. Thomas Paine showed that he understood this in the quotation given earlier: "Great part of that order which reigns among mankind is not the effect of government. It has its origin in the principles of society and the *natural constitution* of man. It existed prior to government, and would exist if the formality of government was abolished." (Emphasis added.)

The interesting problem is: which alternative—anarchy or minarchy—is most likely to respect and preserve liberty,?

The limited-government response is that only a state can have the checks and balances and the separation of powers required to safeguard liberty. This was Madison's response. But this answer implies that those things cannot exist in an anarchy. Why not? The assumption that they cannot is another instance of the myth that the constitution and legal system are outside society. Just as a state can be imagined without checks and balances, so an anarchy can be imagined *with* them. "Far from eschewing checks and balances," Long wrote, "market anarchists take market competition, with its associated incentives, to instantiate a checks-and-balances system, and to do so far more reliably than could a governmental system.... Separation of powers, like federalism and elective democracy, merely simulates market competition, within a fundamentally monopolistic context."

Of course, libertarians would be the first to point out that the U.S. Constitution's system of checks and balances hasn't exactly been effective. "There has been sufficient convergence of interests among the three branches that, occasional squabbles over details notwithstanding, each branch has been complicit with the others in expanding the power of the central government," Long wrote.

Would anarchy fare better? All signs say yes. Market anarchy would feature a competitive legal system, which means individuals could freely enter the market for security and dispute resolution. No monopolist could exclude rivals. Competition is the ultimate check and balance. Just as competition in the market for goods is a unique "discovery procedure," as F. A. Hayek called it, so would competition in the market for dispute-resolution, security, and remediation be a unique source of discovery. Hayek wrote: "I propose to consider competition as a procedure for the discovery of such facts as, without resort to it, would not be known to anyone, or at least would not be utilized." This inestimable epistemological function cannot be simulated by a monopoly, something libertarians should already understand. (See Hayek's "Competition as a Discovery Procedure," in *New Studies in Philosophy, Politics, Economics, and the History of Ideas*, 1978, and Gregory B. Christainsen's "Law as a Discovery Procedure," *Cato Journal*, Winter 1990, online at tinyurl.com/hkl9h9g. Also see Gustav de Molinari's "The Production of Security," online at praxeology.net/GM-PS.htm.)

But how do we know that we'd discover the right things, namely, how to protect liberty and do justice, rather than the wrong things, namely, ways to aggress and exploit? Again, we have no guarantees (nor with a monopoly either, need I say?) because people have volition, but we can judge our chances as favorable compared to our chances under monopoly. Conflict is expensive, not to mention off-putting to customers, and unlike with government, people in a competitive market who perpetrate violence would have to bear the expenses themselves because they could not tax or conscript the population—a pretty strong disincentive.

Thus Long summed up:

Anarchy thus represents the extension, not the negation, of constitutionalism. Instead of thinking of anarchy as a situation in which government has been squeezed down to nothingness, it might be more helpful—at least for minarchists—to think of anarchy as a situation in which government has been ex-

tended to include everybody. This is what Gustave de Molinari, the founder of market anarchism, meant when he wrote, in 1884: "The future thus belongs neither to the absorption of society by the State, as the communists and collectivists suppose, nor to the suppression of the State, as the [non-market] anarchists and nihilists dream, but to the diffusion of the State within society."...
      Anarchy is the completion, not the negation, of the rule of law.

Every problem that the advocate of monopoly government hurls at anarchy comes back like a boomerang. For example, in anarchy competing concepts of proper law may arise, but that's also true with a state, particularly under federalism (states of the union do not have identical laws) and a system of checks and balances. If an aggressor organization were to set up a protection agency or court system, people would be free to resist it. The gang would have no monopoly on the legal use of force and no mystique of the state with which to assert supremacy. But what happens when a state turns into an aggressor (beyond its minimum inherent aggressiveness)? We know what happens. For the most part, people suffer under it, if for no other reason than that they are bound to be outgunned. (While revolutions happen now and then, the potential is limited by collective-action problems. Individuals are reluctant to be the first to rebel, even though they'd be willing if they knew many others would join in.)

Another example: Anarchy cannot offer absolute finality to dispute resolution, but neither can a state. Yet anarchy is likely to provide reasonable finality because customers of dispute-resolution firms would value that feature. The spontaneous private transnational mercantile dispute-resolution process that arose after the fall of the Roman Empire (the Law Merchant) featured practical finality because a perpetual appeals process would have been prohibitively expensive for the courts' customers, who needed to get on with their business. This is also true with private arbitration. A process that went on forever would lose customers to competitors who offered better service.

The claimed superiority of minarchism, Long concluded, is merely the belief that government, unlike anarchy, can "magically" deliver what it merely *declares* it will deliver. The real world is messier both in states and anarchies. But at least in anarchy, the emergent, evolving rules and incentives are aligned constructively. Entrepreneurs make profits by solving problems. Government agencies get larger appropriations when they are problem-plagued. (See David Friedman's "Do We Need Government?" online at tinyurl.com/hu4zk.)

To recap, the American counter-revolution represented by the U.S. Constitution need not sour us on the idea of a constitution, checks and balances, and separation of powers because natural-law market anarchy delivers these, and does so better and more justly than a monopoly government. We can have a constitution and our freedom too!

But how do we get there? The insight into the true nature of a constitution holds a clue. It was grasped by the German anarchist Gustav Landauer (1870-1919), whom Long quoted: "The state is a relationship between human beings, a way by which people relate to one another; and one destroys it by entering into other relationships, by behaving differently to one another."

Credits

Quotations from historical figures were drawn from the Federalist Papers, various collections of Anti-Federalist writings, and the following books:

Max M. Edling, *A Revolution in Favor of Government: Origins of the U.S. Constitution and the Making of the American State* (2003).

Arthur A. Ekirch Jr., *The Civilian and the Military: A History of the American Antimilitarist Tradition* (1972).

Arthur A. Ekirch Jr., *The Decline of American Liberalism* (1955/1967).

E. James Ferguson, *The Power of the Purse: A History of American Public Finance, 1776-1790* (1961).

Merrill Jensen, *The Articles of Confederation: An Interpretation of the Social-Constitutional History of the American Revolution, 1774-1781* (1940).

Merrill Jensen, *The New Nation: A History of the United States During the Confederation, 1781-1789* (1950).

Ralph Ketcham, *James Madison: A Biography* (1971).

Richard Labunski, *James Madison and the Struggle for the Bill of Rights* (2006).

Pauline Maier, *Ratification: The People Debate the Constitution, 1787-1788* (2010).

Edwin J. Perkins, *American Public Finance and Financial Services: 1700-1815* (1994).

Herbert J. Storing, *What the Anti-Federalists Were For* (1981).

William Earl Weeks, *John Quincy Adams and American Global Empire* (1992).

William Appleman Williams, *Empire as a Way of Life* (1980).

Gordon S. Wood *The Creation of the American Republic, 1776–1787* (1998).

Gordon S. Wood, *Empire of Liberty: A History of the Early Republic: 1789-1815* (2009).

Gordon S. Wood, *The Radicalism of the American Revolution* (1991).

Many chapters of this book originated as columns in my TGIF (The Goal Is Freedom) series, which ran on the website of the Foundation for Economic Education (fee.org), 2006-2012, and then continued on the website of the Future of Freedom Foundation (fff.org), 2012-2015, specifically:

Foundation for Economic Education/The Freeman

"Lost Articles," January 26, 2007, http://fee.org/freeman/detail/lost-articles

"History Lesson Lost," October 6, 2006, http://fee.org/library/detail/history-lesson-lost

"The Decline of American Liberalism," March 23, 2007, http://fee.org/articles/arthur-ekirchs-the-decline-of-american-liberalism/

"Where Is the Constitution?," July 28, 2006, http://fee.org/library/detail/where-is-the-constitution

"The Constitution Within," August 18, 2006 http://fee.org/freeman/detail/the-constitution-within

"The Constitution or Liberty," December 7, 2007 http://fee.org/freeman/detail/the-constitution-or-liberty

"Was the Constitution Really Meant to Constrain the Government?," August 8, 2008, http://fee.org/freeman/detail/was-the-constitution-really-meant-to-constrain-the-government/

"That Mercantilist Commerce Clause," May 11, 2007, http://fee.org/freeman/detail/that-mercantilist-commerce-clause

"Is the Income Tax Unconstitutional?," September 1, 2006, http://fee.org/articles/is-the-income-tax-unconstitutional/

"Don't Repeal the 16th Amendment," May 23, 2008, http://fee.org/freeman/donapost-repeal-the-sixteenth-amendment/

"Congressional Generosity," April 1, 2007, http://fee.org/articles/congressional-generosity/

Future of Freedom Foundation/The Future of Freedom

"James Madison: Father of the Implied-Powers Doctrine," July 26, 2013, http://fff.org/explore-freedom/article/tgif-james-madison-father-of-the-implied-powers-doctrine/

"Beware Income-Tax Casuistry, Part 1," August 1, 2006, http://fff.org/explore-freedom/article/beware-incometax-casuistry-part-1/;

"Beware Income-Tax Casuistry, Part 2," September 1, 2006, http://fff.org/explore-freedom/article/beware-incometax-casuistry-part-2/

"Beware Income-Tax Casuistry, Part 3," October 1, 2006, http://fff.org/explore-freedom/article/beware-incometax-casuistry-part-3/

"Empire on Their Minds," March 14, 2014, http://fff.org/explore-freedom/article/tgif-empire-on-their-minds/

"The War of 1812 Was the Health of the State, Part 1," February 27, 2015, http://fff.org/explore-freedom/article/tgif-the-war-of-1812-was-the-health-of-the-state1/

"The War of 1812 Was the Health of the State, Part 2," March 6, 2015, http://fff.org/explore-freedom/article/tgif-war-1812-health-state-part-2/

About the Author

SHELDON RICHMAN is a senior fellow of the Center for a Stateless Society (c4ss.org), chair of the Center's trustees, and a contributing editor at Antiwar.com. He is the author of three other books: *Separating School and State: How to Liberate America's Families* (1994); *Your Money or Your Life: Why We Must Abolish the Income Tax* (1999); and *Tethered Citizens: Time to Repeal the Welfare State* (2001), published by the Future of Freedom Foundation (fff.org). From 1997 to 2012 he was the editor of *The Freeman*, published by the Foundation for Economic Education (fee.org), following which he edited *Future of Freedom* for the Future of Freedom Foundation. Previously he was an editor at the Cato Institute, the Institute for Humane Studies, and *Inquiry* magazine. Richman's articles on foreign and economic policy, civil liberties, and American and Middle East history have appeared in *Newsweek*, *The Washington Post*, *The Wall Street Journal*, the *Chicago Tribune*, the *Chicago Sun-Times*, *USA Today*, *Reason*, *Forbes*, *The Independent Review*, *The American Scholar*, *The American Conservative*, *Cato Policy Report*, *Journal of Economic Development*, *Journal of Palestine Studies*, *Washington Report on Middle East Affairs*, *Middle East Policy*, *Liberty*, and other publications. He is a contributor to the *The Concise Encyclopedia of Economics*. Richman is a graduate of Temple University in Philadelphia. He blogs at *Free Association* (sheldonrichman.com).

I called out as I tossed the bird feed a[nd] chickens clucked hungrily, but I only had [eyes for him.] He dazzled me with a lazy half smile. Slowly, he sauntered over.

"Hey, Addison," he said with a drawl. "I was just thinking about you."

Instantly I felt my face heat up, but managed to smile sweetly. "What a coincidence. I was just thinking about you, too." I stepped toward the fence that enclosed the coop and leaned against it.

"Thinking anything in particular?" he asked.

"Oh, you know, nothing specific. Just general thoughts, really." I gave him a smile.

He watched me in amusement and I could tell he wasn't buying my indifferent act. "Nothing specific, huh?" he asked.

I stifled a giggle at the expression on his face, but continued on with the game, shrugging nonchalantly.

"That's too bad," he responded. "I was hoping you were thinking about last night, and how you feel about me today."

I bit my lip hard, trying to hide my smile. "Well, you *are* pretty charming."

"I knew it! These cowboy boots have never let me down."

strawberry wine

DARLY JAMISON

ZEBRA BOOKS
KENSINGTON PUBLISHING CORP.
http://www.kensingtonbooks.com

ZEBRA BOOKS are published by

Kensington Publishing Corp.
119 West 40th Street
New York, NY 10018

All Kensington titles, imprints, and distributed lines are available
at special quantity discounts for bulk purchases for sales promotion,
premiums, fund-raising, educational, or institutional use.

Special book excerpts or customized printings can also be created
to fit specific needs. For details, write or phone the office of the
Kensington Sales Manager: Attn.: Sales Department. Kensington
Publishing Corp., 119 West 40th Street, New York, NY 10018.
Phone: 1-800-221-2647.

Zebra and the Z logo Reg. U.S. Pat. & TM Off.

First Printing: February 2017
ISBN-13: 978-1-4201-4164-1
ISBN-10: 1-4201-4164-3

eISBN-13: 978-1-4201-4165-8
eISBN-10: 1-4201-4165-1

10 9 8 7 6 5 4 3 2 1

Printed in the United States of America

For my husband and children:
Thank you for loving me and all of my crazy ideas

ACKNOWLEDGMENTS

I've always heard writing is a solitary act, but somehow I never feel alone.

First things first, thank you to Wattpad: the staff, readers, and writers. Without you, this would still be some far-fetched fantasy.

Thank you to my writing group, the Wattpadres, who've left a lasting impression on me: Debbie, Amber, Sarah, Lindsey, Jessica, Tim, Josh, Vic, Farah, Melanie, and Nicole. Long live our Tuesday Twitter chats! *takes a deep breath* Thank you to Tammy, Kristin, Gaby, Keri-Lee, Liz, Katie, Leah, Jill, and countless others (my deepest apologies if I didn't include your name, there are just so many of you!). You are all blessings to me and I'm happy to have met each one of you.

Thank you to my family and non-writing friends. Even though you may not understand this new world I've immersed myself in, your encouragement and support mean everything. I couldn't do this without you.

And finally, thank you Tara Gavin, Jane Nutter, and everyone at Kensington for trusting me to pull this off! I am forever grateful. XO

Prologue

There were two things I knew for certain. Frilly necklines and ball gown silhouettes would likely be the death of me, *and* I was in desperate need of coffee—stat. Technically, there was an acute awareness of a third and even more powerful sensation wreaking havoc on my sanity. I was in love—off the charts, can't-wipe-the-silly-smile-from-my-face-in-love—but that fact went without saying.

I sat in the softly cushioned bistro chair and waited, rather impatiently, for my best friend and future matron-of-honor to bestow upon me a steaming hot cuppa joe. It had been a long day, and it wasn't over yet. I would need to ingest copious amounts of caffeine if I was expected to push forward, clinging to the goal of crossing at least one more item off my super-sized list of things to do. My thoughts raced, just as they always did these days, overanalyzing everything I still needed to accomplish.

Staring out the quaint café window into the midday Georgia sun, my eyes followed the golden rays as they danced carelessly above the tree line, playing peek-a-boo with the leaves as if they didn't have a worry in the world, while I had the weight of the Appalachian Mountains riding on top of my shoulders.

It was still so hard to believe I was actually getting married. Me, Addison Victoria Monroe, about to tie the knot! The very idea made me light-headed. Everything needed to be perfect, and thanks to my crippling OCD, I was devoted to seeing that intention through until every task was complete. However, shopping for wedding dresses on my day off was starting to feel like Chinese water torture.

"God, would you get a grip?" I scolded, covering my mouth with one hand so no one would notice my one-sided conversation. "You act as if you're the first bride to walk the face of the earth!" Letting out a drawn-out sigh, I pushed my fingers through long, sun-kissed locks while the other hand focused on rubbing out the microscopic scratch that marred the mosaic-covered table I sat at.

"Talking to yourself again?" Ruby asked, as she handed me my caramel brûlée latte. I hadn't even heard her approach. "You know, they say that's an early warning sign of schizophrenia."

Ruby Sinclair-Matthews gracefully situated herself into the seat across from me and I cringed as she took a sip of her green kale smoothie. "I don't need you to remind me I'm going crazy," I politely informed her, taking in the softly scented steam. "I'm already well aware." I watched with distaste as she delicately dabbed a napkin at the corners of her mouth, wiping away the nonexistent remnants of her latest obsession.

"What?" she demanded defensively. "Why are you staring at me like I just ate a puppy?"

"Seriously, I don't understand how you can drink that stuff."

Ruby tossed long, pale blond hair over one shoulder and threw me one of her infamous looks of superiority. "I told you, Addy—I'm turning over a new leaf. I am the official poster child for healthy living from here on out. My ass is already the size of the *Titanic*, and I'm not about to let it get any bigger. And my breasts," she said, glancing down at the girls, "I've never had cleavage like this before!" Her honey-brown eyes widened and she nodded in my direction. "I don't know how you can drink *that*." Ruby stared accusingly—or was it longingly—at the large decorated mug positioned tightly between my trembling hands. "There's enough sugar in that thing to send a baby whale into a diabetic coma." The girl should know. It had been her drug of choice up until a few short months ago, when she decided to become Health Nut Extraordinaire.

I covered my laugh by taking a long swig of warm, caramel-flavored yumminess. Sugary treats always had been my weakness, I'm not gonna lie, but I couldn't help it. The delicious sweetness enveloped me like a soothing embrace, and what I needed right now was a little Southern comfort. It was a miracle I didn't weigh a ton and a half after all the self-comforting I'd been doing.

When Ruby had said planning my wedding would be fun, she'd obviously been lying through her teeth. Ripping out my nails one by one sounded more fun than the torture I'd been suffering through. All I wanted was the final outcome, being wife to the man of my dreams, so why was I expected to jump through all these hoops to get there?

"Now," Ruby began, setting down her pulverized vegetables. "Are you excited?"

"To look at more wedding dresses?" I gave her a shrug and rolled my eyes. "To be perfectly honest, it's ranking right up there with getting a Pap smear. I'm exhausted! We've been shopping all day and I haven't found a thing. Tell me again why I can't just elope?"

"Because this is the *biggest* day of your life, Addy! No eloping aloud. You need to have a proper wedding, with all the bells and whistles," she insisted. "Your family and friends deserve that, don't you think?"

"But I'm not really a bells-and-whistles kinda girl."

"So you'll make an exception," Ruby deadpanned, glaring at me with a long-suffering look perfected from years of practice. "You have to be excited, Addy. You're getting *married*! I'm telling you, we need to go to Kleinfeld in New York City. I heard Angelina Jolie was spotted there right before her top-secret wedding to Brad Pitt. You know, with her figure she totally should have gone with—" But I'd already tuned her out. I really had no interest in who went shopping where, or for what. I had too many other things to consider. Of course I was excited, how could I not be? But there were a million tiny details that needed to be addressed before my big day, and I felt as if I needed a personal assistant just to keep track of them all.

"Earth to Addy." Ruby sighed with annoyance, bringing me back to the coffee shop. "Are you even listening to me?" She waved a manicured hand in front of my face, snapping me back to attention.

I studied the perfect pout on my best friend's lips and silently cursed myself for having drifted away from the conversation. Ruby had been my closest confidant since preschool, and now that we were adults we didn't get to see each other nearly as much as we would've liked. Even though we both lived in Atlanta, she was busy tending to her husband and successful party planning business, and I had my blossoming career at the hospital that kept me busier than I cared to admit. Being a physician assistant was a time-consuming responsibility, but luckily I worked with an amazing medical team who made all the hard work worthwhile.

"I'm sorry, Ruby. I've just got a lot on my mind today. With the wedding plans and long hours at work, not to mention volunteering at the medical clinic and packing my things to move to the new house, I'm ready to pull my hair out!"

"Now, don't do that. Your veil can only hide so much." Ruby flashed me a sympathetic smile and reached over to touch my hand. "I really don't know how you do it," she said, suddenly shaking her head. "You've got so much going on. You're busier than a one-legged man in an ass-kicking contest!"

I let out a laugh, nearly choking on my coffee. Leave it to Ruby to drop the perfect one-liner; she'd always been a hard-core fan of tasteless jokes. "Well, I couldn't ask for a more satisfying job, you know that. We're just a little short-staffed at the moment. And I can't wait to get married," I admitted, smiling at the thought. "It's just— it all seems so surreal, you know? There's so much to do, so many things to work out . . ."

Ruby nodded as she absentmindedly twirled the giant rock on her own ring finger. "Believe me, I know how you feel. Planning a wedding can make you feel like you got the shit kicked out of you—in the best possible way, of course. Luckily, you have me to help, and as you know, I am an *expert* when it comes to party plans! Between choosing the right venue, picking out the flowers, and finding the perfect dress, it's no wonder every bride isn't committed before it's all said and done! You know, not every girl has what it takes to put this kind of thing together. But, oh, Addy," she breathed wistfully, clasping her hands together, "when you're standing next to your new husband, everything else just seems so . . . unimportant. And all the stress you put yourself through to get there suddenly feels pointless. But it's worth it—I *promise* you it's worth it."

The truth is, I didn't need Ruby to tell me that, I already knew it. Getting married was not something I took lightly. It was the sacramental union of two souls that were meant to be together forever, officially joining as one. I was about to become half of that magical kind of fusion, eternally secured to the man who'd stolen my heart. Soon, my life would be so closely interweaved with someone else's that people would have a difficult time making out where one person ended and the other began. God, that sounds so clichéd, but it's true. When you get it right, and I *finally* did, it's like a fairy tale. And I was hell-bent on getting to my happily-ever-after.

We took our time finishing our drinks and stood up to leave. The wedding boutique was just a couple doors down and it would be our second to last stop of the day, but my hopes of finding the perfect dress had been lost somewhere between shops six and seven, and I wasn't sure I had it in me to sift through yet another store—even on a caffeine high.

"I remember when I married Tommy," Ruby went on, as we made our way inside the whimsical boutique. "It was the most fantastic day of my life. You know, it's already been five years, but it stills feels as if we're on our honeymoon. You would never know we've been together since high school! Not that we haven't had our share of ups and downs . . . But thank God the highs have far outweighed the lows." Ruby's cheeks flushed bright pink as she gushed on about the summer she fell in love with Tommy Matthews. It wasn't the first time she'd been in love, but lucky for her it had been the last. They complemented each other perfectly. Ruby, so comical and fun; and Tommy, so devoted and supportive—not to mention secure enough in his manhood to deal with the likes of Ms. Ruby Sinclair.

I remember that summer very well. It'd been almost ten years earlier and was the first time I'd found myself in the throes of passion. It was also the summer I'd had my heart broken, and a tiny piece of it had been whisked away to Texas. There's something about first love that tends to stick with a person, even years afterward. People often say that time helps you let go of the pain of that inevitable heartache, but I disagree. Time might change you, make you a little wiser, but it can never erase the feelings of that first touch, that first kiss.

Of the first *time* . . .

I'd been thinking about that summer a lot lately, indulging in the delicious memories of those few special months. Maybe it was because of all the planning and decision making that would change the course of my entire life, or maybe it was the unavoidable loss of innocence that continued to reel me in. Sometimes, I just needed an escape from the chaos, and my thoughts quickly retreated to a time when life was simple and everything was new. There was something sublimely powerful about my first love. The way the hot Georgia sun caressed his face, the gentle way the breeze swept through his tousled, dark waves.

Jake . . . Always on my mind, it seems. For as long as I could remember, he'd been the star of my young adult fantasies, and the slightest reminder of him still caused my heart to skip a beat. *How is that possible after all these years?*

The chiseled features, those eyes, *that body* . . . And enough charm to bewitch even the most seasoned female. Jake was the complete package—and then some. It was no wonder he had gotten under my skin.

Once again, Ruby and I began the task of searching through dresses. I wasn't entirely sure what I was looking for, but I trusted I would know the instant I found it.

"Oh, Addy! This one is absolutely gorgeous!" Ruby exclaimed, jarring me from my reflection and holding up a showy sheath with lots of built-in bling.

I wrinkled my nose. "That's more your style, Ruby. It would look silly on me." My best friend always did have a flair for flamboyant clothing, but that just wasn't my taste. I preferred something simple, something that felt good when I wore it, like an old pair of jeans. Above all, I wanted to feel comfortable on what would be the most important day of my life.

My hand skimmed along an array of delicate fabrics, each gown more brilliant than the last, and I felt a rush of blood surge through my veins. *What if I never find it?* A familiar twinge of panic consumed me as I carefully analyzed every garment. This was impossible! How could I be expected to find the perfect dress in a sea of gaudy designs?

Biting my lip, I chose a dress with a high jeweled neckline and several layers of tulle and lace, and held it up against myself to undergo Ruby's expert inspection.

Two carefully shaped eyebrows shot up into perfect arches. "Oh—my—God. You can't be serious!" she exclaimed, a tortured expression emphasizing her point.

"It's heinous. I would rather gouge my eyes out with a rusty fork than be seen in that thing!"

I couldn't hide my amusement and smiled in spite of myself as I returned the ornate dress to its resting place. I hadn't really been serious about it, I was just hoping to sneak in a laugh. With her lively ways, Ruby was like a walking variety show. She'd always excelled at distracting me.

"I'm going to pretend like that never even happened," she declared in disbelief, turning away with a huff to continue filtering through the different patterns. "We've been best friends for how many years? You would think *some* of my fashion sense would have worn off on you by now."

Hiding my smile, I couldn't help but keep up the charade. "Sorry to disappoint you, but you need to remember— *I'm* the one who has to wear this dress, not you."

"Yes, I know that," she sighed, baffled by my lack of style savvy. "But as your matron of honor, it's my job to make sure you do not look like a raving idiot," Ruby stoically assured me. She took her best friend responsibilities very seriously. "Besides, I *cannot* be seen standing next to you if you insist on wearing something that gross."

"Gee . . . thanks," I deadpanned. Whether she knew it or not, I was in charge, no matter how unstable I might seem. And even though she was a wee bit theatrical, I knew she had my best interests in mind.

"Hey—remember our shopping sprees back in Lakeside? When you maxed out your parents' credit card with your obsessive need to be a trendsetter?" I asked, giggling at the thought. "We rarely did see eye to eye on fashion, even back then."

Ruby nearly collapsed in a fit of laughter, grasping my

arm to remain upright. "Like our junior year when we went shopping for prom? I spent way too much on my dress and my dad forced me to get a job to pay it off. As if that was supposed to teach me some sort of lesson or something!"

Tears spilled over my eyes and rolled down my cheeks as I recalled Ruby's ridiculously extravagant purchase of a name-brand gown and matching stilettos. She was the only teenage girl in attendance wearing an ensemble that cost nearly as much as my first car! I'm not sure who was more livid: her parents for having realized they raised a daughter who obviously did not understand the value of a dollar, or Ruby because they'd forced her to take a summer job at the local farmer's market to pay off her debt. To this day, Ruby still has expensive tastes, but at least she'd learned to practice self-control—most of the time, anyway.

Ten years . . . It seems like just yesterday, I observed, slipping easily back into the past. *So much has changed since then.* It was the summer I turned eighteen, not really a child, yet not quite a woman, and I had no idea what was waiting for me during those steamy months ahead. I hadn't expected anyone to come along and sweep me off my feet, but that's exactly what had happened. And as fate would have it, I wasn't entirely opposed.

I continued to browse through dresses, distracted, as bittersweet memories played through my mind.

PART ONE

Chapter One

Jake Grady was every eighteen-year-old girl's wildest dream. He was tall and broad shouldered, with dark wavy hair that fell carelessly over his tanned forehead, and piercing blue eyes that crinkled slightly at the corners every time his lips curved into a sexy smile. He had the easy confidence of a man who had grown up knowing he was attractive, yet modest enough to not come across as arrogant. Combine those swoon-worthy qualities with some well-developed muscles and a cowboy hat, and you've got the first guy I ever fell in love with.

Sounds like a heartbreak waiting to happen, right? Come to think of it, I don't know many who can say their first love *didn't* end in heartbreak. Other than my grandparents, but that's another story.

Summer had just begun and I had plans to make it my best vacation ever. Come August, the chaos of college applications and essays would begin, along with researching scholarships and grants and the unending deadlines that would inevitably follow. I felt I owed it to myself to get in as much fun as possible while I didn't have the responsibilities of higher education looming overhead.

Basically, my summer agenda consisted of lazy days at the lake, bonfires at night, and a whole lot of living in between.

Jake spent the summer I turned eighteen employed at my family's farm. He was going to be starting his junior year at the University of Houston that fall and was hoping to spend his time off working and saving money. Shoveling horse manure wasn't a glamorous job by any means, but it paid the bills—and his scholarships only went so far.

Gramps would never admit to it, but I know he was impressed with Jake. He didn't offer just anyone an icy beer after a long day slaving away in the hot Georgia temperatures, but Jake managed to sit and enjoy a cold one with my dad and grandpa almost every night after the sun went down. Now, that's really saying something if you know the men in my family.

The women in my family sang a different tune. "A nice, ambitious, and respectful young man, that Jake is," Mags was fond of telling me. "He's got a good head on his shoulders, too, Addy."

Mags was what I called my grandmother. Apparently as a toddler I had a hard time pronouncing Grandma Maggie, and somehow it just came out as Mags. Anyway, it stuck, but she didn't mind. She was one of the most important influences in my life, growing up. She never treated me like a child, and I could go to her with just about anything, and believe me . . . I did! You know, people always say you never know what you have until it's gone. That woman was nothing short of amazing. God, how I miss her.

The sun was already high in the sky that morning he pulled up to my grandparents' house. For some unknown reason, I had managed to crawl out of bed before noon, and I sat with Mags on the front porch, watching his beat-up old Ford truck leave a cloud of dust as it made its way up the long gravel drive. It was a dull shade of blue with a thick horizontal white stripe going down the center of each side. *What a hunk of junk!* I thought with a huff. I didn't realize it at the time, but I would be getting to know the backseat of that old truck very well during the course of that summer.

The opportunity to meet Jake came later that same day, when Mags convinced me to offer him a glass of lemonade. Looking back on it now, I'm pretty sure she was trying to play matchmaker. She had an endearing habit of trying to mingle in a person's love life, but this was the first time she had taken an interest in mine. I remember walking up to him on that sunny afternoon with an ice-cold glass of lemonade dripping in my hand.

"Hey there," I called out. "You need a drink?"

Jake turned to me with that lazy smile of his and looked me up and down. Slowly. Suddenly, I felt naked. As if the flimsy cotton sundress I wore had disappeared into thin air. If I hadn't been holding that damn glass of lemonade, I would have folded my arms across myself to conceal what I knew he was scrutinizing. Instead I just stood there, like an idiot, with my hand dripping wet.

"Well, I don't know," he drawled. "What did you have in mind?" Jake leaned casually against the digging fork he had been using, his eyes squinting slightly in the hazy afternoon sun. He looked as if he had just stepped right out of a sexy cowboy postcard. You know, the kind that say "Wish you were here" in big, bold letters? An unfamiliar feeling of lust stirred as I gaped at his confident sapphire gaze. Was he trying to make me uncomfortable? If so, it was working.

"This," I retorted, shoving the glass at him. Our fingers

brushed together as he took the drink from my hand, and I quickly pulled mine away, shocked by the electric sensation that shot up my arm. I was hoping Jake hadn't noticed my reaction, but I suspected he had when he let out a chuckle.

My mouth felt as dry as the Sahara. Good gravy, was he hot! I tried to overlook his annoying self-assurance and decided to introduce myself. "Um, we've never met before," I began, painfully stating the obvious. "My name's Addison Monroe, but everyone calls me Addy."

"It's very nice to meet you . . . *Addison*." He rewarded me with the sexiest smile I'd ever seen in real life. "Thank you kindly for the drink." He downed the pale yellow liquid and handed me back an empty glass. Then he tipped the brim of his sandy brown hat and turned to walk away, leaving me standing there with my mouth wide open. A swarm of bees could have attacked and I still would have stood rooted to that spot, staring after him. I'll be honest, my first impressions of Jake were stuck somewhere in between lust and frustration. I frowned to myself and finally marched back toward the house, my brunette ponytail swinging impatiently behind me.

"Did he like it?" Mags asked in amusement as I passed by.

My eyes rolled toward the sky as I played back the scene that had just taken place. "Something like that."

I heard her laughing as I stomped into the house.

"Need a lift?"

I turned and saw an old blue pickup following behind me down the long dirt driveway as I walked home that afternoon from my grandparents'.

Jake . . .

My pulse quickened and I tried to think of something clever to say. "I don't get into cars with strangers," I answered, and gave myself a mental high five. I was used to having smart remarks present themselves well after the moment they should have been made, so my quick wit in this moment pleased me no end.

"Well, I'm not a *total* stranger," he said, his lips tilting up into a lazy grin that revealed a tiny dimple in his right cheek. "You did offer me a drink this afternoon, remember? Thanks again for that, you came along just in the nick of time. It was awfully hot today."

Oh no . . . I thought, shaking my head. He was not going to charm me that easily!

"You never even introduced yourself," I shot back, trying to ignore the way his eyes danced as he watched me.

Jake raised his brows in surprise. I guess he wasn't used to having teenage girls resist his down-home, country-boy ways. "I'm sorry, ma'am," he confessed with just a hint of Texas twang. Not so much that it hit you in the face, but noticeable enough to make a girl weak in the knees. "Allow me to properly introduce myself. My name is Jake Grady, and I am very pleased to make your acquaintance," he said, tilting his cowboy hat slightly. "May I offer you a ride?"

And just like that, it was over. Hook, line, and sinker. I never stood a chance.

I couldn't take my eyes off him. Even after working outside all day in the harsh Georgia sun, he still managed to look incredible. He embodied every single teenage fantasy I'd ever had about impossibly hot, too-good-to-be-true Texas cowboys. I took a deep breath before I climbed into the passenger seat of the truck, shutting the door carefully behind me. I noticed Mags waving good-bye to us in the rearview mirror, but pretended I didn't see. I knew she would give me the third degree over what had transpired the next day, so I decided not to give her the satisfaction of acknowledging her sly smile.

Glancing around me, I was surprised at how clean the inside of his pickup was, not even one discarded fast food wrapper in sight. And the smell made me feel dizzy—in a good way—like a mixture of pheromones and Calvin Klein.

"You know," I began, struggling to ignore the building apprehension I felt at being this close to an impossibly attractive, older male. "I really don't need a ride. I just live next door."

Jake gave me an irresistible crooked smile as he pulled out of the drive. "I know where you live, Addison," he said, slightly emphasizing my name, letting me know he had no intention of calling me Addy. "I'm in the mood for some ice cream. I was wondering if you would be interested in helping the new guy in town find his way around?"

"Are you asking me out?" I questioned in disbelief. My eyes felt like they were going to pop right out of my head and land on the floor of his immaculately clean truck.

"I guess I'm asking you if you want to get some ice cream." He laughed lightly. "I promise, you won't need to clarify when I ask you out."

Holy crap. Did he really just say that?

Looking straight ahead, I tried to play it cool and not act like a total spaz. Like getting asked out by a drop-dead gorgeous college guy happened to me every single day of the week. "Sure, I'll show you where to go for ice cream." I shrugged with indifference. I sneaked a peek over at him just in time to catch him quietly chuckle.

Oh my God, I sighed to myself. *He probably thinks I'm such a child!*

It wasn't like I didn't know how to talk to boys. I had started dating that year. Group dates, but dating nonetheless. Not to mention I'd had three different invitations to prom that spring. Believe me, I was no slouch when it came to talking to the opposite sex!

But Jake was not at all like the other guys I knew. I'm not sure if it was his ceaseless self-confidence or the fact that he was a college man, but he had me slightly unnerved.

"Why are you off work so early anyway?" I asked, trying to find something to talk about. "It's not like Gramps to finish up at this hour. It's not even four!"

Jake removed his cowboy hat and laid it down gently on the seat between us. "The tractor I was using took a turn for the worse," he explained gravely. "Your grandpa's working on it now. I offered to stay and help, but he insisted I come back in the morning." He cocked his head, presenting me with a slow, lopsided grin, and a nest of butterflies promptly moved into my stomach.

Taking a deep breath, I tried to ignore my nerves and began asking Jake questions about himself, even though I had already grilled Mags earlier in the day about every tiny detail she could recall. As it turned out, he was invited to stay with his aunt and uncle in Lakeside, Georgia, a small farming community nestled in the foothills of the Blue Ridge Mountains. That's where I lived. Jake's family went to church with mine, and they had somehow managed to convince my grandpa Henry to hire him for a few months during his summer break.

Completely engrossed by his husky voice and the

casual way in which he spoke, I hung on to every word that came out of Jake's mouth. He could have been singing the alphabet in pig Latin and I would have felt compelled to listen. I gave him directions through the small tourist town, pointing out any landmark I thought might be of interest to him. The remaining drive to the ice cream shop was filled with witty banter and sideways smiles, and my confidence began to build.

Until we arrived at our destination.

Chapter Two

As we pulled into the gravel drive, I noticed half of my senior class loitering in the parking lot. A feeling of unease ripped through me and I sat up a bit straighter.

Since when did this become a high school hot spot? I grouched to myself. Living in a rural community, everyone seemed to know everyone else's business, and I was not looking forward to explaining who I was with to my friends, especially since I was just getting to know Jake myself.

"You know," I began, praying my voice wouldn't crack with trepidation, "there's another ice cream shop just around the corner. Why don't we go there instead?" I suggested, trying to make it sound like a good idea.

"Why?" Jake questioned. His eyebrows knitted together in confusion. "We're already here, and this seems like a perfectly nice place." And with that he pulled his pickup into a parking space and turned off the engine.

I took a deep breath and hopped out of the truck.

A large group of kids outside stood around together, laughing and goofing off as they listened to country music blaring from someone's car stereo.

For a split second, the thought of making a break for the cornfield situated behind the parking lot filtered through my mind. If I ran fast enough, maybe no one would see me and I could avoid the embarrassing scene I knew waited for me once everyone got an eyeful of Jake. The only thing that stopped me was the fact that I would seem like a crazed lunatic in front of the guy I was trying to impress, a look I definitely wasn't shooting for. Instead, I bit the bullet and decided to act like a mature adult.

Smoothing out the wrinkles in my sundress, I attempted to put on a nonchalant expression and walked quickly toward the entrance before anyone noticed. Jake stepped ahead and opened the door to let me in first.

"Such a gentleman." I couldn't help but smile at the polite gesture and Jake threw me a half grin, making my heart officially skip a beat.

When we walked into the ice cream shop, a waft of cool air and regret hit me square in the face. At least a dozen kids I recognized were hanging out inside. *Perfect. Here's the other half of my class.*

The noise level in the small shop was at an all-time high as laughter and conversation took place around us, but one mocking, male voice stood out from the rest. "Hey there, Addy." My eyes followed the source of the greeting and I was dismayed to find Brett Lawrence, captain of the varsity football team, checking me out with approving eyes. My chest tightened and I stopped dead in my tracks.

"Hi, Brett," I answered cautiously as goose bumps made their way up my arms. Brett had been my chosen date to the junior/senior prom a couple of months back, and the night hadn't ended very well. I quickly discovered that Mr. Hotshot Football Player liked to pressure his dates into something more than what they were ready for, and that unfortunate evening *I* happened to be on the unlucky end of that exchange.

I'd ended up storming out of the dance with my high heels in hand, one broken spaghetti strap, and an insurmountable amount of humiliation sitting on my shoulders. Brett followed me out into the parking lot and continued his pursuit, forcing me to sideswipe his head with the heel of my shoe. I had done a pretty good job of avoiding him ever since.

Until now.

I turned quickly toward Jake and asked again, "Are you sure you don't want to go somewhere else? This place is so . . . crowded," I lamely pointed out. I suddenly felt queasy, realizing I was now stuck in the same establishment as the guy who had tried to force himself on me. But it was too late. The group of teenagers was upon us, spewing out more questions and comments than I could keep up with.

"Who's your boyfriend, Addy?" someone asked.

"Oh my God, I *cannot* believe you missed my bonfire last weekend! You could have brought your *friend* along," stated another.

"Damn, girl," came one more observation. "Looks like you've already grown a cup size this summer . . ."

Blah, blah, blah . . .

I sighed heavily and attempted to study the menu that hung on the wall. Glancing sideways at Jake, I could tell he was amused by the scene unfolding. Reluctantly, I made the introductions and answered all of the questions— ignoring the one about my bra size.

"Addy—who is this guy and *why* haven't you mentioned him to me before?" my best friend, Ruby Sinclair, sneaked up and whispered fiercely into my ear.

"Shhhh!" I glared back at her as discreetly as I could and threw a glance over my shoulder to see if Jake had overheard. Luckily, he only had eyes for the assortment of frozen flavors displayed in the freezer case in front of us. "I only just met him. My grandparents know him. He's working at their farm this summer."

"How convenient . . ." She smiled coyly. Her perfectly plucked eyebrows rose to an annoying height that made me want to slap them back down to their normal resting place.

"Hey, can't a girl get some ice cream around here without being accused of some seedy under-story?" I hissed back. Seriously, Ruby could be so dense sometimes.

"Not when that girl is my very best friend and just happens to be with one of the most *gorgeous* guys I have ever seen!" She then turned on her heel and pranced off triumphantly, leaving me standing there staring after her.

"Do you know what you want?" Jake asked suddenly, distracting me from my best friend's drama attack. He had left his cowboy hat in the truck, and his dark waves fell casually across his tanned forehead in a way that made innocent girls like me dream of doing not-so-innocent things. He looked like he belonged in a sexy ad for Levi's and not standing in an ice cream parlor with a self-conscious high school senior. But before I could answer, Brett was upon us again with his cocky grin and arrogant attitude.

"Whatcha doin' later, Addy?" he leered, standing a little closer than I cared for him to be. "Wanna come hang out with me for a while? My parents are out of town this week. We would have the whole place to ourselves." My stomach clenched tightly and I caught a mild whiff of beer sitting on his breath.

I glanced nervously at Jake, trying to gauge what he was thinking. How could that idiot ask me out right in front of him?

"No thanks, Brett. I'm good," I replied, moving slightly closer to Jake.

"Ahh, come on! We can finally finish that date we started a couple months back." He smiled suggestively and reached for my arm.

"I said *no*, Brett." I squirmed quickly away from him. He lunged toward me anyway and my heart dropped, just like it had done at prom when I was forced to fight Brett off.

"Oh, come on! You're such a dicktease—" he began.

"I think she wants you to leave her alone," Jake interrupted, stepping forward.

Brett stopped, dumbfounded, and looked Jake up and down as if he had just noticed him for the first time. It was an obvious attempt to decide if he could take him on. "And who are you, her boyfriend?" he finally accused.

"No, I'm not her boyfriend."

"Then I don't think it's any of your damn business," Brett retorted, and turned back toward his group of friends with a chuckle. But no one laughed.

"Looks like I just made it my business," Jake challenged. His eyes were hard and steady as he stared Brett down. If I had not been the cause of the tension, I would have thought that Jake looked pretty damn cute when he was acting all tough. But since I was the cause . . .

Jake glanced over at me and our eyes collided.

"Hey!" a short, round man called out from behind the ice cream shop counter. "I don't want any trouble in here."

Jake tore his eyes from mine and spoke to the employee. "Sorry sir, there'll be no trouble," he promised and gently took my elbow, steering me toward the door. "Come on, Addison, let's get outta here."

The sun was high in the afternoon sky as we walked out into the parking lot, and the kids from my school were still positioned in the same spots as when we'd first arrived. I lifted my hand to my eyes to block the bright sunlight and looked up at Jake. "I'm so sorry," I apologized, feeling like an idiot. What a way to impress the new guy.

"It's all right. Don't worry about it." A lopsided grin spread across his face, revealing that small dimple in his cheek. For one brief moment I thought about touching it, but quickly pushed those kinds of crazy thoughts from my mind. Jake stared at me through thick lashes. "Do you think we'll be safe if we go somewhere else for ice cream, or do you suppose you might have fans there, as well?"

Thank God he's not upset. I sighed inwardly and gave myself a mental kick in the ass. "We should be good." I smiled back at him, relieved to be leaving the disastrous trip behind.

Or so I thought.

"Hey," a loud voice called out suddenly, causing me to flinch.

We turned back toward the door and saw Brett swaying toward us and I froze, my heart racing in my chest.

"Where do you think you're going?" he asked, walking forward and looking Jake square in the eye.

"Look, we don't want any trouble," Jake began. "We're just—" But before he could finish his sentence, Brett hauled his fist back and punched Jake right in the jaw.

Jake staggered backward and I heard myself scream. A pins-and-needles sensation made its way throughout my whole body and the tiny hairs on the back of my neck raised, every single one of them standing at attention. Suddenly, Ruby was at my side, pulling me out of harm's way. I hadn't even seen her come out of the ice cream shop.

The kids in the parking lot stopped what they were doing and started to head in our direction, smelling a fight. They circled Jake and Brett and began to cheer them on, not really caring who won. Jake regained his footing and stepped toward Brett with renewed confidence. Now that he knew what he was up against, he was on top of his game.

"So do all high school guys around here bully teenage girls, or is it just you?" Jake demanded, pushing wavy black hair off his forehead, oblivious to the crowd around them. His pecs stood out impressively as they strained against the thin fabric of his T-shirt.

Brett's face drew into a scowl and he lunged toward Jake again, but he missed and tripped over his own feet.

Jake tossed his head back and let out a husky laugh. "Sorry there, big guy. I guess maybe drinking in the middle of the day should be left to the men who can handle their liquor." He smiled smugly and looked down at Brett, who lay sprawled among the gravel. He must have smelled the alcohol, too.

"You asshole!" Brett shouted, struggling to get up. He steadied himself on his feet and lunged at Jake once more. This time, Jake was ready and threw a swift upper-cut, hitting Brett just under the chin. Brett landed back on the ground, unconscious.

The ice cream shop door flung open and the little round man called out, "I'm calling the cops!"

Everyone scrambled about, leaving Brett on the ground.

Jake grabbed my elbow and steered me toward the truck. "Let's go!" I couldn't believe what had just happened. Finally, someone stood up to Brett! I gave Ruby a quick wave before we hopped into the truck and sped off, leaving a cloud of dust in the parking lot.

"Oh my God!" I breathed when we were on the road, I hadn't realized I'd been holding my breath. "I can't believe that just happened!"

Jake rubbed his jaw and I could see it had already turned a soft shade of pink from where Brett's fist had met his chin. "Are you hurt?" I asked, suddenly feeling guilty. No one had ever gotten into a fight for me before.

"No, I'm fine. It's just a little tender is all." He looked over at me with apologetic eyes. "Addison—I'm really sorry. I hope you're not good friends with him."

I shook my head, surprised he felt the need to apologize. "I'm not anymore," I assured him. "Brett's changed a lot this past year. He's become a bully. You're the first person I've ever seen stand up to him like that. Except for me," I added softly. I'd never told anyone about what had happened that night at prom, not even Ruby.

"You?" He looked over at me with an arched eyebrow.

"Yeah." I gave him a shy smile. "Let's just say this wasn't the first time Brett's been hit in the face in a parking lot."

Jake regarded me closely with wide eyes. I could tell he wanted to ask more, but he didn't pry.

"Maybe I'll tell you about it someday, but right now you promised me ice cream," I playfully teased, trying to lighten the mood . . . and change the subject.

"Yes, ma'am," he returned with a mock salute. Jake offered me an amused smile and a wink. "Where to next?"

The rest of the afternoon was uneventful, as far as nosy friends and fistfights go, and Jake dropped me off at my doorstep just before dinner. I watched from my front porch as his blue pickup pulled out of my parents' drive, and I shivered with anticipation. I knew, beyond a shadow of a doubt, that I was in for the summer of my life.

Chapter Three

The next morning my cell phone alarm shrieked at the crack of dawn, waking me from a dead sleep. Without hesitation, I jumped out of bed and primped and preened to the sound of the roosters, determined to look perfect for when Jake arrived to work.

I made the walk over to my grandparents' house in record time and greeted Mags as she was making breakfast in their large country kitchen, complete with a double oven. As soon as I stepped through the door, I was bombarded with an assortment of delicious aromas, and my stomach gurgled eagerly in response.

"Well, good morning there, sunshine," Mags greeted me with a surprised grin. "To what do I owe this pleasure?"

"What?" I responded innocently. "I was just in the mood for your pancakes."

Mags eyed me suspiciously over her angular glasses. "This early-morning visit doesn't have anything to do with the fact the boys will be joining us for breakfast here in a few minutes, does it?"

I attempted to pull off an angelic expression but

suspected she saw right through my façade. Every morning Mags made a smorgasbord of dishes to feed the hungry farmhands before they went out to work in the fields. She was a firm believer in the whole "breakfast is the most important meal of the day" bit, and she made sure she treated the hardworking men right.

I looked at the long table in front of me and my mouth began to water. It held an array of choices, from her famous fluffy pancakes and sausage gravy casserole to tomato cheddar strata and everything in between. Mags was a genius in the kitchen, and everyone always looked forward to her delicious, made-from-scratch recipes. It was a real treat to be invited to my grandparents' table and I had plenty of happy memories sitting there, surrounded by family, friends, and the most delectable meals in all of Georgia.

As if on cue, the back door swung open and the men started pouring in. I smiled at the usual familiar faces. There was Frank, a boisterous, middle-aged man who had been working for my grandparents since he was in high school; Kevin, an on-again, off-again farmhand with a colorful past but sweet demeanor; Miles, a cranky old-timer who'd had a penchant for pessimism that Mags found oddly endearing; and newcomer Jake, looking especially fine in a tight white T-shirt and some comfortable-looking Wranglers, his unruly dark waves falling casually around his too-good-to-be-true face.

"Mornin' there, Maggie," Frank bellowed as he planted a kiss on my grandmother's cheek. "And, Addy! What're you doin' here this early? Shouldn't you still be countin' sheep?"

I felt a slow burn take over my cheeks and I looked at the floor, struggling to come up with a believable excuse.

"Oh, you let her be now, Frank," Mags answered for

me with a scolding shake of her finger. "I asked Addy to come and help me with breakfast this morning. Do you know how much work it is feeding you men all the time?"

Mags slipped me a discreet wink and I smiled in relief.

"Nonsense, Maggie!" Frank laughed. "You could make breakfast, run the farm, *and* keep all of us in line with one arm tied behind your back."

I glanced over at Jake and noticed he was already looking at me, the corner of his mouth tipping up into a slight smile. Our eyes locked and my heart skipped a beat.

The boys sat down just as my dad and Gramps walked in. They each went over and kissed Mags on the cheek, then joined the rest of the men at the table. I busied myself, setting out the food for my grandmother; it was the least I could do after she saved my butt.

"I'm surprised to see you up at this hour, baby girl," my dad said, smiling at me.

"Mags asked me to help with breakfast today," I explained, keeping in line with the story. I gave him a quick good morning hug before returning to my task.

He looked over at my grandmother in surprise, and she confirmed with a slight nod of her head.

"Addy-Cake," said Gramps, helping himself to a giant portion of cheesy hash browns. "It's good to see you up and at 'em so early. I like seeing your beautiful face first thing in the morning. Makes me feel like I'm starting my day out right."

"You know, I may have her help me out here a little more this summer," Mags mentioned as she handed out servings of crispy bacon. "I'm not getting any younger, and these boys sure do know how to eat."

Frank started to whoop again. "What's gotten into you today? You could run circles around us, Maggie! Every person in Lakeside knows that."

"Well, either way, it'll be nice to have the extra help." She wiped her hands down the front of her apron and gave me a knowing smile. See, I told you she was the best.

Frank became distracted as he took a big bite of pancake. "I swear to you, Maggie, someday I'm gonna figure out your pancake secret," he gushed, shaking his head in delight. "I think you sprinkle a little bit of magic inside every bite!"

Mags let out a hearty laugh as we settled in at the table with our plates. "Oh, Frank! It's called *love*," she teased back lightly.

After we finished up with breakfast the guys started to make their way out the door, heading toward the fields. Jake was still at the table talking to Gramps when I walked out onto the beautiful wraparound porch. The warm morning air was already getting sticky and I lifted my hair off the back of my neck, wishing I'd put it up in a ponytail. I sat down on the wooden swing and slowly began to sway, waiting for Jake to make his appearance.

Moments later, the front door opened and Jake sauntered out, cowboy hat in hand. When he walked up to the swing and sat down next to me, my breath caught in my throat and I vaguely wondered if I would lose my breakfast.

"I wanted to thank you for showing me around yesterday," he said, giving me a lopsided grin.

I found myself staring at his utter perfection and had to force myself to answer. "You're welcome," I finally choked out. "How's your jaw?"

Gingerly, he lifted his hand to his chin and rubbed the spot where Brett had punched him. "Tender," he answered, smiling ruefully. "For a drunken asshole, that guy sure can hit."

I let out an amused laugh and some of the tension lifted from my body. I still couldn't believe he had gotten into a fight for me.

"So . . . what are your plans later?" he asked, pushing his hand through his dark waves.

I gulped. *God, would you get a grip, Addy?* I mentally scolded myself. "I'll be around." I shrugged, pretending to be cooler than I actually felt.

"Good. Maybe I'll see you then?" He dazzled me with a brilliant smile, put on his cowboy hat, and stood up from the swing. As he made his way down the front porch steps, he turned and looked back at me one last time before walking away. His blue-eyed gaze was intense and I felt completely seduced.

He wants to see me again!

I inhaled through my nose and swallowed hard. A slow smile took over my lips as I began to fantasize about our next meeting, and I couldn't help but giggle at all the possibilities.

The rest of the morning I busied myself in the kitchen, helping Mags clean up after breakfast. As always, I was impressed by her tenacity. Mags paid close attention to detail with everything she did, and that included making gigantic breakfasts from scratch to cleaning every nook and cranny afterward. She did not believe in taking shortcuts.

My cell phone beeped for the millionth time from my back pocket. *Ruby.* I rolled my eyes and sighed, staring at the lit screen. She'd been relentlessly texting questions about Jake all morning. I ignored her latest inquiry and went about my work but couldn't avoid her. Moments later I heard my phone ring. Reluctantly, I pulled it from the back pocket of my shorts. "Hello, Ruby," I said.

"Why didn't you answer my text?" she demanded in a high-pitched voice.

Oh no, I groaned, preparing myself. *Not another Ruby rant.*

"I've been waiting *forever* for you to respond, and you know I'm not a very patient person," she whined. "You can blame genetics—I get it from my mother."

I stifled a giggle as I thought of Ruby's mom. Mrs. Sinclair was as pretty as a picture, but she was notoriously chatty and very demanding. Forever hounding Ruby about what clothes to wear and how to act, she was not someone you wanted to get stuck alone with for a long period of time. If you did, you would no doubt be forced to listen to the story of how she was named Strawberry Queen three years in a row, finally losing out to my very own mother. And believe me, bad blood still ran rampant.

"Ruby, I have answered all of your texts, with the exception of the latest one. And that was only because I was in the middle of something," I lied patiently.

"Anyway," she carried on, not missing a beat, "do you want to go shopping with me? I need a swimsuit and I want to check out that cute new boutique downtown."

Downtown Lakeside was typical of any small town. Picturesque shops lined brick-covered Main Street, with perfectly placed flowering trees tucked in between. Lakeside Park, home of the famous Strawberry Festival, was proudly featured in the center with the inviting white sandy shores of Lake Lanier in the background. It was a beautiful and charming area, and we would oftentimes find ourselves hanging out there over the summer months.

Hmmm . . . Can I find time to go shopping with Ruby in between stalking Jake?

"When were you thinking of going?" I asked cautiously. As long as it was after lunch and before the end of the workday, we should be good.

"Maybe around two?" she suggested.

"I think I can make that happen," I agreed, slowly. "You're picking me up, right?"

"Do I have a choice?" she responded sarcastically. It was a well-known fact that there would be no driving for me any time soon. My parents had this overwhelming fear of me getting into an accident, and as I was their only child, they kept fairly tight reins. "Be ready by two," she warned firmly, and we hung up.

Unfortunately, lunch came and went with no sign of Jake. Apparently, he had to run an errand in town during his break, so I never even got to talk to him. I was still sulking when Ruby picked me up.

"What's your problem?" she asked as I hopped into her brand-new white convertible. My best friend could read me like a book.

"What makes you think something's wrong?" I asked, brushing away an imaginary piece of lint from my camisole.

"'Cause you look sadder than a fat woman in a G-string!" Ruby laughed hysterically. She had a thing for making really bad jokes, with no regard for the subject matter.

I tried hard not to smile, but failed miserably. "I am *not* sad," I insisted in my most convincing voice.

"Then what's the prob?"

I shrugged. "I was just hoping to talk to Jake on his lunch break, but didn't get to see him," I explained as offhandedly as I could.

"Oh my God, that boy is so fine! I can't believe you

get to spend the whole summer watching him with his shirt off."

"I *never* said he takes his shirt off," I answered haughtily. "Besides, you can't do that on a farm. It's an occupational hazard," I lied.

Ruby rolled her eyes and cackled with delight. "A girl can dream, can't she? Guess I could learn a few things from the Future Farmers of America."

I threw her a dirty look. A few years back, my parents had bullied me into joining the FFA at school. Ruby still loved to tease me about it whenever the opportunity presented itself, which seemed to be rather frequently.

"Come on." She playfully pushed my arm. "Lighten up! We're about to spend money!"

We arrived downtown in style, with the car top down and the radio turned up. Ruby pulled into a parking space and we hopped out, ready to begin our shopping adventure. And shopping with the privileged Ruby was *always* an adventure. Her parents had blessed her with a credit card all her own, and she wasn't afraid to use it. She simply adored the sound the card made as it swiped over and over again at the register.

"Where to first?" she asked with an excited grin. "And *do not* say 'ice cream.' I've had enough to last me all summer, and it isn't even July yet," Ruby complained, grabbing an imaginary roll of fat from her slender thigh. "Cheerleading practice cannot start soon enough. I'm going to turn into a hog before senior year even begins!"

"You're right, Ruby." Carefully, I scrutinized her perfect size two frame, admiring her pale blond hair and striking honey-colored eyes. She was the picture of pure perfection. Ruby was that kind of annoyingly flawless girl who unintentionally made normal girls, like me, feel homely in her presence. But with my sun-kissed brown hair and light gray eyes, I was pretty in my own right. Of course, back then that was hard for me to see through all of my teenage insecurities and overwhelming self-doubt.

"What?" Ruby shrieked. "Do I look like I've put on weight?" she demanded in a panic, examining herself in the window of the closest shop.

I couldn't contain my laughter and doubled over in agony. "I'm only kidding, Ruby! That's what you get for making the FFA comment," I responded, holding my aching stomach. She was ridiculously easy to rile up.

"You're such a jerk!" Ruby laughed and swung her designer purse at me. I remember that stupid bag cost a very pretty penny.

Who needed enemies when you had a best friend?

Chapter Four

The afternoon flew by, and before I knew it my cell phone read 5:45 p.m. "Oh my God!" I exclaimed. "Look at the time!"

"I didn't realize you had a curfew," Ruby teased.

I playfully nudged her shoulder with mine. "I don't. I was just hoping to get back before Jake left at six."

"We're never going to make it back by then, Addy," she reasoned. "Let's just enjoy ourselves."

I realized she was right and slumped my shoulders in defeat.

"I'm starving," Ruby announced, looking at her watch. "We could grab a bite to eat?"

I shrugged gloomily and let her steer me toward the Sandcastle Café, a popular diner overlooking the lake. I wasn't very hungry but I tried to be good company anyway, even though it was difficult. I really had my heart set on seeing Jake and had secretly hoped he would want to hang out again after work.

"Don't worry," Ruby soothed, reading my mind. "You'll see him again tomorrow, *and* every day for the rest of the summer," she reminded me, her hand settled reassuringly on my arm.

Of course I knew it was true, I just couldn't help the mounting disappointment I felt. "You're right." I nodded and tried to change the subject. "You know, I really do love your new swimsuit."

"I know, right? It's so cute!" she enthused, successfully distracted. "Do you think Tommy will like it? He invited me to the beach with him this weekend."

I threw her a wry smirk. "I think every guy on the beach is going to like it."

Ruby dissolved into a fit of giggles. "Well, I hope they don't like it *too* much. I would hate for Tommy to get jealous! On second thought," she added slyly, tapping her manicured nails against the tabletop, "maybe it would do him good—remind him of what a catch I am."

I snickered at the predictability of her comment. My best friend fell in love every other week, and this time she had set her sights on Tommy Mathews. He wasn't at all like the typical smooth-talking, football-playing studs she normally preferred. He was a really great guy, very quiet and down-to-earth, and not too shabby to look at either.

We talked about our plans for the upcoming weekend as we paid the bill and prepared to leave. The sun was already setting on the horizon as we made our way out of the small diner and down the darkened street toward Ruby's car. A smattering of tourists littered the downtown area, wandering through shops and taking pictures. I looked around appreciatively, relishing the lake breeze. I always did love summertime in Lakeside. We were so busy with our carefree chatter that I didn't even notice him until he was right on top of us.

Brett . . .

Fear gripped my chest as I was thrown back two

months . . . prom night. I stopped short before he could purposely bump into me, but it was too late. Brett's shoulder collided roughly against mine.

"Hey, watch where you're going there, little girl," he blurted out.

Ruby and I exchanged a nervous glance as we attempted to walk around Brett and his friends.

"Where ya goin'?" he called after us. "You're not leaving on our account, are you?" I heard him laugh callously.

We quickened our pace and didn't look back. I could just make out Ruby's white convertible in the distance and tried to stay focused on our destination, hoping Brett would lose interest.

I was not so lucky.

I felt a hand creep up behind me and pull at my long hair. "Leave us alone, Brett," I responded, trying to sound braver than I felt.

"I have a bone to pick with you, Monroe," he said, stepping in front of us.

"You're such an ass!" Ruby exclaimed, trying to push past him. "What's your problem, anyway, Brett? You're such a jerk these days."

"Wait a minute, Ruby, this doesn't concern you. Why don't you take off? I'll make sure Addy gets home safely," he offered with a wink. His friends hovered hesitantly in the background.

A shallow breath caught in my throat and my heart started to beat so fast I felt like it was going to burst. I shot Ruby a worried glance and saw that she was nervous, too.

"I'm not leaving Addy," Ruby responded venomously. She grabbed my elbow and tried to hurry me along, but Brett was having none of it.

"I don't think you're going anywhere," he threatened, stepping in front of us again.

My nose burned from the offensive smell of alcohol on his breath, and against my better judgment, I spoke up. "You smell like your parents' liquor cabinet," I sneered.

"What can I say? Nothing says 'summer vaca' like some underage drinking."

Suddenly, I felt myself being pushed against a wall, my body pinned tightly against Brett's. One arm held me in place while his other hand started to travel slowly up my midsection and underneath my thin shirt. A strangled noise escaped from my mouth, but I was determined to look him in the eye and not cower. "What do you want?" I asked, my voice betraying the brave act I was trying to retain.

"You know what I want, Addy," he hissed quietly, his hot breath inches away from my face. "It's what I've wanted ever since you left me stranded at prom."

"Don't do this," I pleaded, but my words were somehow lost between us. Trapped under his weight, I turned my head and squeezed my eyes shut as he lowered his hot lips to my neck, disgust rising in the back of my throat. Panic raced through my body as I realized what he meant. I was unable to move, just like on prom night when he'd had me pinned against the wall of the deserted coatroom. His hands violating me, ripping the strap of my beautiful dress. I had told him "no" then, too. But just like now, he refused to listen.

My muscles locked as a feeling of dread took over. I forgot where I was or that there was a crowd surrounding us. I felt alone, just like before. It was prom night all over again.

Please, no . . .

Just then, I felt a cool rush of air and was suddenly free

from Brett's firm grip. It took me a moment to comprehend what was happening. Had one of Brett's friends seen enough and decided to intervene?

With shaky legs, I stepped away as two bodies struggled violently along the sidewalk. Ruby was at my side immediately, securing a protective arm around my waist. I strained my eyes under the dimly lit lamppost to get a better look at my rescuer. It wasn't until Brett stilled under the weight of his assailant that I finally recognized the other male.

Jake.

Jake's flushed face came into view as he stepped into the light of the streetlamp. "Are you, okay?" he asked, his voice laced with concern. I looked to the side and noticed Brett lying still on the concrete, a thin stream of blood flowing from a cut on his lip where he'd been hit. In that moment, I realized Jake had saved me from Brett not once, but twice, and in as many days. Tears welled in my eyes, threatening to spill over onto my cheeks. I tried to answer but a cry caught in my throat and I broke down, my knees buckling underneath me.

Suddenly, I was enveloped in Jake's strong arms and a feeling of relief spread throughout my entire body. Oblivious to the commotion going on around us, I inhaled his masculine scent and gave into the safe feeling he provided. It wasn't until Ruby tentatively rubbed my upper arm that I came crashing back to reality.

"Addy? There's an officer here. He wants to speak with you." Her voice sounded just as shaky as my legs felt.

Reluctantly, I pulled away from Jake and looked up at him. With a gentle hand, he carefully brushed the tears from my face.

"It's okay," he reassured me with a soft smile. "You need to talk to him. I'll be right here."

Fear and embarrassment burned like an inferno in the

pit of my stomach, and my mouth struggled to form words. I felt myself begin to tremble as I attempted to move toward the police officer.

"Addy!" I heard Ruby shout, but it sounded muffled, almost like a dream. Without warning, I found myself sitting on the warm pavement of the sidewalk.

"Are you all right?" I heard an unfamiliar voice ask.

My head was spinning and I instinctively knew it was because I had been breathing much too quickly. I tried to take deeper breaths in an attempt to push away the panic I was feeling. I closed my eyes and concentrated on inhaling slowly and exhaling . . . Inhaling . . . Exhaling . . .

When my eyes fluttered open, I saw Jake, Ruby, and the officer kneeling down next to me. Ruby was holding my hand, a worried expression shadowing her pretty features. "Addy?" she asked with caution. "Are you all right?"

Slowly, I nodded and took a shaky breath. "I'm fine. I just felt dizzy," I explained, and struggled to stand. "I'm better now."

The officer and Jake each took an arm and helped me to my feet. Nervously, I looked over to where I had last seen Brett lying dazed on the ground. He was still there but sitting in an upright position, another officer crouching next to him. A small crowd had gathered, and I lowered my head in a lame effort to conceal my identity.

This can't be happening . . . My lower lip began to tremble.

"My name's Officer Kent. My partner and I were in the area when we saw the altercation. Can you tell me what happened?" the police officer asked kindly.

Goose bumps covered my arms as I slowly began to recount the evening's events. With my eyes cast down, I told the officer everything that had happened, and about the incident with Brett at the ice-cream shop the day before.

"Is this the first time this has happened?" the young cop asked, writing everything I said down in a notebook.

I glanced hesitantly at Jake and he nodded in encouragement. Swallowing hard, I whispered, "A couple of months ago, Brett and I went to prom together. He came on strongly that night, too." I explained how he'd forced himself on me at the dance and how I had left him, walking four miles home alone in the dark.

A small gasp escaped from Ruby's mouth and I looked up. Realization washed across her face as she put the missing pieces together from our prom night several weeks ago. She sensed something serious had happened when she discovered I'd vanished halfway through the evening, leaving Brett at prom alone. I'd ended up feeding her some bullshit story about not feeling well. I figured she wouldn't buy it, but surprisingly she never prodded for more information.

"Addy, I'm so sorry! Why didn't you tell me?" A mixture of hurt and concern in her voice.

"It wasn't one of my prouder moments," I admitted feebly, giving her a small smile.

Full of emotion, she reached over and hugged me tightly. "You should never feel embarrassed to tell me anything," she whispered. Fresh tears blurred my eyes as I weakened in my best friend's embrace.

"Would you like to press charges?" the cop asked, interrupting us.

I turned quickly toward him, horrified by his suggestion. "No! I am *not* pressing charges," I stated firmly, wiping at the tears that were now falling freely down my cheeks.

"Are you certain?" He looked skeptical. "You wouldn't

want this to happen again, to you or to anyone else for that matter, would you?"

I considered what he'd said, but couldn't convince myself to go through with it. Life would be hell living in the small town that we did, having to attend school every day with the person I had charged with assaulting me. Silently, I also worried about the repercussions that would surely await me if I did.

Absolutely not—my mind was made up. I shook my head.

"All right then." The cop sighed wearily. "Let's go talk to him."

I looked over at Ruby and Jake and felt my breath begin to quicken again. The last thing I wanted to do was confront Brett. Jake smiled at me with gentle eyes, and I felt his hand grab mine and give it a squeeze. Inhaling deeply, we walked over to where Brett and the second officer were talking. Brett was standing up now and I could tell that Jake had roughed him up pretty good. He gave me a blank stare as we approached them.

"This young lady is not willing to press charges at this time," Officer Kent began, looking directly at Brett. "But I want you to know that we're making an unofficial file, and this incident is going straight into it." I wasn't sure if they could do that or not, but I hoped it was enough to scare Brett. Maybe he would finally leave me alone.

Brett nodded in agreement, an expression of relief covering his face.

"If we hear that you've been involved in any more trouble, no matter how small, I promise the next time you will not be so lucky," the officer threatened, looking Brett square in the eye. "Unless you don't mind a domestic abuse charge going on your permanent record. Your parents will also be notified of this situation."

Brett's eyes widened in alarm. "Do you have to tell them? What if I just promised never to talk to her again?" he pleaded desperately.

Officer Kent shook his head, his eyebrows raised. "Oh, *I'm* not going to tell them. *You* are."

Brett looked over at me with an emotion I was unable to read lurking in his eyes. He caught Jake's gaze and their eyes locked, contempt covering both of their faces. Blind to the silent conversation taking place, the officers exchanged words with each other and then turned back toward us.

"I understand that your parents are out of town this week?" Officer Kent asked, looking directly at Brett.

"Yes, sir, they are," he answered, dragging his eyes away from Jake.

"In that case, you're going to have to come to the station with us and we'll give them a call from there. You can find a ride home afterward."

I looked around and for the first time noticed that Brett's friends were nowhere to be seen. Their presence had dissolved, along with the rest of the crowd. Brett was left all alone. I hoped he would have to walk home from the police department, just as I had walked home from the dance.

"You let us know, miss, if there is any more trouble," the second officer said to me. They turned and guided Brett toward the awaiting police car, leaving words like "Breathalyzer" and "underage drinking" in their wake.

I somberly watched as their vehicle pulled away, taking my assailant with it. Vaguely, I wondered how our circle of friends would react when they caught wind of what happened.

"I'd like to take Addison home, if you don't mind," I heard Jake say to Ruby.

My eyes widened as I looked back and forth at them.

"That is, if it's okay with you," he asked, turning toward me.

I closed my eyes and raised a shaky hand to my head. *What is he going to say to me? What am I going to say to him?* I sighed warily.

"Addy, are you all right?" Ruby asked anxiously. "Do you want *me* to take you home instead?"

I opened my eyes and gave her a tight smile. "No, it's okay, Ruby," I answered, shaking my head. "I'll be fine."

I need to get this conversation over with now instead of having to face him tomorrow, I reasoned.

She gave me another hug before walking to her car. "Call me when you get home," she added protectively. Ruby glared at Jake for a moment before pulling away.

Alone in the street, we stood there awkwardly and stared at one another, neither of us knowing what to say next.

Chapter Five

I cleared my throat, "I just want to thank you—again—for dealing with Brett." I addressed Jake with averted eyes.

"Addison," he began, and then hesitated.

I looked up and noticed he was struggling for words, his eyebrows creased with uncertainty. "How long has this been going on, your trouble with Brett, I mean?" Jake looked down at me in concern.

I shrugged, avoiding his gaze. I didn't want to admit that things had gotten increasingly tense since prom night. "He's just upset about what happened at the dance." I shrugged, trying to make light of the situation.

"And you think that excuses his behavior?" he asked in surprise.

"No! Of course not. But what am I supposed to do, Jake? Things are different when you live in a small town. There are politics involved. He would make my life a living hell if I gave him trouble."

"So you're just going to let him get away with harassing you? Spend the rest of your life looking over your shoulder?"

I swallowed hard, overcome by my own guilt. "That

won't be an issue. Next year I'll be in college, far away from this place. Once Lakeside's in my rearview mirror, everything'll be fine . . ." My voice trailed off.

Jake let out an ill-humored laugh and ran a tanned hand through his hair in exasperation. I watched him intently and wondered why he even cared. After all, we had only just met.

He looked back at me with intense eyes. "You think you'll be free from assholes like Brett once you're in college?" he asked. "Have you even told your parents?"

"God, no! Are you crazy?" *What is he thinking? I could never tell my parents.*

"Look, I want you to tell me if you have any more problems with him. Promise me you will, Addison," he added urgently. "I mean it."

I rolled my eyes and reluctantly agreed, completely embarrassed by the conversation. I felt like a child; defiant, stubborn, and completely unskilled at dealing with problems. After a minute of standing there, I broke the awkward silence. "Can you please take me home now?"

Suddenly, he shot me a funny look. I looked away, not ready for a lecture. "Do you have to leave right away?" The promise of something more laced in his voice.

My head turned back toward Jake so quickly I could practically feel the whiplash from his abrupt change in mood. "Why?" I asked suspiciously. "You want to lecture me some more?"

"I thought maybe we could hang out. I came downtown to grab a bite to eat before heading home. Besides," he added, regarding me through long, black eyelashes, "I was hoping to see you again."

I stared at him, open-mouthed. *Breathe, Addy,* I reminded myself, and quickly tried to regain composure. "I think I might have some time." *Real smooth, Monroe.*

"Are you hungry?" he asked, the hopeful look on his face reminded me of a child on Christmas morning, and I had a hard time believing he was actually talking to *me*.

I felt my face grow warm at the prospect of eating an actual meal with him, never mind I had just walked out of the café. "I could eat," I said cautiously. "So . . . is this a date, then?"

Mischief and utter mayhem filled his gaze and he laughed lightly. "Unofficially."

I could feel my eyebrows hitch together in confusion. *What does that even mean?*

Jake and I ran into the Big Cheese and ordered a pizza, then headed out to the lake to have an impromptu late-night picnic. We settled down on an empty wooden table overlooking the shore. Goose bumps covered my bare arms as I bit into my warm slice of pie. I wasn't sure if it was due to the soft breeze blowing off the lake or because of the company I was keeping.

"Hey, this pizza's not half-bad," I commented, at a loss for clever conversation.

"What? Don't tell me you've never had a supreme before?" he asked in surprise.

"Nope," I answered, shaking my head. "I'm what you would call a pizza minimalist. Ham and bacon, occasionally onion . . . but that's as adventurous as I get."

"So, what's gotten into you tonight?"

I laughed and tossed my hair over my shoulder, just as I had seen Ruby do when in the presence of an attractive guy. "I guess it's because I don't want to be difficult. I've already caused enough trouble this evening. If I start acting like a princess, you might never ask me out on another *unofficial* date again," I teased.

"Addison, what would you say if I asked you out on a real date?" he asked, suddenly serious.

I tried to swallow the bite of pizza I had in my mouth before I choked. "You mean a real, *official* date?"

"A real, *official* date." He nodded.

"Where you pick me up, pay for dinner and *everything*?"

"Wait a minute! I paid for this pizza," he said defensively.

"Unofficially," I shot back with a cocky smirk, and pretended to think carefully for a moment. "I think I would say yes. Does this mean you're asking?"

Jake's mouth tipped into a lazy grin. "Not yet," he responded, with just the right amount of charm.

I threw him a smile, hoping to appear nonchalant, as if the game of cat and mouse did not affect me in the slightest, but my insides were turning into a gelatinous mess. *Oh. My. God.*

"Do you want to go for a walk?" he asked casually, but I had a feeling he had more than a walk on his mind. Or at least I hoped he did.

Nodding in agreement, I caught my lower lip with my teeth—a nervous habit I've had since I was a child. We set the pizza down and removed our shoes before heading toward the shoreline. The gentle waves and full moon added to the moment, and Jake must have felt it, too. He reached for my hand and grasped it gently. I tried not to let it affect me, the feel of his skin against mine, but in that moment all I could do was focus on the pressure of our hands intertwined. Shyly, I looked over and found him watching me. My God, he was so perfect! I couldn't believe I was there with him, walking hand in hand along the lake.

We walked for a while, neither of us saying a word. Suddenly Jake stopped and turned to face me. Our eyes locked underneath the moonlight and my heart started skipping like a deranged madman in my chest. He stepped closer and gently brushed the back of his fingers against my cheek, causing me to bite my lip . . . again.

He gave a soft chuckle and slowly rubbed the pad of his thumb over my mouth, forcing me to drop my lip. "Is this okay?" he asked huskily, closing the gap between us. The intimate gesture caused my head to spin, and I vaguely wondered if I had pizza breath.

Numbly, I nodded as my heart began to race. He leaned in and gently lowered his mouth onto mine. His mouth was amazingly soft—for a rugged, hard-working cowboy—and I felt myself sigh. The way our lips teased each other, his stubble tickling my face—I had never experienced anything like that before in my life. I could have stood there for days kissing him, but I suddenly swayed backward, and the moment was over.

"Are you all right?" Jake asked, concern covering his features.

"Um . . . yes," I admitted, slightly embarrassed. "I think I forgot to breathe."

Jake laughed and put a well-toned arm around my shoulder, steering me back toward the lights of downtown. "Come on, Addison. Let's get you home."

No! Damn it . . . I sulked all the way to his pickup.

The next morning, I woke up to the sound of my cell beeping repeatedly, alerting me to several new text messages. *What the heck?* I wondered crankily, and reached for my phone.

Well??? What the hell happened last night?! the message screamed back at me.

"Ruby," I seethed under my breath. *Doesn't she know what time it is?*

Sleepily, my eyes wandered over to the clock at the

side of my bed. *Ten o'clock! Oh my God—I missed breakfast!* Jake would already be hard at work and I had missed my one opportunity to see him before he started. "Maybe that's for the best," I said out loud in my best big-girl voice. "I need to play it cool."

"My night was amazing; it was incredible; it went better than I ever expected!" I texted back, my finger positioned on the answer button, waiting for the phone to ring. Ruby did not disappoint.

Ring! Ring!

"Hello, Ruby," I said, smiling into the phone.

"Oh. My. *God!* What happened, Addy? Did you guys go out? Is he going to kick Brett's ass? Did you kiss him?" She bombarded me with an onslaught of questions.

"Nothing much. Yes. No, but I think he wants to. And yes, definitely, but it was the other way around."

"He *kissed* you? Holy shit! Was it amazing? Tell me *everything*!" she shrieked in a voice that reminded me of a mouse with its tail caught between the sharp teeth of a hungry feline.

Laughing at her excitement, I answered, "Ruby—it *was* amazing! *He* is amazing!" I blushed with pleasure as I thought of my night with Jake. Sighing with satisfaction, I admitted, "I think I'm in love."

"Oh, Addy, it's not love. It's way too soon for that—believe me, I know. Infatuation, maybe. Or lust."

It felt like all three, but reluctantly I had to agree with her. It couldn't possibly be love.

"Have you spoken with him today?"

I stretched in bed and shook my head, my hair tumbling around me in tangled waves. "No, I overslept. He's already working. Maybe it's for the best, you know." I shrugged. "I don't want to seem overeager."

"Overeager? By a phone call?" Ruby dramatically

exclaimed. "You need to mark your territory, Addy. Jake is *way* too cute to stay single for long in this small town. And you *know* hospitality runs rampant in the South . . ." Her voice trailed off triumphantly, proud of her wise observation.

I felt an uncomfortable prickle crawl up my skin as I contemplated Ruby's reasoning. It was true; Jake was unbelievably attractive, and Southern girls could be particularly . . . friendly. But he was not in Lakeside looking for love. He was here to work. Or at least that's what I kept telling myself. "I don't know, Ruby . . ."

"At least text him! Tell him to have a good day or something. Or tell him you had fun last night! You're a resourceful girl, Addy—think of something! But don't *not* talk to him—you'd be digging your own grave!" she emphasized.

Ruby was making some good points, but I was unsure. I didn't want Jake to believe I was some silly, immature high school girl. I wanted him to think I was a mature woman who knew how to handle herself—even if it *was* just an act on my part. I chewed on my lower lip, trying to decide what to do next.

"Stop chewing on your lip, Addy. I can feel you doing it from miles away," Ruby blurted out suddenly. "I know! Invite him to the Friday Night Bonfire at my house tonight!" she exclaimed, using the title we'd given her weekly summer ritual.

"Oh, shit, the bonfire! I totally forgot about that."

"What?! Don't think for a second you're getting out of it again, Addison Victoria Monroe," she scolded, using my full name, indicating she would have my head if I was a no-show. "You missed my last one. You *have* to be there tonight!"

"You know, Ruby Nichole Sinclair, you have them

every Friday night. I may not be able to make it to every single one," I patiently explained. Ruby lived on Lake Lanier and she loved showing off her family's excessive property. Although I had to admit, it was pretty impressive. Ruby's parents were both real estate moguls, and Ruby's spoiled ass always reaped the annoying benefits.

"You'd better be there," she warned again. "The pool is open and you haven't even come over *once* since school let out. Besides, you can check me out in my new suit."

I rolled my eyes, remembering Ruby's latest purchase when a horrifying thought came to mind. "If I *am* going to invite Jake, *I* need a new swimsuit!" In a panic, I jumped out of bed and began searching for clothes through a freshly laundered pile on my bedroom floor. I didn't have much time to shop if I was going to get back in time to invite Jake to Ruby's.

"I'll be there in thirty," Ruby offered without hesitation.

As aggravating as she could be sometimes, I could always count on my best friend to have my back. "You're a lifesaver! But we have to make it quick. It can't be like last night when I totally missed out on getting back here before Jake left."

"Yes, but it all worked out—didn't it? Getting sexually assaulted by Brett was awful, but then came Jake—the best thing that ever happened to you," she remarked sweetly.

I growled at the memory. "I wouldn't go that far, Ruby. But it did all seem to work out in the end," I admitted with a frustrated sigh. Even though the incident had passed, the thought of Brett still weighed heavily on my mind.

"And don't worry. I am an *expert* when it comes to speed shopping," she said, ripping me away from the unpleasant memory.

"You're an expert when it comes to any kind of

shopping," I snorted back. We hung up and I dressed quickly, then ran down stairs for a quick bite to eat, almost running right into my mother.

"Whoa—slow down there, Addy! You nearly knocked me over," Mom said with an exasperated gasp. "What's the rush, anyway?"

"Sorry, Mom," I answered, sticking my head into the fridge, searching for something cold to drink. "Where's the orange juice?"

"I have to go to the store today. I'll add it to the grocery list."

I pulled out the milk and grabbed a box of cereal from the pantry, pouring the contents into a bowl.

"So, why are you in such a hurry?" she asked again, as I stuffed a large spoonful of toasted oats into my mouth. "You may want to take it easy there, Addy; you're going to choke . . . and I still need to renew my CPR certification," she added as an afterthought, walking to the counter and jotting down a reminder on a piece of scrap paper. Mom worked part-time as a nurse at the local hospital, and there always seemed to be some kind of certification she needed to get renewed or class she had to attend.

I swallowed hard and tried to answer in between bites. "Ruby's on her way over and we're going shopping. Her bonfire is tonight and I need a new swimsuit."

Mom raised her eyebrows in response. "What about your bathing suit from last year?"

I scrunched my eyes in disgust. "Ugh! That was *last* year's suit. I need a *this* year's suit! Everyone has already seen the other one," I explained. *Doesn't she understand fashion?*

Mom threw her hands up in mock exasperation. "Sor-ry. I didn't realize it was taboo to wear last year's suit."

"Well, it is," I informed her, stuffing another bite into my mouth. Just then, I heard a car horn honk from the driveway. I jumped up and threw my bowl into the sink and began to search for my purse.

"It's in the hallway closet," Mom called after me.

How does she always do that? I grabbed my bag and ran over to kiss her on the cheek.

"Do you have money?" she asked, giving me an amused smile.

"Yes, my babysitting money," I answered, nodding.

Mom stood in front of me, regarding me with a funny look on her face. "Addy—are you going to go shopping looking like that?"

I threw her a frown and walked over to the hallway mirror in confusion. "My hair!" I laughed, giving my tangled mess a toss. "What? You don't like it?" I asked, looking back at her over my shoulder.

"I don't mind it, but if I know Ruby, she'll throw a fit!"

Giggling, I opened my purse and scrambled around for a comb. "Love you, Mom!" I said on my way out the door.

"Love you, too, Addy. Have fun." I heard her laughing as the door closed behind me.

Chapter Six

Ruby and I made it back from swimsuit shopping in record time, and I had to admit, I was very pleased with my purchase. I settled on a pale blue bikini with a halter top and bottoms that tied on each side. It fit like a glove and I decided I would change into it at Ruby's, just in case my mom wanted to see it. I had also found some amazing cowboy boots. They were made of red leather and were the sexiest things I had ever owned—besides the new bikini. They'd also cost me my entire savings.

I made it to Mags's in time for lunch and offered to tend to the chickens for her, hoping to run into Jake. And my devious plan worked.

"Hey there, stranger," I called out as I tossed the bird feed around me. The chickens clucked hungrily, but I only had eyes for Jake as he dazzled me with a lazy half smile. Slowly, he sauntered his way over to the coop.

"Hey, Addison," he said with a drawl. "I was just thinking about you."

Instantly I felt my face heat up, but I managed to smile sweetly. "What a coincidence. I was just thinking about you, too." I stepped toward the fence that enclosed the coop and leaned against it, batting my eyes in a way I hoped was seductive.

"Thinking about anything in particular?" he asked, his gaze heavy with delight.

"Oh, you know, nothing specific. Just general thoughts, really." I gave him a sly smile and lifted my hand, shielding my eyes from the bright afternoon sun.

He watched me in amusement and I could tell he wasn't buying my indifferent act. "Nothing specific, huh?" he asked.

I stifled a giggle at the expression on his face, but continued on with the game, shrugging my shoulders nonchalantly.

"That's too bad," he responded. "I was hoping you were thinking about last night and how enamored you must feel toward me today."

I bit my lip hard, trying to hide my smile. "Well, you *are* pretty charming," I admitted with a nod.

"I knew it! These cowboy boots have never let me down."

I laughed at his joke and took a deep breath as I prepared to ask him out. On a date. With me. "Actually," I began nervously, "I really *was* thinking about last night. I had a very nice time. . . You know, after the whole Brett incident," I added, rolling my eyes. "I was wondering if you'd like to hang out again?"

One corner of his mouth tipped up into a smirk, and I instinctively knew the answer would be "yes."

"I don't know," he slowly teased. "What did you have in mind?" Locks of dark hair fell across his forehead, and he removed his cowboy hat to brush them away. I couldn't tear my eyes away as he lifted the hat back to his head in a way I found incredibly sexy. The way his muscles moved underneath his shirt had me thinking thoughts I had no business thinking. Not standing in my grandparents' yard, anyway. It felt almost sacrilegious.

"Well, um, my friend Ruby is having a bonfire tonight at her place. She has one every Friday," I explained, trying to regain my composure. "Her pool is open, too. I missed last week's party, so as her best friend I'm sort of obligated to go to this one. I was wondering if you'd want to come with me?" I rambled on nervously.

"Will your friend Brett be there?"

My smile faded. "He's not my friend," I reminded him. "And the answer is no."

"And you'll be wearing a swimsuit?"

I felt a blush color my cheeks, and I fought to look him in the eye and not down at the ground. "Of course," I said. "How else would I go swimming?"

His eyebrows shot up in amusement as he watched the embarrassment spread across my face. "I can think of other ways." I swallowed hard and looked away, wondering if I was ready for a college man after all. What if going out with Jake turned into more than I could handle? What if he expected certain things from me? Admittedly, the idea had me terrified, and undeniably interested.

"Relax, Addison," Jake laughed. "I'm only teasing you. I'm not like Brett—I swear." He took his right index finger and crossed his heart, signifying a promise. "I'm sorry, I didn't mean to make you uncomfortable. What I said was out of line and it won't happen again."

Regarding him seriously, I considered what he had said. I sensed he was telling the truth and gave him a small smile. Grown-up boys with grown-up jokes, something I seriously was not used to.

"I would love to go with you, and I promise to behave. Unless you ask me not to," he added with an ironic smile.

"Sorry, I'm not trying to be creepy, but I had to put it out there just so you know."

Grinning back at him, I decided to let the comment slide. "Would you be able to pick me up? My parents don't allow me to drive yet."

"Sounds like a plan."

"Can you be ready by eight?" I asked, absentmindedly twirling my hair.

"Eight o'clock it is. And, Addison?" he added, looking into my eyes.

My heart began to flutter at his intense scrutiny and the butterflies in my stomach threatened to jump out of my mouth. "Yes?"

"I'm looking forward to seeing you again."

Jake turned to walk away and I bit my lip. Slowly, I wandered back toward the house, debating whether or not I should tell Mags about the date. She was always full of good advice and had never steered me wrong before.

What if she thinks he's too old for me? I worried. But hadn't it been *her* idea to introduce me to Jake in the first place? Curiosity won out and I decided to speak with her.

"Hey, sunshine." Mags grinned when I walked into the kitchen. "What's up? You look perplexed." She knew me so well.

"Grandma," I began, nervously tugging on the hem of my shorts.

"Uh-oh. I know it's serious when you address me formally," she said, her lips twitching, trying not to smile. She pulled out a kitchen chair for me to sit in and sat down in one herself.

I nodded and made myself comfortable at the large wooden table before speaking. I brushed at some non-existent crumbs and my eyes wandered around the room, looking everywhere but at her. "What do you really think of Jake?"

Mags inhaled deeply before answering. "Is this just about what I think of Jake, or what I think about *you* and Jake?" she asked knowingly.

Shyly, I confessed, my eyes meeting hers. "Me and Jake."

"I see." Slowly, she brought her hands up to the table and folded them in front of herself. "I think Jake is a lovely boy, and he's pretty easy on the eyes, too." She chuckled lightly and observed me over the rim of her glasses. "I've watched him around the farm. He has a strong work ethic—that says a lot about a person right there. Plus, he's a good boy from a good family. It's true, he *is* a little older, but older doesn't have to mean bad. Your grandfather is older than me, and we've always gotten along famously."

I nodded in agreement, although I was a bit confused over what she was trying to say. Her speech so far wasn't exactly satisfying my question. And I needed answers. Fast.

"Your father would have a fit, bless his heart, but oftentimes men have a distorted way of looking at things. Especially when those things involve their teenage daughters." She smiled ruefully. "Sometimes, in order to be with a really good man, you have to be courageous. You have to take risks. Every struggle is a step forward. Just remember in your heart what is good and moral, but never be afraid to stumble and fall. And be true to yourself, Addy. Your relationship with yourself is just as important as your relationship with others. Does this make any sense?" she asked, laying her hand affectionately on mine.

I nodded and gave her a grateful smile. What Mags had

said was starting to make more sense, but I also noticed she was still sidestepping what I really wanted to know. I wanted her to tell me what to do. I wanted her to lay out the plan I was supposed to follow, complete with notes in the margin and wise little tidbits she knew I'd find helpful along the way.

As if reading my mind, she shrugged her shoulders and continued, "I can't make decisions for you, but I can try to equip you with what you need to make the right decisions for yourself. You're a good girl, Addy," she said, her eyes lighting up with love. "You're bright, you're beautiful, and you're caring. You are going to make a wonderful wife and mother someday—not that you're thinking of those things right now. Just promise to remember your worth. Spread your wings and fly—within reason, of course—and settle down after you've experienced everything your heart desires. One day you'll want something more. And when that time comes, you need to choose wisely. Pick someone who loves you as much as your granddaddy loves you, someone who provides for you the way your father does, and someone who makes you laugh as if you're with your best friend. In the meantime, experience life to the fullest, while remaining true to yourself. What's meant to be will eventually be. Just make sure you enjoy life in the meantime."

Thick emotion made its way up my throat and I swallowed back a sob. Crying was not something I typically did, and I wasn't about to start now. I threw my arms around Mags's neck and gave her a squeeze. Finally, I understood what she was trying to tell me. Embrace new experiences, they're a natural part of life; don't let fear stop me from trying new things; and never compromise my beliefs or integrity—for anyone, no matter how gorgeous they might be.

"I love you, Mags," I said, as I tightly clutched her neck. "Thank you."

"Oh, Addy! You're welcome." She chuckled. "And I love you, too. So very much. Now, you're gonna have to loosen your grip unless your intention is to choke me."

My heart felt lighter as I trudged my way home that afternoon. Admittedly, the idea of Jake was a little scary. But he was a good guy with a good head on his shoulders—he'd already proven that. I decided to move forward with wherever this was going, yet not burden myself with expectations. I was going to enjoy my summer and everything it had to offer.

And that included the handsome cowboy.

Chapter Seven

I was ready by seven forty-five and sat in my bedroom watching the driveway, anxiously awaiting Jake's arrival. I had chosen to wear my favorite burgundy dress with the spaghetti straps. It flattered my slim figure without making me look tacky. Plus, the rich color brought out the gray in my eyes.

Yeah, like he's going to be looking at my eyes. I snickered. Pulling my long hair up into a loose bun, I headed downstairs ready for the night to begin. I decided to wear my swimsuit under my dress after all, and just hoped Mom wouldn't ask to see it.

My parents were in the family room, relaxing in front of the television when I walked in. "Ruby's bonfire tonight?" my dad asked, barely glancing up from the Friday-night lineup.

"Yeah. I missed her last one, so I have to show up tonight or she'll revoke her best friend status."

Dad chuckled and finally moved his eyes from the TV, noticing for the first time my choice of clothing for the evening. His eyebrows shot up in surprise. "You're kinda overdressed for a bonfire, wouldn't you say?"

I felt the familiar sting of blush rush over my cheeks, but before I could answer, my mom piped in with a question of her own. "What's up with those boots? They're a little too . . . red . . . doncha think?"

I twisted my leg to the side and looked down, admiring the soft leather. "What, you don't like them?"

Mom stared at me warily and chose not to answer. "Is Ruby coming to pick you up?"

Just then, I heard a horn honk, and I felt my stomach twist into a million intricate knots. A moment later there was a knock at the door, and my heart flip-flopped as I suddenly realized I couldn't put off explaining who was chaperoning me any longer. "Uh—no, Ruby's not picking me up tonight. I invited Jake."

My parents noticeably stilled and regarded me with identical shocked expressions. "Jake, as in *college boy* Jake?" Mom asked with trepidation while Dad sat like a statue on the sofa, eerily quiet. In the meantime, the doorbell rang out and I began to fidget nervously.

"I thought it would be nice to introduce him to some people," I explained quickly. "After all, he *is* new in town." I gave them my best "duh" expression, and just before I left the room to answer the front door I noticed Mom give Dad "the look," and my heart sank.

What if they say no? I worried. *Would they do that to me?*

Upon opening the door, I immediately decided that whatever amount of discomfort I had to go through with my parents concerning the evening ahead, it would all be worth it. Standing before me was what could only be described as a Texan god. Strong, tanned, and wearing the sexiest smile in all of Georgia—and quite possibly the Northern Hemisphere—was Jake.

His eyes traveled leisurely up my body and I felt my

breath catch in my throat. Annoyed by the obvious effect he had on me, I sighed inwardly and forced myself to greet him. "Hey, Jake." I smiled sweetly before biting my lip. "Thank you for picking me up."

Wow.

"You're welcome, Addison. You look amazing," Jake responded, looking sincere. "Those boots are incredible. And your dress . . . It really brings out the color of your eyes." The impact of his words caught me off guard and I barely heard my parents come into the room.

Breathe.

"Jake," my father stated, using his I-am-the-boss-and-you-should-be-scared voice. He walked over and grasped Jake's hand in a firm shake.

"Mr. Monroe. Thank you for allowing me to accompany Addison this evening. It was so nice of her to offer to introduce me to her friends. I really haven't had the opportunity to meet anyone yet." My jaw dropped in awe. Somehow, he had known the perfect thing to say without me having to coach him.

My dad visibly relaxed and a friendly smile covered his face. "How many times do I have to tell you, Jake? Please, call me Carl. Have you met my wife, Renee?"

Mom smiled politely and took the hand Jake offered her. "Not officially," Jake replied with a charming grin. "It's nice to meet you, ma'am. I can see now where Addison gets her pretty gray eyes," he drawled, his Texas accent just a touch more noticeable than normal.

Mom absolutely beamed. "Well, thank you, Jake. It's nice to meet you, too."

Is she seriously blushing right now?

"Well, we'd better get going. Ruby's going to have a conniption if I'm not there soon," I said quickly, grabbing Jake by the elbow and guiding him toward the door.

"You'll be home at the usual time, right?" my mama called after us.

"Yes, one o'clock," I answered with a mischievous wink.

She rewarded me with her all-knowing mom expression. "I think you mean twelve thirty."

"Oh yeah. Twelve thirty." I at least had to try, right?

"Don't worry, Mrs. Monroe. I promise to have Addison back in one piece *and* on time." Jake smiled at my parents and waved as he opened the truck door for me. I slid into the passenger seat and noticed that Mom and Dad looked suitably appeased, if not downright impressed, as they returned his wave.

Jake came around and hopped into the driver's seat. He turned the key and slid the truck smoothly into gear— as smooth as an old truck could slide, anyway. Giving me a sideways smirk, he asked, "Are you ready?"

Smiling back, I couldn't help but acknowledge his velvety interaction with my parents. "You think you're pretty charming, don't you?"

"What do you mean?" he asked coyly as he pulled out onto the road.

"You know exactly what I mean. You practically had them eating out of the palm of your hand!"

"Maybe I'm just good with parents?"

"Or maybe you're just really cheesy?"

"Cheesy? I'm offended you think so little of me, Addison," he teased. He'd left his cowboy hat at home and his dark hair fell casually over his forehead in the most appealing way. The urge to reach out and brush it away from his eyes was intense, but I forced myself to stop thinking crazy. "You really do look great, by the way," he said again, giving me a long look. "Those boots are . . . *really* something else."

A jolt of electricity shot through me and I smiled shyly

at his compliment. The pounding in my chest was at an all-time high and I vaguely wondered if Jake knew CPR. My heart could only take so much . . .

A short while later, we pulled into Ruby's winding driveway, and Jake surveyed the property with appreciation. "Wow, this is nice," he commented as he took in the fantastic view.

"Pretty impressive, huh? It's great having a best friend whose parents are loaded."

"I bet," he agreed. "What do they do for a living?" he asked, turning his eyes toward me.

"They both sell real estate."

"They're making this kind of money in Lakeside?" he questioned, completely bewildered.

"Not just here. They own their own company in Atlanta."

He nodded his understanding and continued to take in the enormous plot of land overlooking the lake. Several familiar cars were already parked when he pulled his truck into an empty spot. Shutting off the engine, he turned to me with a grin and said, "Wait right there." He hopped out of the old Ford and came around to my side, opening the door for me. I gave him a big smile as my stomach began a series of somersaults.

As we made our way up the beige and gray stone walkway, I admired the creeping ivy climbing up the front of the stately older house. Ruby had been my best friend for years, yet I always felt like I was visiting a fancy beachside resort every time I came to her home. It was that beautiful. We walked onto the porch and I rang the doorbell, patiently waiting for someone to answer. Moments later, the knotty pine door opened, revealing a beaming Ruby, dressed in her new bikini and a long, flowing sarong.

"You made it!" she screeched, enveloping me in a cloud of her mother's Chanel No. 5. "God, I love those boots! They're even more fantastic than I remember!"

Laughing, I untangled myself from her arms. "I said I would be here." We stood smiling at each other, relishing the close camaraderie we felt. "Ruby," I began, taking a deep breath. "You remember Jake?" I knew very well that she did. No teenage girl in her right mind would be able to forget his dreamlike perfection.

"Yes, Jake. It's nice to see you again." She smiled graciously, always the perfect hostess. "Welcome to my home."

"Hey, Ruby. Thanks for having me," Jake responded in his polite Southern drawl. "This is some place you have here."

Ruby stood transfixed for a moment longer than she should have and I thought I noticed a slight blush color her cheeks. I shook my head in amazement. It was really unlike Ruby to be rattled by a guy. Before I could make a confirmation, she straightened her shoulders and regained her composure. "Oh, thank you. Come this way."

Ruby led us through the spacious house toward French doors that opened onto a large cedar deck. An elaborate Polynesian cabana and six-man hot tub was nestled along the side, and an outdoor bar was stationed across from it. Off the deck sat an imposing in-ground pool, showcasing a rock cave with a fountain and water slide. I heard Jake let a quiet whistle under his breath and couldn't help but smile. It wasn't often I got to witness a first reaction to Ruby's house. It seemed everyone in our small town had been to the Sinclair estate at one point or another growing up.

"I hope you're hungry." Ruby smiled and gestured toward a long table that was set out in a buffet.

"I'm starving," I answered, wasting no time diving into the generous spread. We heard a doorbell ring in the distance and Ruby excused herself to greet another guest. "Are you hungry?" I asked Jake as I began to pile a mound of sugared strawberries onto my thick plastic plate.

"Always. Thank you," he said when I handed him a plate of his own. "I just cannot get over this place. I didn't think *real* people actually lived this way. It's like something you'd see on a reality show."

I shook my head in understanding. "I'd say it's not fair, but the Sinclairs work hard for what they have. Ruby spends a lot of time alone because her parents are so busy all the time. I would love to live in a house like this with all of its amenities, but I wouldn't trade it for having my family around." I thought I saw a look of approval flash in Jake's eyes, but what I said was true. No amount of money would be worth having to spend most of my time alone. Sometimes I felt as if Ruby was closer with my parents then her own, and the very idea stung. It was one thing to make a living to provide for your family, but completely another to spend all your time doing it.

"I agree with you," Jake observed. "But once you have all of these luxuries, it would be hard to give them up."

We filled our plates and made our way toward a large patio table with a beautiful citronella candle in the center. I looked around at the festivities in place and couldn't help but wonder how the night would end. Would Jake try to kiss me again? God, I hoped so.

"Maybe we shouldn't eat so much," Jake suggested as we sat down. "That pool looks amazing and I can't wait to dive in. I don't want to have to worry about saving your life because you stuffed your face full of food and ended up with a cramp."

"Hey!" I laughed and swatted at him. "What about you? Maybe you'll end up the damsel in distress and *I* your knight in shining armor." I knew that was a crock. The thought of saving a floundering Jake practically had me snorting unattractively.

Jake shook his head as he took a bite of pasta salad. "Not a chance. I'm on the university swim team and I work as a lifeguard at the pool during the school year. Or at least I used to." His eyes clouded over momentarily. "I'm sort of taking a break right now." He turned and gave me a smile.

"So, Mr. Lifeguard, have you ever saved any lives?" I playfully teased.

Suddenly, the smile on Jake's face faded and I instantly regretted asking the question. His whole demeanor changed, and I knew something was very wrong. "You never remember the lives you save, only the one you didn't," he confided quietly.

I shifted uncomfortably in my seat as a prickly sensation came over me. "Someone drowned while you were working?" I whispered, shocked by his revelation. Jake looked away and was silent for a moment, and I wondered if he was going to answer me. Finally, he nodded, lowering his thick lashes.

"It happened this past spring at the UH pool," he began softly. He avoided making eye contact and instead stared in the direction toward the lake. "It was free swim and people were playing games and splashing around— you know, just having a good time. Exams were finally over and everyone wanted to let off some steam. I didn't see her at first because of all of the commotion, and it wasn't until her friends started calling out for help that I realized there was even a problem." He paused and I could tell it was hard for him to talk about. His usually bright eyes were full of regret and I wanted more than anything to reach over and hug him, to chase the bad memories away.

"When I made it over to her, I could see she was having a seizure, and her friends were struggling to keep her head above water, but it was too much for them. I managed to drag her to the side of the pool where the other guards helped pull her out. She wasn't breathing so we started CPR, but she never regained consciousness— even after the paramedics arrived."

Jake continued to avoid my gaze and finally I reached out and touched his hand. At last, he turned toward me and released a sad smile. "I'll never forget the look she gave me when I first reached her. I felt like we made eye contact, but I don't know if she actually saw me or not. It was just before she stopped breathing. Her eyes still haunt me. They were so vacant . . ." His voice trailed off, his struggle with what happened apparent. "It's actually how I ended up here in Lakeside. I needed to get away for a while. It's been a difficult few months."

I stared at Jake, not knowing how to comfort him. "I'm so sorry," was all I could manage.

He glanced back at me and then gave a wistful sigh. "That's life, right?" he asked with a shrug. "Everyone dies eventually."

I knew he was deeply burdened by what happened, but was trying to make light of it. I smiled back. "Jake—you did the best you could. You know that, right?"

And just like that, the cloud passed and a smile took over his handsome features. "So, do *you* like to swim?" he asked, changing the subject.

I gave a nervous laugh and wished he hadn't asked that question. "I'm, um, not the strongest swimmer," I confessed, not willing to admit what a huge chicken I actually was. I was able to swim but had never even jumped into a pool and had no intention of ever doing so.

"*Addison*," Jake teased, an amused smile playing on his lips. "Are you afraid of the water?"

Hesitating for just a moment, I chose my words carefully. "I'm *not* afraid of the water. I guess you could just say that I'm *extra cautious*." I looked down at my plate and moved some strawberries around with my fork, hoping we would move on to a more comfortable topic. Instead, he laughed quietly under his breath.

"Yep, you're afraid."

I was just about to respond when a group of friends came over and I began introductions. I noticed several appreciative glances from the girls as the guys regarded Jake with skepticism. Ruby made her way over eventually, with her date, Tommy, on her arm.

"Jake, I would like to introduce you to Tommy," she said and stepped aside so they could shake hands. "Maybe we can double date sometime?" she suggested with a smile.

I narrowed my eyes and tossed Ruby a discreet snarl.

"I'm sure Jake gets lonely around here not knowing anyone," she offered sweetly, the poster child for innocence.

"That's very kind of you, Ruby. It sounds like a great idea, that is, if Addison doesn't mind . . ." He gave her a smile and I noticed the small dimple in his cheek appear, causing Ruby to practically swoon.

"Oh, *Addison* doesn't mind," she said, enunciating my formal name. "We're best friends. We do *everything* together! Now, who's ready to swim?" she asked, turning toward the crowd.

I laughed at her audacity and shook my head. I could never stay mad at her for long. Ruby and Tommy meandered off, searching for participants in a pending game of water basketball, and I gave Jake an embarrassed smile. "Sorry. She can be a little overwhelming at times."

"It's fine." He laughed. "She's sweet. Are you ready to swim?"

It's now or never . . . I nodded and hesitated slightly before kicking off my boots and pulling the dress I wore over my head. I had never felt so self-conscious about my body before! I took a deep breath and glanced over at Jake, who threw me an approving smile. The butterflies instantly returned to my stomach, making it difficult to breathe. Slowly, he began to remove his black T-shirt, revealing an impressive six-pack underneath. Seriously—none of the guys we knew had washboard stomachs like that. When Jake removed the rest of his clothing my heart about stopped. I had only ever seen a body like that on MTV! His swim trunks hung dangerously low on his hips, my God were they low, revealing those manly pelvic muscles I had never actually seen before in real life. My heart thundered in my chest as I tried not to drool, and I distracted myself by hanging the dress I'd been wearing on the back of the patio chair.

I noticed Ruby gawking ridiculously from across the large yard and silently promised to kill her later. She caught my eye and mouthed, "*Holy hell!*"

I gave her a look. *Real discreet, Ruby*, I thought, when suddenly I realized she wasn't the only one staring. Several of my female friends gaped open-mouthed at the sight of half-naked Jake, and before I could help it, an intense bout of self-doubt threatened to consume me. Without warning, Ruby's prediction about Southern hospitality filtered through my thoughts. I clung to the fact that Jake was there with me and no one else. Not with Ruby, or any other beautiful girl, for that matter.

He likes you, I reasoned, but my stubborn teenage angst persevered. *If you're going to get through this night without running for the hills, you'd better get a grip!* I turned toward Jake and found him watching me, his sapphire eyes penetrating mine. An exhilarating tingle crawled across my skin and I felt myself tremble slightly. The look on his face said it all.

Jake wanted *me* . . .

Chapter Eight

"Are you ready?" Jake asked as he took my hand, leading me down the steps and into the pool. I gasped when the cool water hit my midsection and hoped Jake wouldn't try to pull me into the deep end.

He sank into the water, executing a perfect dive from inside the pool. I watched in grateful awe as firm muscles moved smoothly underneath flawless skin. I could not get over how beautiful he was, and he was with *me!* The very idea was laughable.

"Do you plan on getting wet?" Jake teased when he brought his head up from underwater, his dark hair smoothed back, away from his face. His gaze flickered over me and the droplets of water that clung to his hair glistened in the sunlight.

"I *am* wet," I responded defensively, acutely aware of everyone watching us, then I blushed at the innuendo. Good Lord, what had I gotten myself into? I had no idea how to entertain a college man. None whatsoever! What made me think I'd be able to handle this?

He gave a little laugh and reached for my hands.

"What are you doing?" I asked, trying to keep the panic from my voice.

"Bringing you in deeper."

"Deeper? I don't think I want to go in any deeper." *I knew this was going to happen.* I silently cursed myself for being afraid.

"Come on, Addison. Don't you trust me?" He grinned, allowing his dimple to peek out again.

Reluctantly, I nodded and sighed. Jake laughed quietly and walked up to me, so close I could feel the heat radiating from his body. "I have an idea," he said huskily, and gently grabbed my hands again.

"Wait . . . Now what are you doing?"

"Relax. Hold on to my shoulders," he instructed and placed my hands around his neck. Then very slowly, he let his hands slide down my wet arms. I hoped he wouldn't notice the goose bumps that covered my skin in the wake of his touch. He gave me a smoldering look, then turned away from me, sinking deeper into the water.

I let out a little yelp as the cool water covered my bare shoulders, but couldn't complain about being in such close proximity to Jake. It felt like an electric current was traveling between our bodies, and I was certain my face was on fire. As much as I enjoyed staring at his perfect features, in that moment I was so thankful he was not facing me. Jake slowly made his way out toward the deep end of the pool, ignoring my quiet protests along the way.

"It'll be better out there, I promise," he responded softly, glancing back at me.

I held on to Jake tightly and let him take me to the far end, away from the traffic of the party. Alone in the corner, he turned around and placed his hands on my waist. We moved in the deep water, staring at one another silently.

"See," he said finally. "This isn't so bad."

A nervous giggle escaped from my lips as I struggled to relax.

"I love the sound of your laugh," he said suddenly, his gaze locking with mine.

Abruptly I stopped giggling and my stomach began its familiar roller coaster of flip-flops. Jake inched in a little closer and I backed up against the side of the pool. It felt safer along the edge, knowing there was a small ledge I could rest my feet on if I needed to. Jake looked at me intensely, his eyes heavy as they bore into mine.

"Your eyes are a very unique color, Addison, more gray than blue. They're really beautiful," he said, then softly added, "*You're* beautiful." Gently, he raised his hand to my face and brushed some hair behind my ear. His touch was gentle, gentler than I'd expected, and I felt it resonate through every inch of my body. I was certain my heart would explode in my chest, but forced myself to be brave.

Make your move! It's now or never.

My breath quickened as I boldly wrapped my legs around his waist. Jake looked at me in pleasant surprise, and a lazy smile played at the corner of his mouth.

"You have no idea what you do to me," he said softly. "Do you?"

I wasn't sure how to respond. He couldn't be serious. I wondered desperately if this was the line he used with all the girls he dated, or if there was a possibility he meant what he said. But how could someone like me possibly have an effect on someone like Jake? There were years and most likely a huge amount of experience, or inexperience in my case, between us. There really was no way for me to know for certain, so all I could do was trust my instincts. I stared at his mouth as my body filled with a strange new sensation. I had never before experienced such a feeling of . . . *need*. My gaze met his and passion swamped me.

Slowly, he leaned in closer and brushed his lips against mine. He pulled back momentarily, then our mouths met again and I released a small moan as the kiss deepened. My fingers tangled eagerly in the back of Jake's dark hair and I could feel his body pressing into mine, pinning me against the wall with his weight. Suddenly, he looked at me with a question in his eyes and I worried the kiss would end, but instead he whispered, "Addison." Our lips met once again, and this time his warm tongue gently probed its way inside.

My insides turned to mush as I lost myself in the most amazing kiss I had ever experienced . . . up until that point, anyway. Jake moved both of his hands up to the sides of my face, and it felt sweet and erotic all rolled up into one electrifying gesture. I didn't know what to do with my hands, so I laid them on his tanned chest. As much as I wanted to explore Jake's body, I forbid myself from doing so, not wanting to send out mixed signals. Even though every inch of me protested, I didn't want him to think he was going to do anything more than kiss me.

His hands found my hips and he pulled me closer to him, revealing his excitement. I gasped inwardly and quickly moved away. Jake's confused eyes peered into mine. "Are you all right?" he asked softly.

"Yes, I'm um—I'm okay. It's just that . . . we're moving so quick."

Jake looked away and I worried I had ruined the moment. Not that I would have given into anything I wasn't ready for, but the kiss had been so magical I hated to see it end.

"Have you ever been with a guy before?" he asked, looking at me with curiosity.

I swallowed hard. No one had ever come right out and asked me that. Slowly, I shook my head and briefly dropped my eyes to the water.

"Shit," he whispered underneath his breath. His gaze softened. "I'm sorry, Addison. I don't want you to feel pressured. It's just—you do things to me . . ." His voice trailed off into a flustered chuckle and I prayed he would finish his sentence. But he didn't, he left me hanging.

"I'm sorry. I was enjoying the kiss too much. I just don't want you to think I'm *that* kind of girl—" I broke off, embarrassed.

Shaking his head, he responded firmly, "Addison, you have nothing to apologize for. This is my fault. I need to learn to control myself better around you."

Control himself? Around me? I repeated in my head, incredulously. I just could not get over the fact that drop-dead-gorgeous Jake would even be attracted to innocent, eighteen-year-old me. I stared at him dumbfounded as he released my hips and planted a small kiss on the tip of my nose.

A mischievous smile suddenly highlighted his face. "Are you up for some basketball? I saw a hoop at the shallow end of the pool," he suggested, indicating the water hoop set up in the corner. A game appeared to be just starting.

"Sure," I answered with a small smile. Jake brought my arms up around his neck and turned away from me, leading us toward the game. I couldn't help but smile behind his back. Even though I was nervous in the water I knew how to swim, but wasn't about to let on.

I was enjoying the ride way too much.

The pool party eventually progressed to the large bonfire already started near the lake's edge. Ruby continued to give me googly eyes throughout the entire evening; it was obvious she wanted me to pursue Jake. And Jake, as it turned out, was quite charming. He had managed to enthrall the rest of the partygoers with his easygoing and confident sense of humor. He'd gotten along with all of my friends, both male and female, and had found a couple admirers along the way.

"Hey, man, I heard about what happened the other day between you and Brett," my friend Eric commented to Jake, slapping him on the back with proud-male sportsmanship. "I hear you kicked his ass!" He laughed loudly. "That bastard deserved it, too. I would have done it myself a long time ago, but I've never actually gotten into it with him. I just try to keep my distance."

Jake shrugged off the compliment. "He had it coming. If I hadn't done it, someone else would have. Probably Addison, here," he suggested, giving me a sideways wink. "I hear she's got a mean right hook." Everyone laughed as I slugged his shoulder. It was just like him to take the attention off himself.

"Brett's parents are on vacation this week, and he's been partying at his house every single night. Have you seen him lately?" Eric asked, looking around at the crowd. "He's a wreck."

Suddenly, Matt, another friend, started laughing. "His mom and dad aren't on vacation—he just said they were! Brett's mom is visiting her parents back in Ohio, and his dad is in Mexico with his new girlfriend." He cackled again. "Didn't you hear? They're getting divorced."

Everyone gathered around the fire began laughing, but I didn't think it was very funny, and judging from the look on Jake's face, neither did he. Making fun of someone else's misfortune wasn't my idea of a good time. Picking up my boots, I started heading back toward the house, leaving everyone to their mean jokes.

Suddenly, I heard a rustling noise approaching from behind. I turned to find Jake following, a frown covering his face.

"Hey, Addison," he called after me. "Are you all right?"

Why did I feel like he was always asking me that?

"I'm fine." I released a heavy sigh. "Sorry. I just don't want to talk about Brett. I'd like to forget he ever existed."

Jake looked down at the ground and fell in step beside me. "I understand." He nodded. Shadows from the moon danced across his face, obscuring his features. "It's interesting about his parents, though, don't you think? Maybe it explains some of his inappropriate behavior. Divorce can really screw a kid up."

I shrugged my shoulders, trying to dismiss the whole topic.

He gave me a funny look. "You know, when my parents divorced, I was messed up for a long time. Not that I'm saying it excuses his behavior," he added, looking at me with an intense expression. "Nothing excuses the way he treated you."

I supposed he did have a point. If there was trouble at home, that could be why Brett was acting out. Still, I didn't want to talk about him. "I'm sorry, I didn't realize your parents weren't together."

"It happens. I guess nothing in life is a guarantee," he said, shrugging one shoulder. "Hey—what do you say we get out of here?" Jake asked suddenly, changing the subject.

"I can't," I responded with a wicked grin, even though

I was already sold on the idea. "What about Ruby? She'd kill me."

"Shoot her a text. Tell her you'll see her tomorrow. Besides, I don't think she'll even realize we've left. Did you see the way she was snuggling up to that Tommy guy?" he asked with an amused expression. "I have a feeling she's going to be too busy to think about us."

I started to laugh. I had noticed that, too. "So, what do you want to do?"

Jake shrugged, but there was a distant gleam of delight in his eyes. "I don't know, but I'm sure we can think of something."

The promise of adventure hung heavy in the air, and I felt a shiver of excitement race through me. I was up for *almost* anything he had in mind. Without hesitating, I gave him a nod.

"Let's get outta here, then." He smiled down at me and reached for my hand. His grasp was warm and comforting. We walked quickly toward his truck so we could escape before anyone noticed. I stole a sideways peek at Jake and marveled again at his handsome features. He was truly the most gorgeous guy I had ever seen in my life.

I'd been a little nervous about introducing him to my friends, but realized it had been a good idea after all. It'd been a long time since we had a newcomer to our group, and the prospect of meeting someone different—and older—had left my friends duly impressed. Jake opened the truck door for me and I hopped inside, anxious to see what kind of plans he had in mind for the rest of the evening. I didn't have to be home until 12:30, and the night was still young. He slid into the driver's seat and regarded me with a slow smile.

"Let's go," he said, turning the key and putting the truck

into gear. We sprung forward down the drive and I looked out the window into the side mirror at my reflection. I was happy to see that the breeze from the lake had given my long hair an attractive, tousled appearance. I glanced back at Jake and found him staring at me.

"You look very pretty," he said, then reached for my fingers and brought the back of my hand to his lips. He planted a small kiss and gave my hand a gentle squeeze. Suddenly, I wondered if *he* had any idea of the effect he had on *me*.

I hated to admit it, but I was falling fast.

Chapter Nine

A short while later Jake and I pulled up to a modest yet appealing Cape Cod–style home.

"Where are we?" I asked.

"My aunt and uncle's house." Jake pulled into a parking space and killed the engine. "But don't worry," he reassured when he saw the look of alarm on my face. "They go to bed early. There's no way they're still awake."

I wasn't sure if that made me feel better or worse.

I slipped on my boots and Jake walked around and opened my door. We left the truck and walked up the steps to a small front porch. Jake pulled out a key and opened the door, leading me into a beautifully decorated—and completely empty—house. My pulse kicked up a notch wondering how he planned to occupy our time.

"Do you want to make some ice cream?" he suggested, looking at me with childlike excitement.

Ice cream? I breathed a sigh of relief. "You mean, do I want to *eat* some ice cream?"

"Well, yes, eventually we'll eat it. But first, we have to *make* it."

I smiled at his enthusiasm, albeit a bit reluctant. "Wouldn't it just be easier to go *buy* some ice cream?"

"I suppose. But where's the fun in that?"

I followed him into the kitchen and he turned on a soft light, illuminating the room just enough, but not too much. The low light added to the chemistry I felt growing between us. Abruptly, I put my hand to my mouth to cover a giggle.

"What's so funny?" he asked, his head buried in the pantry. Jake turned toward me, balancing bags of sugar and salt in his arm. He carried a small bottle of vanilla and a can of condensed milk in the other.

"This just isn't how I expected the night to go. I mean, coming back to your house and making ice cream."

"Hey—don't knock it till you try it, Addison. I promise you, this will be the best ice cream you've ever had," he countered, flashing me the smile that made my insides dance.

He set down the ingredients and reached back into the pantry, pulling out an ancient ice-cream maker.

I started to laugh. "Are you sure that thing is going to work? It looks ready to retire."

"I will have you know that while very experienced in the art of ice-cream making, she still has lots of years left in her."

"*She?*"

"Yes, she." He smiled, the tiny dimple appearing in his cheek. Jake added the ingredients into a bowl and took out a mixer. Turning it on, he began to smooth together the contents.

"So, did you have fun tonight?" he asked, his eyes never leaving his project.

I shrugged and pulled up a stool. Sitting down on it,

I answered, "I did, for the most part, anyway. How about you?"

"Sure. Your friends are very nice." Sliding the mixer over, he said, "Okay, now it's your turn."

I took a spoon and moved it over the sides of the bowl, carefully making sure all of the ingredients were mixed together evenly.

"You know," I said thoughtfully, "I could really use some ice cream right about now."

"I thought you might. For some unknown reason, frozen globs of sugar tend to have magical healing properties."

I watched as he poured the mixture into the ice cream maker, adding a pinch of salt and splash of milk. Retrieving a bag of ice from the freezer, he added that as well. He pulled up another stool and began rotating the crank on the old machine. I was surprised to see how easily it turned in his grasp.

"So. Did you like him?"

"Did I like who?" I asked, already knowing the answer.

"Brett," he responded. "I mean, you agreed to go to prom with him. Does that mean you liked him?"

I thought for a moment before answering. "I liked him as a friend. A few different guys had invited me, but I said yes to Brett because—because there was something about him," I admitted. "He had that bad-boy edge that was sort of intriguing. It's not that I *liked* him liked him, but honestly, he'd been somewhat appealing. More so than the other guys who invited me, anyway. I wasn't interested in a relationship with him, if that's what you're asking. I mean, I guess I could tell he was attracted to me, but I just thought maybe we would have a good time together."

Jake gave me a silent look and I could tell he wanted me to continue.

"Brett's always had a strong personality. Either it seems people like him or they don't. But he's really changed over the past few months."

Jake was quiet as he processed the information I gave him. He looked as if he wanted to say something but remained silent, keeping his thoughts to himself.

"I guess I know now he has some problems at home," I went on, feeling relieved to finally get it all off my chest. "And while I can sympathize with his struggles, I just want nothing to do with him."

"I agree with you, Addison," Jake said, pausing at the ice cream maker. He got up from the stool and added more ice to the mixture. Sitting down again, he began to crank the machine. "I think you should stay away from him. Brett's a mess. He's drinking; he's bullying girls. He may have his problems—and that's unfortunate—but he's dangerous. *And* unpredictable," he added.

Giving the ice cream a couple more cranks, he announced, "I think it's ready."

My desire to taste the homemade concoction grew when he handed me an ice-cream-filled bowl and spoon, and I dove right in.

"Wow!" I exclaimed. "This *is* amazing!"

He smiled and said, "There's nothing quite as good as homemade ice cream." And with that, he lifted a giant spoonful into his mouth.

"Where did you learn to make this?"

"My grandpa George taught me when I was thirteen. I spent a lot of time with my grandparents growing up, especially after my parents divorced." His blue eyes clouded over and I sensed he wanted to talk about it. It was the second time he had mentioned their separation this evening, so I very gently prodded, giving him permission to vent.

"When did they divorce?"

Taking another bite, he answered, "They separated when I was ten, but divorced when I was twelve. I had a rough few years after that. Joint custody is tough on a kid, your time being split between two parents and all."

Jake sighed and looked off in the distance. I didn't like the serious expression that covered his normally smiling face. It made me feel sad.

"Your schedule is always changing and you never really settle into a comfortable routine. Nothing is consistent, and that includes rules. So naturally, I liked to see how much I could get away with. It took me a long time to not feel so angry with my parents. Back then, I thought they had ruined my life."

I watched him as he reflected on his past and couldn't help but notice how different we were, and yet how very much the same. I had a hard time imagining what it would be like to split my time between two parents. It seemed confusing.

"Do you still feel that way about them?" I asked curiously.

"No," he said after a moment. "I understand them better now. I know they didn't divorce to ruin my life. It was something they needed to do for themselves. To make *them* happy. But it's hard to see that when you're an angry teenager. My brothers had an easier time dealing with it than I did. I think it was because they were quite a bit younger than I was when Mom and Dad separated." He looked at me and smiled. "We're all pretty close now. My parents may not have made good partners, but they make amazing friends. They've both remarried, and believe it or not, they all hang out together."

"They *all* hang out together? You're kidding!" I laughed in shock. "That seems a little weird."

"I suppose it would seem that way from the outside looking in. But it works for us. So," he said, changing the subject. "You really like the ice cream?"

I nodded. "Absolutely! It's really good. You're right—I've never tasted anything like it before."

We spent the next hour devouring the remaining dessert and talking about my childhood. He seemed a little reserved when I discussed family vacations and whatnot. I imagined he felt like he had missed out on some things growing up.

When Jake dropped me off at home—fifteen minutes early—he walked me to the door and planted a soft kiss on my lips, careful not to overstep any bounds.

I gave him a little wave as he walked back toward his truck. Suddenly, he turned around and called out, "I'm busy tomorrow, but can I call you on Sunday?"

I shook my head and smiled. "I was hoping you would."

He gave me a lopsided grin before hopping into his pickup and driving away into the night.

Chapter Ten

Sunday morning after church found me with my cell phone glued to my hand, awaiting Jake's promised call. I'd had an amazing time with him Friday night and was anxious to get together again. I hoped he felt the same way. His call finally came shortly before noon.

"Are you busy?" he asked after I picked up. "I was hoping we could get together later. Maybe dinner and a movie?"

"I think I can manage that," I responded coyly. I could practically hear Jake grin on the other end.

"There's an old show playing at the drive-in. Have you ever seen *Casablanca*?"

Suddenly, I burst into laughter.

"What's so funny?"

"I thought you were going to say *Godzilla* or something," I responded, taken by surprise.

"Do you really think I am so shallow I would rather watch a cheap cinematic horror film as opposed to one of the greatest romantic melodramas of our time?" Jake exclaimed, in mock disbelief.

"I'm sorry," I teased. "I'm having a difficult time understanding your educated college lingo. I am, after all, an immature teenager, and classic *Godzilla* would be the preferred choice among most people my age."

"Well then, please allow me to enlighten you with my more advanced taste." He laughed. "Seriously, Addison, if you've never seen it, you don't know what you're missing."

I thought for a moment before responding. A drive-in movie seemed a bit dangerous—from a parent's perspective, anyway—and I didn't know if mine would allow me to go.

As if reading my mind, he suggested, "I can talk to your parents, if you like. Ask their permission? That way they don't get the wrong idea."

I smiled into the cell phone. "I'm going to take you up on that. I don't want to see their faces when they find out their baby girl, *and* only child, has been invited to the drive-in by a college man."

I heard him chuckle on the other end. "Okay, so it's settled. I'll pick you up at five thirty."

"You're awfully confident. You haven't even asked them yet."

"I'm not worried," he responded boldly.

An hour later, my mom approached me as I was reading a book on the back deck. Completely absorbed in Bella and Edward's love affair, I didn't hear her walk onto the patio.

"So," she began, clearing her throat. "I hear you're going to the movies tonight with Jake?"

I looked up from the story, my eyes wide with surprise. "Really? I'm allowed to go? You and Dad don't mind?"

She gave me a small smile and held my gaze. "Yes, you can go. But Addy—we need to have a talk." She walked closer to me, but did not sit down. I could tell something serious was on her mind. "Jake's an older guy," she began, hesitantly. "And while he seems like a perfectly nice young man, college guys sometimes have ideas . . ." She trailed off, clearly embarrassed.

I felt my face flush at the prospect of the difficult topic. "Mom, he *is* a nice guy. And he would never expect anything more from me than I was prepared to give."

Nervous, she cleared her throat again. "It's not so much Jake I'm worried about, honey. I mean, don't get me wrong—I'm concerned. But your father seems to like him, and that's saying a lot. Honestly, it's *you*."

My jaw dropped in astonishment. My mother didn't trust *me* with Jake?

"I've seen the way you look at him, Addy. And he *is* an extremely handsome boy. I know you're growing up and I can't watch over you forever. I just need to know that you're going to make smart choices."

I fought the urge to bring up my lunch. Was she saying that she didn't *trust me*? The shocked expression on my face must have given me away.

"It's not that I don't trust you, honey—I know you have a good head on your shoulders. But this is your first *real* date, without a group of your friends nearby. Eventually, there will be decisions you're going to have to make. Just remember, when you make certain choices, it's impossible to go back to the way things used to be."

Uh-oh. We were actually going to have the *sex* talk. Embarrassed, I looked away from her. We'd spoken about this before, first when I entered high school and again before prom last year. It seemed silly to rehash the conversation, especially when it was obvious she'd been watching me *look* at him.

"Addy, I'm not trying to make you uncomfortable . . ."

"I know, Mom," I interjected.

"But there are some things I need you to hear. I'm not going to lecture you on . . . taking precautions. We've already had that discussion years ago. But you need to keep in mind that decisions you make today can affect your entire life."

"Mom, please! I'm not going to have sex with him!"

Mom looked uncertain. "Maybe not today, and maybe not tomorrow. But there is a strong attraction between the two of you—I can *see* it. And you're practically an adult. What kind of mother would I be if I didn't bring these things up?" she asked gently. "It's just as uncomfortable for me to talk about this as it is for you to hear it. When I look at you I still see my little girl, with scraped knees and pigtails in your hair. But you're not a little girl anymore, Addy. You're turning into a beautiful young lady. And you're smart, too. So much smarter than I was at your age."

I looked at her carefully, trying to read between the lines. What was she admitting to? We had never discussed Mom's life before Dad.

"I had an older boyfriend when I was in high school, and he broke my heart," Mom admitted, as if she could read my mind. "And I need you to understand that when you make grown-up choices, you can never take them back. I'm just afraid you're going to get in over your head." Suddenly, her eyes filled with tears, and a wave of empathy washed over me.

"Mom," I began, standing up and walking over to her. "You don't need to worry. I'm not planning on having sex right now. Not with Jake or anyone else. And yes, someday I will have to make certain choices. But I promise you those choices will not be made tonight." I heard Mom sigh softly in relief.

But if we were going to have this talk, it was best to just lay it all out on the table because no way did I want to have to do it again.

"And when that time comes," I continued, "I will take into consideration every possible consequence that accompanies my decision. You and Dad have done a good job raising me, and now you have to trust me to do the right thing. Maybe you won't always agree with my choices, but I promise you I will not compromise myself or my beliefs."

Mom smiled at me and wiped a stray tear from her cheek. "I love you, Addy," she said, pulling me into a tight hug. "And your father and I *do* trust you." After a long moment, she pulled away and held my face in her hands. "You make us so very proud."

I returned her smile and planted a kiss on her cheek. "I love you, too, Mom."

Jake arrived promptly at 5:30, just like he promised. After he exchanged pleasantries with my parents, we were on our way to our first *official* date.

"So, what's for dinner?" I asked after we settled into his truck. The evening was heavy with humidity and I pushed my hair away from my face, wondering if I should have thrown it up into a messy bun.

He smiled. "I don't know. What are you in the mood for?"

I pretended to think, although I already had dinner planned out. "Ice cream," I stated, firmly.

"Ice cream?" His eyes shot up in amusement. "For dinner?"

"Not *just* ice cream," I answered, as though he should know better. "Sweet Retreat has *the best* walking tacos, and I've been craving Mexican food and a chocolate milkshake all day!"

Jake chuckled. "That's one thing I like about you, Addison. You're not afraid to eat in front of me."

I laughed out loud and gently shoved his shoulder, pretending to be offended. "So, what's *Casablanca* about anyway?" I asked.

He gave me a look of exasperation. "I can't believe you've never seen it."

I shrugged my shoulders and gave him a cockeyed grin.

"It takes place in early 1940s North Africa. It's about the owner of a popular café named Rick who runs into his old love, Ilsa. But she's married now to someone else," he explained. "They'd met years before in Paris and were planning to escape together because the Germans were about to invade France, but she never showed up."

I frowned. "That sounds really serious."

"It's one of the greatest movies of our time." He shrugged. "Everyone needs to see it at least once."

"And how many times have you seen it?"

"*Including* this time?" He gave me a sideways smirk. "Once."

"Wait, what?" I shrieked. "You've never even *seen* this movie?"

Jake started to laugh. "Not straight through, only in bits and pieces. But I've always wanted to."

"You made it sound as if you knew what you were talking about."

"I *do* know what I'm talking about. I studied *Casablanca* in Film Education. Only, I missed the class when they watched the movie from beginning to end—I skipped that day," he added sheepishly. "My bed felt way too cozy."

I stared at him for a long moment before dissolving into a fit of giggles.

"What's so funny?" he asked.

"You! You're so full of crap. You intentionally misled me."

"I didn't mean to, Addison. I really do want to see this movie. And I'd like to see it with you," he added with a smile.

Naturally, my stomach did a flip-flop. Would I ever get through a night with Jake without being assaulted by butterflies?

We devoured our meals at the Sweet Retreat and pulled into the drive-in just as the sun was beginning to set in the west.

"Have you ever been here before?" Jake asked.

I nodded. "We used to come here a lot when I was a kid. I loved it," I said, reflecting on the happy memories. "It always felt like a special treat."

"I've never been to a drive-in before," he confessed. "Would you like some popcorn?"

"Sure. What's a movie without popcorn, right?"

I stayed in the truck as he left to get popcorn and drinks. Pulling a small mirror out of my purse, I ran my fingers through my windblown hair and reapplied some lip gloss. My stomach felt a little nervous. I knew tonight might be a changing point in our relationship. Not that I had plans of taking things too far. I meant what I had said to my mom earlier about not giving in to anything before

I was ready. But I knew our relationship would undoubt-edly progress a little further, and I was okay with that.

Jake arrived back to the truck just as the movie was starting. Placing the drinks in the cup holders and holding the popcorn in between us, he scooted a little closer and gave me a small smile. I nervously wondered if he'd any expectations for the night.

We shared our snack and watched a couple of ads before *Casablanca* flickered to life on the screen. The black-and-white images danced before us and I gave Jake a look. "It's in black and white?" I asked with un-certainty.

He chuckled softly. "Don't worry, Addison, you'll survive." He set the popcorn off to the side and shifted closer, putting his arm around me.

I snuggled up to him and tried to hide my apprehen-sion. I could feel Jake's warm breath against my ear and turned slightly to look at him. His blue eyes gazed at me warmly and I suddenly felt very unsure of myself. "Did you know that all blue-eyed people are descended from one common ancestor who had a genetic muta-tion?" I blurted out. *Oh my God, what are you talking about?*

Jake gave me an amused smile. "I *did* know that."

"Did you also know that blue eyes are more sensitive to light than darker-colored eyes? It's because they don't have as much melanin." *Thank you freshman science class!* I swallowed hard.

Jake nodded his head, his eyes latching onto mine, then he leaned in closer, making me feel warm all over. "Of all the gin joints, in all the towns, in all the world, she walks into mine."

"Wh-what?" I whispered, completely confused.

Suddenly, his lips met mine and our mouths moved tentatively, exploring one another. "Is this okay?" he asked, touching his forehead to mine.

I felt my heart rate quicken and inched closer toward him, our mouths meeting again. Jake kissed me slowly, bringing his hand up to the side of my face, and I wrapped my arm around his neck, tangling my hand in the back of his hair—*Casablanca* a distant memory.

I never did find out if Ilsa and Rick ended up together.

Chapter Eleven

After our first official date, Jake and I spent as much time together as we could. We fell into a comfortable pattern of getting together after he finished work during the week and making plenty of time for fun on the weekends.

I introduced him to a secluded location on the beach— a spot rumored to harbor the occasional skinny-dipper—and we would park there for hours, watching the gentle waves of the lake and talking about everything, from our very different childhoods to plans for the future. We began to call it "our spot," and it felt like a secret only the two of us shared.

July rolled in with the usual festive cookouts and get-togethers, and I invited Jake to every single one. He happily accepted my invitations and easily fit into my circle of friends, as though he had been there all along.

Predictably, Ruby decided to run for Strawberry Queen at the annual Lakeside Strawberry Festival. She wanted to follow in her mother's footsteps, and Mrs. Sinclair couldn't have been more proud. Ruby was worried sick about winning the title, but I knew all along she had it in the bag. She was everything a Strawberry Queen should be—smart, pretty, charismatic. And her parents owned half the town, which didn't hurt her chances, either.

I was thoroughly enjoying the lazy pace of summertime, my last summer as a high school student, just as I promised myself I would. Admittedly, I was enjoying the company I was keeping even more. I felt myself growing fonder of Jake with each passing day, and whenever the thought of him returning to college arose, I firmly pushed it into the back of my mind. I just couldn't bear to think about it.

My parents, surprisingly, seemed to warm quickly to the idea of Jake and me being together. With the exception of the sex talk the night of our first date, my mom accepted the fact that we were dating and she played the gracious hostess every time Jake came to the house. Dad, on the other hand, was the biggest surprise, maybe because he had gotten to know Jake on a different level because of working together at the farm, but he welcomed him as if he were extended family. I knew they shared a great deal of respect toward one another, and I guess that's why it was easy for Dad to understand my attraction toward him.

I couldn't get over all of the new emotions I was experiencing. Jake was the first boy who had ever sparked such strong feelings, and sometimes, they were too much to deal with on my own. To make sense of it all, I turned to Mags for support. I admired her so much as a person and respected her opinion of my very first grown-up relationship. I continued to help her out every day at the farm, although I'd given up assisting with early-morning breakfasts. No one should have to wake up at that hour. I used my time there to give her the third degree.

"So, you really think Jake's nice, Mags?"

"I *really* do," she answered, smiling.

"Do you think he's cute?"

"I think he's *very* cute."

"And you think he's a good person?" I shamelessly prodded.

"I think if he *wasn't* a good person, you wouldn't like him so much," she wisely advised. "You're a smart girl, Addy. You need to trust your instincts. What do *you* think about him?"

"I think he's amazing," I sighed. I felt like a babbling idiot! What was Jake doing to me?

Mags laughed. "You two make a cute couple."

I stopped dead in my tracks. It was the first time anyone had referred to us out loud as a *couple*. Suddenly, it all felt so *real*.

Mags must have recognized the look of panic in my eyes. "Addy, everyone falls in love for the first time, eventually. And when it's true love, you just know. It will feel right. Now it's your turn to experience it. In my humble opinion, you couldn't have chosen more wisely. Jake is a wonderful boy."

But I had already tuned her out.

Love? was that what this was? The constant flip-flops in my stomach? Lying awake at night thinking about him? The stupid grin I couldn't wipe off my face?

Me, Addison Monroe—in *love*?

"You're what?" Ruby shrieked as we lay in chaise lounge chairs next to her pool.

"In love," I said, looking around nervously. I wasn't interested in broadcasting my news to the whole world. "At least Mags seems to think so."

"Well, what do you think?" she asked me wide-eyed.

I shook my head and gave her a shrug. "Love is a strong word. I'm not sure what to think. I *do* know that I've never felt this way before."

"I can't believe you're in love!" she sighed. Listening was never Ruby's strong suit.

I rolled my eyes and decided not to argue. "Why not? You've been in love a million times."

"Yeah, but that's me. You're supposed to be the level-headed one." Ruby frowned. "So, now what?"

"What do you mean?"

"What happens when Jake goes back to Texas?"

It was a topic I didn't like to think about. "I'm not sure," I admitted, taking a deep breath. "I guess I'm not going to take things too seriously. He's here for the summer and then he'll be gone," I added, trying to sound nonchalant. But inside, my heart sank.

Ruby shook her head emphatically. "I don't know how you're gonna do it. It's a tragic love story—like a modern-day Romeo and Juliet."

"Let's not get carried away! It's just a simple summer fling." I laughed at her analogy. "There will be no poison involved, I can promise you that."

"I'm pretty sure you're not supposed to fall in love with 'a simple summer fling,'" she retorted, bending her fingers in air quotes.

I swallowed hard and reached for my glass of lemonade, attempting to look unaffected. I should have never even mentioned it. The best thing to do at this point was to distract Ruby and get her talking about herself.

"So, what all do you have to do for this Strawberry Queen thing?"

Ruby sat upright and her expression turned animated. "Can you believe I have to have a *talent*?"

Distraction successful.

I stifled a laugh. As smart and pretty as she was, Ruby was known for her lack of coordination.

"Maybe I should dance?" she suggested.

The thought of Ruby cutting a rug was too much. "Ruby! You have two left feet!" I giggled. "After you and Eric went to prom last year, he said his toes felt broken from you stepping on them so much."

Ruby looked at me through narrow slits. "He was exaggerating."

"I don't think he was. I was there, remember? He limped for a week."

She let out a dramatic sigh. "All right then, maybe I could sing?"

Slowly, I shook my head. "Remember in sixth grade when you tried out for Dorothy in *The Wizard of Oz*? It didn't go so well."

Ruby blushed at the embarrassing memory. "Okay, maybe singing's not such a good idea either. God, Addy! What am I going to do?" she asked dramatically. "The pageant is next week! If I can't find a talent, I'm going to have to drop out."

I racked my brain trying to come up with a solution. "What did your mom do when she tried out for queen?"

Squinting from the sun's bright rays, Ruby lifted a hand to shield her eyes. "She had a ventriloquist's dummy."

I wasn't sure I heard her right. I just couldn't picture Mrs. Sinclair playing with a puppet!

"What?" I questioned. "Are you sure?"

Ruby rolled her eyes. "Yes, she performed with it all three years she tried out. And she was crowned queen every single time."

I raised my eyebrows in disbelief but a plan was already forming. "Does she still have the puppet?"

Shrugging, she answered, "I think so. I remember seeing it a few years ago in the attic. Why?" she asked suspiciously.

"Just hear me out before you say anything, all right?"

Ruby stared at me with a painful expression on her face.

"Your mom won Strawberry Queen three years in a row, right?"

She nodded her head. "You know she did. She tells us that story every single summer."

I ignored her impatient tone and continued. "And didn't she say the pageant judges told her a few years ago that no other Strawberry Queen had ever compared to her?"

"Yes. They said no reigning queen has even come close to beating my mom's record of community service hours. Plus, they still rant over her talent act. Apparently it was the first and only time they ever had a ventriloquist on the stage." Ruby ran a hand through her long blond hair. "What's your point, Addy?"

"My point is, the judges remember your mom fondly—which means they're probably excited you're trying out," I explained. "What if you borrowed your mom's dummy and performed as a ventriloquist? I think it would go over really well."

I studied Ruby's face as she pondered my suggestion. I had to admit it, the idea was genius. Now I just needed to convince Ruby.

"That is so random! Besides, I'm not a ventriloquist. I don't know the first thing about talking to a puppet," she wailed.

"Come on! I'm sure your mom would be happy to teach you what she knows. Plus, she'd be flattered. And I bet the judges would be thrilled. Remember, *they* are the ones you're trying to impress. You'll probably win just because you carried on your mother's tradition. Old people love that sorta stuff."

Ruby still looked unsure, but I could see her wheels spinning.

"I think my mom still has the scripts she used. Maybe I could get ideas from those?"

"Absolutely!" I encouraged. "Besides, what are your other options?"

Ruby looked at me and smiled in relief. "I'm going to do it!" She jumped up and gave me a hug. "You and Jake will be there, right? I can't do it if you're not there for me!"

I untangled myself from her arms. "Of course we'll be there. You're going to be amazing!"

We spent the rest of the afternoon brainstorming ideas with her mom, and just as I suspected, Mrs. Sinclair was elated her daughter wanted to borrow her act.

My plan for distracting Ruby from my situation with Jake worked better than I had anticipated.

It had distracted me as well.

Chapter Twelve

The night of the Strawberry Queen Pageant found Ruby a nervous wreck. I tried to soothe her frayed nerves, but she was impossible to deal with.

"I can't do it!" she stubbornly insisted. The pout that played on her full lips would have made even the most spoiled princess look like an amateur.

"Yes, you can, Ruby. You're the most confident person I know," I answered patiently.

"Oh, you have to say that," she wailed. "It's in our best friend contract."

I rolled my eyes at her dramatic outburst. She might not be coordinated enough to sing or dance, but she would certainly win an Academy Award if given the chance.

"You are going to be amazing, Ruby," Mrs. Sinclair offered, giving her daughter a reassuring hug. The two had spent a lot of time together rehearsing over the past week, and the bonding had done both of them good. They absolutely beamed—that is, when Ruby wasn't throwing a fit.

"I don't know. I've never been so nervous before!"

I looked around the pageant dressing room at the other contestants. Every single participant looked absolutely beautiful, but none compared to Ruby. It amazed me that she wasn't able to see that.

"Look at how you won over the judges with your talent," Mrs. Sinclair reminded her.

Ruby had owned the stage during the talent portion of the contest held earlier that day. She'd borrowed her mother's ventriloquist act and had stolen the show. She even won a standing ovation at the end of her performance.

"I did do that, didn't I?" Ruby questioned, her eyes shining bright with enthusiasm. Ruby would never admit it, but she adored the spotlight.

"Yes, you did," her mom answered with a comforting rub on her shoulder. "And you can do this, too."

Ruby drew in a shaky breath and nodded, her blond hair piled high in an elegant updo. She looked down at the long emerald green dress that clung to her slender frame and gave it a twirl. Finally, she touched her painted nails to the delicate diamonds hanging on her ears and smiled. "Okay, I *think* I'm ready," Ruby announced nervously.

"Girls!" a plump lady called, clapping her hands together. "Get in your places. It's almost time to go onstage."

Ruby turned toward her mom, a frantic look decorating her pretty face.

Mrs. Sinclair gave her another hug and held her face between her hands. "You are smart and beautiful, Ruby. You can do this. No matter what happens out there, you will always be a winner to me."

Ruby took one last deep breath and grinned, an

expression of serenity taking over. Maybe that was all she needed to hear.

She turned on the heel of her stiletto and found her place among the long line of pageant entrants. She gave me a quick wave before I returned to my seat in the audience.

"How is she?" Jake leaned over and asked after I sat down next to him.

I let out an agitated sigh. "A nervous wreck."

An amused look covered his face. "You're nervous, too, aren't you?"

"Of course I am! Ruby's my best friend."

"I think that's cute," he said, his smile growing wider.

I couldn't help but giggle. "Have I told you how happy I am that you didn't make me come to this thing by myself?"

Jake grasped my hand in his and flashed a mischievous grin. "Don't worry. You can make it up to me later."

I elbowed him in the side just as the auditorium lights dimmed, indicating the intermission was coming to an end. Lights flooded the stage as the contestants took their places in front of the large audience.

"Ruby really does stand out," Jake whispered as the girls stood before us. I gave him an appreciative smile. He didn't have to come with me to watch a bunch of high school girls compete for some silly title, but he did. And he hadn't complained once.

"Ladies and gentleman," the plump lady announced grandly from center stage, "I would like to introduce you to this year's Strawberry Queen."

A little girl in a fancy white dress approached the emcee with a small card in her chubby little hand. The plump lady took the envelope and nodded toward the child.

"A round of applause for my young granddaughter, please." The crowd erupted in praise, making the small girl blush. She scurried off the stage quickly.

"Now, for the moment we've all been waiting for," the woman declared dramatically. "These exquisite ladies you see standing behind me are all fine examples of young women today. Each one has shown an amazing amount of maturity and showmanship. But as you know, only one can win this year's title of Strawberry Queen." She made an exaggerated gesture toward the nervous teenagers waiting patiently in the background.

Ruby's eyes met mine and I gave her a wink. Pride swelled inside me as I watched my very best friend stand before the daunting audience, looking as radiant as the queen I knew she was.

"And the winner of the fifty-eighth annual Lakeside Strawberry Festival is . . ."

A hush fell over the crowd and I glanced over at Mr. and Mrs. Sinclair, sitting a row ahead of us in the auditorium. I wasn't sure who was more excited, Ruby or her parents.

"Ruby Sinclair!" the emcee released.

A standing ovation commanded the room as applause thundered around me. I watched intently as last year's queen placed a bouquet of flowers in Ruby's waiting arms and a small crystal-encrusted crown on top her head.

This was Ruby's moment, and she was eating it up. She radiated on the stage as she waved to the crowd that stood clapping before her. She found her parents sitting in their chairs, tears shining in their eyes, and she blew them a kiss.

I couldn't help but laugh at the scene unfolding around me. You would have thought Ruby was being crowned

Miss Universe! I wiped away happy tears of my own and looked over at Jake. He was watching me with a smile.

Without warning, he leaned over and planted a soft kiss on my lips, causing me to stare back at him in awe. All of these beautiful girls surrounding us, and Jake only had eyes for me.

I couldn't have been more thrilled.

Later that evening, when Jake dropped me off at home, we found ourselves walking along a path at the farm, the crunch of the dirt underneath our boots. Twilight was falling over the pasture and the sky was beautiful as it swirled into shades of purple and orange.

Jake reached for my hand. "What are you thinking?" he asked.

Reluctantly, I shrugged. "The Strawberry Festival means that summer is winding down." I turned to look at him. "I guess I've been having so much fun, I hate to see it end."

Jake's gaze dropped to the ground and the muscle in his jaw flexed. "It's been a nice summer." He gave my hand a squeeze. "I have you to thank for that."

Suddenly, my heart raced uncomfortably, pulling inside my chest. The last thing I wanted to think about was when Jake would be leaving to go back to Texas. I couldn't stand the thought of saying good-bye. A thick lump began to form in my throat and I swallowed hard, trying to wash it away. "Come on," I said, trying to change the subject. "I want to show you something."

Jake followed behind as I pulled him toward the barn. We opened the big wooden door, and Jake reached inside to turn on the light. I crossed the dirt floor and led him to the horse stall at the end. Along the wall sat a tier of shelves, each rack holding a series of trophies. "What's this?" he asked, reaching for one.

"They're mine."

He looked at me for a moment, then back at the souvenir in his hand. "Supreme Performance Champion?" He looked back at me. "I didn't know you rode."

I nodded and smiled. "I used to. I don't anymore."

"Why not?"

I shrugged my shoulders. "I guess I grew out of it. After my horse Black Jack died, I lost interest."

For the next several minutes, Jake studied the trophies on the wall, occasionally picking one up to get a better look. "Did you win all of these with Black Jack?"

"I did. The one you're holding right now I won a few years ago, right before we had to put him down. I was almost fifteen. It was actually one of the last times I rode."

"What happened to your horse?" he asked quietly.

I took a deep breath. "He hurt himself on a jump. Broke his leg. For some reason, it just didn't want to heal." I paused, turning to look at the last stall. "He was getting older, I guess. He didn't spring back like the younger ones do."

Jake placed the trophy on the shelf and was suddenly behind me, his arms wrapped around my waist. "Was this his stall?"

My breath caught at the feel of his lips touching my ear. "It was."

Slowly, Jake turned me around to face him. "I'm sorry about your horse."

He pulled me closer and I wrapped my arms around his neck. When his lips met mine, I closed my eyes, savoring the feel. His hand trailed up my spine until it cupped the back of my head, somehow bringing me closer. His tongue slid against mine, and my insides stirred with anticipation.

Just then, a noise outside the barn separated us. "Someone's coming," I whispered, my eyes wide with surprise.

A slow grin appeared on his face and he held his finger to his lips. "Shhh. Follow me."

I smiled as he grabbed my hand, pulling me to a ladder that led up to the hayloft. He helped me on and followed me the whole way up, pausing so I could haul myself to the top. When we were both safely concealed, we looked down below and saw Gramps open the door and come into the barn, a look of confusion across his face. Finally, he turned off the light, leaving us in shadows.

I stifled a giggle. "He doesn't know we're in here."

"Yeah, let's keep it that way. I don't want him to think I'm molesting his granddaughter."

"But weren't you?" I whispered, giving him a long, heated look.

When our eyes met, I saw a desire like I'd never seen before. We fell into each other's arms and then to the floor, my back pressed up against a layer of hay. A reckless, swooping sensation hit my stomach when his lips grazed my neck and I relented to the fact that this might actually be love. Real, true, honest-to-God love. With one hand tangled in my hair, I felt Jake's other hand slide up my midsection and rest just below my breast. It was shocking yet tender, sending shivers of pleasure straight to my core.

Our lips met again, and after a long while, he pulled away, resting his forehead against mine. His hot, labored breath mingled with mine, and he planted one last kiss on my lips.

I lifted my hand to his face and stared into his eyes, and the world stood still. Jake smiled, then covered my hand with his. Very gently, he brought it up to his lips and then sighed. "I better get you home."

Chapter Thirteen

Friday morning greeted me with sunny skies and comfortable temperatures. It was the perfect day to kick off the Strawberry Festival. My little Georgia town was extremely proud of the annual event and spared no expense at making everything just right.

Festival patrons traveled from far and wide to experience the many pleasantries Lakeside had to offer. From the much-anticipated Strawberry Pancake Breakfast that signaled the beginning of the fair, to the scores of strawberry treats and goodies offered throughout the entire downtown area, including the homegrown strawberry wine. The festival was, without a doubt, the highlight of the summer.

Even Gramps and Mags took the day off from the farm to commemorate the affair. They always helped out at the breakfast, whipping up the hotcakes and serving them to the guests. And I was looking forward to wandering around the festival with Jake, as both my parents and his aunt and uncle would be preoccupied with the weekend celebration. It would feel as if we were on our own, with no one to answer to but ourselves.

My first responsibility, however, was to make sure Ruby was all set with her designated royal responsibilities. She was expected to make an appearance at the pancake breakfast and charm those in attendance. But Ruby hadn't been awake before noon since summer vacation started, and I knew I would have to serve as her wake-up call. After my third attempt, I was starting to get nervous. I let the phone ring as long as it would, when finally she decided to pick up.

"Rise and shine, Queen Ruby," I called sweetly into the phone.

"Ugh. What time is it?"

"It's time to get up. That strawberry breakfast isn't going to wait for you to get there, you know."

"Do I have to?" she whined into my ear.

"Yes, you have to. You wanted this, Ruby, now you have to follow through."

"You sound like my mother."

I rolled my eyes. The last thing I wanted to do was argue with Ruby that early in the morning.

"You're coming to pick me up, right?" I asked, changing the subject.

"Do I have a choice?"

"If you would rather attend the breakfast on your own, I would be happy to go back to bed." I had to smile, knowing I had her.

I heard her sigh in defeat from the other end. "I'll be there. Give me forty-five minutes."

"I don't want to be late. If my pancakes are cold, I'm going to kick your royal a—" But she had already hung up.

I showered and dressed in record time, finally making my way downstairs to wait for my ride. My parents had already left to help out with the breakfast, so it was just me alone with my thoughts. I sat in a comfy chair near the front window and twirled my hair around my finger. My mind drifted to Jake, as it always seemed to. I was excited to be meeting up with him later—it was all I could think about. Every time I pictured his lips touching mine, my stomach would tighten. Was this normal? Did he get butterflies when he thought of me, too? Probably not.

Our relationship was moving along rather smoothly and I couldn't help but wonder what this weekend had in store. I knew that we would be left to our own devices and I wasn't sure how I felt about it. On one hand, I was really looking forward to being alone with him. I loved everything about him. His sense of humor, his kindness, the way that he looked. And the way he looked *at me*.

On the other hand, I was scared to death. I felt like a fish out of water. All of these feelings I had for him were so new to me. I talked to Ruby about it a little, but even then I held back. It felt so personal.

Jake and I had discussed the future of our union, as well. He always made sure that I felt comfortable and that things weren't rushing along too quickly. He was a gentleman, in every sense of the word.

But something was coming, I could sense it.

There was a part of me that still could not believe my good fortune for having met Jake. My girlfriends were always prodding me for more information about him, but I just didn't want to talk to them about it. They would get so frustrated by my lack of cooperation—we would always gossip about the guys that we liked before! But this was different. I didn't want them to know how I felt about Jake. Or how we would spend hours at the lake, listening to music and talking. And I certainly didn't want to regale them with the stories that emerged from the backseat of his truck! I'd barely even shared those intimate details with Ruby. All of those reasons were what forced me to believe that this relationship was different. That *he* was different.

I had not yet told Jake that I loved him, or that I *thought* I was in love with him, but I could tell he already knew. I guess when it really *is* true love, you know it. Just like Mags had promised.

Chapter Fourteen

Ruby really came through as the reigning Strawberry Queen. She had the breakfast crowd captivated and left them wanting more. I watched her shine from my chair, nestled safely in the corner, far away from the limelight. She was a natural; if her mom could have made it she would have been proud.

"Are you having a good time?" Ruby asked me, in between mingling with the guests.

"I'm having a blast," I told her.

"Oh, come on! You could at least be social, Addy," she retorted with raised eyebrows.

"I don't want to be social, Ruby. This is your affair. I'm just along for the ride."

"Suit yourself," she exclaimed, and turned sharply to greet a well-wisher.

"Not having any fun?" A deep voice came from behind me.

There were those pesky butterflies again.

"Jake," I breathed and turned toward him. He was wearing my favorite outfit, a tight black T-shirt with jeans that hugged his frame and those worn-in cowboy boots.

He grinned back at me and leaned in closer for a peck on the cheek. I watched Mags across the room smile at us and then turn quickly away, not wanting to be caught. I thought I was going to die.

Please, God, don't let my parents be watching!

I felt my cheeks warm as I looked down, embarrassed by the public display of affection. What I would have given for a rock to climb under.

Jake chuckled and brushed away the hair that fell into my face. "Are you ready?" he asked. "I can't wait for you to show me around."

The awkwardness passed and I once again had a hard time hiding my enthusiasm. I'd been looking forward to this weekend for so long! What made it even better was knowing that I would be able to share the excitement with Jake. I had our whole day planned, from sampling all of the strawberry treats, to listening to live music play at the gazebo in Lakeside Park. I was also looking forward to the arts and crafts area. The festival always displayed an impressive amount of work from local artists, including paintings, sculptures, ceramics, and woodwork. But my favorite section was photography. Lakeside was such a beautiful area, and I was always amazed by the sights captured on film.

"So, what's first on our itinerary?" he asked.

I looked at him sheepishly. "Don't laugh, but every year I get a caricature."

Jake looked skeptical. "You're kidding, right?"

I shook my head. "No, I'm not. I have an album full of them at home, starting from the time I was about four years old on up. It's just what I do," I answered haughtily.

"All right now, don't go getting all defensive on me, Addison," he said, playfully nudging me in the ribs. "I want to do whatever you want to do."

"Okay then, caricatures it is!" I linked my arm through his and we started walking toward the door.

"And where do you think you're going?" I heard a brassy voice call from behind. We turned around to find Ruby with her hands on her hips, glaring at us.

"I'm going to show Jake around the festival."

"You're not going to leave me here on my own, are you?" She pouted.

"You're not on your own, Ruby. You have a roomful of adoring fans. Besides, it's almost noon. I've been here with you for hours!"

She attempted to hide the smile forming on her lips, but failed miserably. "They really do like me, don't they?"

"What's not to like?" Jake piped in. "You make a wonderful queen, Ruby. Probably the best Lakeside has ever seen."

Ruby's cheeks turned a dark shade of pink which, of course, complemented her complexion perfectly. I still got a kick out of watching her swoon over Jake.

"Thank you, Jake. That is so sweet of you to say," Ruby gushed.

"Well, it's the truth," he continued. "Addison promised to show me around, but we'd like to catch up with you later if you have time. How about you text her when you have a free moment? In the meantime, I see several people waiting to get their picture taken with you."

Ruby turned around and smiled at the small gathering lingering patiently behind us.

"I guess you're right!" she exclaimed. "I'd better go. Have fun, you two!" And she was off.

I gave Jake an impressed smirk and shook my head. "You're so good with her."

"Oh, she's not so bad. She just likes the attention." He laughed.

"You know how to sweet-talk her. She's putty in your hands."

"I don't know about all that," he said, still chuckling. "Now enough talk about Ruby—let's go have some fun!"

I smiled up at him and let him lead me out the door into the bright summer sun. Inhaling deeply, I felt on top of the world. Nothing was going to ruin this perfect weekend. As we walked through the decorated downtown area, I noticed the appreciative glances from the females we passed, and had to stifle a giggle. I was walking with the most handsome guy at the fair, and everyone knew it.

Suddenly, my nerves took over. What was I doing? How could I have let myself fall in love with Jake? He would be leaving town in just a few shorts weeks. How was I going to manage without him? I stopped to blindly study a ceramic cat displayed at one of the artists' booths.

"Hey," Jake said quietly, interrupting my thoughts. "Are you okay?"

There was that question again. The same one that had popped up so many times during the short period of time I had known him.

I looked up at him and felt my eyes fill with tears. "I'm fine," I squeaked.

A soft smile lifted his lips. "I think you're lying."

I shook my head in protest, but could feel the lump in my throat growing larger.

"What are you thinking about?" he prodded.

I swallowed hard and wiped at a tear that had escaped. "Nothing," I insisted.

He turned, taking me gently by the shoulders, forcing me to look him in the eye.

"What's going on?" Jake asked again.

Without warning, my tears spilled over like a faucet, betraying me.

"Addison?" he questioned, his voice laced with concern.

"I'm sorry, I can't help it," I sniffed, horrified by my reaction. I owed him an explanation, and not being very quick on my feet, was unable to come up with a suitable lie. "I was thinking of you leaving next month," I blurted out, surprisingly relieved by my confession.

Jake let out a small sigh and regarded me carefully. "I've been thinking about that, too," he admitted.

Shocked, I looked up at him. Was he serious?

"I wasn't expecting to come to Lakeside this summer and fall in love."

My heart sank into my stomach. Did he just say what I thought he said? Did he love me the way that I loved him? His admission didn't make me feel any better— only worse. To know that he returned my feelings was almost too much to bear.

A depressing melody from an instrumental band wafted across from the park, adding to my misery. "I'm so sorry," was all I could think to say.

He laughed lightly and brought his hand up to my cheek, causing my heart to skip a beat. "What are you sorry for? I wouldn't trade this for the world." He smiled down at me, his eyes soft and moist.

"I've never felt this way before . . ." I was unable to complete my sentence. The butterflies in my stomach were fluttering much too quickly. I was starting to feel nauseous.

"Neither have I."

Slowly, he lowered his lips onto mine. It was the softest, most meaningful kiss I had ever received, even more special than the ones in the barn.

Jake pulled away after a moment and looked deep into my eyes. I suddenly felt self-conscious and wanted to turn away, but I was more intrigued by the sadness that covered his face. It was hard for me to believe that he felt the same way I did.

He glanced off into the distance and then smiled. Pulling his eyes back toward me, he said, "Come on. Let's go get that picture."

He laced his fingers through mine and we set off down the road. I was so distracted by my thoughts, I barely even noticed the artwork we were passing—the pieces I had been looking forward to seeing. The weekend I had been waiting impatiently for suddenly seemed bleak and depressing. I sighed, wondering if I had ruined the mood.

Jake gave my hand a reassuring squeeze. "Let's make today special," he offered, as if reading my mind. "Let's fill it with happy memories, not sad ones, okay?"

I nodded, knowing it wouldn't be entirely possible. We started walking again, past all of the artists and the beautiful pieces they had on display.

"This is pretty impressive," he said after a while. "There's a lot of talent in this little town."

"There *is* a lot of talent here," I agreed, trying to snap out of my mood. "This section is one of my favorite spots at the whole festival. I love looking at all of the art."

"Are you involved in art at school?"

I started to laugh. "No, I'm not very creative. I have more of a scientific mind, I guess. But I appreciate those who are artistic. I think it's amazing that someone can take a blank piece of paper or clay and turn it into something so beautiful."

Jake looked down at me with a smile, then wrapped an arm around my shoulder, bringing me in close to him. I inhaled deeply, loving the way that he smelled, like a mixture of soap and citrus. It was a heady combination.

"Here we are," I announced as we approached the caricature artist.

The man was working with a customer, so we wandered around the small display, looking at some of the pictures he had created. There were drawings of individuals and couples, and entire families as well. I had been going to this artist every year since I was a little girl, and I preferred his work because he didn't sketch his subjects so far-fetched, like most caricaturists practiced. Instead, his work took on a more serious tone, making the artwork beautiful and not overly distorted.

"He's really good," Jake commented. "I wasn't expecting the portraits to look so . . . normal. I imagined they would be crazy exaggerations of the people he drew."

"They're a little abstract, but not in really silly ways."

"Hello, Addy!" the artist said, turning toward us and smiling. He had just finished up with his last subject and was giving us his full attention.

"Hi, Mr. Potter."

"I see you have a guest with you this year. Will he be joining you in the picture?"

I looked over at Jake and raised my eyes in question.

Jake caved, just like I knew he would. "Yes, I'll be joining her."

I clapped my hands together, then threw my arms around him, squeezing him tightly. "Thank you," I whispered.

"You're welcome," he said quietly back to me.

"All right then. If you two want to be drawn together, you're going to have to stop staring at each other." The artist chuckled.

I could feel my face turn red and I gave Mr. Potter an embarrassed smile. We took our places in front of his easel and he started to draw our portrait.

* * *

"It really turned out great." Jake held the picture up for us to admire.

"I love it! This is by far my favorite portrait." I looked over at him and smiled. "I'll treasure it forever."

Jake bent closer and gave me a kiss on the cheek, taking my hand in his. We walked toward the music playing at the gazebo.

"Addy!" I heard a loud voice call from behind us. We turned around to see Ruby racing toward us, her tiara gleaming in the sunlight. "What are you two up to?"

"We're just wandering around," I said, once she reached us.

"You won't believe what they want me to do," she whined, her face mangled in disgust.

"What?" I asked curiously.

"I have to announce the winners of the poultry and swine competitions!" she complained.

I frowned, not understanding what the big deal was.

"It's going to be so stinky!" she exclaimed, as though I should have known better.

"It is stinky work, but no one ever said that being a queen was going to be easy, Ruby," Jake sympathized. "I imagine they chose you because they figured you could handle it."

Ruby nodded gravely. "I had no idea it was going to be this difficult."

I snorted under my breath. My best friend could be so utterly clueless sometimes. You shouldn't complain about stinky animals to people who spent their days working knee-deep in horse manure.

"I have to get going," she groaned. "I'll call you later, okay?" she asked.

"Yep. Have fun, Ruby," I said, smiling sweetly.

She rolled her eyes and turned around, walking toward the 4-H section of the festival. Her shoulders were slumped in defeat.

"Guess she's getting more than she bargained for, huh?" Jake laughed lightly. "Hey, what's this?" he asked, dragging me toward one of the vendors.

"Strawberry wine," he read to himself, picking up one of the bottles and turning it over in his hands.

I nodded. "It's one of the most popular items at the fair. The strawberries are grown locally at a vineyard not too far from here. I've heard it's really good. Ruby's parents always have several bottles stored in their basement."

"Have you ever tried it?" he asked, looking over at me.

I laughed. "No! Her parents would never let us."

"Do you *want* to try it?"

My face grew serious. "I've never tried alcohol before," I whispered to him.

Jake gave me a slow smile. "One sip won't hurt anything. I mean, if you *want* to try it—I would never force you."

I thought for a moment. I secretly had always wanted a little taste. And he was right, one drink wouldn't be a big deal. I wouldn't be driving, and I certainly didn't plan on making it a habit. I kind of liked the idea of sharing my first taste of wine with him.

I bit my lip. "I *am* sort of curious."

Jake showed the woman at the vineyard stand his ID and paid for the bottle of wine. She wrapped it carefully in a brown paper bag and we walked away from the tent.

"You look like an alcoholic with that bottle hiding in the bag like that," I said with a laugh.

"Maybe I should run it home? I really don't want to

carry it around all day—especially if it makes me look like a lush! Do you mind?"

"Nope, I don't mind."

"Maybe we can open the bottle when we get there? I'm dying to try it out."

I shrugged my shoulders, hoping I didn't look too excited. I was dying to try it, too. Just a *little* taste.

Chapter Fifteen

I swirled the wine around in my glass, just as I had seen Ruby's parents do on so many occasions, and stared at the pink liquid that I was, admittedly, a little nervous to sample.

"I'm sorry I don't have wineglasses," Jake apologized. "My aunt and uncle never drink." But I was barely listening.

I brought my nose to the rim and inhaled the pleasant aroma. Glancing up at Jake, I noticed he was watching me, carefully gauging my reaction. I gave him a small smile before touching my lips to the glass, tipping a small amount of wine into my mouth. I whirled it around before swallowing, reveling in the crisp yet smooth feeling it left in its wake. I took another big swallow and felt a warm sensation pool in my stomach.

"Well?" he asked. "What do you think?"

"It's delicious," I exclaimed, reluctant to drag myself away from its fruity flavor. I had never tasted anything quite like it before, and felt very mature sitting there with Jake, drinking it.

I watched him take his first sip, admiring the way his muscles moved underneath his shirt as he lifted the glass to his mouth. I smiled in anticipation as I waited for his reaction.

"This *is* good," he said finally, after finishing half of what was in his cup. "Probably the nicest wine I've ever tried. You got lucky, Addison. My first sip of wine tasted like teriyaki sauce."

I laughed and swallowed down what was left in my glass, then held it up for him to pour more.

Jake gave me a reluctant look. "Are you sure, Addison? I don't want you to overdo it. You're not used to drinking, so it probably wouldn't take much to, um, make you feel funny." A slow blush covered his cheeks. I couldn't help but grin at his discomfort, enjoying the fact that it was him for a change.

"Come on," I persuaded. "Just a little more. It tastes so good!"

He smiled skeptically and poured a small amount more into my cup. We brought our glasses together for a quick toast before I drank it down, marveling at the slightly euphoric sensation taking over. I knew better than to ask for more.

"I'm sorry—I can't give you any more," Jake said regretfully. If I didn't know better, I would have sworn he was psychic.

"That's okay, I'm good." I smiled at his sense of responsibility. How many guys would act like that? I set my glass down on the counter and walked over to Jake, enveloping him in a hug. "Thank you."

"What for?" he whispered into my hair as he wrapped his arms around me.

"For everything. For just being you. For making this the best summer of my life. For letting me fall in love with you, and for loving me back. And for giving me my first

taste of wine—I'm so glad I got to share this with you."
I smiled into his chest, loving the way we fit together.
"I love you."

Jake pulled away and brought his hand up to my face,
slowly brushing my hair behind my ear. His eyes were
tender as he stared down at me, and I felt myself melt. I
definitely wasn't drunk, but I had to wonder if it was the
wine that brought out the honesty, or just the fact that I
really wanted him to know how I felt.

"I love you, too," he responded quietly.

I inhaled deeply, suddenly needing to hear more.
"Why?"

His mouth twitched. "Why what?" A look of confusion covered his face.

"Why do you love me, Jake?" It felt like a perfectly
normal question to ask at the time, but I could tell it had
caught him off guard.

He paused before bringing me back into his chest and
holding me tightly. "I love you because you make me
feel . . ." His voice cracked slightly. "You make me feel
like I've never felt before. I love you because you're the
first person I want to talk to when I wake up in the morning and the last person I want to talk to when I go to bed
at night. I love you because you're smart and witty. I love
the way you make me laugh. I love your innocence and
naivety. And I love how you always want ice cream." He
chuckled quietly. "I love everything about you."

My heart swelled. I looked up at him and felt more
love than I ever knew was possible. Everything about
him was so perfect and I was so lucky to be a part of his
life, even if only for a short while.

He brought his forehead down and rested it against
mine. "I love you, Addison," he repeated. They were the

sweetest words I had ever heard, and I knew I would cherish the moment for as long as I lived. No matter how much time passed and what happened afterward, those words would forever be burned into my heart.

"I love you." I sighed, bringing my lips up to his.

Jake's hands traveled down to the small of my back, and I twisted my hands into his hair. When an involuntary moan escaped from his mouth, I felt my stomach leap.

I needed more.

"I want to be with you, Jake," I said, after he brought his lips down onto my neck.

I felt him still.

Oh no! Had I said the wrong thing? Would he not want me the same way I wanted him?

Jake pulled away from me and looked deep into my eyes. He seemed conflicted, as though he were struggling with something internally. Was he trying to figure out how to let me down gently? I had to force myself not to take it back; not to say "just teasing."

"Addison," he began. "I'm not so sure that's a good idea."

"Why?" I asked him. "Don't you want me?"

He brought his forehead back to mine and quietly chuckled. "I want to be with you more than you know," he whispered.

I let out a breath, thankful he was not rejecting me. "But I love you. Why isn't it a good idea?"

"Look at me," he encouraged softly, tilting my chin upward. "Once you make that decision, there's no going back."

"You sound like my mom." I shook my head vigorously.

"I won't want to go back. I promise! I love you, and I want my first time to be with you."

Jake gave me a smile, but still seemed hesitant. "I just want to make sure that you're ready . . ." His voice trailed off with uncertainty.

"I *am* ready, Jake. I'm *more* than ready. I'm eighteen years old! And you are *not* just some random guy I'm dating. I'm *in love* with you!"

"And I'm in love with you," he answered firmly.

"Then what's the problem?" I asked, not caring if I sounded like a child.

"It's just a big decision, that's all. And I don't want you to regret it."

"I'm not *going* to regret it," I insisted, grasping his face between my hands and looking him square in the eye. "I'm only going to regret it if I *don't* do it. Once you leave for Texas—who knows when we'll see each other again. If ever . . ." I fought a shiver that threatened to take over my body. I didn't want to think about him leaving.

My words seemed to resonate with him. His face relaxed and he released a long, drawn-out sigh. Finally, his lips met mine for a slow kiss. I smiled against his mouth as I waited for his next move.

"What's so funny?" he asked, returning my smirk.

"I'm just excited," I announced bravely.

"Addison." He laughed lightly. "What am I going to do with you?"

I raised my eyebrows and laced my fingers through his. "I can think of something."

Jake led me into his bedroom and closed the door behind us.

* * *

"You're so beautiful," Jake murmured, his blue eyes blazing with lust. His fingers worked their way down along the curve of my stomach. Sharp tingles shot throughout my body and spread to my core in electrifying waves. How was it possible to feel scared and exhilarated all at once?

I tried not to let my eyes linger, but I had never seen a naked man in real life before. I'd seen a picture once in a magazine when I was thirteen that Ruby had found from God knows where. I remember we sat there laughing at it for what felt like hours.

I was not laughing now . . .

As we lay in his bed, Jake began to move the soft pad of his thumb in slow circles below my belly button, causing the tingles dancing through my body to intensify. Every part of me was responding to his touch in ways I was completely unfamiliar with. I forced myself to take a deep breath, but it did nothing to calm my nerves.

His experienced hand moved up my body with a slow, languid pace until it reached the swell of my naked breast. When his fingers brushed the sensitive bud, I felt a rush of sensations in lower regions, sensations that were very new to me. I tried desperately to pretend I was the kind of girl who knew exactly what to do in situations like this, but failed miserably when I cried out as Jake lowered his head, closing his mouth around the tender pink tip.

"I love you," he said quietly, and his tongue continued to torture me. But I couldn't respond. I let my hands flutter to his hair and tried not to embarrass myself.

After a long moment, Jake let his lips scorch a path upward until they brushed against my ear. "Addison," he whispered, his voice thick with emotion. "Are you sure you want to do this? We can stop if you want to."

His words sent shivers up my spine. I wanted nothing more than to surrender to the feelings that were stirring inside me. No way was I turning back now. I moved my head to look at him and our eyes locked. "I'm positive," I promised.

Jake's eyes centered in on my lips and he moved his arms around my waist, closing what little distance there was between us. His breath was warm as his mouth pressed against mine, slowly taking its time.

Every inch of my body awoke and all I could do was think about how much I wanted him, how much I needed him. With his gentle kiss, an agonizing warmth spread across my chest and trailed down my body.

Jake released me slightly and reached into the wallet on top of his dresser, removing a small, square package. He brought it closer, releasing the condom that was nestled inside. I tried to quiet my breathing. After he slipped it over his length he moved on top of me, his mouth once again finding mine.

My breaths were ragged as I kissed him back, wondering if my inexperience would ruin the moment. The last thing I wanted to do was disappoint him. But the low growl he let escape confirmed Jake was enjoying himself just as much as I was.

Moving his lips along my jaw, Jake traced a fiery path down my neck, and when his mouth found mine again it was more urgent than before. He slipped his tongue inside, exploring every inch. I clung to him tightly as he moved on top of me and I could feel his arousal pressing against my middle. I sucked in my breath, knowing what would come next.

Was I really going to go through with this? You bet I was.

Fire raced through my veins as Jake gently pushed into me. He moved in deeper, then slightly pulled away, raising himself onto his elbow. Jake lifted his hand and caressed wavy strands of hair from my cheek, then carefully brought his fingers beneath my chin, tilting my face up to meet his. Sapphire eyes bored into mine and his expression was so gentle and sweet I could feel my own eyes fill with moisture.

"Are you okay?" he asked quietly, his eyes never once leaving me.

I nodded, not trusting myself to speak.

Jake captured my lips in a heated kiss as he settled back between my legs. His hand brushed the swell of my breast as it made its way around to the back of my thigh, raising it slightly allowing him to move in deeper. Our hips rocked together, back and forth, finding a comfortable rhythm. I marveled at the shock of pleasure and pain I felt. I'd never really given much thought to how it would feel to actually make love. And that's what it was. Love.

I let my hands slide up his smooth, tanned skin that stretched over rock-hard muscles, until my fingers tangled into his tousled hair. Electrifying sensations raced through my body, building in intensity toward the center of my core. Jake's hand was on the move again, making its way up my midsection until it finally found my hand. When our fingers entwined, the connection I felt with him in that moment became so powerful, so real, I had to remind myself to breathe.

Jake's gaze caught mine and he held it tightly. I was unable to look away. My pulse raced as heat began to build deep inside my stomach. Jake clung to his rhythm and his fingers grasped mine tighter, his breathing becoming quicker, more jagged.

Suddenly, a glorious warmth exploded in my center and rushed through every limb in my body, causing me to cry out at the exact same moment as Jake. We lay together, tangled in each other's arms, as our breathing began to slow.

Jake had been so gentle, so careful with me, and somehow I found myself loving him even more.

Chapter Sixteen

The next morning I lay in my bed, reminiscing over the previous evening's activities. I couldn't help but alternate between a giggle and a blush when I thought of how sweet and gentle Jake had been. It was everything a first time should be, and the butterflies in my stomach were working overtime as I mulled over every last detail.

When I trudged down the stairs for breakfast, I wondered if my parents would be able to tell that my whole life had changed; that I was no longer the little girl they undoubtedly perceived me to be.

But they carried on as if nothing had happened—much to my relief.

"Are you going to the festival today?" my dad asked over his morning cup of coffee.

"I am. Ruby is coming to pick me up soon."

"Does she have many royal responsibilities today?" Mom questioned with a laugh in her voice.

I smiled and rolled my eyes. Ruby's imperial position had brought about several new jokes in my house. My parents loved her dearly, but couldn't resist getting in a good jab every now and then.

"She has some free time until this afternoon," I explained. "We don't want to miss our annual pig-out session at the shortcake stand." Ruby and I had always made it a point to devour as many pieces of strawberry shortcake as we could before the nausea kicked in, forcing us to swear off pastries forever. Or at least for a few hours.

"Will you be seeing Jake later?" my mom asked, a tiny smirk playing upon her lips.

The familiar feeling of warmth spread across my face as I forced myself not to throw up. "Yes, I'm going to meet up with him later."

"You two sure have been seeing a lot of each other lately," my dad observed, opening the morning paper. I suspected his intent was to sound casual, but thick curiosity laced his voice.

"I suppose." I shrugged. Maybe they could tell what I had been up to after all? That wasn't possible, was it? I wanted to die.

"What time is it anyway?" I asked, holding out my wrist to look at a watch that was not there. "I better hop in the shower—Ruby will be here soon!" And I raced off, relieved to be away from their parental scrutiny.

"You didn't even eat!" I heard my mom call after me.

"I'm not hungry," I answered. Shutting the bathroom door behind me, I ignored the pains of starvation as I turned on the shower and attempted to drown out my anxiety.

I heard Ruby honk about an hour later and ran down the stairs, hoping to avoid my parents. Thankfully, they were nowhere in sight.

"I'm leaving," I called over my shoulder and shut the door behind me.

This would be the true test. If *anyone* would notice that something had changed with me, it was Ruby.

"Hey, girl!" she chirped, as I slid into her convertible. "You ready to binge on strawberry shortcake?"

"You know it," I said, smiling back and buckling my seat belt. Ruby acted completely natural, as if she had no idea that my world had been knocked off its axis—in the best possible way.

"So how did the rest of yesterday go?" I asked. "I take it you made it through your many obligations okay?"

"Ugh—barely! I was up to my knees in pig poop and chicken feed!" she exclaimed dramatically. "I swear, I have taken two showers since then and I can *still* smell their animal stench on me!"

"What's on your agenda today?" I asked, laughing at her drama-infused tale.

"I get to host the pie-eating contest!" she announced with a smile. "It should be more fun than passing out a bunch of 4-H ribbons, anyway. Plus, Tommy entered it," she swooned. Things were starting to heat up between Ruby and Tommy Matthews, and I couldn't have been happier for her. I hated to admit it, but I was shocked that things were going so well. Tommy wasn't the usual type of guy Ruby fell for. He was much more laid-back and low-key, not her typical crush material. I guessed it was true what they said about opposites attracting, or at least I hoped so for her sake.

Ruby pulled her car into the festival just as the late-morning mob was starting to arrive. Saturday was usually the busiest day, and I felt we were lucky to have found a decent parking space.

The crowd was thick as we made our way through the fair, and we ran into several friends along the way. The atmosphere was relaxed and we were enjoying ourselves immensely, until a familiar voice rang out from the army of festival-goers.

"What's up, Monroe?" I would recognize that patronizing tone anywhere.

Brett.

"Just ignore him," Ruby advised, grabbing my elbow and steering me in the opposite direction.

"Hey, you two!" I could tell his voice was getting closer as we attempted to make our way through the horde of people. "Where do you think you're running off to?"

Before I knew it, he was standing in front of us with his friends, preventing me and Ruby from moving forward.

"Leave us alone, Brett," Ruby demanded. "Remember what the cops said the last time you got in our way?" It wasn't so much a question as it was a threat.

A slow smirk spread across Brett's face as he smugly lifted his chin.

"Oh that! My uncle cleared up that little *misunderstanding*," he sneered. *"*He works for the police department and took care of everything for me. He explained how things were gonna go down to those two rookie cops. They won't be bothering me anymore." He nudged his friends and they all began to snicker.

I swallowed hard as I felt a cold sweat come over me. What did that mean? That he could bully me any time he wanted without repercussion? My heart fell into my stomach as I tried to decide how to handle the situation. "I don't want to argue with you, Brett," I pleaded quietly.

"Well, I don't want to argue with you, either," he said sweetly, but the look on his face said otherwise.

"I just want to go home and pretend like nothing ever happened," I continued, my voice shaking slightly.

"Go ahead," he countered. His words didn't sound menacing, but they came out like a dare.

"Come on, Addy," Ruby said, grabbing my arm again. She pushed through Brett and his friends and we quickly made our way past them. I wanted to look over my shoulder but fought the urge. We walked for a couple of minutes in silence, then finally I couldn't take it any longer. I had to know if he was following us. And sure enough, he was.

Brett waved to me as we made eye contact, and I saw him quicken his pace.

"He's following us," I said in a panic, looking over at Ruby.

We lengthened our stride as we weaved through the crowd, Brett and his friends hot on our tail the entire time.

"He's crazy," Ruby blurted out, but I was too afraid to respond. My voice wouldn't work. I saw her look behind us again and then she called out, "Come on!"

The fear in my chest mounted, and my only thought was to run as fast as I could.

When the base of the festival came into view, I began to search for Ruby's car. I turned around one last time, hoping to find that we had lost Brett through the maze of people, but he was still behind us, getting closer.

As we exited the fair, a small noise escaped from the back of my throat, finally breaking the silence. I tried to call to Ruby, but was unable to form any words, yet I could sense that she was running alongside me.

Once the crowd was no longer a hindrance, we broke into a sprint. Relief washed over me when Ruby's car came into view. We were almost there. I was so focused on our escape that I didn't see the SUV until it was too late. The last thing I remember was hearing Ruby scream. Then everything went black.

Chapter Seventeen

"Addy, Jake's on the phone," Mags said. She poked her head into my room. Both of my parents were working, so Mags had volunteered to stay with me until they came home.

I looked up at her from my spot on the bed. The same spot I had been lying in for what felt like an eternity. I shook my head and returned to the book I was reading. When I didn't hear her leave, I cocked my head back in her direction. She was still standing there.

A sad, knowing smile covered her face. "This is the third time he's called today, honey. Don't you think you should talk to him?"

I swallowed the lump that was forming in my throat, but wasn't able to speak. All I could do was shake my head again as tears filled my eyes.

Mags was at my side immediately, sitting on my bed and taking me in her arms. It felt so comforting to have her there with me. I realized that I had not hugged her like that since the accident, and I collapsed into her warmth. Suddenly, my turmoil spilled over, bringing with it all of the tears I had been suppressing.

"It's okay, Addy," she said softly, stroking my hair. But it didn't feel okay. Nothing felt okay. Everything felt wrong.

"He's worried about you. You know that, right?" she asked.

All I could do was nod.

"You're going to have to talk to him sooner or later."

"Later," I cried, my voice muffled against her neck.

She pulled away from me slightly and looked me in the eye, wiping the tears that fell down my cheeks. "You owe him that much, Addison. He cares a great deal about you—and you care about him."

I hated it when she called me "Addison." It was her way of saying "and I mean it." And I didn't want to hear that, even though I knew she was right. She gripped my shoulders gently and then trailed downward, her left hand resting on the cast that covered my right arm.

It had been three days since the accident, and three days since I had last seen Jake. I just couldn't bear to look at him, I was so embarrassed. I knew it didn't make any sense. It wasn't my fault that Brett had chased me, or that I had been hit by the SUV. And it certainly wasn't my fault that I had ended up with a broken arm and concussion. But I felt humiliated all the same.

A lot had transpired in the days following the accident. I ended up having surgery to repair a closed arm fracture and spent the night in the hospital so that the doctors could keep an eye on my concussion. I had to speak with the police—and received an earful from my parents for not having told them what was going on sooner—and then was forced to face the disappointing news that Brett really hadn't done anything wrong by chasing me. I couldn't prove that he had ill intent.

My dad did, however, exchange words with Brett's parents, and I found out from Ruby earlier that morning that Brett had left to stay with his grandparents in Ohio. His mom would be joining him shortly after her divorce was final. I did sigh in relief over that bit of news.

Jake had come to the hospital as soon as he heard what had happened. He stayed all the while I was in surgery and into the night. I barely remember him being there—I was only awake for short periods of time—but the look on his face was seared into my memory. It was a mixture of emotions, ranging from worry and fear to anger and hate. I knew he blamed Brett for what had happened—I blamed him, too. But a lot of good that did me.

I told my mom the following day that if Jake stopped by, I didn't want to see him. I told her to tell him that I was "too tired" or that I didn't "feel up to it." She tried to protest, but I didn't care what she said—I just didn't want him there. The thought of facing him was too humiliating.

So, the only piece of unfinished business that remained now was Jake—yet I still couldn't bring myself to deal with it.

"I know what you're doing," Mags said, bringing her hand to my face. Very gently, she tucked my hair behind my ear.

I wiped at the tears rolling down my cheeks. "What do you mean?"

"You're pushing him away," she said quietly. "You have always been so independent, and you hate to let people see how you feel. But you don't have to be afraid to let yourself love him."

"But he's going back to Texas soon," I whimpered, my tears falling faster.

"That doesn't mean time and distance can't make the heart grow fonder."

"I'm too afraid. I don't want a broken heart."

Mags grasped my hand in hers. "We can't go through

life afraid of getting hurt. Letting ourselves fall in love means taking a risk. You'll never know what can become of it unless you try. In the long run, getting your heart broken would be so much better than never knowing what could be. Just think about that before you do anything rash."

I nodded and tried to smile.

"I'd better let him know you won't be coming to the phone," Mags said, getting up from the bed. "Are you sure you don't want to speak with him?"

I shook my head. "Not right now," I answered. "But please tell him I'll call him later."

There—I was one step closer to tackling the situation. I had listened to every word Mags had said, but for once in my life, I questioned her judgment. I had to talk to him, there was no avoiding that, but what the hell was I going to say? I knew I had made things even more uncomfortable by avoiding him, and I hoped he would understand. But it was Jake—and I knew that he would. He was amazing that way.

Mags smiled and gave me a nod, then turned to leave, closing the door behind her. I lay back in my bed and stared up at the ceiling.

I never expected to fall in love with Jake, or anyone, for that matter. I always figured love was something that would happen to me when I was a little bit older, maybe sometime in college. And even as I was falling, I didn't realize it. Not until Mags had pointed it out. And still, I could hardly believe it. Falling in love with Jake had happened too easily and felt so right—almost like breathing.

We had just spent an almost perfect summer together, and I had tried so hard not to think about the future and him leaving. But the truth was it had always been there, looming overhead, like a giant black storm cloud ready to burst. I had fallen in love with a boy I couldn't be with. And I kind of felt like if I leaned on him now—when I actually needed him the most—I would only grow to love him more. And I wasn't sure I could take that kind of pain.

Sighing deeply, I wiped at the tears that had started falling again. What was I going to do? I sat up in bed and reached for my cell phone. The only thing I could do was hit the problem head-on and stop being such a wimp.

I found Jake's number and hit Call.

I waited anxiously in the front room for Jake to arrive, reciting in my head over and over again what I would say to him. Now that I knew what I had to do, I didn't want to wait.

"Are you sure you're going to be okay?" Mags asked before she left for home. My parents were still working and I think she wanted to give me some privacy.

"I'm going to be fine," I reassured her.

She gave a smile before shutting the door behind her.

I took a deep breath and sighed, flopping down into the chair to watch for Jake's truck. When I saw it approaching the house, I felt the butterflies in my stomach increase.

After he parked, Jake slid out from the driver's seat, still wearing his cowboy hat. He took it off and tossed it into the front seat before shutting the door. My heart fluttered as I imagined falling into his arms and inhaling his intoxicating scent. It seemed so weird that I had not actually spoken with him since that day at his aunt and uncle's house. The day we had been together for the first time. This had been the longest we had been apart since we'd met at the very beginning of summer.

I'd waited for him to knock at the door, not wanting to appear too anxious. But when I saw the look on his face as I let him in, I melted.

"Addison!" he exclaimed, engulfing me in a gentle hug. His scent was just as wonderful as I imagined it would be. He buried his head in my hair and I felt him inhale. "I've been so worried about you. Are you all right?" he asked, pulling away from me, his eyes scanning across my arm in the sling.

I swallowed hard, wondering for the hundredth time if I was doing the right thing.

Yes, I definitely was. There was no other option. "I'm fine," I replied, giving him a small smile.

"Are you in much pain? Here—why don't we sit down?" he suggested, guiding me into the living room and toward the couch. His eyes were etched with concern and I felt so guilty for having put him through what I did.

"I'm so sorry, Jake," I began after we sat. "I should have called you sooner."

"No, don't worry about it. I understand," he said quickly. "You've needed your rest, and all I would have done was kept you up. I'm just so glad you're okay."

I sighed as he gently brought me into his chest.

"I am so sorry this happened to you, Addison," he continued. "I've been beating myself up over it. I should have been there with you. It never would have happened if I'd been there . . ." His voice trailed off.

I sat up straighter. "No, Jake. This isn't your fault. Please, don't blame yourself."

But the look on his face said it all. He *did* blame himself. And there was nothing I could say to change that.

"Jake, please!" I pleaded with him desperately. "I won't be able to live with myself knowing you feel guilty for what happened." No one was to blame. No one except for Brett—and he wasn't going to be a problem anymore.

"I suppose this needed to play out," I reasoned. "If it hadn't, Brett would have bullied me until one of us moved away for college. This is *not* your fault."

He sat up and brought his hand to my face, just the way I had always loved. Sighing, I leaned my cheek into his palm, relishing the sensation. I knew it might be the last time I would ever feel it. Without warning, he leaned in close, taking my breath away with a slow, deep kiss.

No, I could not let him distract me from what I needed to do.

"Jake, we need to talk," I said, pulling away from him.

He looked confused as he waited for me to speak. But suddenly, I found it difficult to say anything.

"What is it, Addison?" he asked after a moment.

I closed my eyes. I couldn't bear to look at him. "I don't think we should see each other anymore."

When I finally stole a peek at him he was staring at me, a look of hurt covering his face. "I don't understand."

"It's not that I don't love you, because I do. But you're leaving soon, and I just can't—" But I couldn't continue. How could I tell him that I needed to protect myself? It seemed so selfish, and I knew that it was. "I'm so sorry," I mumbled feebly, looking away.

When he spoke again, his voice was no louder than a whisper. "So, it's over? Just like that?"

It's for the best, Jake. Please understand. "Yes."

When Jake's eyes met mine, my heart dropped. Our relationship hadn't ended the way I'd always assumed it would, with Jake breaking up with me. Instead, *I* had broken up with *him*. Guilt washed over me as he stood up from the couch. Jake wasn't one to argue. There was nothing left to say.

"Please tell me you understand, Jake. You would have to end things anyway once you leave. I'm just trying to save you the trouble."

When I walked him to the front door, he turned to me. "Thank you for giving me a wonderful summer, Addison. I'll never forget you." He leaned down and gave me a soft kiss.

"Will you call me before you go back home? I'd like to say good-bye."

A muscle twitched in his jaw. Jake gave me a small smile and nodded. And then he was gone.

Tears pooled in my eyes as I watched his old blue pickup pull away for the last time.

I spent the next several days torturing myself, wondering over and over again if I'd done the right thing. It felt as if there was a giant empty spot where my heart had once been. Mags watched me quietly, but let me be. I knew she was wondering why I had done what I'd done, but what could I say? Letting Jake go sooner rather than later made sense at the time. But now, I wasn't so sure.

All I could think about was how hollow I felt. How ending things with him only made me feel worse. Locking myself in my room, I dialed the number for Jake's aunt and uncle's house, determined to make things right. It didn't take long before his aunt picked up the phone.

"Hello, Mrs. Grady. This is Addy Monroe. Is Jake there?"

"Addy, it's so good to hear from you! How's your arm? I heard you had a bit of an accident."

I cleared my throat. "It's doing better, thank you. Is Jake there?" I asked again.

There was an uncomfortable moment of silence on the other end. "I'm sorry, sweetie. Jake's not here. He drove back to Texas early this morning. Didn't you know?"

"What?" My heart plummeted. "Are you sure? He said he would call first before he left."

"I'm so sorry. He's gone. Why don't you call his cell—" But I had already hung up.

Jake left town? How could he have left town? He wasn't supposed to leave for another couple of weeks! Sobs racked my body as I lay back in bed, and a moment later Mags appeared in my doorway asking if everything was okay.

"He's gone, Mags," I cried. "He already went back to Texas."

She rushed to my side and sat on my bed, enclosing me in her arms. "I know, honey. I'm so sorry."

I pulled away, my eyes swollen from crying. "You knew?"

She nodded her head. "He left this morning."

"Why didn't you tell me?"

She cupped my cheek with her hand. "Would it have done any good?"

I shook my head, then buried my face in her neck.

"Shh," she soothed, rocking me in her arms. "Everything will be okay."

"I love him."

"I know you do."

"I made a huge mistake."

Mags leaned back, her eyes holding mine. "Addy, why don't you call him?"

I shook my head. "No, I can't do that."

She searched around in her pocket and handed me a handkerchief. "Why not?"

"Because I ruined everything! He left earlier than he was even supposed to. It's because he hates me." I blew my nose loudly.

Mags gave me a smile and touched my hair. "Oh, sweetheart. Jake doesn't hate you."

"You don't know that. I broke up with him and now he went back home. He doesn't want to hear from me."

"He loves you, too. That much I do know." She gave me a sympathetic smile. "This might be hard to hear, but you don't drown by falling in the water, you drown by staying there."

I shook my head again and lowered my gaze to the bed. "I just can't do it."

"Give it some time. Maybe you'll change your mind in the morning."

She gave me another hug and then left the room and I sat on my bed, wondering how I would ever survive losing my first love.

PART TWO

PART TWO

Chapter Eighteen

"Young lady, what in heaven's name are you still doing here? Shouldn't you be long gone by now?"

So much for a quick getaway. I took a quick peek at my watch before turning on my heel to greet Mr. and Mrs. Venkrackel as they shuffled hand in hand down the hospital corridor.

"I'm actually just about to leave," I answered with a smile. As sweet as the elderly couple was, I had plans I was already running late for, and I needed to get out of the hospital if I was going to make them before the restaurant closed. "What are you doing out of bed, Mr. Venkrackel?" I asked, walking toward them. "I thought I told you to take it easy today. You can tackle the hospital hallways tomorrow. Right now you should be getting rest." I raised my eyebrows and gave the eighty-six-year-old patient my best I-am-the-boss-you-need-to-listen-to-me-face that I learned from my dad. "How do you feel? Any dizziness?"

"Oh, I feel fine," he grumbled through a swollen, split lip. "I just had a little fall, that's all. No big deal. I don't understand why you're making me stay in this god-awful place overnight. I'm better off in my own bed. At least I won't be exposed to hospital-acquired illnesses there." The old man stared me down, the hematoma surrounding his right eye the color of a ripened eggplant.

"Oh, Walter," sighed his better half as she fluffed her stark white curls. "You have a concussion, for goodness sake! Stop giving the poor girl a hard time. She's just doing her job. Isn't that right, Addy? I told him this wasn't a good idea, but you know Walter."

I squared my shoulders and stuffed my hands into the deep pockets of my calf-length lab coat, ready to rumble with the feisty patient. "You should listen to your wife," I agreed, throwing Mrs. Venkrackel a grateful wink. "We need to monitor you for a while. I studied long and hard to become a physician assistant, and I know what I'm talking about." I lifted my chin, attempting to flex my authority. "Now, how about we get you back into bed?" I turned the couple around and began guiding them down the long hallway toward the in-patient rooms.

"What's the matter, Dr. Monroe?" asked Mr. Venkrackel with raised brows. "You don't trust me to get there on my own?" An ornery gleam twinkled in his hazel eyes as he continued to give me a hard time.

"I'm not a doctor, I'm a physician assistant. And you are one of my favorite patients, Mr. Venkrackel. I just want to make sure you get tucked in properly. That's part of my job, you know." I purposely widened my smile, hoping it would be charming enough to soften the blow. It could be a challenge at times getting older patients to take me seriously, especially when I was younger than most of their grandkids.

"Addy, really, you don't need to walk us back. We'll find our way just fine on our own," assured his wife over the rim of her rose-colored bifocals. "I've been tucking this old goat into bed for the better part of sixty years! I've gotten pretty good at it, if I do say so myself. Besides, I'm sure you'd like to start your weekend. Any special plans, dear?"

I gave the stubborn couple a smile and continued forward, glancing down at their wrinkled hands tightly grasping one another. I felt my insides soften at the sight. "As a matter of fact, I do have special plans. I'm having dinner with my best friend tonight, and then I'm taking my fiancé home this weekend to meet my family. We're going to tell them we're engaged."

Saying the words out loud still felt unreal, as if I was telling someone else's story instead of my own. Twenty-eight years old and I was finally tying the knot! I'd been waiting a long time to find my Prince Charming, and now that I had, I wanted the world to know.

"Congratulations!" Mrs. Venkrackel gasped, engulfing me in a toxic cloud of perfume and mothballs. "You're going to make one beautiful bride, Addy." She stepped back, her seasoned gaze meeting mine, and clutched my hands in hers. "Your family is going to be thrilled! And where is home?" she asked, smiling at me warmly and releasing our grasp, reaching once again for her husband's waiting hand.

I returned her wide grin with one of my own as we returned to our walk. "Lakeside. Near Lake Lanier. My family owns a farm there."

"Lakeside!" She cackled with delight. "We know exactly where that is, don't we, Walter?" She turned toward her husband. "We spent summers there when our kids were small. Such a lovely little town. Tell me, do they still have their annual Strawberry Festival?"

"They do." I nodded, suddenly filled with nostalgia. "It's one of the biggest events of the summer. I always looked forward to it while growing up." Memories of shortcake and caricatures flashed across my mind, and the desire to fill my lungs with country air grew more intense with every breath. You know, what they say is true. You can take the girl out of the country, but you can never take the country out of the girl.

"Did he at least ask for your hand in marriage?" Mr. Venkrackel chimed in, fiddling with the neckline of his starched hospital gown and pulling me away from visions of cold glasses of lemonade and sultry nights on the farm.

"Excuse me?"

"Your fiancé. Did he ask your parents first for their blessing?"

"Oh, Walter!" Mrs. Venkrackel scolded. "Stop being so nosy. Things are different these days. Kids aren't expected to ask a parent's permission first. It's so old-fashioned." She flashed me a knowing smile and nodded, indicating she had my back should her husband decide to protest.

"Nonsense, Helen! There is nothing old-fashioned about practicing good manners. It's the proper thing to do. Any respectable man should know that," he announced doggedly, rubbing an agitated hand over his thinning hair and throwing me the stink eye. "So—did he?"

I cleared my throat and glanced hesitantly at Mrs. Venkrackel, hoping she would honor the silent promise she'd just made and rescue me from the tongue-lashing I would likely receive. "Well, no he didn't. But that's only because Christopher's never met them before. I'm sure under different circumstances he would have asked for their blessing first."

"Christopher," Mrs. Venkrackel repeated, mulling over the name. "That's nice. Strong. Masculine. He sounds like a young man you can have lots of babies with."

I felt a blush move across my cheeks and forced a smile. Looking straight ahead, I nodded politely—what else could I do?—and avoided her gaze.

Out of the corner of my eye, I saw Mr. Venkrackel shake his head. "It doesn't matter. Everyone knows that asking the parents' permission first is one of the oldest rules in proposal etiquette. It's a fine tradition, one that shouldn't be broken. Whatever happened to honoring tradition?" he mumbled to himself, drifting off into a hushed tangent.

"Behave, Walter," Mrs. Venkrackel scolded, ignoring the quiet protests of her husband. "So, what does your Christopher do, dear?"

Ushering the couple inside the empty hospital room, a rush of pride washed over me, just as it always did when I spoke of Christopher. "He's a doctor. He works in Internal Medicine."

"A doctor, just like you! That sounds lovely. I bet he's wonderful."

"I'm not a doctor, I'm a physician assistant," I gently reminded her. "And he absolutely is. He's very dedicated to his practice." I flipped on the overhead light and walked over to the bed, turning down the top sheet. "Time for beddy-bye," I announced, turning toward a disgruntled Mr. Venkrackel. He threw me another dirty look but followed my instructions and slid into bed. I tucked the blankets tightly around him, just as I promised to do, and planted a kiss on top of his nearly bald head.

"You are so good to us, Addy. Are you this sweet with all of your patients?" Mrs. Venkrackel asked, her wrinkled face a mask of love as her gaze moved from me toward her husband.

"I treat every patient like family," I said, thinking of my own family back in Lakeside. I couldn't wait to get home to see them. "I never want to lose sight of why I first went into medicine. Having the opportunity to help people is such a blessing, one I'll never take for granted."

"You tell that Christopher he's a lucky young man," Mrs. Venkrackel said before I left the room.

"I will. And you two take care of each other. I'll see you when I get back into town."

Half an hour later, I pulled my silver Volvo into a parking space at Uncorked and headed straight for the bar. If I knew my best friend—and of course I did—she would be parked right where the action was.

"*You* are late, missy," Ruby announced, as she stood up from her bar stool and swallowed me in a tight hug. Her pale blond hair was swept into a low bun and she wore a form-fitting violet dress that covered her curves in the most jaw-dropping way. And I wasn't the only one who noticed. I observed more than one appreciative glance from the males scattered around us as she leaned into our embrace. "Thank God you're here," she whispered loudly as we settled into our stools. "The male population is getting pretty creative with their pickup lines these days. You wouldn't believe the crap that just assaulted my ears. I swear to God, doesn't anyone see the rock on my finger?" She visibly shuddered, reaching for her glass of white wine and taking a long sip. "Anyway, how are you? You look fab."

I set down my purse and waved to the bartender, summoning him over to take my order. "Thanks, so do you." I smiled at the barman as he handed me a glass of Riesling. I inhaled the sweet scent as I brought the rim to my lips, swirling the crisp taste around in my mouth. "And I'm good. Sorry I'm late, you know how it is." Ruby was well aware that my hospital rounds didn't usually end when they were supposed to. Oftentimes I stayed late, making sure every one of my patients was well taken care, questions answered, and Plans of Care up to date. It all came with the territory, and I was nothing if not thorough. "So, you're drinking tonight? I must admit I'm shocked."

Ruby threw me a disappointed smile and shrugged. "Yeah. I just started my period, so I figured why the hell not? Guess I'm not knocked-up this month—not for lack of trying," she announced, taking a sip of what I assumed was Chardonnay. "Speaking of which. Did you know that ovaries have a life span? Yeah, my doctor dropped that little bombshell on me at my last appointment. I mean, what the hell! Right? I'm starting to think mine might have aged prematurely. Tommy and I have been trying for a baby for almost a year now. You're in the medical field, Addy," she said, staring at me with desperate brown eyes. "Do you think my ovaries are over the hill?"

I bit the inside of my cheek and tried hard not to smile. I knew Ruby and her husband had been trying to get pregnant for quite a while, but these types of things had a mind of their own. You just couldn't rush fate, but telling Ruby that was not something I intended to do. "I think your ovaries are just fine. Try not to get all worked up, okay? Stressing out about it isn't going to do you any good."

But Ruby was not about to let the subject drop. "My mom said fertility patterns tend to run in families. My parents became pregnant with me on their very first try. And Nana and Grandad were the same way. What's the matter with me, Addy? Why are my ovaries trying to ruin my life?"

I stared at Ruby's crestfallen face and offered a

sympathetic smile. "It'll happen, I know it will. You'll get pregnant when you're meant to get pregnant, and not a moment sooner. Have some faith."

She shook her head, her eyes scanning the crowded restaurant. "I *told* Tommy he should be wearing boxers. If his sperm quality has diminished because of those ridiculous tighty-whities he insists on wearing, I'm going to be so pissed off!"

"That's enough." I laughed and held my hands up in surrender. "Too much information. You're going to make my ears bleed."

Ruby swallowed the rest of her wine and gave me a sheepish grin. "Sorry, but you know how much this means to me. I would give anything to have a baby."

My heart swelled thinking of my best friend as a mother, and I covered her hand with mine. "And you will. Just give it some time. I know it will happen for you."

The tips of Ruby's lips turned up slightly. "I suppose. I'm just not a patient person—you know that."

That was an understatement if ever I heard one.

"Well," I began, taking a deep breath. "You're further ahead of the game than I am. But . . . I'm closing in on you."

Confusion pinched Ruby's face as she contemplated my words. "What are you talking about, Addy?" she asked slowly, her voice deep with suspicion.

I held up my left hand, my ring finger catching the light in the most magnificent way.

Ruby gasped and reached out, grasping my fingers between her own to get a closer look at my engagement ring. "Addy, oh my God!" She stared at the three-carat emerald-cut that adorned my finger and let out a slow breath. "How did I not notice this? I always knew Christopher had amazing taste! This is absolutely beautiful.

Come here, you!" she shrieked and threw her arms around my neck for the most bone-crunching hug I'd ever received. "I can't believe you're getting married! Tell me how it happened. I want details!"

Laughing, I untangled myself from her arms. "It happened a couple of days ago, when I met him for dinner after work."

"A couple days ago? And you're just now telling me?"

"Well, I needed a moment to let it all sink in, you know?" I shrugged. "If it makes you feel any better, you're the first person I've told, other than the Venkrackels, but they don't count. Not really, anyway."

Ruby's perfect eyebrows crinkled in confusion. "The Ven-what-els?"

I waved my hand, dismissing what I'd just said. "It doesn't matter. You're the first person I've told that really matters."

A smile reappeared on Ruby's face and it was wider than before. She brought a manicured hand to her chest and sucked in her breath. "Oh, Addy. I'm so happy for you. You're going to make a stunning bride." She lifted her hand and brought it to my hair, gently pushing a soft caramel wave away from my face. "So, how did he ask? Did you know it was coming?"

"We looked at engagement rings last week. He didn't have a clue what I would like, so he wanted me to give him some ideas."

Ruby's smile fell. "You're kidding. You picked out your own engagement ring? That's not very creative."

I shrugged my shoulders. "You know Christopher—he's not big on surprises. He'd rather know what to expect. Plus, he wanted to make sure I liked my ring." I couldn't wipe the silly grin off my face. "Which brings me to why I invited you here tonight."

Ruby's eyes widened and she leaned closer toward me. Her expression was hungry, and I suspected she already knew what I was going to say next. "You've been my best friend for as long as I can remember—and really I think of you more as family. Would you please consider being my matron of honor?"

A loud shriek filled the small restaurant as Ruby jumped up from her seat again and wrapped her arms around my neck. "Oh my God! Yes, of course I will, Addy!" She stepped back, her hands still grasping my arms. "And I'll help you plan everything! Don't worry about a thing—I've totally got this." Her eyes were bright with enthusiasm.

I let out a relieved sigh. "I was hoping you would say that. You're the master when it comes to party plans. I totally suck." The last time I tried to organize an event, everyone left before the cake was cut. Well, that might be a slight exaggeration, but not by much.

It was my grandparents' fiftieth wedding anniversary, and I decided to have it outdoors. It wasn't my fault a small tornado passed through town that day. It didn't do much damage to the farm, aside from the cake table tipping over and a few small trees were cracked in half, but the party had dissipated just the same. Planning a wedding sounded terrifying and better left to a professional who knew what they were doing.

Ruby rolled her eyes. "I wouldn't go that far. I mean, yeah, that party was a disaster, but you can hardly be blamed for an act of Mother Nature."

"Still, I'd rather have your help, as long as you don't mind."

"You know I don't mind! I love weddings, they're my specialty. Just promise me right now you'll trust whatever I say. I already have so many ideas to share with you!

How do you feel about destination weddings? Like say, Playa Mujeres? Or maybe even Europe? You know, I planned *the* most fantastic wedding in Anguilla a few years back. It was absolutely gorgeous! There's just something magical about saying 'I do' in paradise." She paused. "Internists make a lot of money, right?"

I saw a dreamy haze cover her eyes and I knew I was in trouble.

Chapter Nineteen

When I got home later that night, I was met by a dark house. Christopher still hadn't made it back from his rounds at the hospital, even though it was going on eleven, but I understood it came with the territory. He had a heavy patient load, and a few of those patients had been stuck in the intensive care unit for the past several weeks, clinging to life.

I'd been working in the medical field for just over a year before I met Christopher. He was one of the youngest doctors making rounds, and without question the most attractive. And it wasn't just me who thought so. Every time he came by, the nurses, young and old alike, seemed to come out of the woodwork like hungry ants flocking toward sugar and gather at the nurses' station, shamelessly offering coffee and pummeling him with whatever questions that came to mind. "Dr. Bennett, would you like to order a CBC for that patient? Dr. Bennett, do you want Mr. So-and-So on a cardiac diet? Dr. Bennett, do these scrubs make my butt look fat?"

A few of the braver ones would try to cross that professional/friendship line, sharing what they had done over the weekend and trying to learn more about his personal life. But Christopher was smart, he kept the vultures at bay—which had earned him a bit of a reputation with some of the more aggressive and husband-hungry staff members, because God forbid a man didn't look at them twice. The nurses who shared the dream of landing a doctor didn't appreciate the brush-off and worked tirelessly to be the one to break through his tough shell.

However, Christopher had a strict policy of not mixing business with pleasure, especially after one of his doctor friends had hooked up with a medical surgical nurse. The affair had lasted all of five months and didn't exactly end well.

The couple found it next to impossible to keep their relationship professional while at work and on more than one occasion had been known to air their dirty laundry in front of their peers. After the affair fizzled, they were still forced to see each other several times a week at the hospital, and there was no escaping the gossip and accusing stares he now received from the nurses and their loyal aides.

So when Christopher finally asked me out, I hadn't seen it coming. He was breaking all of his rules. We had spoken briefly on a number of occasions discussing the status of this patient or that, and he'd always been very friendly. But I'd heard the whispers that took place between the nurses, dissecting the reasons why he never engaged them in conversation—he was already in a committed relationship, he was stuck-up, he was gay—and it never occurred to me that perhaps he might be interested. Then again, I'm not exactly known for grasping the obvious, even when it's staring me in the face.

One date led to two, led to three, and before I knew it we were house hunting—which really didn't sit well with many of the nurses. Getting married was the next logical step in the life we were building together, and I couldn't have been happier.

After I entered college, I'd gotten very involved in campus life and my studies before finally deciding to major in medicine. I dated quite a bit during those years, but never really had gotten serious with anyone—not until I met Christopher—and it felt good to finally be in a loving, committed relationship.

Everything was coming together perfectly, just the way it was supposed to. I had the perfect job, the perfect house, the perfect fiancé—even if he was a little busier than I liked him to be. But how could I not be proud of his dedication to his patients? We'd both gone into medicine for the same reason, to help those in need, and Christopher excelled at it. I looked up to him on so many different levels. He was smart and compassionate, exactly what a doctor should be. Christopher put his patients first, and I felt lucky he was mine.

My bags were already packed for the upcoming weekend in Lakeside, and all I really wanted to do was hop in the shower and climb into bed. There was no telling what time Christopher would make it home, especially since we'd be out of town all weekend. I knew he wanted to tie up loose ends and make certain everything was taken care of at the hospital before making the two-hour trek to see my family.

I hopped into the shower, washing away the stress of the day and contemplating the weekend ahead. Introducing Christopher to my family had me so nervous! I was certain they would all get along, but the gesture felt so . . . final. This was a huge commitment, and one I didn't take lightly.

Marriage is a sacred event, made in front of God and

our families. It's more than just companionship; it's an act of total self-giving. It's a man giving himself completely to his wife and a woman giving herself completely to her husband, in such a way that the two become one. I'd gone through *Cosmo* and every woman's mag I could get my hands on, taking every test I found confirming he was *the one.* And nine times out of ten proved I'd found a perfect match—why that one didn't agree was beyond me.

The water started to turn cold by the time I stepped out. Turning off the shower, I heard familiar footfalls coming from the bedroom and I realized Christopher must have arrived. I ran a fluffy peach towel through my hair, then wrapped it around myself before opening the door of the master bath.

"You're home," I said, crossing the room. "I wasn't sure when to expect you."

Christopher looked up from the suitcase he was packing, a slow smile spreading across his face. "Yeah, I was hoping to get here earlier, but it wasn't in the cards."

He reached toward me, pulling me close, and I stood on tiptoes to wrap my arms around his neck. Our lips met briefly before I pulled away. "How was your day?"

"Busy. We almost lost Mrs. Davenport today. She has pneumonia now. The poor thing—she can't catch a break. Plus, I had patients to see at two different hospitals, *and* I needed to stop by the office to take care of a couple things before we left town. But it's over now," he said with an exasperated sigh. "How was your day? Did you get everything taken care of?"

He looked at me with those kind, brown eyes and I couldn't help but smile. He had an irresistible boyish quality about him, with a classic, chiseled bone structure and very short brown hair that tapered down to the nape of his neck. I knew exactly why the nurses did a double take every time he walked past them. Christopher was very handsome, intelligent, and driven. He had a confident air that was impossible to miss.

"I had a good day, thanks. Took care of everything I needed to. Now I can go to Lakeside without a care in the world. I'm ready for a little getaway."

"Hmmm . . . I know, it's been a while, huh?" he said, returning to the clothes he had stacked in neat piles on the bed. "Did you meet with Ruby? Will she be our matron of honor?"

"Of course! How could she say no? We've been best friends forever. And on top of all that, she offered to help me organize! Thank God, I'm really no good when it comes to planning parties."

Christopher nodded but didn't look up from his packing. "Yes, I remember your grandparents' anniversary. Thank goodness they're forgiving people."

I rolled my eyes. "My party was crashed by an unwanted guest—I didn't send that tornado an invitation. By the way, we need to make plans to visit your parents next." I didn't want to get too involved in wedding plans before both of our families knew what was going on. It was then that I noticed the TV in the bedroom was on and an old black-and-white movie was playing. "What're you watching?"

Christopher glanced up from his clothes and gave a little huff. "Well, I'm definitely not watching it, you can change the channel if you like."

I studied the picture on the screen and noticed it seemed familiar, as if maybe I'd seen it before, only I couldn't place it. "What is it?"

"Only the worst movie ever made. *Casablanca*. You've never seen it?"

Casablanca. I hadn't thought of that story in a while. A smile tugged at the corners of my lips. "Yes . . . no . . . well, sort of. Not really."

Christopher laughed. "Either you've seen it or you haven't."

"Then I guess I haven't."

"Well, you're not missing much, I can tell you that. It's the most overrated film in the history of cinema."

"You think so? I thought it was one of the best. Doesn't it have some of the most memorable quotes ever written?"

"Yeah, if you like garbage. You can tell a movie is going to be bad when it starts out with that cheesy 1940s narration. The plot is slow, the acting is mediocre. It's really not worth the trouble."

"So, you don't think it's romantic . . . giving up the person you love for the good of your country?"

"Are you kidding me? There are so many plot holes you can hardly take it seriously. Hey—I thought you never saw it before? You seem to know an awful lot about it." He set down the shirt he was folding and turned toward me.

I shrugged my shoulders and wrapped my towel closer. "A friend told me about it once, but he thought it was one of the most iconic movies ever made."

"It might be iconic, but that doesn't mean it's good." Christopher placed his hands on my shoulders and turned me until we were face-to-face. Out of nowhere he asked, "You're happy, right?" He pushed a damp lock of hair behind my ear.

"Of course I'm happy. I'm about to marry my best friend."

Christopher chuckled. "Well then, Ruby's a very lucky lady."

I laughed. "Stop it! I wasn't talking about her. I was talking about you, silly."

Christopher cupped my cheeks in both hands. "I love you. You know that, right?" he asked, a serious expression covering his handsome features.

I searched his brown eyes and knew he meant every word. Christopher did love me, I knew that was true. He might be busy with his work, but he always took the time to make me feel important.

"I know. And I love you, too."

"Have I ever told you how cute you look in a towel?" he asked, changing the subject. His eyes took their time as they swept over my towel-clad body.

A pleasant sensation swirled in the pit of my stomach and I closed my eyes as Christopher planted a kiss on top of my nose. "I don't think so."

Wrapping his arms around my waist, he pulled me closer. "Well, you look *very* cute. Scrumptious, in fact."

I let out a giggle as he bent his head and kissed my neck, his lips leaving a trail of moisture as he made his way toward my ear. "Scrumptious?"

"Absolutely delicious." His mouth met mine and he kissed me slowly, releasing the towel I had tightly fastened around my chest and letting it drop to the floor. "Do you promise to walk around like this for the rest of my life?"

"I do."

I felt Christopher smile against my lips before we made our way to the bed.

* * *

"Oh my God, I can't wait to get home," I said the next day as we were packing our suitcases into Christopher's black Audi. "It's been so long!"

"It hasn't been that long. You just went for a visit a couple of months ago."

I loaded my accessory tote into the trunk and closed the door. "Two months is a long time to go without seeing my mama," I said, gathering my hair into my hands and twisting it up into a messy bun. "I hate to be away for too long. We need to think about going to Pittsburgh. If we want to start planning the wedding we can't keep putting it off. It'll only take us about eleven hours to get to your parents, and I think it'd be nice to spend a few days, don't you? I'd love to meet your whole family and take a tour of the town where you grew up."

Christopher came around and opened the passenger door, and I settled into the front seat and fastened my seat belt. "That would be nice. I haven't been home in a while." He bent down and gave me a quick kiss before shutting the door and walking around to the driver's side.

"Then it's settled. Maybe we can go within the next couple of weeks?" I said, once he was seated in the car.

He put the key in the ignition and brought the engine to life. "I'm not so sure that's gonna work, Addy. I have patients to see. I'm already going to be away from the office for the next few days. I can't keep taking time off."

I scrunched my eyebrows. "But I'd like to meet your family and tell them in person we're getting married."

"I'd like that, too. And we will, I promise. I'm just not sure when I can get away next." He pulled the car onto the street and turned to me and smiled. "But we'll invite everyone we know to the wedding. We'll do it up right, okay? I want to show you off to the world."

Nodding, I rolled down the window and leaned back into the seat, enjoying the breeze as the city of Atlanta passed by. How different Atlanta was from Lakeside, with its urban design and grand architecture. Atlanta was a town rich in history and spilling over with residents. It was a far cry from the fifteen hundred acres of corn, hay, and cattle where I had grown up.

I watched Christopher out of the corner of my eye as he maneuvered the car in and out of traffic. As if he felt me staring, he turned his head and gave me a smile. "Whatcha doin'?" he asked softly.

Taking a deep breath, I gave him a shrug. "Just wondering what it'll be like to be married."

"I imagine it'll be a lot like it is now. We already live together, so I don't think we'll be too surprised by each other's idiosyncrasies—unless you're hiding something from me?" he teased, glancing over with an amused grin.

I shook my head. "Nope. My life's an open book. I have nothing to hide." And I didn't. Levelheaded and logical, right down to my sensible shoes. That summed me up in a nutshell.

"So, tell me," he began as he rolled up my window and adjusted the thermostat in the car, "what's the farm like?"

Though I'd been home often, Christopher had never visited. A sudden prick of homesickness poked at my heart as I envisioned the area where I grew up. As a teenager, I'd always figured I would leave Lakeside as I searched for bigger and better things in the city, but the reality of a more populated area quickly lost its appeal. As much as I adored my life in Atlanta and taking advantage of the active nightlife, residents had to keep in mind that there was crime—a side effect of overpopulation I was not accustomed to. Crime in Atlanta was above the national average, a sobering statistic to a country-raised girl like myself. The most dangerous thing that ever happened in downtown Lakeside was the occasional pothole marking the street.

"The farm's great. It's been in my family going on three generations now. My grandpa Henry inherited it from his parents, and my dad is slowly taking over more responsibilities these days. I imagine someday the torch will be passed on to me."

"Be passed to you?" he asked, a look of shock covering his face. "No offense, Addy, but what would you want with a farm?"

I gave him a funny look. "What do you mean?"

"I mean, you're not a farmer. What're you going to do with it?"

I opened my mouth and then closed it. What did he mean by that? "I don't know. I've always loved it. I hate the thought of it going to total strangers. I guess I'll decide what to do when the time comes." I turned toward him in my seat and tucked one leg under me. "I get the feeling you don't like the thought of owning a farm."

Christopher shook his head. "The idea of becoming a farmer doesn't sound very appealing—to me anyway," he added. "Some people are just not cut out for that type of thing, and some people are. I'm not so sure I'm one of them."

I considered that for a moment, supposing he must be right. Not everyone was meant to live in a small town, and I was not about to make a big deal out of something that wasn't even an issue yet. "So, where do you see us in ten years? Or twenty?" I asked, changing the subject.

He shrugged. "Not too far off from where we are now, I guess. Maybe I'll own my own practice one day. And maybe I'll hire the best-looking physician assistant in all of Atlanta to come work for me," he said, throwing me a lopsided grin. His soft hand reached over and rubbed my knee. "Tell me more about the farm."

Pursing my lips, my mind wandered over the details of the property. "I've always thought it was beautiful. The fields stretch on for miles and the Blue Ridge Mountains surround the whole area. And the smells," I said, breathing in deeply, "the scents in the air are amazing."

"The smells? What do you mean, like manure?"

I let out a laugh. "No, not manure—I mean, you can smell that sometimes, too. But I was talking about the alfalfa hay that the horses eat. It smells so sweet, there's nothing quite like it. Haven't you ever been to a farm before?"

"Not since I was a child. And all I remember about it was that a blood-hungry goat tried to eat my jacket. I never wanted to go back after that."

"Because a goat took a nibble at you?"

"Hey, I was like three years old at the time. It was a traumatic experience!"

"Well, you won't have to worry about the goats at my family's farm. They're exceptionally well-behaved."

"Well-behaved goats?" He raised an eyebrow. "Is there even such a thing?"

"Of course. Mags wouldn't have it any other way. She's got everyone and everything in tip-top shape. No one dares fall out of line—human and beast alike."

"She sounds like an amazing woman. I'm excited to finally meet the famous Mags."

"You should be," I teased, throwing him a wink. "She's really looking forward to it, too. I just spoke with her the other day. She wants to know why I haven't brought you home sooner."

Christopher gave me a crooked smile. "Did you tell her I was in high demand?"

"Of course. I told her the nurses couldn't bear to part with you." I looked down and saw my hands were trembling slightly. I guess I was more nervous about bringing Christopher home than I thought. It was strange; I wasn't normally an anxious person, but then again I'd never taken a man home to introduce as my fiancé before. I had this gut feeling, an unnerving inkling in the back of my mind, that things were not going to go as smoothly as I would like. But that was crazy, Christopher was wonderful. There was no reason in the world why my family wouldn't love him just as much as I did.

A couple hours later, we entered the booming metropolis of Lakeside, Georgia, population 9,523. Everybody knew everybody here—the side effect of living in a small town—and if you weren't up to date on all the local gossip, then you must be living under a rock. Teenage me hated that part of country life. I preferred to fly under the radar and couldn't wait to get the hell out of Lakeside, just to enjoy some anonymity. Knowing that everyone knew your business was unnerving, and the world was so big. I couldn't imagine staying in one tiny town for the rest of my life.

Leaving behind the beautiful scenery and my close-knit family was the unfortunate technicality.

As I took in the lush landscape and majestic beauty of the Blue Ridge Mountains, I felt a deep sense of appreciation and longing. The chaos of the city was far behind me now, and only peace and relaxation lay ahead. Suddenly, I ached to go horseback riding along one of the many local waterfalls or feel the thrill of a whitewater rafting adventure.

Lakeside might be a small farming community, but it

was overflowing with the splendors of tradition and culture. I felt a rush of pride as we drove through the downtown area, passing the great white gazebo in the park and the art gallery and specialty shops that lined Lake Lanier. Already I felt as if my spirit was renewed, and I hadn't even made it to the farm yet.

I saw Christopher's eyes widen as we turned down the road my parents' house was on. "This is the farm?" he asked, his voice full of surprise. "Your family takes care of all *this*?"

"This is it."

My parents' home was adjacent to my grandparents' farmhouse, and the rolling fields spread out behind them as far as the eye could see. I couldn't help but smile.

Growing up, I had my share of responsibilities. When you're born into family farm life, you have no choice but to get involved, so I really didn't know any other way. Not every kid I knew lived on a farm; actually very few of my friends did, and I always felt as if they were missing out. I couldn't imagine not waking up to the sound of the roosters every morning, or going horseback riding whenever the urge struck. It was safe to say that farm life was something I'd been missing since I moved to Atlanta, but judging from the look on Christopher's face I knew he wouldn't understand.

"It's so . . . big. How does your family do it?"

"Well, they do have help. There are several farmhands that work here in the fields, taking care of the animals and the crops. It's run just like any other business," I said, rubbing the back of my fingers against his smooth cheek. He looked slightly unnerved, and I suppose I couldn't blame him. He was about to meet my entire family for the first time, and he'd just learned that I—*we*—would be inheriting 1500 acres of profitable land someday. That was a lot to take in.

I sat quietly in the passenger seat as Christopher maneuvered the car into a parking space, then sucked in an enormous breath after I realized my lungs were void of oxygen. *Now's not the time to quit breathing*, I reminded myself. There hadn't been many times in my life I could remember being that nervous. I bit the inside of my cheek, not knowing if I wanted to laugh or cry.

The sound of my heartbeat crashed in my ears as we slid out of the car and walked to the stairs of the porch. I inhaled deeply, allowing the scents I had missed to fill me. Putting on my most reassuring smile, I reached for his hand and turned to him. "Here we go. Remember, my parents' names are Carl and Renee. Now don't be nervous, I know they'll love you."

"I'm not nervous, Addy. And I am not going to call them by their first names. It would be rude. I'd like to make a good impression."

"Christopher, they're easygoing people. They would probably feel weird if you called them anything but!"

"I'm sticking with Mr. and Mrs. Monroe until they invite me to call them something otherwise."

Hiding my smile, I squeezed Christopher's hand as we made our way up the front porch steps. It was funny; for as long as I had known him, I'd never seen him act out of place before. Even now. After getting over the initial shock of seeing the farm for the first time, he was the picture of calm confidence—it was as if he didn't know any other way. Never once had he shown his vulnerable side, and I was starting to wonder if he had one. I suppose that's what happened when you grew up in a family of doctors. Both of his parents were surgeons and his older sister was, as well.

It was Christopher who didn't go the surgical route. Life had always been simple for him, according to what he had shared with me about his childhood. Family vacations to Europe, private schools growing up. Things always seemed to come easy for him; he didn't know any other way.

We climbed the steps and before we even made it to the door, it opened wide and my parents stepped out.

"Addy," my mother said, pulling me in for a tight hug. "It's so good to see you, honey!"

I let her swallow me up, then stepped back and smiled. She was as pretty as she was when I was a child. There were just a few smile lines lingering around the corners of her eyes and mouth, but other than that she seemed untouched by the years. Her dark blond hair was still long, and she wore it up in a ponytail, giving her a youthful appearance.

"It's good to see you, too, Mom! And Dad," I said, turning toward my father and falling into his embrace. I tucked my head into the crook of his neck and sighed, that gnawing, homesick feeling melting away.

"You look happy, baby," he whispered into my hair.

"I am, Daddy." I looked over my shoulder and stepped back. "I'd like you both to meet Christopher, my boyfriend." Stepping aside, I smiled as my father reached for his hand.

"It's good to meet you, Mr. Monroe. Addy's told me a lot about you."

"It's good to meet you, too. And please, call me Carl."

The corner of Christopher's lips turned up and he turned toward me with an expression that screamed, *I told you so.*

I rolled my eyes just as my mother went in for the kill. "Christopher, it's so nice to meet you! I'm Addy's mom, and you can call me Renee." She threw her arms around his neck and brought him in for a healthy dose of Southern hospitality.

"It's nice to meet you, ma'am. You have a lovely home."

My mother was a big fan of the Colonial my father and she had built after they got married, and she loved nothing more than giving tours. "Well, come on in! I'll show you around." She smiled sweetly, looping her arm inside Christopher's, guiding him inside. My dad shot me an amused look as we followed behind.

It was good to be home.

Chapter Twenty

Dad checked the time on his wristwatch. "Okay, your grandparents are expecting us to be at their house for lunch. Let's get a move on." He grinned. "Have you shown Christopher to the guest bedroom?"

"Mom's showing him now. I think she likes him." I smiled and rolled my eyes toward the heavens.

Dad dropped his voice to a whisper. "I like him, too. You did good, baby girl."

I felt the smile on my face spread from ear to ear. There's just something about having your daddy's approval that makes a girl feel like a princess. I couldn't stop the tears that filled my eyes. "I'm so glad," I said, throwing myself into his arms.

Dad stumbled backward and laughed. "Hey, is everything okay? Did you think we wouldn't like him?"

I shook my head against his chest. "No, it's not that. I knew you'd like him. What's not to like, right? He's amazing. And he's so good to me."

Dad pulled me in tighter and kissed the top of my head, just like he used to do when I was little. "I'm glad you found someone who loves you. You deserve every happiness this world has to offer."

Closing my eyes, I felt the tears slide down my cheeks, getting the front of my father's flannel wet. "Thank you, Daddy. It's good to be home. I've been missing Lakeside a lot lately. Atlanta's great and all, but it's not the same. I miss small-town life."

He ran his hand down the back of my head in one comforting gesture, and instantly my heart felt full in my chest. "I don't know how you do it. Every time I'm away from the farm for too long, I feel as if I'm suffocating. You're braver than I am, leaving home the way you did."

"That's because you raised me to be sure of myself. I never would have been able to move if it hadn't been for the love you and Mom have shown me."

"Maybe we did too good," he said into my hair. "I miss you being here."

And just like that I felt my eyes fill again. "I love you."

"I love you, too, Addy."

"Hey, guys." Mom stood in the doorway. "Can I get in on that?"

Dad opened the hug and invited her inside. "Just like when I was little," I said with a laugh, wiping my eyes. "A family hug."

"God, Addy, I have missed you so much!" Mom said, pulling me in tighter. "And I like him. He seems very sweet."

I laid my head on her shoulder. "He is."

"Speaking of Christopher, where did you put him?" Dad asked Mom with a smile in his voice.

"He's getting the bags from the car. You know, he said I could pass for Addy's older sister! He won me over right there!"

"But, Mom, I don't have an older sister."

"Oh, stop! You know what I mean. He's definitely a keeper, Addy. I'm glad you brought him home. It's about time someone caught your eye."

"And on that note, we need to get going. I'm starving," Dad said, breaking apart the family hug. "Addy, why don't you help Christopher take the bags to your rooms and then meet us at your grandparent's house, okay?"

"Sounds good to me."

Mom and Dad turned toward the door just as Christopher walked in with our suitcases.

"Christopher," Mom said, placing her hand on his arm. "We're going to head next door. You and Addy can catch up."

Christopher nodded his head. "We'll be right behind you."

We waved good-bye as my parents left, and I took my suitcase from Christopher and led the way up the stairs to the bedrooms. We made a quick stop at the guest room, dropping off Christopher's suitcase, then headed into my room.

"So, this was your bedroom, huh?" he asked, leafing through the papers and books that still lay on my desk. "It's not at all what I pictured."

"No? What do you have against navy blue?" I looked around at the walls I'd painted in the days leading up to my senior year of high school. The dark color reflected the mood I was in at the time: reserved, quiet, reflective. I wanted to start over, to begin the school year with a clean slate, and for some reason indigo seemed like a good place to start. Looking around now, the color seemed a bit depressing.

"I don't have anything against navy blue. Just seems sort of . . . inappropriate for a young girl's bedroom. Especially when the rest of the house is so light and airy."

"I was making a statement."

"I guess." He walked over to me and wrapped his arms around my waist. "Your parents are great," he said, brushing his lips against mine.

Leaning into his kiss, the nervousness I had felt earlier slipped away. "They like you, too. Both of them. You've already won them over."

"Just like that, huh?"

"Just like that," I said, smiling against his lips. "They know a good thing when they see it. And I can't wait for you to meet my grandparents. If I know Mags, she's prepared a feast. I hope you're hungry."

It was then that I noticed the bottle in his hands. "What's that?"

He held it up so I could get a better view. It was a bottle of expensive wine, his favorite. "I thought I'd give it to your grandmother. Perhaps we can have it with dinner."

A smile spread across my face. "Nice touch. You sure know how to woo my family. They love wine, living here in Lakeside near all the vineyards."

"So it was a good idea?"

"I think so. They're going to love it, and you." I stood on tiptoe and gave him a kiss.

A few minutes later we walked hand in hand across the field of white clover that led to the farmhouse, while birds called to one another as they swooped overhead.

I pointed out the different areas of the farm along the way. "Straight ahead, that's where the hay fields are, then behind us is the corn. And over there are the cow and horse pastures, and that smaller area over there is for the goats. The chicken coop is next to that, and on the other side of the farmhouse is the pond," I said, making certain

I mentioned every nook and cranny. "See, that's not so bad. You'd be a pro in no time."

Christopher shook his head and laughed. "I don't know about that," he said, and for a moment, I detected a sliver of unease. He shielded his eyes from the midday sun and turned toward the sprawling fields. "This is pretty overwhelming to an urban guy like me. My family moved from the inner city when I was little into the suburbs, and I remember that being a huge adjustment. Country life seems incomprehensible. I'm not sure how anyone does this." He brought my hand to his mouth and gave it a kiss. "But I love that this is where you come from. I think it's our differences that brought us together. I've always believed that opposites attract."

Our eyes met and I gave him a small smile, but the pit of my stomach felt a bit uncomfortable. A subtle breeze moved past us as we continued our walk, and the air began to feel thick and heavy. An American flag swayed gently on the flagpole in front of Mags and Gramps's house as a couple of farmhands worked in the distant fields.

My family's farm had always been a huge part of who I was, even as a teenager when I wanted to escape. It wasn't so much the way of life I was looking to get away from, it was the thought that I was missing out on bigger and better things.

As we approached the farmhouse, the smell of lunch wafted in the air around us and suddenly I felt my insides rumble.

Christopher's face lit up as he caught the scent on the soft breeze. "Is that your grandma's cooking I smell?"

"It is," I said, climbing the stairs to the back porch. Before opening the door, I turned around and gave him a hug. "Thank you for coming here with me. Everything is starting to feel so real, you know? Like we're not playing house anymore."

I felt him kiss the side of my head. "There's no place I'd rather be."

Peeling myself away, I opened the back door and entered the large country kitchen alive with the aroma of home cooking. As I took in the various dishes that were already set out, my mouth began to water. Mags had spared no expense, just as I'd figured.

The large rectangle table was draped in a white linen tablecloth with diverse concoctions spread out from one end to the other. The lunch menu was vying with the breakfast menu for most important meal of the day, especially when there were only six people invited to the table.

I peeked over at Christopher and watched as his eyes danced over the plates of hand-breaded fried chicken, mashed potatoes and corn bread gravy, cobs of white corn and homemade sweet rolls. And to satisfy the sweet tooth, a double-layer chocolate cake and strawberry pie piled high with whipped cream. To wash it all down, two bottles of white wine from the local vineyard sat chilling in buckets.

"Mags, you shouldn't have gone through all this trouble," I said, enjoying the look of surprise that crossed her face as she turned away from the countertop.

She began walking toward me, arms outstretched. "Addy! Come give me a hug, beautiful girl." I laughed as she wrapped her arms around me and pulled me in tight.

This . . . *This* was what it was all about. Love and laughter and family and fun. Family is always there for you, no matter what, even if you're the black sheep and move far away. They love you enough to let you leave and are overjoyed every time you return. No one will ever support and love you the same way your family will, it's a special connection you won't find anywhere else. Now it was time to introduce them to the newest member.

"Mags," I said, stepping back from our embrace. "I would like to introduce you to Christopher." I noticed the crow's feet at the corner of her eyes seemed a bit deeper than the last time I had seen her, yet her presence remained strong and confident, unaware of her advancing age.

Without hesitation, Mags enclosed him in her arms. "It's so good to meet you, Christopher. I've heard so much about you."

"It's good to meet you, too. Addy thinks very highly of you. I've heard nothing but wonderful things. I've been looking forward to getting to know you and your family. I'm grateful to finally have the opportunity." He held out the bottle of wine he'd brought with him. "This is for you."

Mags reached forward and took the bottle, then placed her hand on his cheek, her smile as genuine as the hot Georgia sun. "Thank you so much, that is very generous of you. We feel so grateful to meet you, Christopher. It's not every day our Addy brings home a friend. You must be very special to her." The look in her eyes told me she already knew what our trip was about. There was no getting past Mags. She placed the wine in the bucket to chill.

"Hey, there, Addy-Cake. How's my girl?" Gramps walked in from the family room with my parents trailing behind him. "I hear you've brought company with you."

I slid over and gave him a hug. "I have. Gramps, I'd like you to meet Christopher Bennett. Christopher, this is my grandpa Henry."

The two men exchanged handshakes and smiles. "It's

nice to meet you, sir. Your farm is quite impressive. Addy was pointing everything out to me on the walk over."

"Oh, yeah? You a country boy, son?"

Christopher laughed. "I'm afraid not. I grew up in Pittsburgh. It's a far cry from Lakeside. But Addy here has told me all about growing up on the farm. I especially enjoy hearing her stories of the farm animals, like when she was little and was chased by the chickens, or when she was kicked by a temperamental cow! I never get tired of her farm tales."

"You wouldn't think it was so funny if it were *you* who got kicked by the cow," I said, needling him in the ribs with my elbow. "In fact, if I'm not mistaken, you were afraid of a baby goat nibbling on your jacket when you were little!"

"What can I say, I was in foreign territory." Christopher smiled and put his arm around my waist. "I'm really looking forward to seeing the sunset while I'm here. I bet the view is amazing."

"You bet it's amazing," Gramps said. "You haven't seen a sunset until you watch it from the swing on our front porch. The crimson blaze just above the horizon as it gives way to a violet sky. I'll tell you what, you've never seen so many stars like what we have here at the farm."

"I'm looking forward to it, sir."

"Please, call me Henry."

"All right," Dad said impatiently from the background. "Let's get on with lunch, I'm starving!"

Mags gave a silvery little laugh. "Okay, the plates are at each seat and there's a serving spoon in every dish. You make sure you save room for dessert, Christopher.

I make the best chocolate cake this side of the Blue Ridge Mountains."

The conversation flowed easily as we loaded our plates and settled into our seats. I listened to the relaxed banter that went around the table and smiled to myself. God, I missed being home, surrounded by the people I love the most. And every time I came for a visit, the longing to be back grew stronger and stronger.

"Addy told me once before what kind of doctor you are," Mags said, addressing Christopher, "but I can't remember. What exactly do you practice?"

"I specialize in internal medicine. Basically that means we care for the whole patient, across the spectrum, not just in one concentrated area. We provide long-term, comprehensive care of both acute and chronic illnesses. It's my goal to one day run my own practice." Christopher turned and looked at my mom. "Addy tells me you're a nurse. What department do you work in?"

"I've been in obstetrics for almost thirty years. I was in nursing school while Addy was still a baby. Those were crazy days," she said, rolling her eyes. "Having an infant while you're still in nursing school is not something I would recommend!"

Christopher smiled. "I can imagine. I hear the nurses at work talking about surviving nursing school. I can't even begin to imagine how difficult it must be to juggle school and a family."

"Speaking of families," I said, pouring myself another glass of wine, "we have something we'd like to share with you." I looked around the table at the expectant eyes of my family and held out my left hand. "Christopher asked me to marry him and I said yes."

"That is, if we have your blessing," he added quickly.

A loud shriek went up and before I knew it, my mom was on top of me, hugging me until it hurt. Out of the corner of my eye, I saw Christopher shaking hands with first my dad, then Gramps while Mags stared on with a distant smile. Everyone took turns congratulating us and then finally I came face-to-face with my grandmother.

"Congratulations, Addy," she said softly, gathering me in her arms. "I'm so happy for you. I love you so much."

My eyes clouded over. "I love you, too, Mags."

"This deserves a toast!" Dad said, grabbing more glasses from the cupboard. "What do we have to drink besides wine? Do we have any champagne?"

Mags laughed. "Heavens no, Carl! Who do you think we are? I'm afraid all we have around here is another bottle of wine from the local vineyard. Had I known we would be celebrating, I would have been better prepared." She gave me a crooked smile. "Is that okay with you, Addy?"

"That would be perfect, Mags. Wine and dessert go hand in hand."

Wedding talk flowed casually over dessert, and afterward we stood up from the table and began to clear our plates. "I'll help you clean up, Mags," Mom said, planting a kiss on my grandmother's cheek.

"Nonsense, Renee. You go into the family room with the boys. Addy will stay and help," she said, looking over at me. "Won't you, honey?"

It wasn't really a question. "Of course I will. I was planning to anyway."

The smile on Mags's face grew wider and a hint of secrecy gleamed in her eyes. I knew exactly what she was up to, and I wasn't at all opposed. Some of our most memorable conversations had taken place over a sink full of dirty dishes, Mags washing and me drying.

First menstruation, first kiss, that porno magazine my innocent eyes had witnessed when I was a mere thirteen—there was no such thing as a taboo topic when it came to girl time with Mags. Mom and I exchanged a knowing look as she took her cue and ushered the men into the next room. I turned and gave Christopher a quick kiss before he followed the herd from the kitchen.

"So, a doctor, huh?" Mags said as she turned on the water to fill the sink. "That's a pretty good catch there."

I poured more wine into my glass and nodded. Following her lead, I began to slide the dirty dishes into the warm water. "I'm pretty lucky. He's amazing," I said, taking a glimpse into the next room. Mom, Dad, Gramps, and Christopher were seated in the plush cushions of the couch, the hum of the TV in the background, but no one seemed to be paying attention. Waves of laughter and easy conversation drifted in as the four carried on comfortably with one another.

Mags and I switched sides at the sink as we began our normal routine; she washed and rinsed a plate, then passed it on to me to dry. "Christopher is great, Addy, he really is. But you're engaged pretty quickly, don't you think?" she asked, slipping me a sideways smile. She was never one to mince words; it was one of the things I loved most about her.

"I know it may seem rushed, but we've known each other for quite some time now. We were friends of sorts before we began dating, and that's how it should be, right?"

"I don't disagree with you. You should most definitely be friends first." Mags was quiet for a moment as she washed and rinsed the next plate, and I took a quick sip of wine before she handed me the dish. "Now, don't get mad, Addy, but I have to ask—are you certain you're getting married for the right reasons? You're not pregnant, are you?"

I choked, nearly spitting the wine out of my mouth. "What? No, I'm not pregnant! Of course not! Oh my God, Mags," I hissed, looking over my shoulder into the next room, making sure everyone was out of earshot. Leaning in closer to her, I felt a slow burn crawl over my cheeks. "I'm happier than I've ever been. I have a career that I love, a beautiful home, and a wonderful man I'm about to marry. This is just the next step. What more could I ask for?"

Setting down the plate she was holding, Mags stared at me over the rim of her glasses, an expression I couldn't quite read covering her face. "It's one thing to be happy, it's another to feel satisfied. Christopher loves you, that much is obvious, but . . . do you love him? I mean, *really* love him? Do you feel satisfied?"

"Mags!" I responded, my eyes wide with surprise. "What's gotten into you? I don't understand where this is coming from. Do you not like Christopher? Is that what this is about?" The desperation in my voice was evident, even to me. What would I do if she didn't approve of my fiancé? I had never in my life doubted the advice Mags had given me; I trusted her more than I trusted anyone.

This . . . *this* . . . couldn't be happening.

"Of course I like Christopher, he's a lovely young man. It's just . . . I see the way you look at him, it's like you're not really seeing him. It's as if you're going through the motions somehow, but not really feeling them. Happiness is about being happy in your life, but satisfaction means feeling happy *about* your life. It's about the big picture. I can't explain it, but there's something about your eyes. They just don't light up the way they should. The way I've seen them light up before."

I stood there for a moment in total shock. *What is this? What is she talking about?* It felt as if Mags had just toppled over a complicated puzzle I had carefully constructed, spewing the tiny fragments everywhere. And the pieces, no matter how hard I tried to fit them together, just weren't making any sense. My eyebrows hitched together in confused offense. "Then you need to get your glasses checked, Mags. They seem to be a bit foggy."

Mags arched her brows. "Addison Victoria! Have you forgotten that I have known you since the day you were born? Your expressions have always told a story—whether you've intended them to or not—and I've become an expert at reading them. We have a shared history, you and me, and I know you just as well as I know myself. I've seen you in love before, Addy," she continued, her gaze softening as she watched me. "This isn't it."

Oh God, she was not about to bring up the past, was she? What happened when I was a child was irrelevant! My eyes suddenly felt wet. "Christopher is a wonderful man. I don't know what you mean."

Mags looked at me intently, her gaze almost desperate. "He *is* wonderful, I can see that. But I think you do know what I mean."

I knew exactly what she meant, and it wasn't fair. "Mags, you're being silly! I was a teenager then. I'm an adult now. You saw me fall in love for the *very* first time, when everything is new and exciting. Christopher's not my first boyfriend; it's not going to be the same. I'm more experienced now, more mature. Please don't turn this into something it's not."

Mags adjusted the glasses on the bridge of her nose. "I know Christopher is not your first boyfriend, but that doesn't mean it shouldn't feel new and exciting. When you're in love—*really, truly* in love—those feelings come hand in hand. I've been in love with your grandfather for over fifty years now, and every day when I wake up to him lying next to me it feels new and exciting."

I shook my head in disbelief. "But that's you and Gramps. You two have been in love forever, you're child-hood sweethearts! It's not fair to make that comparison."

"It doesn't matter if you've been together for fifty years or fifty minutes, Addy. True love shines through. It's impossible to miss."

My jaw jutted forward and I dropped my gaze to the floor, not knowing how to respond. Mags reached over and brought me into a tight hug. We stood there for a moment, the sound of our breathing the only thing heard.

"I'm not saying this to upset you, honey. Please know that," she finally said, putting her hands on my shoulders and stepping back to look into my eyes. "I would never want to hurt you."

"I know that." I quickly wiped a tear from my cheek. Swallowing hard, I felt my throat ache as I fought to hold back the flood that threatened to spill over.

"You may not understand this, but I *know* you. Inside and out. You're so much like me. And I wouldn't feel right if I kept this to myself. I *have* to tell you what I see. Even if you don't agree with me, even if you can't under-stand what I mean. I wouldn't be able to live with myself if I kept quiet. You care about Christopher very much—*I know that*. I just need to make sure you're positive he's the one. *Before* you do something you regret. I love you with all my heart, Addy, and I just want you to—"

"To be happy," I said, quietly finishing her sentence. The corner of Mags's lips tipped up into a small smile and she nodded her head. Placing her hand on my cheek, she wiped away a stray tear with the tip of her thumb.

"I love you, too, Mags. So much. You mean the world to me. And I understand what you're saying, and I appreciate it. I have always gone to you when I've had a problem and you've helped me work through it. In many ways, you're my best friend—just don't tell Ruby." I attempted a slight laugh. "But I *am* happy with Christopher. And I need you to trust me."

"I do trust you, sweetie, and I know you'll do the right thing. You're such a smart girl, ever since you were knee high to a cricket. And I am so proud of the woman you've grown into. You amaze me every single day. I never had a daughter of my own, just a bunch of boys," she said with a grin. "And you are so much more than a granddaughter to me—you're my best friend, too. I just want you to think about this. Okay? Promise me you'll consider what I said. And afterward, if you tell me you are a hundred percent positive Christopher is the one, I'll accept that and never doubt it again." Mags brought me in for another hug and I felt her sigh deeply against me. "We can talk more tomorrow, if you like."

I nodded. "I promise. I'll think about it."

"Thank you, Addy, that's all I ask." She was quiet for a moment before speaking again. "But I'd like to leave you with something . . . You never did answer my question."

I searched her expression, looking for a clue to what she meant. "What question is that?"

Mags's face softened as tears glistened in her eyes. "You never said you love him."

I dropped my gaze to the floor, the heaviness of the conversation taking its toll. Looking back up, I took a deep breath. "We'll talk more tomorrow," I promised.

Only, we never got the chance.

Later that night, while I slept in the bedroom where I had grown up, Mags passed away peacefully in her sleep.

Chapter Twenty-One

The entire morning was a blur. After my mother woke me to share the news, I felt my entire world crash down around me in tiny pieces. It couldn't be true. Mags couldn't be gone. Only, she was. And nothing I did or said would ever bring her back.

Gramps had found her just after the sun came up, when he realized it was seven a.m. and she had not yet awoken. She was lying in their bed, a peaceful expression eased across her face. She looked as if she were sleeping, but when he nudged her, she didn't move.

Instinctively, he knew she was gone. Not knowing what to do first, he called 9-1-1, then proceeded to call my parents to tell them what happened.

We raced over, still in our pajamas, and sat with Mags until the paramedics arrived. After listening for a heart-beat and feeling for a pulse, examining for signs of breathing and pupil reaction to light, Christopher confirmed her death, stating she must have had a heart attack in her sleep.

He assured us that she felt nothing, no pain or fear,

and that much was evident by the look of serenity that marked her features. Mags and Gramps had always been so happy, smiling and laughing together, but this time Gramps's expression didn't mirror hers. He looked like half the man he had been only the night before, when life had been almost perfect.

After they entered my grandparents' home, the paramedics contacted Medical Control, and before they transported her to the nearest facility, they allowed us some more time to sit with her, praying, crying, and holding her hand.

The aftermath of her death felt unreal, as if I were watching a movie and it was not actually happening in real life. *My* life.

I left the room so Gramps and my parents could say their good-byes in private and waited patiently for my turn. Sinking deep into the cushions of the couch, I listened to the sounds of life happening around me. The chirps from the orioles outside the window and the quiet echo of conversation taking place between Christopher and the paramedics felt mocking. Especially now, as death hovered in the farmhouse like an unwanted thief, snatching Mags away in the middle of the night while the rest of the world slept, unknowing.

When my parents entered the family room, their eyes were red and swollen. The pain of losing Mags was thick in the air, mind-numbing and suffocating, and I felt something flare deep in my chest. I stood up and walked to them, hugging both tightly. "Daddy," I whispered, my head tucked into the crook of his neck. "I'm so sorry."

His embrace loosened and I felt him crumple. I had never seen him cry before but he shook now, his sadness getting the better of him. Emotions clouded my mind but tears never came. As sad as I was, I couldn't cry. Not that day or the next. It was as if I couldn't believe what was happening, like none of it was real. Even when my grandfather came into view, appearing older and smaller than I had ever seen him look. The shock of white hair on top of his head shot out in opposite directions, and the corners of his mouth appeared weighted down, as if he would never smile again.

"I'm so happy you had the chance to see her one last time, Addy." Dad whimpered quietly into my hair, his tears wetting the long strands, matting them against my face.

"Me, too, Daddy." I kissed his cheek and went over to hug Gramps.

I wrapped my arms around my grandfather's neck and could feel him quivering softly. "I love you, Grandpa." He tightened his hold around me, but never said a word.

It was so difficult to see the strongest men I had ever known appear as vulnerable and fragile as children. I knew that no matter how much time had passed, we would never be the same; our family would be forever changed. Mags was our rock. She was the strong, stable matriarch every one of us depended on. She was our foundation, and every part of our family was connected to her in ways that couldn't be replaced. Mags lived for our family. She was the calm in the middle of the storm. She made everything better. *She* made things right, not because she fixed my problems but because she taught me how to deal with them, how to fix them myself. And now she was gone.

"Honey," my mother said quietly, placing her hand on my shoulder. "Do you want to say good-bye before they take her away?" Her voice caught in her throat as she choked out the last words.

I gave Gramps one last squeeze and turned toward my mother, nodding.

"Go take your turn, Addy. Mags would want that," she encouraged, giving me another hug.

I caught Christopher's eye from across the room and he nodded. Stepping back, I gave Mom a small smile. "Thank you," I said, and disappeared down the hall. I must have been in that hallway a million times before, playing hide-and-seek with my cousins as a child or just walking down it throughout the years to admire the cluster of family photographs that decorated the walls. Pictures of me growing up, of my parents, of my grandparents' other children and their wives and offspring, of Mags and Gramps and the farm. The celery green walls that had always seemed so relaxing and cheerful now lacked the lightheartedness I had known before. Everything felt dark and empty.

Slowly, I entered my grandparents' bedroom, my eyes on the still figure lying underneath the sheets. I walked up to the side, my breath hitching when Mags's face came into view. Swallowing hard, I grasped her hand as I settled down in the chair next to the bed.

Her fingers felt cool and rigid inside the warmth of my grasp. Thanks to my medical background, I had an understanding of what was going on, of the changes that were taking place inside her body as the minutes and hours slowly ticked by.

In a dreamlike state, I studied her outline and the fine lines that etched her face. Memories of Mags came racing back like waves rushing toward the shore. They crashed around me in a resounding roar, filling my ears and throat, suffocating me with their intensity.

I recalled an incident when I was a child, when Mags let me help her make an open-faced pumpkin pie the day before Thanksgiving. I watched closely as she kneaded the pie dough, tucking it inside the silver tin, then it was my job to fill the center with the homemade pumpkin filling. But the bowl was heavier than I expected and it fell out of my hands, its contents splashing all over the floor. Immediately, I began crying, worried that Mags would be upset. I sank to the floor, trying to clean up the mess I had made when suddenly I felt her soft hand cup my cheek. I looked up and Mags was grinning.

"You know what I do when things don't go exactly as I plan?" Sniffling, I shook my head. "I eat ice cream." She helped me off the floor and sat me down at the large rectangular table, placing a big bowl of chocolate fudge swirl in front of me.

"Now, you eat up," she said, "But don't tell your parents—they'll have my head if they knew I gave you a treat before dinner." She sat down with me and we shared the ice cream, laughing about the different fumbles she'd made in her life.

"We all make mistakes, Addy. The most important thing is that we learn from them and we never allow them to keep us from trying again." By the time we got around to cleaning up the pie, the filling had dried and crusted against the floor.

This is really happening . . .

"What am I going to do without you?" I finally choked out. Everything I wanted to say suddenly felt trapped inside my throat, as if speaking the words out loud would make everything real. And I didn't want it to be real. More than anything, I wanted to wake up in my bed and find it had all been a dream.

That Mags was still alive and well. That she wasn't lying lifeless before me. I didn't want to think about how she wouldn't be there to help me with my problems or to see me get married. That my future children would never have the chance to meet the woman who had influenced my life more than anyone ever had or ever would.

The thought that continued to play over and over in my mind was did she know how I felt about her? Was she aware of how deeply I loved her? The idea of never being able to tell her again . . .

"I can't believe this is happening . . . One minute you were here and the next minute you were gone. It's not fair!" I took a deep breath, wondering if I would be able to go on. "You mean everything to me, and I will always treasure the wisdom you have passed on. You've taught me to believe in myself and to look at the bright side of things, even when everything seems impossibly dark. You taught me to speak my mind, no matter what, even if my voice shakes when I do it. You've helped me to understand the importance of never having regrets, and how everything in life has a lesson, even if we can't see it right away. And you taught me how important family is, and that we should never take them for granted. Knowing you won't be here anymore, it hurts more than anything I've ever experienced before."

I felt my eyes moisten, but still the tears wouldn't come. Closing my eyes, I leaned back into the chair and shook my head, trying to wake up from the nightmare. But I couldn't. I was awake, possibly more awake than I had ever been, and this nightmare wasn't going to go away. I looked down at Mags, whose hand was still in mine, and noticed the beds of her nails were starting to turn a bluish-gray.

"I can't say good-bye to you." I winced, the words coming out of my mouth feeling unnatural and ugly. "You once told me that if I couldn't find a happy ending, maybe it was time to look for a new beginning. How is anything supposed to be happy now?" Anger started to bubble in the pit of my stomach, and before I could stop, it consumed me. "This isn't fair!" I said again, louder this time. "You're the strongest person I know. How could this have happened?"

I stood up and sat on the edge of the bed, trying to get closer. "And now I have to let you go. How am I supposed to do that?" I asked softly. "You're my best friend. I can't do this without you. I'm not even sure how to try!" I took a deep breath, letting the air fill my lungs until there was no room left. Slowly, I let it slip out, knowing my time was almost up. The memories, the hugs, the "I love yous," they were over. There would never be any more to add to the list we started twenty-eight years before. "I have never known pain like this before, Mags. And as much as it hurts, if I had the chance, I would do it all over again. You are the most amazing woman I have ever met, and I'm a better person because I have felt your love."

My shoulders tensed as I stood up from the bed. Bending down, I kissed the top of her head and walked out of the room, not looking back.

I entered the family room, my eyes searching for my parents. Devastation lined their faces in a way I had never seen before. The happy, contented expressions they'd been wearing the night before were replaced now by dark shadows and lines. They looked older somehow, broken by the void that now sat in their hearts.

And Gramps. Just the sight of him shattered me. He and Mags had been together since childhood; they had never even dated anyone else. He looked small and fragile as the paramedics went to the bedroom to lift Mags onto the stretcher. I couldn't even begin to imagine what he must be going through. The weight of his loss weighed heavily on him, and I wasn't sure how he would survive without the love of his life, the woman he had been with for so many years.

"Addy," Mom said, walking over and putting her arm across my shoulders. "Let's go home for a bit, leave your father and Gramps some time to themselves."

"Are you sure we shouldn't stay? Don't we have to start making arrangements?"

"If there's anything I can do to help, please let me know," Christopher offered, walking over to where we stood. "I can make the initial phone calls, put the wheels in motion. That way your family can grieve without having to worry about arrangements."

Mom placed her hand on Christopher's arm. "That's very nice of you to offer. Let me talk to Addy's father first and see what he thinks. Thank you." Her lips pulled up at the corners but the smile never reached her eyes.

Moving closer to him, I allowed Christopher to wrap me into a tight hug. "How are you?" he asked quietly.

I shrugged my shoulders and leaned against him, shaking my head. "This can't be happening."

Christopher turned his head toward mine, placing his lips on my forehead. "I'm so sorry, Addy."

"Me, too," I said, sighing deeply.

"Are you two hungry?" Mom asked. "Let's go back home and I'll make a late breakfast."

Slowly, we made our way onto the front porch and then through the meadow separating our house from my grandparents'.

Looking out over the fields, as the early afternoon sun shined brightly across the tips of the crops, memories came flooding back to me. Memories of my childhood, memories of Mags. I let out a shallow sigh, my heart plummeting into my stomach. Glancing over my shoulder, I saw the stretcher being raised into the ambulance as we walked through the door.

But still, I couldn't cry. I wanted to. I knew my tears were buried behind my eyes, they just wouldn't come out. They sat like an overwhelming weight inside me, unwilling to budge.

I sat at the kitchen table and watched Mom as she worked over the stove, making a breakfast I knew I would never eat. Occasionally, she would sniffle or raise her hand to her cheek, brushing aside a tear. It was so easy for her to feel the pain. What was wrong with me? If I could just let go, maybe the heaviness that surrounded me would begin to ease. Maybe my lungs would be able to take a cleansing breath, maybe the ache in my heart would calm.

I was vaguely aware of my mother placing a plate in front of me. Numbly, I pushed around the eggs with my fork, not eating or paying attention to the quiet conversation taking place at the table. It wasn't until Christopher squeezed my knee with his hand that I finally looked up. "Hey," he said with a small smile.

"Hey." My eyes scanned over the kitchen and I realized we were the only two there. "Where's my mom?"

"She went to take a shower. I think she just needed to be alone." He nodded his head toward my untouched plate of food. "You're not hungry?"

I shook my head. "Not really."

"You should probably try to eat something."

"I know. I will, just—not right now." I stood up from the chair and spilled the contents of my plate into the garbage. Filling the sink with warm water, I started to wash the dishes from breakfast when suddenly I felt Christopher come up behind me, the warmth of his hands resting firmly on my shoulders.

"Addy, what can I do for you?"

Turning into him, I laid my head against his chest. "What you're doing right now. Just hold me."

We stood for several moments, neither one of us saying a word. Finally, the ring of a cell phone pierced through the silence. Christopher stepped back and reached into the pocket of his shorts, a look of dismay covering his face when he took in the display screen of his phone. "I'm sorry. I have to take this." He gave me an apologetic smile as he walked toward the back door and stepped out into the sunshine, closing the door behind him.

Sinking back into the kitchen chair, I wrapped my robe tightly around me, realizing for the first time I was still wearing my pajamas.

Too exhausted to care, my eyes homed in on a microscopic scrape marking the wall, staring at it until my mind went blank. Avoiding thoughts, I just sat in silence, allowing myself to retreat into the comfortable stillness of the house. My eyes closed as I relaxed against the back of the seat, the rich textures of outdoor sounds filling my senses. The noises didn't feel as mocking as they had earlier, now they were just there. A reminder that life was still going on around me, even though one existence had been cut short.

I could almost hear Mags's voice inside my head telling me things would be okay. "Everything in life is temporary," she would say. "Every time it rains, it always stops. After the darkness, there is always light. Sometimes these things are easy to forget and we get caught up believing our pain will last forever. But it won't. Nothing lasts forever. Even life."

The sound of Christopher opening the back door caused me to open my eyes. "Addy, I'm so sorry to do this to you, but I have to leave." A look of alarm covered his face.

I sat up straight in my chair. "What? Why? Is something wrong?"

He pushed a hand through his cropped hair. "Mrs. Davenport took a turn for the worse. She's not doing well at all."

"But there are other doctors working this weekend. Surely they can take care of things until you get back?"

Christopher paced the length of the kitchen in long strides, his expression torn. "I know, but I'm her primary doctor. No one knows her the way I do."

I held my breath. "When do you have to leave?"

Stopping in front of me, he took my hands, pulling me to a standing position. "The sooner the better."

I opened my mouth to say something, then closed it again. After everything that just happened he wanted to leave? "But what about Mags and my family? What about me?"

Drawing in a deep breath, his gaze met mine and held it tightly. "Addy, this is my job, you know that. I'm never truly off work." He gave me a sympathetic smile and lifted his hand to my cheek. "I am so sorry you lost your grandmother, and I'll do my best to make it back in time for the funeral. But Mrs. Davenport is still alive, and I have a responsibility to take care of her."

"What about your responsibility to take care of me?" I asked, disbelief seeping into my words. "I'm going to be your wife, then *we'll* be family. Will you put your patients before me then? Will you put them before our children?"

"We never spoke about having children."

I felt a rush of warmth cover my face. "We *have* spoken about children! You've always said you love them."

"I do love them, but that doesn't mean I want them." He sighed again, releasing the air slowly. "Look, Addy. My career is very demanding of my time, and I can't choose when emergencies will happen. If you want to have children, that's something we can talk more about, but you have to understand that this is my job. Being a doctor is what I went to school for, it's what I have worked so hard to obtain. There may be times when I have to leave and you need to handle things on your own." His expression softened as he watched his words register. "I love you, Addy, that will never change, but this is who I am. I'm sorry if it upsets you. I know this is the first time we've been involved in a situation like this, and I can't promise it won't happen again."

The honesty of his words sank in. Was he foreshadowing our future together? My gaze fell as I contemplated what to say. "What if you can't make it back in time? What if you miss the funeral?"

Christopher gave me a slight shrug. "Then I won't make it back. Even if I can't be with you, it doesn't mean

I won't be thinking of you and your family." He brought me into his chest and brushed a soft kiss over my forehead. "I'm very sorry."

I bit my bottom lip, not knowing how to respond. Christopher wasn't a bad guy, he was just deeply dedicated to his profession. I couldn't blame him for that. Nodding against the soft cotton of his nightshirt, I felt my breath catch.

"I know you are. I'm sorry, too."

Chapter Twenty-Two

An hour later, Christopher had his belongings packed into his car and said good-bye to my parents, offering his deepest sympathy and apologizing for having to leave so abruptly. They said they understood, sometimes work can't wait, but it was impossible to read their expressions beyond their words. They were caught up in grief, their thoughts on the tragedy that had fallen upon them.

Christopher held me in a tight embrace before settling down into the driver's seat. "Are we okay?" he asked, his eyebrows raised in question.

Stepping back, I nodded. "We're okay. You have a job to do, I understand that."

He adjusted himself in the seat and closed the door, rolling down the window. "I love you. I'll call you tomorrow and let you know how things are going. Maybe by then your family will have a better idea of when the funeral will be."

I nodded again. "That sounds good." Christopher reached for my hand and brought it to his lips, smiling slightly as he gave it a soft kiss. I studied his face. It was obvious he felt guilty about leaving me behind. "Drive safely."

"I will." He gave my hand one last squeeze before letting go.

Standing in the driveway, I watched the black Audi as it pulled smoothly out of the drive, turning onto the street and away from the farm. I swallowed hard, my chest feeling hollow. Unease crept into my thoughts, different from what I had felt that morning after learning about Mags. This new sensation settled in deep, stirring up confusion and debate. The conversation Mags and I had started the night before, when she asked if I was certain about spending my life with Christopher, began to nag at me. I'd blown it off when she'd brought it up, but now it was back, staring me in the face. Trusting Mags's advice was never something I had questioned before; why was I questioning it now? Could she somehow see something about my relationship I couldn't? And now I would never know. The possibility of continuing our conversation had been snuffed out in the wee hours of the morning, when she'd taken her last breath.

There was a point in my life, not very long ago, when I knew exactly what I wanted, but now I wasn't so sure. How could my entire existence fall to pieces in such a short amount of time? It was impossible for me to know if I was questioning my future with Christopher based on a heart-to-heart with Mags, or if I had every right to contemplate it based on his decision to leave me when I needed him most. And I *was* questioning it. Maybe his leaving was a sign.

What if the connection I thought we shared wasn't as strong as I had believed? I understood he had a job to do, and it was an important one at that, but the choice to return to Atlanta cut deep. It stung in a way nothing else ever had. Betrayal and disappointment devoured me, and I couldn't tell if my feelings were justified or if I was being selfish. Either way, Christopher's departure tormented me, and I trembled with the thought of it.

I turned and walked back toward the house, taking my time as I climbed the stairs to the front porch. Sitting down on the top step, I stretched my legs out before me, my nightgown hitching up above my knees. I tilted my head toward the sky, closing my eyes and allowing the soft rays of the sun to warm my skin as they plunged to the earth. The events of the day were taking their toll, and every part of me ached with exhaustion.

I dipped my head to the right and leaned forward, my gaze settling on the farmhouse next door. Gramps was there, all alone, for the first time in God knew how long.

For the past five decades, he and Mags had never been far from one another. Even during the day when he was working in the sweltering fields, she was always nearby, waiting for him to return. Their love was noble and timeless, surviving the ups and downs of life in a way many couples were not able to mimic. What was he doing now? What was going through his mind?

My heart swelled with sympathy and I swallowed hard, trying to relieve the ache in my throat. I was torn between wanting to give him space to grieve and wanting to go to him, to comfort him and let him know everything would be okay. But I couldn't. I didn't know if things would ever be okay again.

So many emotions filtered through my thoughts. This was the hardest challenge I had ever encountered and I felt overcome by shock, confusion, and regret. *Why did I ever move away? How could I have been so selfish? All those years wasted . . .*

I knew I was being silly, that I needed to live my own

life, but I couldn't help feeling shameful at the same time. I felt hungry for answers and solutions I knew I would never get.

Placing my hands behind me, I pushed myself up from the porch and stood, slowly stretching the muscles in my back and shoulders. Every part of me felt knotted and tense, weak with grief and loss. I need time to myself, to process my bereavement, but more important than that, I needed to check on my parents. As hard as losing Mags was on me, I knew they were hurting, as well.

When I walked into the house, soft music wafted through the rooms, a soulful tune I recognized immediately. I never could understand my grandmother's love of old country music. When I would ask her why she listened to it, she would always say it inspired her. At the time I thought she was being silly, but now I could feel it. The passion in the singer's voice was undeniable, and a feeling of longing settled in my chest.

I followed the sound into the kitchen, where I found my parents sitting at the table, their hands folded neatly in front of them on the kitchen table, their eyes staring, unseeing.

"What are you listening to?"

I sat down at the table next to my mom. "Humming-bird cake? I haven't had that in ages."

Mom reached over to stroke my hair, grasping a thick lock and letting it slip slowly through her fingers. "I know. She sure did love to bake." A sad smile played on her lips. "I remember when you were little, you always wanted to help her in the kitchen. You remind me so much of her, you know that? There is so much of Mags in you."

I smiled back, pride swelling in my chest. "Why did you make a hummingbird cake?"

"Well, you know I'm no Mags in the kitchen," she said with a chuckle, "but someone from work was retiring, and hummingbird cake is her favorite. Your grandmother was kind enough to help me make it."

"I'm going to miss her cooking. I'm going to miss everything about her," I said, looking over at my father's expression. His eyes were downcast as a tear slid down his cheek, and my heart broke all over again.

Mom and I exchanged a look, and I saw the worry heavy on her face.

"Nothing will ever be the same," Dad said suddenly. "Dinners, holidays, the farm." His voice cracked with emotion. "And Dad . . . How is he ever going to get by without her?"

I reached over and grasped his hands in my own. "You're right, Daddy. Things will never be the same, but that doesn't mean they can't be good again. It's going to take some time for us to heal. I don't think we ever will entirely, especially when we weren't expecting to lose her so suddenly, but I know Mags would want us to move on, or at least do our best to try. It won't be easy and we'll be lost for a while, maybe a long while, but we'll get through this together. I think we should take comfort in knowing how much she loved us and knowing that she knew how much we loved her. Not every family can say that."

My father lifted his moist eyes until they met mine and he gave me a small smile. "You sound just like her right now." He leaned over and gathered me in his arms. "I'm so glad you're here with us."

I closed my eyes and pressed my cheek against him. "Me, too. I'll stay as long as you need me to."

He kissed the top of my head. "Oh, baby girl. You

have a life back in Atlanta. We'll be fine here. Don't you worry."

"If you change your mind, just say the word and I'll stay." Taking a deep breath, I felt a slight weight lift from my shoulders. If my family needed me, back home was where I would be. Everything in Atlanta could wait. A wave of relief washed over me, and even if it was only for a moment, I welcomed it. A part of me had died that morning with Mags, but I knew now everything would be okay. It had to be.

After removing the pajamas I had worn all day I hopped into the shower, allowing a small amount of anger and pain to wash away as the stream of hot water beat against my body. I knew the respite was temporary— every moment brought on new emotions—but I would take any bit of relief I could find.

When the water ran cold, I stepped out of the bath and wrapped a towel tightly around me, then wandered back to my bedroom. As I opened the closet door, my eyes danced over a wardrobe I hadn't seen in ten years. I pulled out a sundress and my old boots, the red leather soft with age. Dropping the towel, I slipped the dress over my head, the white fabric skimming against my bare skin.

My fingers worked their way through wet strands of hair, releasing the long tangles before they fell in waves around my shoulders. As I slid on my cowboy boots, my eyes caught the reflection in the full-length mirror attached to my closet door.

Standing tall, I walked over to it and stared at the image looking back at me. It had been a long time since I had let my hair flow naturally, without using a straightener to smooth out the waves. The dress and boots still fit comfortably, and seeing them now brought a smile to my lips.

The girl in the mirror looked like someone I had known a very long time ago. Someone who was young and innocent and full of life and enthusiasm, dreaming about the future that lay ahead. She was a far cry from the reserved, coiffed professional whose gaze held mine only the day before.

I reached for the bottle of moisturizer in my overnight bag. I put a big glop in my hand and began to rub it into my skin. I moved around my room as I worked the lotion up my arms, stopping briefly at the pictures lying fanned out across my desk.

Picking them up, I studied the first one, a photograph of Ruby and me during our senior year of high school, for several moments before moving it to the back of the pile.

The next one, I lingered over longer. It was an image of my grandparents' kitchen, the long rectangular table filled with family and friends enjoying the Sunday-night dinner Mags and Gramps hosted once a month.

It was nothing fancy—usually everyone brought a dish and gathered together after church for a quiet, relaxing day free from work on the farm. When I was younger, Mags would always give me important responsibilities, mashing the potatoes or setting the table, and make such a big deal over my efforts, even if I did make a big mess most of the time.

I moved over to the pictures that hung on my wall, getting lost in the memories of my childhood. Photographs of me growing up on the farm and pictures taken during my school years. One of Gramps kissing Mags on the cheek and another of Mags and me at my high school graduation, her arm wrapped tightly around my shoulder and a look of pride across her face.

There were even some taken of Ruby and me at the Strawberry Festival, including the year she'd been crowned queen.

I walked to my bookshelf, pulling out a leather-bound album, and sat on my bed. Turning the cover, I slowly flipped through nearly eighteen years of caricatures, my smile growing wider with each one.

Until I came to the final one drawn of me the summer before my senior year. My fingers traced the outline of the person sketched next to me, the only time I'd ever had company during a sitting. The dark waves and brilliant blue eyes stared back at me, and a feeling of nostalgia took me by surprise.

"Are you okay? You have a funny look on your face."

I closed the album and turned to the sound of my mother's voice. "I'm fine. Just reminiscing is all." I stood up from the bed and gave her a hug. "I'd like to take care of the funeral arrangements." I picked up a handful of pictures. "I'll put together something everyone will enjoy so you don't have to worry about it. Then you and Dad can concentrate on Gramps."

Mom's shoulders sagged in relief. "That would be great, Addy. Thank you. Dad is with Gramps now," she said, shaking her head. "I can't believe how blindsiding this is."

"How are you?" I asked.

She took a deep, ragged breath. "Coping," she said with a wistful smile. "I'm so sorry you lost your grandmother. I know how special she was to you." Her eyes grew misty as they flitted across my face, trying to gauge my response. "You don't have to be so strong, you know that, right? It's okay to cry."

I nodded. "I'm not a big crier, I never have been. You know that."

"I know. You've always handled things your own way. I just want you to know that it's okay. Crying is a release, it's cleansing. We all need to cry sometimes. You don't have to be strong for us, if that's what you're doing." She reached out and rubbed my upper arm.

The corner of my lips tipped up. "Now *you* sound like Mags."

"I wish!" she said, a small laugh escaping her lips. She was quiet for a moment as her face clouded over. "You and Mags were thick as thieves. There were times I felt jealous of your relationship."

My eyes opened wide with surprise. "You were jealous? But why?"

Mom let out a sigh and sat down on my bed. "It just seemed you preferred her to me, sometimes. The way you two would carry on in the kitchen, laughing like schoolgirls. And as you got older, it seemed you shared more with her than with me. I get it now, but back then it was difficult to see. I know kids need someone else besides their parents to talk to, and I am so glad you had Mags. I feel foolish that I ever let it bother me."

I sat down, joining my mom on the edge of the bed. "I hope I didn't make you feel bad. It was never my intention."

"Oh, no, Addy! I never felt bad, just a little left out sometimes. It was silly, I know that now." She took my hand and held it firmly in hers. "I am so glad you had Mags in your life. I know she had a big impact on you, and your father and I are so proud of how you turned out. She helped mold you into the beautiful and gracious woman you are today, and for that I will forever be grateful."

I studied her face, trying to read between the lines of what she said. "You and Dad did that, too. I have learned so much from the both of you. There has never been a time in my life where I felt I couldn't come to you."

Something tugged at the corners of her mouth. She sighed and closed her eyes for a moment, and when she opened them she gave me a wide smile. "I feel so lucky you are mine, you know that?" She leaned in for another hug.

We sat quietly and watched an oriole sing on the perch of the windowsill, its brilliant orange plumage blazing brightly in the sun. Veering back, she studied me with squinted eyes. "I see you've raided your closet," she said with a smile.

I looked down at the dress and boots I wore and grinned. "They still fit," I said, looking up at her. "What do you think?"

Her eyes moved down my frame, taking in my outfit. "I think you look amazing. Just like you did in high school. I'm still not sure about those red boots, though."

Before I could stop myself, I laughed. "You never did like them! Why not? I never did understand that."

A blush covered Mom's cheeks. "I didn't think red was an appropriate color for you. It felt too passionate. I didn't want my baby girl to grow up."

"You know you couldn't stop that from happening. I had to grow up, whether you liked it or not," I said quietly.

"It doesn't make sense, but you'll understand one day when you're a mother."

I felt the smile melt off my face. "I suppose."

Mom pursed her lips and leaned back. "How do you feel about Christopher leaving?" she asked, as if she knew what I was thinking.

I shrugged my shoulders and looked away. "He has an

important job to do. I guess I should get used to that." I looked over at her and thought I saw a shadow pass over her face. "Last night after dinner, when I was helping Mags wash the dishes, she said she wanted me to think long and hard about something. She asked me if I was certain Christopher was the one."

Mom's eyes shot open wide with surprise. "She said that?"

I nodded and looked down at my hands. "At first, I didn't know what to think. Why would she say that? And then today he runs home to his patient, even though there are plenty of other doctors there to take care of her. He left me." I shook my head and looked up at her. "I mean, he apologized and seemed to genuinely feel bad. But he still left. I don't know what to think," I admitted. "I thought I knew what I wanted, but now I'm not so sure. Mags has always been spot-on with her observations. We were supposed to talk more about this before I left, but now—we can't." My heart sank into my stomach.

"My God, Addy. I'm so sorry." She took a deep breath and let it out slowly, then ran a hand through her hair. "You know, I've been employed at the hospital for a very long time and I see how hard the doctors work. I've also seen a lot of other things, too. Modern medicine is a gift, but it can come with a price. Now, I don't want to deter you, you need to follow your heart. But I will say that if you decide to marry Christopher, chances are it won't be like the marriages you've seen growing up." She shifted on the bed, turning more to face me. "Do you remember when you were a little girl and you hated me being on call? Do you remember how you felt when I had to work on Christmas or your birthday?"

I nodded.

"Being a doctor means a lot more on call. It means

dropping everything and rushing to the hospital on a moment's notice, no matter what's going on at home. Holidays, cookouts, the birth of children . . ." Her voice trailed off. "It also means going away to conventions. Early days, late nights, long hours, flirting nurses. You're just getting a taste of that now. Once you're married, once you have children, it's not going to change. It could even get worse. Christopher said he'd like to run his own practice one day. That means more responsibility. You know this, you work in the medical field. Are you prepared for all that?"

I thought for a long moment before answering. "I thought I was. I know how hard he works and I'm so proud of all he's accomplished. I also know it makes him happy. And if it makes him happy, then it should make me happy, too."

It wasn't until I said it out loud that I realized it was a lie. A dirty, nasty, flat-out lie.

Chapter Twenty-Three

When Monday morning came around, I woke up confused. For a split second I thought it all had been a dream, a nightmare, and I was safe in my own bed with everything back to normal. But I wasn't in my own bed. Well, I was, but it was a bed that I hadn't slept in for years. And it hadn't been a dream. Mags was gone. And so was Christopher.

I sat up, my hair falling in tangled waves around my shoulders. Pushing back the knotted strands, I took a deep breath. There was a lot that needed to get done today. The funeral arrangements had been made; now I just needed to prepare.

I wanted to gather as many pictures as I could find, photographs that captured the essence of who Mags was, and put them together to display at the funeral home. I also wanted music to play, her very favorite songs, so I would need to go through her collection to find the CDs I knew she loved most.

This had to be a celebration; Mags would want it that way. She wouldn't want people crying and making a fuss. And if I took care of all the details, then it would save

Gramps and my parents from having to do it. They could just be together and grieve without the worry of needing to get things done.

I stretched my muscles, tight with stress, and swung my legs over the side of the bed. My eyes squinted against the morning sunlight that filtered in through the white blinds on my window, and I folded my hands in my lap sedately. For a moment I felt peaceful, like I had a grip on the situation.

My mind traveled back to the night before, when Mom and I had spoken. Her words played over and over in my mind, about doctors and babies and life. I'd gone over these things before I fell asleep, and I was certain Christopher and I could work things out. After all, we loved each other. And if I told him how his leaving made me feel, he would certainly understand.

Reaching to the bedside table and grabbing my cell, I pulled up Christopher's number and called. The phone rang a few times before sending me to voice mail. I felt my eyebrows crinkle. Christopher always answered his phone, at least when he wasn't working. Tucking a loose strand of hair behind my ear, I dialed Ruby's number. I hadn't yet called to tell her about Mags and now that funeral arrangements had been made, I knew she would want to know.

"Addy," she exclaimed before I could even say hello. "How did it go? Does your family love Christopher? What am I saying, of course they do! After all, he *is* a doctor. They must be ecstatic."

"Hey, Ruby. I have some unexpected news." I took a deep breath. "Mags passed away yesterday morning."

There was silence on the other end, not something I was used to when it came to my best friend.

"Mags?" Ruby finally said. I could hear the shock in her voice. "Oh my God. What happened?"

"We think she had a heart attack while she was asleep." The words sounded foreign coming out of my mouth. "I'm just glad she didn't suffer."

"I am so sorry, Addy," she said, slowly. "I know how close you were. How are you holding up?"

I paused to gather my thoughts. "I'm okay, I guess. Her funeral is tomorrow, and there's a lot I'd like to get done so Gramps and my parents don't have to worry about it."

"God, I just . . . I don't even know what to say. This was the last thing I ever expected." I heard Ruby take a deep breath. "At least Christopher is there with you. I'm happy you have someone not as close to the situation to lean on."

"Christopher's not here," I said, trying to sound casual.

"He's not there? What do you mean he's not there? I thought you two were together to announce your engagement."

I let out a quiet sigh. "We did. He left yesterday afternoon to go back to Atlanta. He has a patient who's not doing very well."

Silence built on the other end of the phone. Finally, Ruby answered. Her voice was slow and measured, but I could hear the disbelief in her tone. "What do you mean, he left for Atlanta? Wasn't there anyone else taking over for him?"

"Yes." I felt my nerve endings prickle. "There was another doctor on call, but he was the patient's primary caregiver. He felt he should be there."

"You mean to tell me he left you alone on the day your

grandmother died? I just can't believe that, Addy. Are you okay with this?"

I hesitated, not expecting the question. "Of course I'm okay with it. What choice do I have? He's a doctor." I sounded more convincing than I felt, but I wasn't in the mood to get into it with Ruby, not yet anyway. Not when there was so much to get done. The last thing I needed was for a big, black cloud of doubt to hang over my head when I had other things to concentrate on. "It's okay, Ruby. Really it is. I'll get through this."

"When did you say the funeral was?"

"Tomorrow," I repeated, shifting my weight on the bed. My head felt heavy with exhaustion.

"Then I'll be there this afternoon. Just give me some time to tie up loose ends."

"Ruby, it's not necessary. I'm fine."

"The hell it's not necessary! You need someone there with you, and if Christopher isn't going to step up and do his job, then I will."

"He *is* doing his job, that's why he left," I said with a sigh, but inside I felt a rush of relief.

"Forget it. I know you, Addy. You always act so strong. Mags meant a lot to you, and I know you couldn't possibly be as together as you sound. It's going on nine o'clock now, I'll be there by one. No way am I going to let you go through this alone."

I thanked her and hung up the phone. Now that Ruby was coming to my rescue, I began to feel better.

Lying back in my bed, I stared at the ceiling, my thoughts traveling over my list of things to do. I'd gotten most of the pictures together the night before. I just needed to finish and go through Mags's CD collection. The funeral had to honor Mags's memory and memorialize who she was in life.

More than anything, I wanted to recreate what it felt like to be in my grandparents' home. To take everyone away from the starched upholstery and sterile disinfectant of the funeral home and make it seem as if they had just walked into the warmth of my grandparents' kitchen. And I didn't just want to have memories you could see, I wanted memories you could *smell*. Decorating the funeral home with candles seemed like a good way to start—especially ones that reminded guests of her cooking, like maybe pumpkin or apple pie. Having Ruby here would be a good thing. Not only for me but for Mags, too. If anyone knew how to throw a party, it was my best friend.

I pushed my hands through my hair before calling Christopher again. This time, he picked up right away. "Addy, I'm so sorry I missed your call. How are you?"

"Better, I guess. I'll be busy today with everything that needs to be done for the funeral. The showing is tomorrow. Gramps only wanted it to be one day, so the burial will be on Wednesday. When do you think you can make it back?"

The line was quiet, and I thought we'd lost the connection. I sat up in bed. "Christopher, are you there?"

"Uh—sorry, I'm here."

"When do you think you'll be able to get here?" I asked again. Suddenly, my stomach felt queasy and I suspected I already knew the answer.

"I'm sorry, Addy. Mrs. Davenport's still not doing well. She has a collapsed lung now. We're having a chest tube inserted today. She's pretty nervous about it, and so is her family. I've been at the hospital all night. I don't think I'll be able to get away."

I sat in stunned silence as I let his words sink in. All at once, my mother's words from the night before came rushing back to me. *"If you decide to marry Christopher, chances are it won't be like the marriages you've seen growing up."*

"Addy, did you hear me?" Christopher asked.

"Yes, I heard you."

"I'm really sorry. I hope you understand."

"I do understand. This is your job. I'm not going to fault you for that."

He breathed a sigh of relief. "I'm glad you get it. Look, I have to get going. I stopped home to eat and shower, now I need to head back. How about I pick you up on Thursday? Will that give you enough time?"

The pain I felt suddenly made me flinch. I hadn't realized I'd been biting my lip. "I think so. I need to go, too. I have a lot to get done."

I stood up from the bed and reached into my luggage, grabbing shorts and a shirt. I searched the floor for the boots I had kicked off the night before.

"Thanks again for understanding, Addy. I love you."

But I didn't answer, I'd already hung up. And he didn't call back.

When Ruby arrived that afternoon, I met her out front, anxious for a hug. I needed to feel something familiar and comfortable, something that would help me feel normal in a world that had suddenly turned upside down.

She wrapped me in a tight embrace, the scent of her perfume surrounding me. "Look at you! You look so different! I miss those waves," she said, touching the soft curves of my hair. "And those boots! I can't believe you still have them." Ruby's eyes moved enviously across the red leather. "I always wanted them, you know that? I was so mad you found them before me!" She stood tall and lean, her long blond hair pulled into a loose ponytail. Her eyes met mine and she gave me a sympathetic smile. "How are you?"

We began to walk toward the porch. "I'm doing okay—busy. There's so much to get done. Will you help me put things together? I'd love for this to feel like a celebration of life and not make it any more depressing than it already is."

"Of course I'll help you," Ruby said, snaking her arm around my waist. She laid her head on my shoulder. "What did you have in mind?"

When we got to the porch, we turned and sat on the steps. "I want it to feel happy, like a party. I want to focus on the things that made us happy, not the things that are making us sad. And it has to feel authentic, not forced. Do you know what I mean? Mags deserves something fun and personal." I turned to her, tucking back a stray strand of hair.

Ruby nodded slowly, her gaze shifting over the farm. "I know exactly what you mean. I was doing some thinking on the drive, since you said you wanted to put it together. I figured you'd want help. I remember the fiftieth wedding anniversary you threw . . ." she said, her voice trailing off, and a smile tugging at the corner of her lips.

I laughed. "Don't remind me."

Out of the corner of my eye, I could see Ruby studying me. "How are you really?" she finally asked, reaching over and placing her hand over mine.

I shrugged. "It sucks. This came out of the blue. I think it's always harder to lose someone when you don't see it coming." I smiled ruefully. "I'm just glad I was here when it happened."

Ruby took a deep breath and let it out slowly, moving

her eyebrows into a high arch. "Yeah, that was some timing. It's still so hard to believe, you know?" She shook her head and pushed back the wispy bangs that swept across her forehead. "I called my parents. They wanted me to pass on their condolences. They'll be at the showing tomorrow and wanted to know if there's anything they can do to help."

"Just show up. My family will appreciate all the support they can get."

"And what about you?" she asked, her brown eyes alive with concern.

My brows crinkled. "I'd appreciate the support, too."

"No, I mean, what's going on? With you and Christopher? Is he going to be here?"

Leaning back, I drew in a ragged breath. "Nope. He's staying in Atlanta."

Ruby's eyes widened in shock. "You've got to be *kidding* me! He couldn't get away for half a day?" She shook her head. I could tell she wanted to say more but stopped herself. Instead, she changed the subject. "How's your family handling this?"

I lifted one shoulder. "Oh, you know. They're a mess. Mags was our foundation. I'm not sure how they're going to cope without her."

"How are you coping?"

I turned and stared at her. "I already said I'm fine."

"I know that's what you said, but is that really true?" She studied me, her eyes squinting in the sun. "Have you even let yourself cry?"

Shaking my head, I snorted a sound of disapproval. "God, you sound like my mother! What does crying have to do with it? It's not going to change anything. It's not going to bring Mags back. All it's going to do is give me puffy eyes and a runny nose."

"Come on, Addy! Why do you always hold everything in?" she asked, leaning her shoulder into mine. "You'll feel better after you cry. It's a stress reliever. I do it all the time. There ain't no shame in my game!"

"That's you." I felt the corner of my mouth lift slightly.

"You are *so* stubborn, you know that? What would Mags say?"

"She'd probably tell me to get over myself," I said, laughing softly. I turned toward her and sighed. "I'll look into it after everything's done, okay? Maybe then I'll be able to squeeze out a few tears." Raising my hand, I shielded my eyes from the brightness of the sky. I didn't want her to know that I was afraid if I allowed myself to cry, I might never stop. "Will that make you feel better?"

"You're hopeless." She stood up and reached her hand out to me. "Come on. Let's get to work before we get wrinkles from all this squinting."

I smiled, peeking up at her through the sunlight, and took her hand.

When I walked into the funeral home Tuesday morning, I heard the bluesy voice of Johnny Cash singing in the background. The pictures Ruby and I had put together were off to one side not far from the entrance, and the scent of pumpkins teased my nose, warm and rich, so much like my grandparents' kitchen on Thanksgiving afternoon.

Ruby and I had worked late into the night, and she'd taken everything with her so she could set up without me, putting pictures in their places and lighting the candles before we arrived.

A pleasurable sensation made its way over me as I took in Ruby's hard work. The memory tables were arranged like stations, each one encompassing a different chapter of Mags's life. One table represented my grandmother as a young and vibrant girl, growing up on the farm her parents had owned. She was youthful, her face cheerful and bright as the unpredictable future lay ahead of her.

Another table displayed pictures of her and Gramps after they got married and the life they shared before starting their family. Settling down on my grandfather's family farm, dancing together on the porch of their home, working hard to foster the roots of a new generation.

My grandparents were so much in love, and had been since they were very young. I could only hope to have a marriage half as happy and satisfying as theirs one day.

The next table revealed Mags as a mother, growing older with her children, relishing the memories they were building together.

The final display represented the extended family Gramps and Mags had helped create, their children and their children's children, extending across the long branches of the family tree that would continue to grow for years to come.

I looked over the tables with pride, taking in the deep impression Mags had made over the years. She lived her life to the fullest, and she did it with such grace and enthusiasm.

"This is amazing, Addy," Mom said, walking up behind me. Her arms circled around my waist and she rested her chin on my shoulder. She sighed softly as she gazed over the tables. "She was an amazing woman."

I turned to give her a hug. "Do you really like it?" I asked, my face buried in the soft waves of her dark blond hair. Out of the corner of my eye, I spied the open casket against the back wall.

"I love it. Everyone will. You and Ruby did such a fantastic job." She pulled away, her eyes traveling across the large room. "I wonder where your grandfather is." She shook her head, worry etched across her face.

"Dad spoke with him earlier," I said, trying to ease her mind. "He just needs some time alone. I think that's why he didn't want to drive over here with us. Some people need more space than others."

Mom turned to me with a distracted smile. "I know, I just can't help but worry. It's the mother in me, I guess." Her eyes continued to look around, sweeping periodically toward the door. Her expression relaxed once my grandfather walked in. "Finally," she said, breathing a sigh of relief. "I was worried he wouldn't get here before the guests. We only get so long to visit with her in private before they arrive."

Scanning the room, I noticed several of my grandparents' closest friends and relatives had arrived while I was looking over pictures.

My gaze finally landed on Gramps. He was a tall man, with strong shoulders from years of laborious work. He carried himself with a dignity learned from years of honest employment and hardships that only other farmers would understand. He'd always said working in the fields was just as rewarding as watching his family grow, and he refused to slow down, even though he was well past the age of retirement.

He made his way toward where his sons stood, hugging each of them tightly before greeting their wives. He looked pale and tired in the black suit he wore, the lines on his face deeper than they'd been the day before.

"I'm going to go see him," Mom said softly as she looked me in the eye. "You should, too."

"I will. Let me just make sure everything is taken care

of." I gave her a smile. "You go ahead. I'll be along shortly."

Spotting the funeral director near the front door, I wandered over to discuss how the day would play out, when the prayer service would take place, and when guests would have an opportunity to share their memories of Mags. After I smoothed over details, I searched for Gramps, wanting to catch him before his time would be monopolized by well-wishers. The funeral home was beginning to fill, and I turned back and forth, trying to locate him in the growing crowd.

"Looking for someone?"

Surprised, I turned to the voice. "Gramps," I said, allowing him to fold me into his arms. "How are you?"

He took a slow, deep breath. "I had an epiphany last night."

"What's that?" I asked, my face pressed tight against the wool of his suit.

"'In the midst of life we are in death.' Have you ever heard that quote before?"

I stepped back and shook my head. "I don't think so."

Gramps's eyes moved across the room and lingered over the casket. "It's a confirmation of our mortality. Your grandmother—she made every moment of her life count, from the second she woke up in the morning until the moment her eyes closed at night. I have never known anyone like her, and I have never known a pain like this. I feel it deep in my chest, I feel it in every bone in my body." He took a handkerchief out of the pocket of his jacket and held it briefly to his nose. His eyes fixed intently on mine. "I sat up last night because I was too afraid to go to sleep. Do you know why?"

I shook my head.

"Because I realized today would be the last day I

would ever see her face again, until I join her in heaven, that is, and I am going to miss that face more than the sun misses the sky at night." He paused. "But at the same time I feel grateful."

The expression of surprise and confusion on my face made Gramps chuckle.

"I have been a very lucky man to have known the love and loyalty of a woman like your grandmother. The happiness we felt watching our crops ripen in the fields, of sharing the splendor of the sunrise with our children before the work of the day began, that's something I will cherish until the day I take my last breath. Not everyone slows down to appreciate such things, but we did. Every single day. Maggie made my dreams come true. She worked tirelessly beside me, even through the disappointments and pitfalls life sometimes brings. And she did it with a smile. That woman never complained," he said, shaking his head. His eyes misted over. "I couldn't have asked for a better partner in life. But like every living thing, we're only allowed to walk in the sun for a short while. I'm happy to have walked with your grandmother. I'm happy she chose me to spend her life with."

A thick lump formed in my throat, and for the first time I was worried I wouldn't be able to stop my tears from falling. I reached up on tiptoes and threw my arms around his neck. "You're a wonderful man, Gramps. One of the best people I have ever known. I am so sorry for your loss, I don't even know what to say." The burning in the back of my throat intensified as I grappled with the reality. I swallowed hard, but the sensation wouldn't disappear. This would be the last time I ever saw Mags, too. In the chaos of everything, I never looked at it that way until that very moment.

"My God, did Maggie love you," he whispered fiercely,

stepping back. With a solemn smile, Gramps reached over and touched my cheek, causing a shiver of emotion to move through me. "From the moment she first saw you, it was as if the stars shined in your eyes." His tired gaze searched my face. Finally, he sighed. "Come on, Addy-Cake, let's go see your grandma. She's waiting to say good-bye." He held out his elbow, and I linked my arm through his and let him steer us toward the casket.

A feeling of panic began to swirl deep in my stomach. I couldn't do this! There was no way I could look at Mags now, not after the moment I'd just shared with Gramps.

How did this even happen? I'd come back to Lakeside to introduce my family to my fiancé, and now I was laying Mags to rest. This was supposed to be a happy time; instead my heart was breaking. Life changes fast, it changes in an instant, and somehow I had to figure out how to make sense of it without the wise words of Mags to carry me through. One minute she was here, happy and healthy, the next minute . . . gone.

The painful realization sank in. Once the glossy cedar casket closed, I would never see my grandmother again. I would never see her smile or get to listen to her clever ramblings. Over time, her voice would be harder for me to remember, and I would eventually forget what it felt like to be enclosed in her arms.

We walked closer to her, my vision clouded by the tears I had not yet shed, until finally we stood at the foot of the bed her body would sleep in for the rest of eternity. I blinked, once, twice, trying to clear away the curtain of emotion.

When my gaze traveled over Mags, I felt like I was trapped in a dream. She looked so much like herself, yet different somehow.

All at once, I lost control. My eyes swam with tears as

I succumbed to the fact that this was it. Pain squeezed my lungs, and as I labored for breath, the room began to spin as the walls closed in around me.

"Addy? Are you okay?"

The sound of my grandfather's voice was muffled and quiet, as if I were listening to him from underwater. "I just need some air," I managed to choke out.

Turning, I ran through the funeral home and out into the sunlight, ignoring the shocked expressions of the people around me. Thoughts of suffocation filtered through my mind as I fought to fill my lungs with oxygen. It was so hard to breath! How would my family react if they'd lost me, too?

Without thinking, I followed the stone walkway around to the back of the building, my eyes reaching out to the empty acreage in the distance. Quickening my pace, my strides widened until I broke into a sprint. I had no idea where I was going or what I would do once I got there, all I knew was that I needed to get away from the casket positioned in the center of the room as if it had every right to be there.

A fire ignited in my chest and spread through my veins as I made my way across the uneven terrain, my ankles twisting against the lumpy ground. The searing pain in my legs intensified as it blanketed across me, forcing me to drop to my knees. The hem of my dress fanned out around me in the dirt. Bending forward, I clutched the earth as I struggled for breath and a loud sob escaped before I could swallow it back. With deep, ragged gasps, a numbness consumed me, the grief I'd been holding in fighting to come out.

You're not allowing yourself to grieve because you don't want to let go. A voice surrounded me and I recognized it immediately. Brushing the tears from my cheeks, I held my breath, waiting for more.

"Mags?" I asked out loud, unable to believe what I was hearing.

Don't hide from your heartache, Addy. It will follow you if you don't let it out. Her voice was so clear and vivid, as if she were standing right there in the middle of the plowed field.

"You're dead," I said, stating the obvious.

I will always be alive in your heart. All you have to do is pay attention and you'll feel me there.

I lifted my head and stared out across the field, wondering if I'd lost my mind. Once people die, that's it. They're gone. They don't come back from the dead to teach life lessons.

"Addison?"

This time, the words came from behind me, but they didn't belong to Mags. They were deep and soft, and my pulse pounded with familiarity. I knew then I had surely gone insane.

"Addison." My name came again, a little closer this time.

My heart froze in my chest. Slowly I turned my head, dragging my eyes to the owner of the voice as a wave of recognition washed over me. "Jake?" I whispered, realizing I must have died from suffocation after all. But thank God I had gone to heaven.

His sapphire eyes bored into mine as he reached down to help me to my feet, and his touch felt so . . . *real*. Before I could stop myself, I brought my fingers to his cheek, the feeling of stubble against my palm. "Are you really here?"

"I'm really here." And his *voice*. Damn it. It was so soothing and familiar. Even though it had been years since I'd heard it last, it still had the ability to send tingles through my veins.

Without warning, my eyes filled, clouding the man that stood in front of me. He opened his arms and I fell into them, allowing my tears to spill over in hot, aching streaks.

Chapter Twenty-Four

With the hot Georgia sun beating down on our shoulders, I cried until I was empty, until the pressure that sat on my chest lifted and the walls of my throat expanded, easing the smothering loss.

And it felt good. It felt good to release the anguish I'd been holding on to. It felt good to be back in Jake's arms. I leaned against him for a long time, my cheek pressed tightly to his chest, oddly comforted by his presence. The thudding of his heart soothed me, calming my pain and drying my tears. He held me, running his hand up and down my back in tender, soothing strokes.

Slowly, I lifted my gaze to his. It was as if I had stepped back in time and the memories that had grown blurry around the edges came back into focus, rushing toward me like a sudden gust of wind.

My breath came out in shallow bursts as I searched his face, every inch of it seared deep into my mind. His hair was a little shorter than I remembered, but still dark and wavy as it tumbled over his forehead. And his eyes, my God, his *eyes*. Just as blue and intense as the ones in my memory. He stood tall and tan, his shoulders broad and his waist narrow, just as they had been ten years before, and the added years on his face only made him more attractive.

But Jake Grady had been so much more than just an attractive face.

The first time I had laid eyes on him, I thought it was love at first sight, not that I believed in that anymore. But the connection we had so many years ago was unlike anything I'd ever experienced before, or since, even while dating in college. And the realization of that now made me shiver. We'd only been kids at the time, young and naive, but I couldn't deny that I had never felt the way Jake had made me feel, not even with the man I was supposed to marry. For a few months, during that long, hot summer, I'd known what it felt like to be completely in love. To feel the raw excitement of so many firsts and the fierceness and passion that came along with them.

Then came the moment everything had changed. A moment I still had trouble believing had happened, and not only that, had been brought on by me.

Breaking up with Jake had been the hardest thing I had ever done, but at the time it had made sense—it was the only thing that made sense. He would be leaving for Texas and our relationship would end, and my heart and pride would have been torn to pieces along with it. Following a breakup a few years ago, I typed Jake's name into Google, shamelessly snooping for information, and what I'd found crushed me. An engagement announcement from the *Houston Times* declaring his upcoming nuptials with a Tamara WhatsHerName, a fashion designer from Dallas whose picture looked more like a supermodel gracing the cover of *Cosmo* than the designer who dressed them. *Of course.* She was exactly the kind of woman I had always imagined him with; it never made sense what he'd seen in me.

So that was it. Jake had moved on, it was time I did, too.

He stared down at me so intently it felt like a caress. "Are you all right?" he finally asked, still holding on to me.

Averting my gaze, I felt a peculiar warmth spread across my cheeks and travel south, consuming my whole body. I forced my eyes back up to his. "I'm . . . um. I'm good. I mean, not right now of course, but in general— I'm good. Before this week, anyway, if that's what you meant." I nodded.

The corner of his lips tipped up into that slow, familiar smile and I felt my knees weaken just a little. "I'm sorry. I know this must be awkward seeing me here after all these years."

"What? Me? Awkward? No. Not at all," I said, shaking my head. "I'm totally comfortable with this. Really. I just . . . I wasn't expecting to see you at the funeral. Or out here," I said, looking around the vast field we stood in. *Oh my God! Just. Stop. Talking.* I bit the inside of my cheek, desperate to keep my mouth from opening again.

The intensity of his gaze was unnerving. He smiled gently, catching a lock of hair that had blown across my cheek and tucking it back behind my ear. "It's been a long time."

Emotion clogged my throat. "Yes, it has," I said, swallowing the burn. "A very long time."

His eyes fixed on mine as he studied my face. "I'm sorry about Mags. I know how much she meant to you. When my aunt told me what happened, I drove in for the funeral. I had just walked inside when I saw you run out. You looked pretty upset. Thought maybe you could use a friend. I hope you don't mind me following you out here."

I shook my head. "No, of course not. I just needed some air." I bit my lip, the unexpected reunion jumbling my brain. "Thank you for driving all the way here. My family will be happy you came. I mean, that you traveled all this way to pay your respects." The thought of him standing there holding on to me was overwhelming; it crowded my mind until I couldn't think straight. I took a step back, breaking the hold. "Mags always did like—"

Searing pain traveled from my ankle up through my leg, forcing my knee to buckle. Jake caught me in his arms and I fell against him. Again. My eyes flew to his face as his expression grew more concerned than before.

"Are you hurt?"

"No, I'm fine. Really." It did hurt. *A lot*. But I wasn't about to admit that to him. *Just walk it off. No big deal.* I stepped away from him, but the burning twinge tore through my ankle, crippling my ability to stand. Once more, his arms reached out toward me, catching me under my arms before I hit the ground. "I can do this," I said, attempting to push him away. Visions of him coming to my rescue all those years before swam before me, and I didn't want him to think I was still that same helpless girl, always in need of a knight in shining armor for protection. I stumbled slightly, trying to stand tall.

"You *are* hurt. Addison . . ." I heard him sigh. "Why are you being so stubborn?" he asked, swinging one arm down under my knees and lifting me up.

I gasped. "Jake—it's just my ankle! Seriously, I have another one. What're you doing?"

"What does it look like I'm doing? I'm carrying you, at least until we get to solid ground. Then we'll see how you do on your own. There's no way you can walk with that ankle through these mounds of uneven soil."

As he began to make his way toward the parking lot, I felt the definition of strong, lean muscles moving underneath his button-up shirt, and a shock of tingles ignited in my center, just as electrifying as they had been when I was eighteen years old. He carried me through the field, not stopping until his feet touched the pavement. Very gently, he set me down. I wobbled slightly but was able to stand on my own through the pain.

"How do you feel?" he asked, watching me doubtfully through long, black eyelashes. "Do you want to get it checked out?"

I swallowed hard. "It's tender but I'll be fine. Just an inversion, I imagine. All I need is some rest and ice." Glancing over my shoulder, I searched for the back entrance of the funeral home planning my escape, but my heart beat wildly in my chest and I wondered how likely I would be to manage a quick getaway in my disadvantaged state. "Thank you for helping me. I'm going inside now." Turning away from him, I swiveled on my good leg and began the long trek back.

"Do you think you can walk, or do you want me to carry you?" he asked, following close behind.

I hobbled slowly, biting my lip to keep from crying out. "I can do it, thanks."

"You really don't look like you can. At this rate it'll take you all day to make it inside." His Texas twang was subtle but I heard it, bringing a rush of goose bumps up my arms.

I stopped walking and glared. "I *said* I'm fine. I can walk there on my own."

Jake's eyes danced with amusement. "Okay," he said,

holding up his hands in defense. "Whatever you say. You're the boss."

Taking a deep breath, I started moving again. I could feel Jake close by, the heat of his body mingling with mine. *Just keep going, get back inside. I'll feel better once I'm there.* But with each step I felt my walls beginning to crumble, and by the time I made it to the center of the parking lot, visions of Mags lying in the casket invaded my mind and a spark of panic slid along my nerves. The humid afternoon air wrapped around me, making me dizzy, and my stomach twisted with a sour sensation. I brought my hand to my head, pushing it roughly through long hair.

"Addison, are you sure you're okay?"

Stopping suddenly, I dropped my gaze to the sun-beaten pavement. "No," I whimpered quietly.

"I can carry you again. Just until we get inside."

My eyes swept up, searching his face, taking in the concern etched deep into his expression. "No. You don't understand. I can't go back in there. I can't look at her in the casket. I just can't do it again."

A frustrated gasp escaped from my lips as I covered my face with my hands. Deep sobs shook my shoulders, and before I knew it I was wrapped in Jake's arms. Silently, I cursed myself. I knew once the dam broke it would be impossible to repair, which was exactly why I hadn't wanted to cry in the first place.

"How about we go somewhere else?" he suggested softly, his lips nearly brushing the tip of my ear.

Wiping my tears, I nodded against his chest. Jake hoisted me up into his arms and carried me through the parking lot to a brand-new Ford truck parked near the entrance. It was sleek and shiny, and black all over, a far cry from the rusty vintage model he'd driven years before.

He set me down and opened the passenger door, then helped me slide inside, his hand brushing against me as he buckled the seat-belt across me. My senses went into overdrive at the touch of his hand, every nerve ending feeling as if it was on fire. I sniffled loudly after he closed the door, running my fingertips across tear-soaked cheeks before he came around to the driver's side. My eyes traveled to a well-worn cowboy hat sitting next to me, and a picture of Jake from all those years before jolted through my mind. My lips parted as my breath hitched unexpectedly.

Jake settled in and gripped the wheel tightly, the knuckles of his fingers turning momentarily white. Out of the corner of my eye, I watched him stare straight ahead before turning to me. "Addison, are you certain you want to leave? I hate to think you'll regret this later."

Was he second-guessing his invitation for my sake or for his? I drew in a deep breath and swiveled my eyes toward him. "I'm positive. Seeing her like that was so much harder than I thought it would be." I shook my head and sniffled again, my hair falling across my cheek. "I just need more time. I'm giving the eulogy tomorrow." *Oh, good Lord, I'm giving the eulogy tomorrow.*

"You are?" he asked, his voice laced with surprise. "Are you sure you're up for it?" Without warning, he slowly leaned toward me, and I felt my heartbeat race. His face was inches away from mine, so very close.

I closed my eyes and held my breath, waiting to feel the tips of his fingers against my skin, just as he'd done in the field when he brushed aside my hair. But the touch never came.

Confused, I opened my eyes and was surprised to find those fingers in the glove box, pulling out a small package of tissues. He handed them to me and nodded his head, his eyes steady as they fixed on mine. "Here you go."

Air punched out of my lungs as I took the tiny rectangular packet. "Um . . . thank you," I finally answered. My fingers fumbled over the wrapping until I managed to slide out a cotton square. I touched it to my eyes, then pressed it under my nose, and before I could stop, my mouth began to move, the first thought that came to my mind rambling its way out. "Today took me by surprise, that's all. I've been so busy with arrangements, it's like the news hasn't sunk in. But tomorrow it'll be better, I'll be prepared. I know I will be." I nodded, trying to convince him—or maybe I was trying to convince myself.

"I hope so." And the way he said it told me he meant it. "So, where would you like to go?"

I took a deep breath and let it out slowly. "I don't know. What do you think?"

Jake thought for a moment, then shrugged. "Would you like to get a drink? I think you could use one."

A drink before noon? I hadn't done that since college. "Sounds perfect."

He buckled his seat belt and put the truck in reverse, backing it up until he could pull out. When he turned onto the road, I unzipped the small purse I wore across me, taking out my cell. "Don't you have to let someone know you're leaving?" I asked, wondering if his wife would mind him taking off.

Jake threw me a sideways glance before moving his eyes to the rearview mirror. "I'll call my aunt and uncle in a bit. They weren't ready to leave, so I drove separately. But you should let someone know you're gone."

I held up my cell. "I was just going to text my mom."

We held each other's gaze for a moment before his eyes shifted back to the road. Turning on my phone, I scrolled through for Mom's number and jotted down a quick message. *Mom, everything's fine, I just can't do it today. Seeing her in the casket took me by surprise. Don't worry, I'm okay. I'll call you later. Love, Addy.*

Before I could tuck my phone away, Mom responded. *It's okay, Addy. I understand. Just take some time. I love you.*

Pushing the phone back into my purse, I zipped it closed and leaned back in my seat, watching out the window as we drove through town. People were scattered about, carrying on as if life hadn't changed. Only it had. For me, anyway.

Lakeside had expanded over the years. It was just as quaint and charming as it had been before, yet the growth of the economy was evident by the new buildings and businesses that comprised the town. The city was booming, in more ways than one. In addition to businesses, families were drawn to the comfort of country living, planting their roots in the rich Southern soil.

All my life I'd been waiting for the day I could escape from my childhood to enter the realm of being an adult— as if going to college made a person an adult. And when that time came I ran as fast as I could toward a bigger and more exciting life in the city. Yet every time I came home to the place I'd grown up, I found an odd comfort driving through the streets, breathing in the new details of a place that felt older than time.

My eyes moved to my ankle, which throbbed, the pain pulsating down my foot, and I noticed it was beginning to swell. I turned my head slightly to study Jake's profile.

The years had been kind to him, that was for sure, but I could see changes now I hadn't noticed before. He'd matured over the years, the sharp angles of his face more defined than before. His nose was straight, his mouth full and soft, and his jaw chiseled, settled into a determined position. But his confidence hadn't changed, and neither had the charm that seeped from him. If anything they were stronger than before, but natural, as if he didn't know any other way. The expression on his face was rigid and controlled; it was an expression that had caught my breath time and time again, and I found it happening now.

He wore comfortable khakis and a white collared shirt, a burgundy tie fastened around his neck. On his feet were brown leather boots, similar to the ones he wore when we were younger, only these appeared new, not as well-worn as the ones from before.

His wife must have stayed in Houston. After all, why would she want to come to a tourist town to sit at the funeral of a woman she'd never even met?

Neither one of us spoke until the truck turned into a gravel driveway. "How's this?" Jake asked, pulling up to an old building on the edge of town. "Looks like the only bar open this early."

"Mad Horse Brewing Company," I said, reading the red neon sign out loud. "This used to be a horse stable; I remember my mom telling me about it. I can't believe I never came by to check it out."

"Well, it is a bit out of the way."

The parking lot was nearly empty as Jake pulled his truck into the spot closest to the entrance. He killed the engine and hopped out, coming around to my side and opening the door. I unbuckled the belt and slid away from my seat, carefully landing on the gravel below. Jake snaked his arm around my waist, helping alleviate the pressure of my weight as he opened the front door. Country music blared from an ancient jukebox, and one patron sat bellied up to the bar.

"We just opened up. Seat yourselves," the lady behind

the bar called out, barely looking up from the drink she was mixing for her only customer.

As Jake guided me to a table in the back, my eyes wandered around the rustic decor, taking in the exposed wooden frame outlining the establishment. The white walls contrasted against the reclaimed woodwork, and the soft lighting wrapped around the scenic pictures of Lakeside throughout. "This is amazing," I said as I settled into the seat Jake pulled out for me.

His gaze drifted across the walls of the tavern, landing on something behind me. "Is that what I think it is?"

When I turned around, my eyes fixed on a large piece of black-and-white artwork hanging on a wall near our table. I followed the lines and curves of the dirt road leading up to a rural barn positioned at the end. "That's my grandparents' barn. I can't believe I didn't know about this."

"That there's the Monroe family farm," came a raspy, female voice. We turned and found the woman who was behind the bar standing at our table holding two menus. "It's about six miles south of here and is one of the oldest farms in the area." She placed the menus on the table, then moved her gaze from the picture on the wall back to me. "You just passin' through town? I don't reckon I've seen you two in here before."

"I used to live here when I was younger. I moved to Atlanta several years ago." I glanced at Jake sitting across from me, his eyes holding me as he watched me speak. "That's my grandparents' barn," I said, nodding toward the framed photo.

Her deep-set eyes widened. "Henry and Maggie are your grandparents? Well, I'll be a son of a gun!" Her weather-lined face released a sympathetic smile. "Then you must be here for your grandma's funeral. I sure am sorry to hear about that. Maggie was one helluva lady." The woman shook her head sadly. "Ya just never know when your time's up."

Dragging my eyes away from Jake, I gave her a small smile. "I guess not."

"So, you must be Addy, then? My God, I haven't seen you in years. You're all grown up! You probably don't remember me. I knew you when you were just a tot. My name's Nell Hartley. I used to sing with your grandma in the church choir. I moved to Alabama for a while, came back a few years ago after my husband died. Didn't see the point in stayin' after he was gone. My heart's always been in Lakeside, anyway."

Her name wasn't familiar, but I didn't tell her that. "It's nice to see you again."

She nodded, then turned toward Jake. "And this young man must belong to you," she said, eyeing him with appreciation. "I'll tell ya what, they sure do know how to grow 'em in Atlanta."

I bit my lip, trying to hide a smile. "This is Jake Grady. His aunt and uncle are John and Kathy Grady."

The woman's smile widened. "Ya don't say! Well, I know them, too. Very fine people. Ya know, that's what I love about livin' in a cozy little town. Everybody knows everybody else. And if ya don't know what you're doin', someone else surely will," she added with a wink. She turned back to me. "I'll be stoppin' by the funeral home after my shift tonight. I really am sorry to hear about Maggie. She's goin' to be missed."

"I appreciate that."

"Now, enough with the chitchat. What can I get for you two?"

"I'll have a glass of white wine," I said, looking up at her. "Whatever you have, I'm not picky."

"Well, in that case, how would ya like to try our strawberry wine? Just got a new order in from the vineyard down the way."

My eyes swiveled toward Jake as a slow burn made its way across my cheeks. I couldn't drink strawberry wine without remembering that afternoon so long ago, and judging from the look on his face now, he knew exactly what I was thinking. "Sure, why not?"

She turned to him. "And what'll it be for you, handsome? Can I interest you in some strawberry wine, too?"

Jake laughed and leaned back in his chair. He lifted his hand to his forehead, pushing away a wave of dark hair. "I'll just have a beer. Whatever you recommend, I'm not picky either." He gave me a look that sent a shiver to my core. "Could you also bring a bag of ice? Addison here twisted her ankle."

"Is that so?" She turned to me with an arched eyebrow. "You got it," she said then walked away, hot pink cowboy boots clicking against the hardwood floor.

Avoiding his gaze, I watched the waitress, averting my eyes only after she disappeared from sight. Without thinking, I picked up a menu and tried to look through it, realizing then that my hands were shaking.

"How long are you in town for?" he asked with a slow drawl.

"I'm leaving on Thursday." I paused, my eyes still buried in the menu. "What about you?"

He was quiet for a moment before answering. "Same here. Are you hungry?"

I lifted my eyes to find him watching me. I'd barely eaten that morning, but no way would I be able to eat now. "Not really, just looking."

We were quiet for several minutes while I looked over the food options, unable to make out any of the words in front of me. Finally, I set it down, placing my hands in my lap so he couldn't see them quiver. "So, how have you been, Jake?" I asked, breaking the silence.

"I've been real good. Keeping busy." He folded his hands in front of him, and I noticed he did not wear a wedding ring.

I felt my eyebrows crinkle slightly and looked up at him. "Aren't you married?" I bit my lip again, unable to believe the question had escaped from my mouth.

Something flickered in his eyes. "I almost got married once, a few years back, but in the end I couldn't go through with it. It didn't feel right, somehow."

His gaze latched onto mine as a slow ache built low in my stomach. I couldn't understand how this man had managed to stay single all these years . . . even with the beautiful Tamara WhatsHerName waiting to claim him.

"What about you, Addison? Are you married?"

Unease pricked at my skin as I shifted uncomfortably in my seat, but I couldn't tear my eyes away from the ice-blue ones sitting across from me. "I'm engaged," I finally choked out. My shoulders tensed as I watched him take in the words. Was there a remote possibility he still might be interested, even after the way I had ended things before? If he was, the look on his face gave nothing away. *Ha, don't fool yourself! He probably hasn't thought of you in years.*

We stared at each other for a long minute, neither one of us saying a word until the moment was broken by the arrival of our drinks.

"Here you go," the waitress said, setting down a glass of wine in front of me. "One strawberry wine for you, and one Mad Horse Bock for you. Now you be careful with that, handsome," she said, setting down a dark-colored drink and giving Jake the eye. "That'll have ya windin' your ass and scratchin' your watch if you're not payin' close attention!" She let out a loud laugh and reached into her apron. "And here's a bag of ice, sweetie. I know how much your grandma loved you, she was always braggin' about her granddaughter in the big city. I'm gonna make sure I take real good care of you."

I thanked her and leaned down to place the ice on my ankle. When I settled back in my chair, I took a sip of wine, anxious to keep my mouth busy so I wouldn't say anything stupid. It had been years since I'd last tasted that particular strawberry flavor, and it was just as delicious as I remembered. Nostalgia and present day began to swirl around me, and I took another drink to calm my nerves. Before I realized it I had emptied the glass.

"I guess you were thirsty," Jake said, amusement thick in his voice.

"I guess so."

Patrons were starting to filter in through the door, settling at tables nearby. When Nell stopped back, her eyebrows shot up in surprise. "Well, would ya look at that? I see you like our wine. How about another glass?"

If I was going to find a way to get through the day, I would need something a whole lot stronger than strawberry wine. "Actually, I'll have what he's having."

"If you're sure, sweetie," she said, giving me a doubtful look.

I turned to Jake to see the same expression plastered across his face. "I'm positive." My eyes followed Nell as she made her way behind the bar. I'd never been much of a beer drinker, but no one here had to know that. "So, Jake. What have you been up to? Are you still living in Houston?"

He nodded, his eyes never leaving mine as he lifted the chilled mug to his lips, taking a long pull. He set the drink down and leaned forward, resting his elbows on the table. "I own a small horse ranch thirty minutes outside of town. I bought the place shortly after college. It's nowhere near as profitable as your grandparents' farm, but I really enjoy the work. I also work as an environmental engineer, so the ranch can't be too big. It's just enough to keep me busy." He took another drink. "I hear you work in the medical field. Following in your mom's footsteps, are you?"

I smiled, my stomach twisting in knots just listening to the sound of his voice. "Yes and no. Mom's a nurse, but I work as a physician assistant. That basically means I can care for my patients without the direct supervision of a doctor."

He looked suitably impressed. "Does that mean you can prescribe medication?"

"I can. I can even assist in surgery if I wanted to."

"Is that the plan?"

I shrugged, trailing my finger over the rim of the empty glass. "I'm not really sure, to be perfectly honest, I've only been working for a couple of years. I haven't given much thought beyond what Christopher wants to do." As I said the words out loud, I realized how lame they sounded and I wanted to kick myself in the shin for letting that information leak out. The last impression I wanted to make was that I couldn't think for myself.

"And Christopher is your fiancé?"

I released the breath I hadn't realized I'd been holding. "Yes. He's a doctor in Atlanta. He's always said he wants to open a practice of his own, and he'd like me to come work for him when he does."

We looked up in time to watch Nell approach with a chilled mug in her hands. "Here ya go, Addy," she said, setting it in front of me. Picking up the empty wineglass, she fastened me with a look. "It's strong, don't say I didn't warn ya. You just let me know if you'd rather have another glass of wine instead."

I smiled, grateful for her concern. "Thank you, Nell. I will."

"And is that what you want?" he asked, after Nell walked away.

"What? To work for Christopher?" I shrugged. The truth was I didn't know what I wanted. "I'm really not sure."

Jake stared at me for a moment, then pushed his chair away from the table. "I'll be right back," he said, standing up. "I just need to make a couple of phone calls."

His torso twisted and he walked away, my eyes following his every step. I propped my elbows on the table and buried my face in my hands, sucking in a slow, deep breath.

So much had changed since we'd last seen each other. Ten very long years had gone by. Yet for some reason seeing Jake had rattled my nerves in a way that felt out of place in my carefully composed life.

Jake Grady was water under the bridge. At least that's what I kept telling myself.

Chapter Twenty-Five

As the minutes ticked by, I sat thinking about the summer I turned eighteen. The summer I'd been bullied by my date to junior prom, the summer Ruby won Strawberry Queen, sultry nights spent at the lake, the moon the only witness to the things I'd been up to. The summer I fell in love for the very first time.

Thoughts of Jake's lips melting into my mine swam before me, and something I hadn't felt in a long time slammed into my chest. Memories of that summer collided inside my head, each one sweeter than the last.

By the time Jake came back into view, swaggering toward me in his confident stride, my heart was working overtime. Each beat pulsed against my chest in a way I found maddening. Reaching for my drink, I took a large gulp, nearly choking on the rich, malty flavor. He sat down in his chair, the corners of his lips tipped up into a lazy smile.

Don't stare at his mouth. Don't stare at his mouth. Don't stare at his mouth. Damn. It was too late. Once my eyes landed on those full, kissable lips I couldn't drag them away, and I was lost once again remembering how they felt brushing up against mine.

"How's your drink?" he finally asked, his expression telling me he already knew the answer, he just wanted to hear me admit it was strong.

"It's great," I lied. "Exactly what I need right now." To drive my point home, I took another large sip of the dark, golden liquid, licking the cold froth away from my upper lip. I took a deep breath and smiled. "It's great to see you again. You've barely changed at all." *Except for the fact you're even more magnificent than before.*

"It's nice to see you, too. The years have been good to you, Addison. You're more beautiful than I remember, if you don't mind me saying so."

Mind him saying so? Yeah, right. "Thank you." I smiled and looked down at my hands clasped tightly in my lap and realized they were moist with sweat. Again, something twitched inside me, something deep and intense. Trying desperately to brush away the frenzy of emotions, I began to question why I was there, allowing feelings from the past to resurface. *What am I doing? I'm engaged to a wonderful man! How can I be sitting here thinking the things I'm thinking?*

But I knew why I was there, and it wasn't just because I needed to get away. I *wanted* to be there. I *needed* to be there. Seeing Jake again after all these years brought back feelings I'd buried a long time ago, at least I thought I had, and I needed to figure out why. Was it because he was my first love, and first loves have a way of rooting themselves deep inside you? Was it because I was disappointed in Christopher? Or was it something more?

My thoughts drifted over the events of the past few days, and I let out an ill-humored laugh.

"Is something funny?" he asked softly. His voice was warm and husky.

I lifted my eyes and locked my gaze with his, mesmerized by his hypnotizing tone. "I was just thinking how our running into each other is only one of several ironic things that have occurred this week." I turned and watched as another couple was seated at a table near ours. Instead of sitting across from one another they sat side by side, holding hands. I took a slow breath. "I just happened to be in town when Mags passed away. Christopher and I came in for the weekend to announce our engagement."

I watched as he listened to what I was saying, his eyes softening with each word. "I'm sorry. I won't pretend to know what you're going through."

Lifting the drink to my lips, I took another swallow. "Thanks, I appreciate that." My fingers tightened around the handle of the mug as pent-up frustration moved over me. "You know what?" I asked, cocking my head to the side. "I don't think Mags liked Christopher. She basically said I was making a mistake. She wanted me to think long and hard about getting married and promised we'd talk about it more the next day. And then she died." I laughed again, this time more bitter than before. "How's that for irony?"

Jake sat there and watched me, not saying a word.

I shook my head, unable to keep the words from falling out of my mouth. "I mean, how can she drop a bombshell like that and then die, for Christ's sake? It's just not fair." I took another drink. It occurred to me that perhaps I was talking too much, but I could feel the alcohol beginning to buzz through me, releasing my inhibitions. My jaw clenched tightly. "I can't believe this is happening."

He pursed his lips as his eyes fell to his drink. "I don't know, Addison. Life's not always fair." He lifted the glass to his lips, allowing the cool beverage to slide inside.

But there was no stopping me, I was on a roll. "Not always fair? You can say that again. The same day she passed away, Christopher drove back to Atlanta, claiming he needed to be with a patient. He left me after this tragedy, and expects me to understand. Can you believe that? How am I supposed to understand?"

Jake raised his eyebrows. "You don't?"

I forced down the last of my drink and shook my head. "Hell no, I don't understand. He knew how close I was with my grandmother. He knew how much I cared about her. How could he just leave? I would have never left him." My eyes searched the room for Nell, and once I saw her, I waved her over. "Can I have another drink? And one for my friend, too."

"Comin' right up." She began to turn on her heel but Jake stopped her.

"Wait a second, Nell." He looked back at me. "Addison, are you sure you don't want something to eat? You just ordered your third drink."

The warm rush moving through me was only getting stronger, but the last thing I wanted to do was eat. Combing my fingers through my hair, I gathered it together and twisted it into a low knot, securing it with a band I found in my purse. "I'm not very hungry; I just want to drink."

The look on his face was difficult to read. I could sense he was amused yet also uncertain. He turned to the waitress. "Could you bring us an appetizer? A sampler platter if you have it?"

Nell's eyes moved from Jake and then to me. "You got it," she said, then turned and walked away.

"I'm sorry." I let out a frustrated sigh. "I've been doing all the talking. Tell me about you, Jake. I'd love to hear more about what you've been up to."

He shrugged his shoulders and looked away, seeming to study the photographs on the wall. "There's nothing much to tell, really. I work for the city as an environmental engineer. I help develop solutions to environmental problems, which is something I've always been interested in. I have an office in Houston but spend a lot of my time working at construction sites. When I go home, I have the ranch to keep me busy. The truth is, I'd rather be there than traveling between construction sites, but all in all, I enjoy what I do." He looked back at me. "It's a good life. I'm very happy."

A feeling of emptiness settled upon me, hungry for him to say more. What had gone wrong with his engagement? Why had he never married after all these years? "Is there anyone special in your life?" I asked, the influence of the alcohol easing my reserve. I had burning questions that needed to be answered. Like now.

Jake shrugged. "I date quite a bit, I've just never met anyone I'd like to settle down with. I thought I had not too long ago, but I was wrong. We broke things off a few months before we were supposed to be married." His eyes suddenly grew serious. "What about Christopher? Is he good to you?"

I didn't answer right away. I'd always believed he was good to me. He was always kind, he would bring home surprises like flowers and small gifts, but in hindsight his presents were a prelude to his absence. "He's a good man, hardworking and dedicated. I'm very proud of all he's accomplished. But I'm beginning to think he likes his job more than me." *Whoa, hold on there! Way too much information shared.* "So, how's your family?" I asked quickly, changing the subject.

Jake opened his mouth as if he wanted to say something, then closed it again. Finally, he gave me a small smile. "They're doing well. My parents still live in Houston with their spouses, and my brothers stuck around, too. They're both married now with children," he said, then swallowed the last of his beer. "It's funny to watch them as fathers. I still think of them as my annoying little brothers." His eyes sparkled when he spoke of his family, revealing the love and admiration he obviously felt. Then he shrugged. "But I guess we all grow up sooner or later."

"Would you like to have kids one day?" I asked, unable to tear my gaze away.

Slowly, he nodded his head. "Kids are great, I love spending time with my nieces and nephews. I'd definitely like to have my own someday."

The desire to know more about him stung like a knife to the stomach, or what I imagined a knife to the stomach would feel like. I wanted him to tell me every single thing I'd missed over the years. How he spent his free time, what he thought about right before he fell asleep.

Biting the side of my cheek, I swallowed the personal questions and asked a safer one instead. "Do you still swim?" I finally asked, wishing Nell would hurry up with the drinks.

Jake toyed with the empty mug in front of him, spinning it in circles before he answered. "I do. Not competitively any more, just for fun, but I've been thinking about getting into coaching. I've always kept up to date on my CPR and First Aid training from when I was a lifeguard. It's something I might try to do someday."

We were quiet as Nell finally appeared with our drinks and a large plate of appetizers. "Let me grab y'all a couple small plates and some napkins. I'll be right back." She took the empty glasses and walked away.

The smell of deep fried awesomeness swirled around me and I picked up a chicken strip and took a big bite. I hadn't realized how hungry I was until that bite hit my empty stomach. "Appetizers were a great idea," I said, popping the second half of it into my mouth. "Good call." Before he could answer, I had already started in on a loaded potato wedge covered in gooey gobs of melted cheese.

The corner of Jake's mouth twisted up into a smirk. "I thought they might be. Especially with the way you're pounding back the drinks." He reached for an onion ring, dipped it in sauce, then stuffed it into his mouth.

I exhaled sharply. "I am *not* pounding back the drinks. I've only had two."

"With a third one sitting in front of you." He tapped his fingers against the side of his glass and watched me with those eyes. Those *eyes,* damn it. They were really unfair. "How's your ankle?" he asked, swiping another onion ring from the plate.

Leaning down, I picked up the ice pack and set it on the table. "It's fine. It doesn't even hurt anymore." I stared at him staring at me and felt a slow burn crawl over my cheeks. "What?" I asked in defense, unnerved by the look on his face. Picking up my mug, I took another healthy swig, willing him to turn away, but he wouldn't. He just kept staring.

"I was just thinking about the summer we met," he said slowly. An expression I didn't understand covered his face. "How much fun we had together. You broke my heart, you know." His lashes swept upward and our eyes locked once again.

An uneasy feeling collected in my stomach, just as it

had done countless times in the past. Every time I got caught up in those bittersweet memories, that same sinking feeling would creep its way back.

Ten years ago, when we were together, the thought of Jake going back to Texas made me feel sick. I'd come to rely on him more than I had realized, more than I'd ever expected I would. And after the accident, I decided I couldn't do it. I couldn't watch him leave knowing he might never be back.

With the help of the alcohol sliding through my veins, I lifted my chin. "If I didn't break your heart, you would have broken mine. I was only protecting myself."

"Addison," he began, and his *voice*. Damn it. So deep and soft. It curled around me, each syllable pulling, unraveling a desire I'd buried a long time ago.

I took another long drink, determined to stay strong. No way was I going to fall for him all over again. "Please don't, Jake. Don't say you weren't going to break my heart, because you were. You had no choice. You were going back to Texas no matter what happened between us. And I would have been left in Lakeside, pining away for you. I gave you a piece of myself," I said, my words beginning to slur. Out of the corner of my eye, I could see the googly-eyed couple at the next table looking at me funny but I didn't care. I obviously needed some kind of closure, and you bet your ass I was going to get it. "I gave you something I'd never given anyone else. God, I was *so* stupid! I should have known better."

"Are you saying you regret being with me?"

No, that's not what I was saying! What the hell was I saying?

"No, I'm saying I shouldn't have fallen in love with you knowing you weren't sticking around." There, I said it. It was out in the open for everyone to hear, including that stupid eavesdropping couple. "And the longer you *were* around, the harder I fell. If I leaned on you after the accident—well, let's just say it would have been too much. Saying good-bye was a defense mechanism. It was the only thing I knew how to do. And it was the one time in my life I ignored Mags's advice."

A shadow of confusion fell over his face. "What do you mean you ignored Mags's advice?"

Shit. What was I doing? I waved my hand, attempting to play down what I'd just said. "Mags was rooting for you the whole time. She told me not to be afraid to love you. That if we were meant to be together things would work themselves out, and something as insignificant as distance wouldn't stand in our way." Her words sounded pointless at the time, but today, under the thick haze of fermented lager, they made perfect sense.

"But you didn't believe her? Or you didn't love me enough?"

Lifting the glass to my lips, I swallowed the rest of my drink. "I didn't believe her," I said, tears suddenly clouding my vision, making it impossible to see. "It was the first time I didn't think she understood what I was going through." I blinked rapidly, clearing away the curtain of moisture. "Hey, why am I the only one drinking?" I asked, noticing he'd barely touched his beer.

Jake glanced at the watch on his wrist. "Because it's still early, and I'm not a very cute drunk." He gave me an amused smile. "You, on the other hand . . ." His voice trailed off.

My face prickled with heat. "Are you saying I'm drunk?"

"I'm saying you're a *cute* drunk."

I cocked my head and fixed him with a look. "I might be a lot of things, but drunk I am not."

His smile grew wider. "You know, you sound strikingly similar to Yoda when you're drunk."

Irritation pricked at me and I straightened in my chair. "Jake! I am *not* drunk!"

Jake laughed and threw up his hands in surrender. "Okay, okay. You're not drunk, I take it back."

An electric charge filled the air around us. Jake stared at me with those impossible blue eyes as I fought to maintain a poker face, but *holy hell* my body was starting to do things—and it had nothing to do with the alcohol. I tried to relax. "So, you think I broke your heart?" I asked, steering him back to the conversation.

Jake took another drink. "I know you did. It took me a long time to get over you."

"But you did. You got over me."

"What choice did I have? You broke up with me."

I started to say something else, something ridiculously not clever, but the look on his face stopped me in my tracks. He looked so exposed sitting there across from me. And so damn irresistible. "Do you think we had a chance? Back then, I mean," I asked quietly, afraid to hear his answer.

Jake was silent for a moment as his eyes traveled around the restaurant. Finally, they landed on me. "I was willing to try, but you wouldn't listen. You were so stubborn. Still are," he said with a slow grin.

I snorted and leaned forward. "*I'm* stubborn? You're the one who won't commit to a relationship—even when it's to a beautiful fashion designer," I said, then quickly clamped my lips together. My eyes widened. *Please, God. I did not just say that out loud!* But the look on Jake's face confirmed I had opened my mouth and inserted my foot—along with a side of swollen ankle.

"How do you know I was engaged to a beautiful fashion designer?" he asked with one eyebrow raised. "I never told you that."

I let out a frustrated breath, realizing I was busted, without question. Caught red-handed, like a dim-witted villain. Unless . . . "People talk. I must have it heard it somewhere." I shrugged one shoulder. "So, what was the problem? Was she too into her looks? Completely absorbed in herself and her career?" Good Lord, why couldn't I shut up?

Jake shook his head. "No, Tamara was great. Yes, she was beautiful, but she didn't act like she knew it. And she did most of her work from home. She was caring and attentive, any guy would be lucky to marry her. It just wasn't working for me." He leaned forward, our faces inches apart from one another. "Maybe I never got over you, Addison."

I sat back in my chair and narrowed my eyes. "Don't you say that. You're not allowed to say things like that!"

Slowly, Jake leaned back, resting one arm on the back of the chair, the hint of a smile dancing on his lips. "But you asked."

He had me there. "That doesn't mean you get to tease me."

"Who said I was teasing you? Maybe I'm telling the truth."

"Don't mess with me, Jake," I warned, shaking my head. "I've had a really screwed-up week and I'm full of shit beer."

Jake's lips pulled into a lazy smile. "I knew that beer was too strong for you."

"I didn't say it was too strong, I said it was shit."

"That's why you keep ordering more? *And* why you are talking so loudly?"

My gaze flickered over to a nearby table. "I am *not* talking loudly," I insisted. Yet the annoying couple-in-love sitting next to us was still throwing me crazy looks.

Nell walked toward us, a tray full of drinks in her arms. "Hey there, you two. Let's try to use our indoor voices, okay? You're already sittin' well outta the way. I don't have a quieter area to put ya in." She set two drinks in front of Romeo and Juliet and walked on to deliver the rest of her orders.

I bit my lip and looked back at Jake, who was quietly chuckling across from me.

"Jake," I hissed. "Why didn't you tell me I was talking so loud?"

He only laughed harder. God, it was the greatest sound. Deep and throaty and sexy as hell. I felt a spasm in my stomach and then much, much lower.

"I *did* tell you, but you didn't believe me."

Turning in my chair, I waved Nell over. "Can I pretty please have another beer if I promise to be quiet?"

Nell looked at me with uncertainty and then gave a reluctant sigh. "You're not drivin', are ya?"

I shook my head.

"Well, in that case . . . Can I get you another one, handsome?" she asked, looking over at Jake.

He shook his head. "No thanks, I'm good."

"Yes, you are," I heard her say underneath her breath as she sauntered off.

I looked back at Jake, who was watching me closely. "What? You don't think I can handle another beer?"

He dipped his head, running a tanned hand along the back of his neck. "I don't know. Do you always drink like this?"

"No. I rarely drink, and when I do it's normally a glass or two of wine."

"I was afraid of that."

"What is *that* supposed to mean?" I demanded, staring at his broad shoulders, the dangerous way his black hair curled across his forehead, his magical eyes that matched the rolling waves of the ocean. Oh crap. "Forget it. I'm going to use the restroom."

Before he could respond, I stood up from my chair and forced myself forward, not knowing where I was going. It didn't take long to discover the room was starting to spin. My eyes darted quickly from one corner of the restaurant to the next, desperately searching for the women's room. When I saw the sign above the entrance, I made a beeline toward it, closing the door tightly behind me.

It was then that I heard an alarm ping from inside my purse. Opening it up, I retrieved my cell phone, my eyes moving over a new text message from Ruby.

Addy, what the hell's going on? Your mom said she saw you leave with Jake Grady! I don't know where you are or what you're up to, but you need to call me this instant!

Oh shit. Mom saw me leave? This couldn't be good.

Ruby, everything's fine. Yes, I'm with Jake. We just sort of ran into each other. I can't talk now, but I'll call you later. BTW, the funeral home looks amazing. You're the absolute best. XO

I leaned back against the oak door and let out a long breath. Hopefully that would be enough to keep Ruby quiet for a while. Before I put my phone away, I turned off the ringer. "What *are* you doing?" I asked out loud. "Besides making a total fool of yourself!"

"You're not makin' a fool of yourself, sweetie," I heard a raspy voice say. "That boy is clearly taken by you."

My eyebrows drew together as I bent down, eyeing the pink cowboy boots in the stall closest to me. The toilet flushed, and Nell walked out, barely looking at me as she made her way toward the sink.

"My only suggestion would be to sip the next drink a little slower. You're startin' to look like a lush." She washed her hands, then grabbed a paper towel, drying them off and discarding it in the trash. She turned to face me. "There are plenty of women in this town who'd be more than happy to get horizontal with that boy—if ya know what I mean, and I think ya do."

God, did I know.

"He's enough to make a good girl forget her reputation. But if ya haven't noticed, he only has eyes for you."

I stepped back, my gaze dropping to the floor. "Oh, uh . . . I wasn't talking about him."

Nell laughed loudly. "The hell ya weren't! Look, I know burnin' loins when I see 'em, and you, girl, have got a ragin' fire on your hands. You're gonna need someone to put out that blaze," she said, arching her eyebrows. "Don't try to kid yourself."

I crinkled my nose. "I'm engaged to someone else. He's a doctor and he loves me very much. Definitely more than he loves his patients." Good gravy, why couldn't I just shut up?

"Hmm, that's too bad. I thought maybe you and that boy had a history together."

I felt my cheeks blush. "We do. Jake was my first love."

Nell gave me a knowing smile. "Ahh, first love. Well, that explains it. A girl never quite gets over her first love.

I know I never did, that's why I married him. May the ol' goat rest in peace."

"Did you always know he was the one?"

Nell looked off to the side, a faraway look in her eyes. "Oh, I always knew he was the one. But then he left town without me to ride the rodeo circuit and I thought I'd never see him again. He found his way back a few years later after an injury forced him to give up ridin'. I snatched him up right away, and the rest is history. We were married for thirty-three years before colon cancer took him home."

She looked at me, her eyes moist with tears. "I don't regret a single day I spent with that man. And knowin' what I know now and all the struggles we had along the way, I'd do it over again in a heartbeat if I had the chance." She pulled a napkin from her pocket and touched it to each eye. "You know, Addy, every moment gives us a new beginnin' and a new endin'. You get a second chance every moment of your life. You just have to learn to make the most of it. Anyway, I gotta get back to work. You take it easy on that drink, ya hear. And on that boy." She walked out of the restroom.

By the time I made it back to the table my stomach was tangled in knots and a new drink was waiting for me.

"Are you okay?" Jake asked when I sat down. "You were gone for a while. I was getting worried."

I scanned the room, searching for Nell. She was behind the bar, chatting away with another waitress. Our eyes met and she gave me a wink. "I'm fine, just ran into someone in the restroom." I tore my gaze away from her and looked at Jake. There was a time when I thought he was the one, or at least thought he could be. Had I ever honestly felt that way about Christopher? Of course,

I loved Christopher, but was I *in love* with him? Or were all of these crazy insecurities brought on by the beer? The longer I sat there, the harder it was to think. "You know, I—"

Just then my hand caught the handle of my mug and it tipped over, spilling the contents all over the table. Jake and I stood up, throwing the stack of napkins on top of the mess. Dark golden liquid gushed way across the table, despite our best efforts to contain it.

A couple of nearby waitresses made their way over, wiping up the spill with large clothes. "I'm so sorry," I gasped. "It was an accident."

"Of course it was, sweetie," one waitress said. "It's happened a million times before and it'll happen a million times again. Don't you worry about it, this is an easy fix. Other things, not so much." She turned to Jake, her eyes moving appreciatively up the length of him. "I'll be right back to clean this up properly."

"Do you think Nell could bring the check?" Jake asked before she left. "I think we've had enough. Is that all right?" He looked back at me, a question in his eyes.

I felt my shoulders fall at the thought of our reunion ending. "Okay." I shrugged, trying to seem as though I didn't care.

"Sure thing." The waitress walked toward the bar and we sat down as Nell made her way toward us.

"Callin' it a day?" she asked.

Jake smiled at her. "I think so. What do we owe you?"

"Here's the check," she said, handing it over. "I took the last drink off since Addy didn't get to enjoy it." Nell threw me another wink.

"Thank you, Nell. I'm sorry I made such a mess."

She waved her hand. "It ain't no skin off my back. No harm, no foul."

Jake reached into his wallet and handed over a few bills. "Here you go, Nell. Thanks for taking care of us. Keep the change."

Nell's face broke into a wide smile. "Why thank you, handsome. I'd say you're a keeper." She gave me a sideways glance, her eyes twinkling mischievously. I returned her smile, hoping Jake hadn't seen the exchange. "Maybe I'll see you two later? I take it you're going to the burial tomorrow?"

"We'll be there," Jake answered. His eyes moved from Nell then back to me. "Are you ready, Addison?"

My lips pursed and I nodded. "Thanks, Nell. For everything."

"My pleasure, sweetie. I'll see ya soon."

"What do I owe you?" I asked Jake, as we stood from our chairs.

"Not a thing. This was on me." Jake rested his hand on the small of my back as he guided me toward the door.

Chapter Twenty-Six

"Well, I don't think going back to the wake is a good idea," Jake said after we settled into his truck. "Your parents will have a fit if they find out you're drunk."

I rolled my eyes and let out a sigh. "I'm not drunk, Jake."

"Oh no? Do you always walk with a wobble?" He glanced at me sideways, a crooked smile playing on his lips.

A wave of heat made its way across my face. "It's my ankle. I guess it's still a little tender." Oh, who was I kidding? If I'd finished that last drink before it spilled, I would have gone from sloppy to completely shit-faced in a matter of minutes. And Jake *knew* it. I wasn't fooling him.

"Well, either way, it's probably not a good idea. Unless you really want to go back?"

Going back to the funeral home was the last thing I wanted to do. A feeling of guilt flowed through me. "Not really," I answered quietly. "Is that bad?"

He shook his head and lifted his hand, unbuttoning the top of his shirt, then gently pulling at the tie until it hung loosely around his neck. "I don't think so. Mags knows you love her. Your family knows you love her. I don't think you have to go to the wake to prove that. And besides, who cares what anyone else thinks? Not everyone handles funerals well. But the choice is yours. I'll take you wherever you want to go."

A needle of reflection pricked at my chest. I knew exactly where I wanted to go. "I want to go to the farm," I said, holding my breath.

I watched Jake turn toward me slowly, an expression I couldn't make sense of covering his face. "Are you sure?" he asked, his brows crumpling slightly.

I nodded. "I'm sure."

Heading west through town, Jake took the rural country road that led to the farm, following the lazy curves until the hull of an old barn came into view.

My gaze flickered over his face as we approached the long drive, taking notice as his jaw clenched when he turned onto the property. "It's been a long time since I've seen this place," he said quietly, parking the truck and turning off the engine. "Hard to believe it's been ten years."

Jake removed his tie and button-up, revealing a tight white T-shirt underneath. I could see the cut of his pecs stirring underneath the thin fabric, and *good gravy*, my pulse kicked up a notch.

Silently, we hopped out of the truck and closed the doors behind us. We began a slow walk along a bush-lined path that forked off to an open pasture. Broken sunlight passed through the scarlet oaks and buckeye trees as a sense of quiet contentment swirled between us. "It's so peaceful here. I feel as if I can breathe. It's like I've been holding my breath without even realizing it, and it finally releases once I'm here. It happens every time I come home." I turned to look at him. "Does that sound weird?"

Jake shook his head. "Not at all. I remember your family's farm fondly, I think it's why I have a small one of my own. There's just something about it that draws you in. I never could understand why you wanted to leave here. At the time, I thought maybe it was because of Brett. But you left anyway, even after he was no longer a threat."

I let out a soft chuckle. "Brett Lawrence—God, I haven't thought of him in ages." A gentle breeze blew across my cheek, and I reached up to tuck the hair out of my face. "I was just a kid. I was convinced there was a big world out there waiting for me. It didn't seem right hanging around a small town."

"Do you still feel that way?" he asked, his gaze locking with mine.

A slow smile eased its way across my face. "I've found a new appreciation for small-town living. Atlanta's just so big and congested. I don't think I'd ever want to raise a family there, not that I'm worrying about that right now. It's just too bad it took my moving away to come to that conclusion. Don't get me wrong, I'm glad I branched out a little. I don't think I would have felt satisfied if I hadn't. If I hadn't moved away, I think I always would have wondered what I was missing, so I guess I have no regrets. It's just . . . coming back here makes me miss the way life used to be. So simple and peaceful. Do you feel like that at your ranch?"

Jake's gaze held mine for an instant longer, then he wheeled around and stared straight ahead. "I love living on the ranch. Having a wide-open spot all to myself with no one nearby to watch over what I'm doing. It gives me a sense of freedom." He looked back at me. "That's how

I felt working here that summer. Like nothing or no one could touch me. It was exactly what I needed at the time."

We followed the path for a while without saying a word and I couldn't help but travel down memory lane, remembering all the times we'd walked there before, spending time together under the warm Georgia sun, falling in love. "I'm sorry about your engagement," I finally said, staring up at him. "I was out of line at the restaurant and I apologize. Guess maybe I did have a little too much to drink."

Jake walked beside me, his arm occasionally brushing against mine, sending a shiver up my skin with each feathery touch. He looked off into the field, his eyes squinting in the setting sun. "No apology necessary. You're right. I won't commit. I've tried to, but something always holds me back." He turned and looked at me, his eyes intense as they bored into mine.

My breath caught just a little and my heart started beating faster than it should have. "Why do you think that is?" Silently, I waited to hear the words I'd dreamed of hearing so many times in my dreams. The words I would have given anything for.

He hesitated a moment before answering, and when he did his voice was thick with emotion. "I think I've been carrying around this illusion of love. I've tried to recreate what I felt once before, but it's never quite the same; it just doesn't match. I always find something wrong with her, or the relationship—or even me. I keep waiting for that *feeling*, only it never comes." He paused. "There was something that kept a distance between me and Tamara, something that keeps a distance between me and any woman I get close to." Jake reached over and tucked a stray strand of hair behind my ear. I closed my eyes against the whisper of his fingers grazing my cheek.

How many times had I silently urged him to do that? How was it possible that one simple gesture could make me feel the way it did? Fulfilled, electrified . . . *alive*. When I opened my eyes, he was staring at me. "You're a hard woman to get over, Addison."

I swallowed hard, consumed by the guilt I'd been holding on to for years. What woman in her right mind would leave this kind of man? "Jake—I'm so sorry, I—"

"It's all right, Addison, you don't need to apologize," he interrupted, not allowing me to rehash my regret. "I understand why you did what you did. I mean, it took me a while to realize it, but eventually I figured it out." Jake looked straight ahead, the muscle in his jaw straining against his skin.

"Why didn't you ever call me? Why didn't you at least try to make me see?"

He sighed, looking as if he was gathering his thoughts. "It wasn't my place. You needed to make that decision on your own, I couldn't make it for you. I just hoped in time you'd realize what you were doing and you'd get in touch with me. When you didn't, I had to move on."

I lowered my head, ashamed. "A couple of weeks after we last saw each other, I did realize what I'd done—what I threw away. Nothing was the same without you, I was miserable. I called your aunt and uncle's house, but it was too late. You'd already left town."

Jake stopped walking and turned to face me. "You called my aunt and uncle's house? They never said anything."

"I asked them not to. I figured it was a sign that you were better off where you were and I shouldn't interfere."

His eyebrows wrinkled with confusion. "But why did you call them? Why didn't you call *me*?"

My breathing became shallow as his eyes pressed into mine, searching for answers he'd waited ten years for. "I was afraid. I was afraid you'd turn me away after what I'd done. And I couldn't take that. I couldn't stand the thought of you breaking my heart." I averted my eyes, embarrassed by my confession.

Jake caught the edge of my chin, forcing me to look at him. "Addison, I could never turn you away. Didn't you know how much I loved you?"

My throat was so tight, but I managed a nod. God, his *eyes*! They were so blue and profound as they drilled into mine. My heart plummeted as I fought for control.

"I'd never felt that way about anyone before, not the way I felt about you. And I've not felt that way about anyone since. I've tried to tell myself I'm being ridiculous, that what we had was just young love, but my heart refuses to believe what my head tries to tell it." Jake looked off into the distance for a moment, then turned his gaze back to me.

"When we met, I felt like we had this immediate connection, and the thing is—I wasn't even looking for it. In fact, it was the furthest thing from my mind. Which is the reason why I knew it had to be real. When I told you I loved you, I really meant it. I'd never said that to another girl before."

My stomach dipped and then tangled into a thousand tiny knots. Whether he knew it or not, Jake had a hold on me—just like he did the first time we'd met—it was as if time and distance had never separated us. The chemistry we had all those years before, it was still there, and I knew he felt it, too.

"I loved you," I finally said, surprising myself by opening up. "I had never let a guy get that close to me before, but you were different. My feelings for you that summer . . . they scared me. And then knowing you were only going to be in town for a short while before heading back to school and the swim team, and the . . . girls." I paused, shaking my head. "I couldn't compete with that."

"You didn't have to compete with that. There was nothing in the world more important than you."

I let out a slow, ragged breath. Why had I been so stubborn? Why couldn't I have just accepted what we had was real, that maybe it could have lasted? Why hadn't I listened to Mags? If I had, who knew what our lives would be like now. "I'm so sorry. How can you not hate me?"

Jake shook his head and gathered me in his arms. "I could never hate you, Addison."

Silence fell between us as we stood holding one another, the evening song of cicadas carrying across the soft breeze. I squeezed my eyes shut, trying to ignore the pain that was making its way across my chest. There was a time when he'd held my heart in the palm of his hand, and when he returned to Texas he had taken a piece of it with him. It was obvious to me now that I'd never gotten it back.

He pulled away, and in the fragile light of dusk, our eyes met. Without another word we began to walk again, the dirt path crunching beneath our feet. Jake reached for my hand and our fingers entwined, just as they had done so many years before. A slow tingle began at my toes and made its way up the length of my body, mixing inside my head until I couldn't think straight. How long had it been since I'd held hands with a man? That was something Christopher and I never did—I'm not really sure why. Holding Jake's hand now felt good, it felt natural, but most of all, it felt *right*.

As the path began to wind down our pace slowed,

turning into a gradual shuffle. *Don't let this get out of control. You have a fiancé at home waiting for you.* My eyes traveled across the jeweled tones of the sky as the sun descended below the horizon, contemplating the situation I was in. Yet no matter how rational I tried to be, the feeling of Jake's body so close to mine was all it took to stir up the memory of him, of kissing him, of touching him . . . When my gaze drifted forward, it settled on the spot where I knew we'd end up.

The barn.

With the red sun declining in the darkening sky, my heart nearly stood still when we entered the building. Jake held the door open, inviting me inside. He turned on a light and I watched as he made his way to an empty horse stall, his hand curving over the edge of the gate.

With him standing there like that, wearing those boots, it threw me back to a certain afternoon we'd spent there, and a shiver of sexual awareness prickled its way up my spine. With his back to me, my eyes roamed around the curves of his body, lingering longer in all the right places. If he wasn't the most gorgeous man I'd ever seen . . .

"Where are the horses?" he asked, interrupting my fantasies.

I sucked in a sharp breath, praying he hadn't felt my eyes secretly molesting him. "Gramps had a new barn built a few years back. It's just a little ways down on the other side of the farmhouse. That's where the horses stay. They store equipment in here now."

Jake nodded his head as his gaze moved around the barn, finally landing on the hayloft above. The corner of his mouth lifted into a slow smile, and when he turned to look at me, his eyes were full of mischief. "Remember that afternoon we spent up there?"

Did I remember? Oh yeah, I remembered. How could

I possibly forget? I nodded as a rush of heat made its way through my body, stirring up tingles in well-hidden places. With any luck, the dim light from the bulbs had concealed the inappropriate thoughts filtering through my mind.

"Do you mind if I take a peek?" he asked, cocking his head toward the ladder.

Visions of Jake climbing into the loft ten years before swam before me. "Not at all."

He took long strides, crossing the room quickly. He moved seamlessly, swinging his leg onto the ladder with the grace of a man who'd done it a thousand times before. As he pulled himself up a couple of rungs, his biceps flexed against the sleeves of his shirt. "Are you coming up?" he asked, looking down at me.

My body thrummed with a feeling I was embarrassed to admit, even to myself. The sleepy memory of our time spent in that loft had been awakened and was having a reckless effect on my good judgment. I kicked off my dress shoes and moved forward, following him up the ladder. When he reached the top, he offered his hand to help me up the rest of the way.

"How's your ankle?" he asked with an easy grin, the dimple in his cheek playing peek-a-boo in the faint light drifting up.

"It's fine, thanks."

Jake reached overhead and pulled a thin chain, allowing a soft glow to illuminate the loft. With bare feet, I crossed the floor and sat down, folding my dress underneath me. I let my feet dangle over the edge of the open hay drop, and stared up at the blackening sky above.

The moon was full and round as it hovered brightly behind a distant tree line, and a silky breeze wafted over the pasture. I heard Jake behind me, the heels of his boots clicking softly against the wooden planks and strands of hay.

After a while, he sat down next to me and we watched as the final rays of sunlight disappeared behind the rolling foothills. "This brings back a lot of memories," he finally said, breaking the silence. "A lot of *really* good memories. That was an amazing summer."

I caught his gaze and held it. "It was a great summer. Probably the best summer of my life."

For the next half hour we revisited those months, laughing easily over the good times we'd shared. We retraced our steps up until the point where the memories became cluttered by heartbreak. The night slowly grew darker and the stars blazed brightly overhead, like a wave of sparkling crystals across the ebony sky.

"I used to love saying things that made you blush," he said, a lazy smile inching its way across his face, making my pulse race just a little faster. "You were so easy to get worked up."

"And you were so charming," I laughed lightly, catching my hair as it fell against my cheek. I removed the messy knot I had made earlier and ran my fingers through the waves until they poured over my shoulders. "You still are."

His eyes met mine and held them, refusing to let go. "I know. It's sort of a curse," he teased quietly, the look on his face saying more than words ever could. Jake leaned back, propping himself up on his elbows, his gaze sweeping across the vast field in front of us. "Do you think you'll be ready for tomorrow?"

My breath released slowly. It was a topic I had pushed out of my mind. "I don't know," I admitted. "I'm not sure

I'll ever be ready to say good-bye." Suddenly, my eyes brimmed with tears and my breathing grew rapid. I turned away, not wanting him to see me cry.

Jake sat up and put his arm around me, pulling me into his chest. "I'm sorry, Addison," he whispered into my hair. "I am so sorry this has happened."

Unexpectedly, my chest tightened and all the times I'd thought of Jake over the years swirled together, creating one big, heavy mass. The heat of our bodies together felt so right, and I began to tremble with need and longing.

Lifting my head off his chest, I looked into his eyes and felt the years that had separated us melt away. Jake lifted his hand and cupped my cheek, then rested his forehead against mine. I felt his breath punch out of him in quick, little bursts and I pushed all thoughts of what was right and wrong out of the way.

My heart was pounding as I straddled his lap, drinking in the desire I saw burning in his eyes. Jake grabbed my hips and pulled me in closer, then lifted his hands to my face as long waves of my hair tangled intimately between his fingers. When he whispered my name I almost came undone, every inch of me wanting to experience more. I pressed into him, desperate to feel the strength and comfort of his body against mine. He tugged gently at my hair, exposing my neck, and the heat of his breath skimmed across my fevered skin. I waited to feel his lips devouring me the same way they'd done before, but they never came. I pulled back, my eyes searching his. The moment was right, *it felt so right*, he had to feel it, too. Didn't he?

Jake opened his mouth and let out a soft breath, hesitating slightly before bringing his lips to mine. The kiss was soft and tender, almost timid, as if we were kissing again for the very first time. His hands dropped to my waist as mine slid through his dark waves and our embrace intensified, causing a series of vibrations to move through my body. I opened my mouth, inviting his tongue inside. Our tongues probed against one another, teasing and enticing, until a pool of warmth gathered low in my stomach.

I melted into him, clinging to his body as if I'd never let go. And in that moment, I never wanted to. Not ever again. Our hips rolled together as his lips moved lower, lower, over the curves of my shoulder. My body went limp, surrendering wholeheartedly to a deep-seated desire.

When one hand moved slowly from my waist, inching its way up to the fullest part of my breast, a spark jolted through me, electrifying and delicious. I threw my head back, a tiny gasp escaping my mouth from the sudden charge. I hadn't expected this to happen, it was never the plan, but now that it had, there was no turning back. I needed Jake in the same way I needed blood in my veins and breath in my lungs. I needed him the same way I knew he needed me.

His lips moved up over my collarbone, brushing against the tender hollow below my ear, and my body ached, thinking of his mouth ravishing the rest of me. I wanted him, more than I'd ever wanted anyone in my life.

My breath rushed in and out as his tongue made slow, excruciating strokes along the arc of my jaw, leaving me dizzy with the memory of him from so long ago. Then his mouth found mine once more and he kissed me, wet and deep, tasting me in a way I hadn't experienced in a very long time. When I caught his lower lip between my teeth, a deep sound of approval rumbled in the back of his throat, sending a rush of molten lava through my veins.

And then without warning, he stopped. Jake pulled away, his breath ragged as he dragged his lips from mine.

Oh no, no, no! Confusion consumed me and I swallowed a plea, my body screaming, crying out for his touch. But when I looked into his eyes I knew something had changed. I wasn't sure what he was thinking but his gaze blazed with intensity, differently than before.

Jake shook his head, his expression apologetic. "I'm sorry, I can't do this."

My breath caught in my throat, threatening to choke the life out of me. "What do you mean?" I whispered, unable to fill my lungs with air.

"Addison," he began, his eyes locking with mine. "I don't want to complicate things for you."

My shoulders slumped forward with the blow of rejection. I shook my head, desperate for him to understand. "Things are already complicated."

"I gathered that." He averted his eyes, his breathing still heavy. "It's natural to want to feel intimacy after the death of a loved one, but that doesn't make what we're doing right. You're in a dark place right now, you're vulnerable, and the man you're in love with isn't here with you—but I am." Jake looked back at me, his deep, sapphire eyes pleading. "As much as I want to be with you, this can't happen. I will not take advantage of you like this."

I leaned back as humiliation sank deep into me.

"Come on," he said quietly. "I'll take you home."

My knees wobbled as we walked back to my parents' house, and Jake's words played over and over in my mind. *"You're in a dark place right now, you're vulnerable, and the man you're in love with isn't here with you—but I am.*" Yet I wasn't convinced that what he said was true. What if the man I loved was standing right here next to me? Maybe I'd been in love with him the whole time. Or maybe I was falling in love with him all over again. I didn't know. Could it be possible?

When we arrived on the front porch, Jake waited patiently while I took out my key and unlocked the door, opening it to the dark, empty house. He leaned forward, his hand traveling along the wall until it found a switch. Then he flipped it up, filling the room with light. Moving back, he stared at me, his expression softening. "I'm really sorry," he repeated. When he came closer, his hand gently grasped the back of my head and he planted a tender kiss on my forehead. "I'll see you tomorrow."

I stood on the porch, my insides tingling with a mixture of emotions. With everything inside me I knew Jake was right. I had no business being there with him; I was engaged. And yet being together had felt so perfect.

The night was soft and dark and the stars blazed brightly lighting up the sky, a spectacular view I couldn't find in the city. But I couldn't appreciate it. All I could think of as I watched Jake's truck disappear from sight was that we weren't finished.

Not even close.

Chapter Twenty-Seven

When the first rays of sunlight trickled in through my window, I'd already been awake for hours staring at my ceiling, rehashing the events of the previous day. Jake Grady was the last person in the world I imagined running into. As many times as I had thought about him over the years, there was never a moment he was further away from my mind.

And then BAM, there he was, in all his hot Texas glory, and suddenly the world made even less sense. It had been nearly a decade since I'd seen him last. A *decade*. Yet at the same time it felt like just yesterday. He was different now, older and more mature, yet somehow exactly the same all rolled into one. And his eyes, his voice, his *mouth* . . . Oh God, his *mouth*.

And what happened last night!

Suddenly, my heart tugged and I flung a bare arm up over my face, covering my eyes as humiliation washed over me once again. Jake's rejection rose up to the surface, through the deep, murky waters of confusion and grief, and bobbed up and down screaming like a banshee demanding to be heard.

I swallowed a moan and rolled onto my side, pushing long, tangled hair away with my hand. What had I been thinking, kissing him like that? Well, technically he'd kissed me, but how could he not after I threw myself at him? Straddling his hips, the feel of his hard body between my legs, the catch of his breath as I—

Oh, God! Just stop it, would you?

I curled into the fetal position and squeezed my eyes shut, praying what happened in the loft had all been a dream. But I knew it hadn't. Not with the way my body hummed now, as if it was hopped up on crack and fifty shades of lust.

For a long while after he left, I sat in a chair and stared out the window into the dark, my mind replaying the image of his truck driving away—and of it driving away ten years before. Jake said I'd broken his heart. That *I'd* broken *his* heart. Who would have thought? That entire summer I'd been consumed by the idea of him breaking mine, it never occurred to me it would be the other way around. I'd been so preoccupied by protecting myself I never once thought about protecting him. And that made me *bad*. That made me *very, very bad*. Even worse than bad. That made me a coldhearted bitch.

Almost an hour went by before the bright headlights of my parents' SUV turned into the drive, snapping me out of my masochistic stupor. I hurried up the stairs, kicked off my shoes, flung my dress on a chair, and scurried into bed, burying myself deep under a mass of thick blankets. A few minutes later, I heard the bedroom door crack open, and the soft light from the hallway filtered inside.

I fought to stay still so they'd think I was asleep, and it worked. My parents closed the door gently and left me alone, alone with my thoughts and the memory of Jake's touch still sending currents of heat to my core.

I rolled onto my back, a frustrated breath depleting my lungs. And today. *Today.* How could I face him again? And how in the world was I supposed to deliver a eulogy for a woman I wasn't ready to say good-bye to? Giving myself a mental shake, I reached for my phone to check the time and noticed I had three missed calls and several texts, every last one of them from Ruby.

Call me as soon as you get this, I don't care what time it is! the final message read. Did that mean right now? Would she really want me to wake her up at 6:30 in the morning? There was nothing my best friend hated more than waking up with the sun; in fact, she designed her whole business around *not* having to do it.

A minute later, I was listening to the ring of the phone, waiting to see if Ruby would pick up. After what felt like forever, she finally came through. "Addy?" she began, her voice thick with sleep. "What time is it?"

"It's about six thirty," I whispered, not wanting my parents to know I was awake. "I'm sorry, I wasn't sure if you wanted me to call you this early—"

All at once, Ruby revived, her voice crisp and clear and laced with a desperate enthusiasm. "No, this is fine. I've been waiting to hear from you all night! What the hell happened, Addy? How did you end up with Jake?"

My heart jumped at the mention of his name, and a series of quivers shifted through me. "I just—we just—sort of ran into each other," I stated lamely.

"You ran into each other? Obviously," she said wryly. "Come on, what happened? Is he still as gorgeous as he was before?"

I sighed. "Even more so."

"*Holy shit*," I heard her say slowly underneath her breath. "So, is he married?"

I shook my head, amused by the irony of it all. "Nope. He's single. And perfect. With an amazing body and features so chiseled they could cut glass." I sighed again, then added offhandedly, "You know, he almost got married once. To a beautiful fashion designer from Dallas. Seriously, beautiful isn't even the right word— maybe breathtaking? Or stunning? Flawless?" I let out an ill-humored laugh. "But he said he couldn't go through with it." I paused, still unable to believe his words. "Ruby—Jake said I broke his heart. He said he never got over me."

I was met by silence on the other end. "Ruby? Are you there?" I asked, shaking my phone. As if that was going to help the connection any, but I wasn't exactly grounded in reality at that moment.

"I'm here," she finally whispered. "You have *got* to be kidding me. I mean, what the hell? I can't believe this is happening now that you're engaged. What are you going to do?"

"What do you mean, what am I going to do?"

"I mean, *what are you going to do*? Did you feel any of the old feelings? Were there any sparks? Would you say you were *hot and bothered* being with him?"

Hot and bothered? Yeah, you could say that. Shaking my head, I sat up in bed and cradled my face in my free hand. "I kissed him."

"You *what*?" Ruby gasped. "*You* kissed *him*?"

"Yes, I kissed him. And then he pulled away."

"*He* pulled *away*?"

"Yes, Ruby. *He* pulled *away*," I answered with a huff. "Would you please stop repeating everything I say? I need to hear words of wisdom right now, not some stupid echo."

"I'm sorry, Addy, I'm just in shock! This is not at *all* what I expected to hear at the ass-crack of dawn! Holy *shit* . . . I'm speechless."

"Oh, great. For the first time in your life you're speechless. Just what I need."

"All right, all right. Just give me a second, okay? What do you expect? You dropped a bomb on me before I was even fully awake. And not just *any* bomb, I might add. A freakin' *hydrogen* bomb!"

Okay, I'd give her that. I waited and waited for what felt like an eternity before she finally spoke again.

"I've got nothing," she said, her voice unusually flat.

Wait. What? "How the hell can you have nothing? You always have *something*—whether I ask you or not!"

"Jesus, Addy! I'm not a shrink!" I heard her release a long, drawn-out sigh. "Let me get some coffee in me, okay? I'll be able to think much clearer after that. In the meantime, do not panic."

Really? Do not panic? That was her advice? I was already *way* past panic. I was quickly approaching strait-jacket time.

"Addy, are you listening to me? *Do not panic!*"

"Yes, Ruby. I heard you. Do not panic. Thanks for that. That's some pretty sage advice there."

"Just give me some time, all right? I promise, I won't let you down."

After we hung up, I didn't feel any better. In fact, I felt a whole lot worse. Flipping onto my stomach, I pushed my face in the pillow and let out a long scream.

Several hours later, I stood at the back of the church with my family, greeting the guests as they made their way inside. So many of them wanted to share memories or little threads of wisdom Mags had imparted over the years. Most of the stories made me laugh, but some made me tear up, and the last thing I wanted was to open the floodgates. After a while, I could barely listen anymore, couldn't let myself feel, or the tears would come and there would be no stopping them.

The casket was centered at the front, near the altar, the top open to allow everyone a final farewell. When Ruby arrived with her parents, I gave each of them a hug before they settled into a pew in the middle of the church. Out of the corner of my eye, I caught a glimpse of Ruby, waving me over. I hurried up the aisle, the hem of my black dress grazing my ankles, and moved into the pew. Ruby shifted down, giving me room to squeeze in.

"I know you're busy," she said quietly, "so I won't keep you. Nice boots, by the way," she said, glancing down at the red leather. "I'm sure your mom's thrilled you decided to wear them today."

I smiled. "You know it. It just felt right. Like I'm supposed to wear them, and I don't care if it's appropriate or not."

"I think you look incredible. Anyway, I just wanted to let you know that you're absolutely glowing."

I sat back, stunned. "Glowing?" I moved my hands to my cheeks. "I'm probably just flushed. It's really humid outside today, I couldn't even straighten my hair," I said, running fingers through persistent brown waves. "It must have rained last night."

Ruby cocked her head and gave me a look. "It's humid, but it's not *that* humid, Addy. You look—I don't know how to say this without sounding crazy. But you look . . . *awakened*, somehow."

"Well, I *have* been awake for several hours now. I barely slept. I must be ruddy with exhaustion."

"That's not what I mean and you know it." She gave me a small smile and touched her hand to my cheek, her brown eyes filled with affection. "Whatever happened last night certainly agrees with you."

I lifted my chin. "Oh, you mean being rejected? Yeah, I think so, too. It feels pretty good, almost like a badge of honor or something."

Ruby dropped her hand and playfully pinched my side. "Stop being difficult, Addy. I'm giving you my advice."

I bounced at her touch, then dipped my head lower as I leaned in close. "Oh, thank God. I'm going crazy trying to figure out how I should handle him today. I made such a fool out of myself last night," I whispered.

Ruby shook her head, her glossy blond hair pinned up into a sleek, classic bun. "I don't think you did. Jake said he never got over you, right?"

I nodded.

"Then he didn't suddenly get over you last night, no matter how big an ass you were." Her eyes widened suddenly and her voice dropped an octave. "Shit—can I cuss in church? Anyway, I imagine you told him about Christopher?"

"Yes, of course I did."

She shrugged one shoulder. "Jake was always the good guy, you know? The noble protector of your good name. I just don't think he wants to get in between you and Christopher. But I definitely don't think you should rule him out."

My eyebrows shot up. "What? How can I not? I'm engaged to be married."

"Yes, but do you even have a wedding date?"

I felt my brows hitch. "No, but what does that have to

do with anything? I have a ring on my finger," I said, holding up my left hand.

Ruby's breath caught as she stared at my diamond, and she lifted a well-manicured hand to her chest, momentarily distracted. "Would you stop waving that rock in my face? It literally takes my breath away. Anyway," she said, shaking her head as I folded my hands in my lap, "maybe this is a sign?"

A sign? Come on! Who believed in that kind of stuff? "Or maybe it's just a coincidence?"

"*Or* maybe it's a signal from the universe trying to get you to understand something? Something you were too dense to pick up on before."

I gave her a scowl, but bit my tongue.

"Maybe it wants you to become aware of your destiny and take action before it's too late." Ruby leaned in closer, her lips close to my ear. "*Maybe* it's a sign from Mags?"

I jolted upright in my seat. A sign from Mags? My eyes drifted toward the casket as I remembered the last conversation we'd shared—the one about my engagement. Had I mentioned that to Ruby? I didn't think I had. Could it be possible that my grandmother was playing matchmaker again, but this time from somewhere beyond the grave? *No, stop it! You're being ridiculous. Don't let Ruby's superstitions wear off on you.*

"Think about it," she continued. "Mags always liked Jake. Maybe this is her way of bringing you two together."

"Are you suggesting she *died* to prove a point? Because that's just sick."

Ruby rolled her eyes. "That's not what I'm saying at all. But wouldn't it be just like Mags to intervene in your life even after she passed?" Ruby and I slowly turned to stare at the casket as silence fell between us. "Love is a matter of following your heart, Addy," she finally said, turning back to me. "We get a second chance every minute of our lives. What if this is your second chance with Jake?"

Oh crap. Where had I heard that before? I slumped back against the hard wood of the pew and took in a deep breath, lost in thoughts of what-ifs and second chances. Just then, Ruby let out a quiet gasp and I followed her gaze to the back of the church.

Jake. Looking downright edible in a pair of pressed jeans, his trademark boots, a navy jacket and tie. I shook my head, attempting to purify my thoughts. *Especially* since we were guests in the house of the Lord, for crying out loud.

"*Daaaayum*," Ruby murmured underneath her breath. So much for not swearing in church.

Ruby and I exchanged a look. "Follow your heart, Addy," she whispered again.

I leaned in and gave her a hug before standing up to walk down the aisle. Jake was shaking my dad's hand when I approached, my mom and his aunt and uncle gathered nearby. It was impossible for me not to stare as I made my way toward him, and when he looked over at me his eyes latched onto mine.

"So, how long are you in town for, Jake?" I heard Dad ask, but Jake was still watching me, his eyes warm and kind. His smile tipped up a notch when I reached his side.

"He's leaving after the burial," Kathy Grady answered before pulling me in for a hug. "Addy, it's been so long! You look beautiful. We are so sorry to hear about your grandma. She was a wonderful lady."

I nodded and returned her embrace, but inside my heart plummeted. What did she mean Jake was leaving after the burial? Was it because of what happened last night? Ugh, how could I have been so stupid?

"Are you at least staying for the luncheon?" I heard Mom ask through the haze. "There'll be a get-together in the church hall after the burial."

Jake pulled his eyes away from mine. "Actually, I've had a change of plans. I'm in town until sometime tomorrow."

"When did that happen?" Jake's uncle John asked. "I thought you had an important meeting in the morning."

"I spoke with my boss yesterday and told him there's no way I would be back in time. I found someone else to stand in for me."

Aunt Kathy looked pleased. "Oh, that's so nice, honey. I'm glad you'll be staying a bit longer. We don't get to see you nearly enough."

But I'd barely heard what she was saying. My mind drifted back to the restaurant when Jake had excused himself to make some phone calls. I'd assumed he'd called his aunt and uncle to let them know where he was. Perhaps that was when he spoke to his boss as well?

Aunt Kathy and Uncle John began to make their way down the aisle, but Jake lingered behind, eyeing me with concern. "Are you ready for today?" he asked, his voice deep and smooth.

I shrugged lightly. "As ready as I'm going to be." My eyes searched his, wondering about his meeting at work. "How can you stay if you're supposed to be back at work tomorrow?"

Jake gave me a smile and I felt my knees weaken. "I thought you could use a friend." He leaned forward, enveloping me in his arms. "Good luck with the eulogy. I'll be here rooting for you." Planting a quick kiss on my cheek, he gently released me and turned to make his way up the aisle. Stunned, I let my parents lead me to our pew.

The church was overflowing, to the point where there was only standing room left in the back, and even that area was crowded with mourners paying their respects. From the altar came the sounds of the church organ playing, as the choir Mags sang in for nearly thirty years softly came in on the chorus.

My family took up the first four rows of seating—Gramps, my parents, me, my aunts, uncles, and cousins. The enormity of my loss threatened to swallow me whole, and I spent the next thirty minutes trying to let the pastor's words comfort me.

And then suddenly it was my turn. My hands shook violently as I unfolded the speech I'd prepared and made my way to the podium on the altar. I passed Mags in the open casket but didn't dare look inside for fear I would lose what little self-control I felt. Climbing the steps, I turned and stood behind the wooden platform, meeting the expectant eyes of the full congregation. Faces I hadn't seen in a very long time, and others I'd seen more recently.

My gaze flickered across my family, and Ruby and her parents. I saw Nell sitting with the choir and a myriad of acquaintances I'd made over the years. Finally, my eyes locked with Jake's and he gave me a nod.

With moist eyes, I looked down and realized I could no longer see the words on my papers. They were a blurred mess of shapes, fuzzy and unclear, and I knew there was no way I would be able to read them. I took a deep breath and folded the sheets, placing them on the raised surface in front of me. Adjusting the microphone to a more comfortable angle, I took another deep breath and cleared my throat.

"When I came back to Lakeside this past weekend to

visit my family, the last thing I imagined doing was giving a eulogy for my grandmother, Magdalene Elise Monroe. But God works in mysterious ways, so here I am, and here all of you are, too.

"My grandmother was one of a kind. She wasn't famous or wealthy, but she was rich in so many other ways—in the ways that really matter. She had the love of her childhood sweetheart, the love of her family, the love of her community, and that's all she ever needed to feel happy and fulfilled. She was the salt of the earth, good, kind, trustworthy. She seasoned the world and everyone in it with her incessant faith.

"Mags was always a mentor to me, and I would take her my problems—always in her kitchen—and she would quietly listen until I was finished spilling my guts. Then somehow she managed to give me exactly what I needed to hear—even when it was something I didn't really want to hear. I have so many happy memories in that kitchen, her teaching me how to cook, and heart-to-hearts over dirty dinner dishes. It's where I've been nourished in so many ways since the time I was very, very young. Mags never held back, she always told it like it was. She didn't believe in sugarcoating anything—unless she was making one of her favorite desserts. Then the more sugar the better," I added with a soft chuckle.

"I think she knew every single person in this town. And she didn't *just* know them, she *knew* them. I mean, *really* knew them. She paid attention to details and remembered important dates like birthdays and anniversaries. She made everyone feel special. And she welcomed her friends into her home as if they were family—because to Mags, everyone was family. She had such a positive influence on the lives of those who knew her, and that's never been more obvious to me than it has been over these past couple of days. Listening to your stories about my grandmother has brought many smiles to my face, even though inside my heart is breaking." I glanced at Nell sitting with the choir and she gave me a wink, encouraging me to go on.

I looked at Gramps, his eyes damp with tears, and I gave him a smile. "Growing up, Gramps would always tell me that my grandmother was the best thing that ever happened to him. And for the longest time I thought he meant because she made the best fried chicken this side of the Blue Ridge Mountains." I paused and smiled. "Eventually, over time, I came to realize he was talking about so much more than just that.

"Mags was an extremely patient woman. She was never one to get angry. In fact, I can only recall one time in my life she was legitimately upset with me. I must have been around ten years old and I let my best friend Ruby convince me that Mags's prize strawberry shrubs needed replanting. And oh boy, did we do a number on them—remember that, Ruby?" I asked, looking at my friend. Ruby laughed through her tears and nodded. "I could tell Mags was really mad, but even then she didn't yell or scream. She just gave me *the look*."

I stood up a little straighter so everyone could see and tried to recreate it. I hardened my eyes while my lips pulled at the corners.

A burst of laughter filled the congregation, and I giggled for a minute, too, lost in the memory, then regained my composure and continued on. "She gave me the look and said, 'What in the good Lord's name is the matter with you, Addy?'" The audience laughed again, a little louder this time.

I shrugged my shoulders, my eyes moving to the open casket. "I'm sorry, Mags, I still have no idea what I was thinking. Thanks for that, Ruby," I murmured, looking back at my friend. Her grin grew wider and she blew me a kiss.

My gaze fell back onto Mags, and my smile slowly faded. "After I found out that Mags had passed, it took a while for me to be all right with it, if that's what you want to call it. Actually, those aren't the correct words at all." I looked back at the crowd. "I'm not all right with it, I don't know if I ever will be. But I know *she'll* be all right. And I know our grief today is for ourselves because Mags is in a good place. God has a plan . . . even if we don't understand it. He loves us. He doesn't like to see us in pain. But that doesn't mean life will always be easy. Every day we are faced with challenges, and we all go through difficult times when the world seems unfair. I've been trying these past few days to figure out what Mags would say right now. What little piece of insight she would pass along if she were here, and I think I've come up with it. I think she would say, there is no right or wrong way to grieve. Grief is as unique as the person experiencing it. Life is unpredictable, and part of life is continuing forward even though you have no idea where you'll end up. Appreciate the times when everything feels beautiful, but remember there is no guarantee how long that will last. Accept that plans change and change can be scary, but it's how we grow. It's how we move forward. There are things that happen beyond our control and our path will shift in ways we never expected. *Embrace it*. Find the lesson and learn from it. Alter the world as you move through it and let your wake be felt by everyone who surrounds you. That's what Mags did. She created waves of kindness and compassion. And we are all better because of it."

My eyes swept over Mags, lying so still. My grandmother. My best friend. The one person in the whole world who really understood me . . . was gone.

I inhaled a sharp, ragged breath as my chest squeezed uncomfortably, and a tight knot of pain formed in my throat. Grief slipped around me like a heavy cloak. Suddenly, I felt weak. My knees buckled slightly as my body fought to maintain control. Somewhere in my heart it was the end of the world. Tears rushed to my eyes and I let out a cry.

Somehow in the haze, I saw my parents stand from their seats, a deep concern carved into their faces. And then there were arms around me, strong and comforting, supporting my weight. The sound of muffled cries resonated throughout the church, but I was unable to see anything as my gaze blurred with tears. I closed my eyes against the sudden burn, when a silky voice made its way through the fog. "It's okay, I've got you."

Startled, I pulled my head back and looked up.

Jake.

His eyes were thick with emotion and his breaths came out in long, even exhales. Leaning into his chest, I allowed myself to collapse. We stood there for a moment as hundreds of eyes watched.

When my sobs finally subsided, I drew in a deep breath and straightened, attempting to stand tall. My eyes flickered over the congregation and I spoke once again into the microphone, my voice unsteady. "My family and I would like to thank you for coming out today. For helping us celebrate the life of one truly amazing woman— the most amazing woman I have ever known. A woman who was always there for us whenever we needed her. Maybe if we learn to lean on each other now, the way we leaned on her, perhaps she won't feel so far away." I bowed my head as fresh tears surfaced.

Turning away from the podium, I allowed Jake to lead me down the steps and toward the seats next to my family. As we passed Mags in the casket I stopped suddenly and turned to face her. "I'm going to miss you so much," I whispered. "I love you." I pressed my lips to my fingers, then softly touched them to the side of her face.

My parents made room as Jake and I slid into the pew, and I was barely aware when they each came forward to give me a hug. The pastor returned to the podium and began to pray, each member of the congregation bowing their head. After the prayer ended, I stole a quick peek at Jake out of the corner of my eye. The muscles in his jaw flexed, but his gaze remained steady on the pastor as he spoke.

And then it was time. Each aisle slowly released as they filtered past Mags, paying their final respects.

I felt Jake's hand planted at the base of my back, warm and steady as he ushered me forward. When she came into view, my breath felt as if it wanted to punch out my lungs, but I hung on to it tightly, not wanting to make another scene. As I walked up to her with Jake by my side, I felt an odd calmness settle over me. This would be the final time I would ever see Mags before the casket was closed. Gingerly, I reached for her hand and gave her a smile.

A gentle touch made its way up my back, rubbing the center in long, smooth strokes. When I turned to Jake he was smiling, too.

We returned to our seats and watched as Gramps and

his children lowered the lid to the casket, closing away the image of Mags forever. My eyes shut as I thought about how there would be no new memories, only the ones I already had left, and I would have to find a way to be okay with that.

The sun poked its way through thick gray clouds and humidity was thick in the air as the funeral service progressed to the cemetery outside. Yet no matter how warm it was, the smoldering Georgia temperature couldn't chase away the chill I felt inside my chest. The sound of soft whimpers floated across the breeze as we watched the casket being lowered into the ground. I held tightly on to my parents' hands as it sank lower, away from our view.

As the graveside service drew to a close, my gaze landed on Ruby and she nodded toward the cemented path nearby. During our funeral planning, we decided we wanted to surprise the guests with something special, something to commemorate the event with a unique perspective. It felt like a good idea to end the service on a positive note, and it was something we thought Mags would appreciate. I followed her nod and discovered several church members wheeling large carts our way, each tier holding dozens of sky lanterns, enough for every person in attendance to send one off.

A wave of pleasant surprise made its way through the crowd as each person stepped forward to claim their lantern. With smiling faces, they helped each other light the lanterns, each one depicting Mags's name and the year she was born and the year she passed.

Mom came up behind me and circled her arms around my waist. "This is an amazing idea, Addy. Such a beautiful way to honor your grandmother."

I turned and gave her a hug. "I'm glad you like it. I hope they like it, too," I said, my gaze shifting to where my father and grandfather stood. They were laughing softly as Gramps held a lantern for Dad to light.

"They love it," she said quietly. "And I love you. Your eulogy was very special, absolutely beautiful."

I laughed and looked down. "Which part? When I couldn't even read the words on my paper or the part where I broke down like a crybaby?"

Mom curled her fingers underneath my chin and forced me to look up. "Every part. The whole thing. It was perfect."

I drew my arms around her neck and held her close until Ruby came by with our lanterns. "Ladies, there will be plenty of time later for hugging. Right now we have a wish to send up." She smiled brightly as she handed us our fragile lamps.

Once every lamp was lit, we released them together, watching the way they filled the afternoon sky, illuminating it against the dark gray of the clouds.

After watching for a while, the crowd began to filter back inside the church and into the hall where the luncheon was being held. Jake kept me in his line of sight the entire time, and I kept him in mine as he made his way through the tangle of people, allowing his aunt and uncle to introduce him to all their friends. My breath caught at one point when I saw him and Ruby talking, and I held it, hoping she wouldn't expose our previous conversations.

"What are you doing?" someone asked from behind me.

Startled, I jumped and turned around. "Dad, you scared me!"

He chuckled softly and folded his arms around me. "Thank you for all of your hard work. You have no idea how much we appreciate it."

"I think I do," I said quietly, planting a kiss on his cheek.

When we stepped back, I noticed him staring at Jake from across the room. "I wasn't expecting to see him here."

I took a deep breath and followed his gaze. "Neither was I."

He was quiet for a moment as he turned back to study me. "What a way to stir things up for you, huh?"

Wait. What? "I'm not sure I know what you mean," I responded, my eyebrows hitching in confusion.

Dad smiled. "I've seen the way you two have been watching each other, and I know how much you cared about him before."

"Daddy," I said, completely embarrassed I'd been caught. "That was a long time ago. We're adults now, *and* I'm engaged."

His gaze flickered back to Jake. "I know. It's just kind of nice how he postponed his trip back to Houston until tomorrow, don't you think? He'd be on the road right now if he hadn't."

I shifted uncomfortably from one foot to the other. "It's very nice." The irony hadn't escaped me. At the first sign of distress, Christopher had made a run right back to Atlanta, while Jake had extended his stay because he thought I needed a friend.

Dad turned and looked back at me, his eyes holding mine. "When you were younger, I always tried to give you advice, tried to help you make the right choices. But you're an adult now, and a mighty fine one at that. And I'm not always going to be around when you need to hear certain things." He stepped forward, his face inching closer to mine. "Just because you make a decision does not mean you can't make another one. Only you know what is best for you. Anyone can come into your life and tell you how much they love you, but it takes someone really special to show how much they care."

A flash of heat rushed across my cheeks. Was he saying what I thought he was saying? My feelings and thoughts twisted into one giant mess. It felt like everyone was giving me advice about Jake, even when I didn't ask for it.

Biting the side of my cheek, I turned and watched Jake, the way he moved through the crowd, the way he stopped and listened when people spoke, the purpose in his stance. Every nerve ending in my body tightened, and for one long moment I could barely breathe.

Feeling the weight of my gaze, Jake turned, his eyes catching mine, and his lips curved into a smile. It was impossible not to stare as he made his way toward me, through the thick crowd gathered at the hall. When he reached my side, my lips parted but no words came out. His grin grew wider.

"It was a very nice service," Jake said, turning to my father. "Maggie would have loved it. Especially the sky lanterns. That was a nice touch."

"That was all Addy's doing," Dad said, motioning toward me. "She put together an amazing celebration."

I looked down momentarily as a blush covered my cheeks. "Ruby helped with a lot of it. After all, she *is* a master party planner. I'm sure she'll expect my first-born," I teased, not knowing what else to say.

When I looked up, both Jake and my father were staring at me. My gaze flickered from one face to the other, then finally at the wall. Well, this wasn't awkward at all.

"I was wondering if I could borrow Addison for the day?" I heard Jake ask. "Unless you have plans for her?"

I swallowed hard and looked back at them. A slow

smile spread across my father's face as his gaze swept toward me. "As far as I know, she's free."

Something deep and warm stirred in Jake's eyes. "What do you say? Would you like to spend the day with me?"

My chest rose sharply as my pulse kicked into high gear. I was just thankful he was even talking to me after last night! "Um . . . Yes, of course."

"Let me just say good-bye to a few people and I'll meet up with you afterward."

Nodding my head, I expelled a long breath and watched as he walked away. A moment later, I felt a soft touch on the side of my arm. Dad's eyes were on me, scrutinizing the expression on my face. "You okay?" he finally asked.

I forced a smile, hoping my lips weren't trembling like my insides were. "I'm good."

A second passed before he spoke again. "Addy," he began softly. "It's better to know and be disappointed than to never know and always wonder. Go. Have fun. Be young." We stared at one another, gray eyes on gray eyes. I didn't know what to say to that. There were no words. "Just make sure you say good-bye to your mother and grandfather first."

My lips twitched slightly. I leaned in and gave him a hug. "I love you, Daddy."

"I love you, baby girl."

Stepping back, I grasped his hands in mine. "I am so lucky you're mine," I said to him, repeating what he'd told me time and time again when I was young.

A smile spread across his face. "I second that."

Grabbing my clutch, I wandered through the crowd saying my good-byes, my thoughts drifting to what had happened the night before, remembering what it felt like to have Jake's lips on my mine. The world seemed to stop spinning. And as wrong as this was, for some reason it felt so right.

Tomorrow we would both be leaving Lakeside and it would be over. But I was determined to enjoy today. Two old friends, hanging out like old times. Well, not *exactly* like old times. And suddenly I couldn't breathe.

But I didn't care.

Chapter Twenty-Eight

The soles of our boots scuffed against the blacktop as we walked, and I could feel the weight of Jake's eyes as he watched me.

"Nice boots," he observed as we made our way through the packed parking lot toward his shiny black truck. His lips curled into a mischievous smirk. "I always did like them. Thought they were pretty damn sexy. I'm surprised you still have them."

I let out a quiet laugh. "I found them buried in the back of my closet the other day. My mama hated them, and I think she still does. You should have seen the look on her face when she saw I was wearing them."

"I can imagine." Jake flashed me his dimple. "I think you look amazing."

"Thank you," I said, a smile tugging at my lips. Somehow I knew he'd be pleased when he saw them, remembering how much he'd liked them before. Not that I had dressed for him or anything. No way.

We were quiet as he opened the passenger door of the truck, letting me slide into the cab first. When he made his way around to the driver's side, he took off his jacket, dress shirt, and tie, laid them in the backseat, then slipped on the cowboy hat I'd seen the day before. His muscles moved smoothly against the restraints of his cotton T-shirt and I turned away, trying not to look. If I didn't know better, I'd swear this was Jake from ten years ago, all hot and tanned and *Texan* in his soft brown Stetson. The way he wore that hat sent my pulse into a tailspin, jarring feelings of desire from so long ago.

"You did a great job today. I mean it," he said softly, looking at me sideways. He eased the truck onto the road and hung a sharp right. "Maggie would have been proud."

Swallowing hard, I looked down and fiddled with the clutch in my lap. "Thank you. And thanks for . . . helping me out earlier." I turned to face him, my throat starting to burn as I drifted back to the moment. "I really made a fool of myself up there."

Jake's eyes were soft as they met mine. "No, you did a fantastic job. Your words were heartfelt and passionate. Your love for her was obvious, everyone could see it. That's nothing to be ashamed of."

Turning away, I stared out the front window, quiet for a long while. "I'm sorry about last night," I finally said. "It was inappropriate. I shouldn't have attacked you like that. I don't know what came over me." Oh, God! Did I seriously just say that? Nice choice of words.

"Attacked me?" he asked with a smirk.

Heat rushed across my cheeks. Really? I had to make myself sound like some sex-crazed lunatic? Even if that was exactly how I felt. "You know what I mean. That should never have happened."

"Come on, it wasn't so bad. Was it?" Jake reached for my hand, our fingers entwining together, and when he spoke again his voice sounded deep and raspy. "Addison, you have nothing to apologize for. Maybe I'm the one who should apologize. I lay awake half the night beating myself up over how the night ended. How *I* made the night end. It's just, seeing you again after all these years, it's so hard to do the right thing. I don't even know what the right thing is, to be honest. I know you're engaged, and I want to respect that *and* you. But at the same time I feel selfish. I still feel a connection to you and I'm fighting hard to stay in control. Stopping what would have happened last night had nothing to do with me not wanting you. You're all I ever wanted." He paused, flexing the muscle in his jaw. "I remember every moment of that summer we were together, and each memory is more powerful than the last. How I felt about you, how I *still* feel about you, it overwhelms me. I never intended to fall in love with you, but I did. And for me, I've only found a love like that once."

Shocked by his confession, I turned to him and our eyes met, and then he looked away. "I'm sorry, Addison. I don't mean to make you uncomfortable."

Make me uncomfortable? Once upon a time those words were all I'd wanted to hear. They consumed my every thought, both waking and sleeping. And now here they were, ten years later, but so much had changed in the meantime. I was no longer that young girl. I was an adult now, and I was engaged. But those facts were blurring quickly.

I shook my head. "You're not making me uncomfortable." I squeezed his hand, encouraging him to look at me. "I know I shouldn't say this, but I feel the same way." I let out an ironic laugh. "My thoughts are so messed up right now, and I don't know how to make sense of them."

Silence fell between us as he took another right turn down a familiar country road. Without having to ask, I knew exactly where we were headed, and I wasn't sure how to feel about it. Neither one of us spoke, caught up in old memories from summers long past. After a couple more turns, I spotted the dirt path we'd driven down many times before, only this time it was concealed by years of overgrown brush. When he veered into it, my breath caught in my throat.

The truck followed the dense undergrowth of the woods until it opened up to Lake Lanier. When he parked near the sand, I hid my clutch in the glove box and we took off our boots and walked to the shore, the cool waves of the water rolling over our toes. I shivered slightly as a sudden breeze swirled around us, drawing our bodies closer together. He was so close, so very close. I tried not to brush against him as we walked along the beach, tried not to notice the familiar scent that danced on his skin, making my heart flutter like it had so many times before.

Jake looked at me, his eyes soft and intimate. "Are you cold?"

I hugged my arms around myself, wondering if it was the breeze from the lake or the way he watched me that sent a shiver along my skin. "It's just a chill. I'll be fine." Looking into the sky, I noticed the gray clouds getting thicker as they loomed overhead.

Jake followed my gaze. "Looks like it wants to rain. Maybe a walk's not such a good idea. Would you like to head back?"

I can end this right now. Stop myself from doing something I might regret. "I don't want to go back." And I meant it. I didn't want this to end. I wanted to stay right where I was, even if it was the last place I should be. And it was. The absolute last place in the world I should be. Not that I was hung up on the past or anything.

"I'll get you my jacket," he said. "Just give me a minute."

Humidity cloaked my skin as I watched Jake head back toward the truck, and my thoughts drifted to places they had no business going. We'd only been together once, so many years before, but it had been the sweetest afternoon of my life. No other time had compared to that first time with Jake. Not with the few guys I'd gotten close to in college, not even with Christopher.

Several moments later Jake was by my side, holding the navy blazer he'd worn earlier at church. He held the jacket up and I turned my back to him, sliding my arms into the long sleeves. The soft cashmere brushed against my bare skin, causing a series of goose bumps to arise. Wrapping it tightly to my body, I closed my eyes and allowed his lingering scent to fill my lungs. It was clean and sharp, like the sunshine and outdoors, and it reminded me of the first time I'd been in his arms. When I swiveled to face him, he smiled and placed his hands on my shoulders, holding me still. "Better?"

All I could do was nod.

As we began to walk again, Jake wrapped his arm around me and pulled me close, and before I could stop myself I leaned into him, resting my head in the crook of his arm. And it felt right, everything felt right. The overcast sky and the sand between our toes. The lake breeze as it spun around us.

With our heads down, we continued along the shore, our footprints leaving deep imprints in the golden sand. "What are you thinking?" Jake finally asked.

Did he really want to know? I took a deep breath and let it out slowly. "I'm thinking about a lot of things." So much had transpired over the past few days. Too many life-changing events swirled inside my head, threatening my common sense.

"Care to elaborate?" The hint of a smile tinged his voice.

God, where do I start? "I'm thinking about Mags. I'm thinking about how I'll never see her again. I'm thinking about Christopher and how he left when I needed him most." I paused for a moment before continuing. "I'm thinking about you, and what would have happened if we'd never broken up. Where we would be right now. If we'd still be together?" We stopped walking and I turned to face him. "Jake, I can't fall in love with you again."

He gave me a weak smile. "I know."

"I'm getting married."

"I know."

"And Christopher's a good man, even if I am disappointed in him at the moment."

He nodded his head. "I hope he is a good man. You deserve a good man. You deserve a *great* man." His fingers grazed my cheek. I closed my eyes and leaned into his hand, my chest suddenly aching.

I looked back at him and stuffed my hands into the deep pockets of his jacket. "Maybe coming to the lake wasn't such a good idea?" I asked, searching the ethereal blue color of his gaze. "It's bringing back too many memories."

"Maybe you're right."

"I probably shouldn't be here right now."

"Probably not." He paused, looking out at the water, the brim of his hat shadowing his face. And then he looked back at me. "Why are you here?"

I shook my head as the air rushed out of my lungs like a deflated balloon. "Because I can't stay away. For some reason . . . I just can't stay away. I don't want to." I drew in a silent breath of willpower, but temptation curled around me like the waves lapping over my ankles.

We stood there, studying each other, drinking one another in, and when thunder clapped somewhere in the distance, I didn't care. I was rooted to that spot as Jake moved in closer and very gently kissed me, the soft brush of his lips against mine. Slowly, our lips moved together becoming familiar with each other again, and after one excruciating moment, he pulled away, his thumb lightly brushing the apple of my cheek, leaving behind a trail of fire.

Searching his eyes, I saw more emotion than I'd ever known before. And when he shifted closer, closing the gap between us, I didn't stop him. His hand snaked around to the back of my head, tangling in my hair, and his heart pressed against mine. I could feel it beating in his chest, just as fast and erratic as my own.

"Addison," he finally whispered, touching his forehead to mine. His hat fell backward behind him onto the sand. "Can I please be selfish?"

My breath caught in my throat, making it difficult to inhale, and I parted my lips, but no words came out. Inching forward, my hands made their way up the curves of his chest, exploring the dense muscles underneath his shirt. I couldn't fight it any longer, I didn't want to fight it. I wanted Jake just as much as I'd wanted him when I was eighteen.

"Yes," I managed to choke out, but I could hardly hear myself against the deafening sound of my pulse.

A warmth slid through my veins and my body tensed as Jake managed to pull me in tighter, with one hand placed firmly on the back of my head, the other wrapped around my waist, the weight of it sending agonizing sensations to my core.

His breath grazed my ear, then across the side of my face as his mouth took its time seeking out my lips. And then he kissed me, slowly at first, but its intensity built with each passing second. The pressure of his lips moving against mine sent a moan through my body that reverberated between us. His tongue swept across the seam of my mouth and I parted my lips, allowing it inside, taunting and teasing me until every nerve ending felt close to combustion.

My hands moved across his strong frame, hungry and desperate, until they twisted in the dark curls at the nape of his neck, and I pressed into him, my body tight to his, frantic for more. I wanted to feel him inside me, moving in unison, the way we'd done once before.

Jake released a long exhale. "Addison . . . You have no idea what you do to me. What you've always done to me."

"I want to be with you," I breathed, my lips close to his, the heat of our breath mingling together.

Suddenly, he stilled and it was then that I realized the clouds had opened up, releasing a whisper of rain. The cool, silky drops caressed my skin, sending a tingle throughout my overheated core. When he looked at me with those blue eyes, those eyes that always seemed to see inside my soul, I felt the gaping hole that had been seared into my heart so many years before begin to fill.

Tormented, I saw his jaw clench, and he closed his eyes briefly. "Are you sure?" he finally asked, his gaze locking with mine.

Sensations raced across my skin as I saw the passion burning in his eyes. "I've never been this sure about anything before," I said, my voice broken by ragged breath.

Thick drops came down now, more insistent than before, but we still stood still, oblivious to the rainfall.

A flash of lightning lit up the sky, and finally we broke eye contact.

"Come on, we better go." Jake reached down to pick up his hat, then placed it on his head. He grabbed my hand as we ran barefoot toward the truck.

I laughed out loud as the rain pelted down, feeling as if I were a teenager again. Tilting my face toward the dark, charcoal sky, I let the drops hit my cheeks, enjoying the way they felt against my fevered skin. I glanced at Jake and he was smiling, too, as rain dripped from the brim of his hat.

When we reached the truck we climbed inside, and I shivered as cold droplets fell from the ends of my hair. Removing my clutch from the glove box, I slid it into the pocket of Jake's jacket, then I leaned back in my seat, feeling more alive than I had in years.

After we buckled our seat belts, Jake followed the narrow dirt path as the rain came down harder, and then he turned left onto the quiet country road. "Where are we going?" I asked, trying to determine what he was thinking. But I didn't have a clue. His expression was set, giving nothing away.

When he turned to me, he lowered his lashes, then finally lifted his eyes to mine. "To my hotel."

Surprise whipped through me and my eyebrows raised. "You're not staying with your aunt and uncle?" I just assumed he was, since that was where he'd stayed before. But *this* . . . This was a pleasant surprise indeed.

Jake shook his head and smiled. "My aunt turned the spare room into Hobby Lobby. There's no place for a bed next to the sewing machine."

Leaning back in my seat, I felt a wave of anticipation pound into me like a tsunami. My body clenched in the most delicious way, realizing I would have Jake all to myself, with no one there to interrupt us. Only two consenting adults alone with their imaginations. And holy hell, was that a good feeling.

My body thrummed impatiently, every molecule vibrating, as I clung to the indecencies filtering through my mind. All ideas of engagements and weddings and fiancés slipped from my thoughts and were replaced by a deep-rooted, decade-old desire. Every inch of him would be mine, at least for tonight, and I knew that even if I tried to fight what was happening, I would surely fail.

Without saying a word, Jake took the rural roads to downtown Lakeside and pulled into a charming inn right across from the town park. He removed his hat and laid it on the front seat of his truck, then we slipped on our boots and made a dash toward the door as rain pummeled the concrete underneath our feet. I clutched the navy blazer against me, trying to shield myself from the storm, desperately aware of Jake's hand on the small of my back.

After we were inside, he reached for me and our fingers twisted together as we moved through the halls, the sexual tension between us increasing with each hurried step.

By the time we made it to his room, I was practically unable to control the urgency I felt. Once inside the dimly lit room, Jake closed the thick mahogany door and we stood still, staring at one another, our hair and clothes dripping wet. But I didn't care. No longer did I feel the chill of the rain against my skin, all I felt was a growing inferno, the flames promising to consume my entire body.

Outside, the unrelenting rain beat against the window, concealing us behind a curtain of moisture. Deliberately slow, I removed the blue blazer, letting it fall in a damp heap to the floor. If Jake leaned in only a couple of inches more, our bodies would connect. Our mouths would come together.

As if reading my mind, he gradually moved forward, erasing the narrow space between us.

"You're so beautiful," he finally murmured, his heavy-lidded eyes never leaving mine. I stepped back until I was flush with the door, my breath catching beneath the longing in his gaze. Jake raised his hands, placing one on either side of me, trapping me against the rich mahogany panels. He lowered his head, the heat of his breath skimming my cheek. "So much more beautiful than I remember. Every time I see you I think I'll be prepared for the way you look, the way you *look* at me, but I never am. Not even close."

Releasing a sigh as his body pressed into mine, I felt my legs threatening to buckle underneath his touch. It felt so good to be in the circle of his arms, my legs captured between the strength of his thighs.

He cupped my face in his hands as his mouth carefully lowered onto mine, the languid strokes of his tongue tasting, tormenting. A coil of tightness began to collect in my stomach. Then his hands progressed lower, slow and methodic, as they traveled down the length of my body while his mouth continued to devour my lips until they felt swollen. When his fingers curled, I felt the veil of my dress skim up past my hips, my stomach, my breasts, until it was over my head, joining the blazer on the floor.

A wisp of cool air swirled around me, tickling my skin, but I quickly dismissed it when his mouth connected with the curve of my shoulder, moving unbearably slow up the stretch of my neck. His hands inched behind me until his fingers found the clasp at my spine and when he released it, my breasts were exposed, my nipples erect under his hungry, sapphire gaze. He enclosed them in his hands and then bent his head, gently taking the sensitive left peak into his mouth. I released a long sigh as my head rolled back, and I was immune to everything but the feathery touch of his tongue as it massaged my skin.

His hips pressed into mine and the fingers of his left hand teased my right breast while his teeth gently closed around my nipple, nibbling and pulling, bringing me to the brink. But before I could succumb, his mouth moved again, making a fiery trail to my right breast where he spent a good amount of time driving me insane.

When he dropped to his knees, I gasped out loud at the feel of his warm breath along the outside of my panties, lingering dangerously close to my core. He reached behind, cupping my cheeks, and he very slowly, very gently buried his mouth in the silky material of my undergarment. And just when I thought I might explode, I felt his fingers graze lower, along the smooth muscles of my hamstrings, until they reached the tops of my boots. Expertly, he slipped them off, one at a time, his hands returning to my backside.

Clutching the back of his head, my fingers spread through his dark hair as his tongue followed the thin seam of fabric along my bikini line. Leaning back, I pressed my head into the door, squeezing my eyes shut as the slow torture continued. After a while, his fingers slipped into the sides of my panties and, oh Lord, the slow drag of lace across my thighs made my stomach clench with expectancy. When the tiny piece of clothing joined the pile already on the floor, I inhaled sharply. His mouth closed around my body like it never had before.

A low growl rumbled from deep inside his chest, causing my breath to race out in quick, shaky gasps. My legs trembled with pleasure as his tongue slowly explored intimate curves, and it was all I could do not to cry out. Tossing an arm over my head, I pressed my lips into the soft muscle of my bicep, hoping the pressure would keep my mouth closed.

Thoughts of how amazing he felt, how I needed to feel him inside me, swarmed my senses. Jake and I against the wall, on the floor, in the bed . . . I wanted him in all those places and more. Nothing mattered but the two of us, and this moment that was so perfect I knew it would be seared into my brain forever. He knew where to stroke lightly and where to apply pressure, and it wasn't long before I felt my insides tighten, then release into a fit of endless spasms.

A rush of molten lava traveled through my limbs, heavy and magnetic, and my pulse began to slow to a half-normal rate. His lips grazed my stomach, the divide between my breasts, and finally brushed against my mouth, warm and gentle. My body felt like putty as he lifted me up, carrying me to the turned-down sheets of his bed.

Very gently, he set me down and I knelt before him, reaching for the hem of his shirt, quickly moving the fabric up and over his head. Wrapping my arms around his neck, we kissed again, and I let out an involuntary breath as his tongue slid against mine. And then he stepped back, away from my grasp, and began to remove the rest of his clothing. The air in my lungs hitched as I soaked in the sight of him. Jake's body was perfect, more perfect than before. Smooth, tight skin stretching over lean, defined muscles. He was flawless, in a way that mythical gods were supposed to be. There was Apollo, Ares, Zeus, and Jake.

The bed dipped under his weight, and he pressed his forehead to mine. "Do you have any idea how I feel about you?" he whispered. The heat of his breath brushed against my lips.

Turning him into the bed, I straddled his hips, our mouths never once leaving each other. Leisurely, I moved lower, letting my tongue glide across his skin, the sharp angle of his jaw, down his neck until finally I lingered on the defined arcs of his chest. As my hands slid against his ribs, the sounds of his breath became ragged and broken. I moved lower, lower, until my mouth closed around him, tasting him the way he'd tasted me.

A moan escaped from his throat and his hands tangled in my hair and never in my life had I ever felt so *aware*, aware of myself, of the man I was with. When our lips met again so did our bodies and we moved together, deeply, precisely, tangling in the sheets, as if we'd known each other our whole lives. And it was even more perfect than the first time, better than all the times rolled into one. The thunder growled outside as our bodies released, our skin damp with sweat. For a long while I lay against his shoulder, our fingers entwined, talking and laughing, and after one more round, we both fell asleep.

A familiar noise woke me up. First I heard it in my sleep, far away like a dream, until its persistent ring broke through the darkness. I sat up in bed, clutching the sheets to my chest. A feeling of unease curled in my stomach when I realized it was my cell phone. I held my breath until the ringing stopped, but after my sigh of relief it started again.

With the thin sheet wrapped around me, I made my way to where Jake's blazer was lying on the floor. I picked it up and pulled my clutch from the pocket, then set the jacket down on the bed. My fingers were shaking as they maneuvered around the zipper, easing it open to reveal my phone. I removed it from the satin confines and looked at the display screen.

Christopher.

My heart rate kicked up a notch as I stared at his name, willing it to go away.

"You'd better get that."

Startled, I glanced at him. Jake was sitting up in bed, his dark hair messy with sleep and sex. My breath exhaled sharply and I looked back at my cell. I closed my eyes as I accepted the call.

"Hello? Addy?"

When my eyes fluttered back open, my gaze locked with Jake's. A thick layer of guilt swept over me, threatening to steal the air from my lungs. "Hello." A prickle of panic raced along my veins.

"I've been trying to get a hold of you. Are you all right?"

He'd been trying to get a hold of me? How many times had he called? "I'm sorry," I said, thinking fast. "I guess I had the ringer turned off."

He sounded relieved. "I'm glad that's all it was. I was starting to get worried. It's not like you to not return phone calls. How did the funeral go? Did your family get the flower arrangement I sent? I was hoping it would arrive in time, but I was late ordering it."

The flower arrangement? What flower arrangement? I had no clue. "Yes, we did get it. It was beautiful," I lied. "Thank you, Christopher." At the mention of his name, I looked back at Jake. He was watching me closely with dark eyes, the corner of his lips turned down.

"On the bright side, Mrs. Davenport is doing better. A *lot* better. I thought we might lose her there for a little while." He paused, waiting for me to respond, but

I couldn't. "Anyway, I'll be there in the morning to pick you up. I hope you don't mind. There's a staff meeting in the afternoon I'd like to get back for. Will you be ready?"

I had almost forgotten he was picking me up. "Actually, that won't be necessary," I said slowly. "I'm driving home with Ruby."

Christopher missed a beat. "You don't want me to pick you up? Is everything all right?"

"No, everything's not all right." I took a deep breath. "Christopher, we need to talk."

My words were met by a moment of uncomfortable silence. "We need to talk, yet you don't want me to come get you? Addy, that doesn't make any sense. If I pick you up we can talk on the way home. I'll be there at seven."

"I said no. I don't want you to come." My lashes lowered with guilt. "I'll call you when I get back into Atlanta." I ended the call, not waiting for a response. I couldn't look at Jake. Not yet. My eyes flickered to the bedside clock. Ten o'clock? Where had the time gone?

"Do you have to leave?" Jake asked after a minute, the sound of regret thick in his voice.

Our eyes met for a brief moment before I turned away. "I probably should."

Quietly we dressed. The air in the room seemed to have been sucked out and replaced with a thick, dense smog. My movements felt slow and heavy as if they were weighted down. And I suppose they were. Weighted down with guilt, confusion, and regret.

"I'm sorry," I said finally, standing in front of Jake. We stared at each for a long moment before he responded.

"I understand. This isn't your fault."

I let out a bitter laugh. "Just like ten years ago when you said it wasn't my fault? Even though it was?"

"That was different." He sighed. "We were kids then and you were scared."

My heart thumped wildly, beating against the walls of my chest. "I'm scared now."

Jake stepped toward me and then stopped himself. "I'm the one who should be sorry. I shouldn't have let it get this far. I knew better. I knew you were engaged, yet I still allowed it to happen. It was selfish of me."

"We both knew better." I looked away, not wanting to see the pain in his eyes. "I guess history does have a way of repeating itself." Suddenly, a small box caught my eye. It was lying at the foot of the bed, underneath his jacket. Reaching down, I grasped the soft burgundy velvet. "Is it yours?" I asked, thankful for the distraction. "I think it fell out of your jacket."

Jake shook his head and sat down on the bed. "It's not mine. It's yours."

I crinkled my eyebrows. Mine? I knew it wasn't mine. I'd never seen it before in my life.

"Go ahead," he said. "Open it."

Swallowing hard, I lifted the hinged top and my breath caught in my throat. I glanced back at Jake and studied him carefully, trying to make sense of the unexpected surprise.

"That afternoon we spent together at my aunt and uncle's house . . . right after the Strawberry Festival, when we shared the bottle of wine," he explained in a soft voice. I knew what he was getting at. "Afterward, I went back to the fair and walked around for a while, trying to clear my head. I knew I was in trouble. I hadn't meant to fall in love with you, that wasn't part of the plan, but I couldn't help myself. It was unavoidable. It was fate . . ." His voice trailed off, thick with emotion.

I sat down next to him. "Jake—I'm so sorry, I—"

"It's okay, Addison. Please, you don't have to apologize again," he interrupted, holding up his hand. "I've already told you I understand why you did what you did. I get it," he offered gently, nodding. "Anyway, I found this and it made me think of you. I wanted you to remember our summer together and how much fun we had, regardless of how it would all end. I wanted to give you something to prove I really did love you."

Tears pooled in my eyes as I looked back at the velvet box. I couldn't believe it. It was hands down the most thoughtful gift I had ever received. I swallowed back a sob and tried to regain my composure. "I don't know what to say," I whispered, not trusting the sound of my voice. My eyes met his. "Why didn't you give it to me?"

"I didn't have the chance. The next time we were together, you broke things off. It didn't seem like the appropriate thing to do."

"Kind of like what's happening now?"

"No, this time I want you to have it. It was always meant for you, no matter how things turned out."

"But, Jake—are you sure?" I asked, trying to read his expression.

Jake reached over and gently took the box from my hands. "Turn around."

Without another word, I turned my back toward him, lifting my hair. He fastened the delicate silver chain around my neck. I swiveled back to face him, my heart breaking. "Thank you." I reached over and gave him a tight hug, barely able to believe the romantic gesture. After he released me I looked down, carefully lifting the small strawberry charm. "Jake, it's perfect. But why did you bring it with you now? How did you know?"

He gave me a small smile. "I didn't know, but I brought it anyway, just in case. It was always meant for you. It never belonged to me." Jake's gaze latched onto mine, a thick veil of emotion in his eyes. "I've always loved you. I never stopped."

A giant, uncomfortable lump formed in my throat, making it impossible to swallow. "I love you, too. I really do. I've never met anyone like you before. And under different circumstances—" Christopher's face danced in front of me as if he were there.

"Shhh, I know." He enveloped me in his arms as tears spilled down my cheeks in long, hot trails. "It's just not our time. Maybe our time was that summer, and that's all it was meant to be."

I nodded against his chest, not knowing what to believe. If our time was only meant to be that summer, why did I feel so sad? His hand moved through my hair in long, comforting strokes, soothing me until my tears subsided.

"I will always love you, Addison, no matter what. And I don't blame you for anything. No matter where life takes us, I will always remember you and what we had together." Very gently, Jake planted a kiss on my forehead, one on the tip of my nose, and then finally on my mouth, his lips brushing against mine carefully. "Come on. Let's get you home."

Epilogue

"Hey, Addy—are you all right?" Ruby asked, bringing me back to the wedding boutique.

I took a deep breath. "I'm fine." Shaking my head, I tried to clear away the attack of emotions. I glanced around the shop, hoping no one was watching me make a fool of myself.

She hung up the trumpet silhouette she'd been admiring and turned to face me. "It's not every day a girl gets married. Believe me, I know how stressful it can be," she said with a sympathetic smile. "But you're happy, right?" Ruby's gaze latched onto mine and her serious tone caught me off guard.

I gave her a smile and nodded, not trusting myself to speak just yet. I took another deep breath, biding my time. "You of all people should know how happy I am," I reminded her. "I'm getting married to the man I'm meant to be with. I've never been this happy in my life."

Ruby's eyes misted over. "Then why do you look so unsure?"

I shrugged my shoulders, my thoughts slipping back into the past. "I was just thinking about life and everything that's happened up until this point." I tried to explain. "You know, it's funny. No matter how carefully we plan our lives, there always seems to be a fork in the road—"

"Throwing everything off course," she offered, softly finishing my sentence. Ruby smiled and enveloped me in a tight hug.

She knew exactly what I meant.

When we pulled away, she gave me another smile before holding up a different dress for inspection. I shook my head. Turning back toward the wedding gowns, I began leafing through them, memories of Jake and the past still clouding my thoughts.

My eyes scanned the row of wedding gowns, finally resting on one dress in particular. Bringing my hand up to it, I let my fingers trail along the beaded bodice, appreciating its simple elegance. With its feminine, off-the-shoulder neckline and stunning Chantilly lace detail, it had a glamorous vintage feel to it I simply could not resist. I had to remind myself to breathe. Gingerly, I lifted it from its place and held it up for Ruby to see.

"Oh, Addy!" she gasped, bringing her fingers to her mouth. "It's perfect." Embracing me once more, Ruby whispered, "Mags would be so happy."

My voice caught in my throat. I knew she was right.

When she stepped back, her eyes glistened with fresh tears. "*I'm* so happy. But I still can't believe you live so far away." Ruby forced a chuckle, trying to keep herself from crying again. "You're a terrible friend, you know that?"

I smiled and reached out to touch her arm. "I miss you, too. But I promise we'll see each other as often as we can."

Ruby nodded and turned away, dabbing discreetly at

her eyes. They say the first trimester of pregnancy can make the mother-to-be very emotional, but Ruby wore it well.

I looked down at the beautiful garment lying in my arms and slowly walked over to the full-length mirror positioned in the center of the boutique. My breath caught as I held the wedding dress up against myself in the reflection. It was as if it had been made for me. Just like Jake.

The next several months were a blur of preparations and excitement, counting down the days until I would marry the man of my dreams. Much to Ruby's dismay, Jake and I decided on a ceremony less elaborate than what she'd had in mind, something that fit us both perfectly. We would be married in Lakeside, a sunset wedding on my grandparents' farm where we'd first met. Our families were elated, and somehow I knew Mags was, too. Come hell or high water, she would be present—if only in spirit.

And she was there, I felt her all around us as my father walked me down the makeshift aisle sprinkled with rose petals. Layers of satin followed behind me as I made my way toward the altar positioned near the edge of the pond.

Mom eyed the red leather boots peeking out from under my dress and shook her head, but her smile told me she accepted my decision. What other shoes could I possibly wear? And Jake had never looked so handsome and happy as he did in his tailored black tux, his dark hair tumbling seductively over his forehead.

Before our loved ones, we promised to cherish each other until death did us part. Then with God as our witness, we sealed our vows with a kiss. I looked into the crowd of beloved faces and knew that moment would be one of the happiest and most memorable of my entire life.

As the fireflies fluttered around us, lighting up the night with their beacons of light, Jake and I shared our first dance as husband and wife. But it was him, Jake, who made the moment so amazing, more amazing than anything I had ever dreamed possible. He was what I had been searching for my entire life. Our connection was unbreakable, and no matter what happened in the future I knew he would always be by my side. Finally, he was mine and I was his, the way it was always meant to be.

An endless sea of stars made their way across the darkened sky as a string quartet carried on throughout the evening, playing one beautiful note after the next.

My parents danced together arm in arm, the happiness on their faces unlike anything I had ever witnessed before. And even Gramps was having fun, smiling and laughing with his friends and family gathered around him. I knew he missed Mags more than anything in the world, but he had learned to live again. He really was the strong, capable man my grandmother always said he was.

"Addy, someone wants to say good night." Jake and I turned to the tiny, sweet face nestled in Ruby's arms, and I felt my heart swell. "We couldn't say good-bye without visiting Mya's godparents first. She'd never let us live it down." I looked into my best friend's eyes, the joy of motherhood shining brightly within them.

I gathered the delicate bundle and cradled her in my grasp, admiring the porcelain hue of her skin and pucker of her tiny rosebud lips. "She's too young to play the guilt card." I giggled softly and kissed the top of my god-daughter's silky blond head, her intoxicating fragrance causing my stomach to stir.

Ruby beamed proudly. "Five weeks old today."

"But you should hear her once she gets going," Tommy Matthews exclaimed, never once taking his eyes off his wife and new baby girl. "My prediction is she'll be giving Ruby a run for her money before too long."

Playfully, Ruby nudged him with her elbow before turning back to me. "Next will be your turn, Addy. You need to make me a godmother. And Mya needs a best friend."

I felt Jake's arm tighten around my waist. Tilting my head up, I caught his gaze and held it, our happy secret bubbling up inside me. It had only been two weeks since the pregnancy test read positive, and we still couldn't believe it. The news hadn't been expected, but we both agreed it was the most wonderful wedding present we would ever receive.

Jake smiled, the dimple in his cheek peeking out. "All in due time." He dragged his eyes away from mine and looked at our friends. "But don't worry. You two will be the first to find out."

"We better be." Ruby gathered the sleeping baby in her arms and handed her over to Tommy, then tucked a soft pink blanket around her. "It's bad enough you lured my best friend to Texas. You can't take that away from me, too." She laughed and threw him a wink.

"I have to say, this is one of the nicest weddings I've ever been to." Tommy adjusted Mya in his arms and looked around in appreciation. "I can't believe the transformation of the farm. It's really amazing."

With narrowed eyes, Ruby looked around with appreciation at the clusters of candles and fireflies as they blinked all around us. "Not exactly what I had in mind, but I have to admit . . . it's perfect. Just like you two." She grinned, the glow from the flames reflecting in her eyes.

"I love you both so much. You know that, right? And I'm so happy you're finally together. It's been such a long time coming."

"Too long." Jake pulled me closer and planted a kiss on my forehead.

"Thank you, Ruby." In a rush of emotion I collected my best friend in my arms. "For everything. For helping me with the wedding, for always being there for me. I love you." Tears pressed against the backs of my eyes and I struggled to keep them from escaping. "You're more than my friend, you're my sister."

I felt Ruby's grip tighten around me, folding me in. Tendrils of pale blond locks tickled my cheek as she held me close. "I love you, too, Addy." After a long moment, she stepped back and pressed her hand to my cheek. "My sister."

Placing my hand over hers, I gave it a squeeze. After Mags's funeral I'd stayed with Ruby for a few weeks, trying to make sense of what I wanted when I realized I already knew. Seeing Jake again after all those years woke me up. It made me feel alive in a way I hadn't in a very long time. And when we were apart, it hurt. Being without him just wasn't right. It wasn't *natural*. And there was no denying it anymore.

Breaking things off with Christopher had been very difficult, but I'd had no choice. I was in love with Jake, and was not about to lose him again. I had learned my lesson the hard way.

And Christopher deserved more than what I could give him. He deserved a wife who would love him, understand him, and support a doctor's lifestyle.

I took a leave of absence from work and, putting my ego aside, located Jake's address—courtesy of Google—and packed an overnight bag, certain Jake would turn me away. Then I gathered my courage and made the twelve-hour drive to Houston, like some dreamy, lovesick teenager.

A million years had passed in the few weeks since I'd seen him last. Fear consumed me, tempting me to turn around as I pulled up to his ranch, but the welcome mat in front of the door beckoned me to stay.

With my heart in my stomach, I knocked on the door. As the seconds ticked by, doubts flooded my mind. Would he be able to forgive me for leaving him again? My eyes scanned the modest farm surrounding the house. Horses galloped in the pasture and a small pond decorated with lush weeping willows sat at the far end. It was as perfect as I imagined. I could practically see Jake hard at work in the field, his cowboy hat shielding his handsome face from the sun.

Maybe this was a bad idea? Uncertainty got the better of me and I began to walk away, the thought of rejection too much to bear. I descended the steps and started toward my car.

"Addison?"

I stopped. Pulse racing, I turned to face him. His sapphire gaze was kinder than it had any right to be, and the sting of tears pooled in my eyes. "Jake, I'm so sorry. I know I have no right to be here, to ask for your forgive—"

He took the steps two by two and swallowed me in a hug, not allowing me to continue. "Don't apologize. You're here now, and that's all that matters." Without another word, he offered me his hand and invited me inside. The passion and intensity between us was stronger than ever and we spent the next two weeks in his bed—in *our* bed—before I finally made my way back to Georgia to gather my belongings.

Amidst words of congratulations, I snuggled into the

crook of my new husband's arm as we said good-bye to our guests, who were just starting to trickle back to their cars. Lacing his fingers through mine, Jake traced the silhouette of my wedding band. "I can't believe the day is already over. It's been a wild ride."

Laughing softly, I looked into the dwindling crowd. "You're not having second thoughts already, are you?"

Jake shook his head. "Second thoughts? Not on your life. There's only one thought going through my mind right now." He dipped his head closer, his breath warm against my ear.

"Yes?" I looked up at him, his eyes holding me captive. The expression on his face nearly took my breath away. "What is it?"

He touched his forehead to mine. "How lucky I am that you're mine. You—and our baby," he whispered. Discreetly, he placed his hand on my stomach, and I felt my heart flip-flop.

A satisfying wave of tingles rushed through me as I sank into his warmth. The ring on my finger caught my eye. I looked down and smiled as it shined up at me, brilliant against the light of the stars. "You know, it's funny," I said, glancing up from the halo of diamonds. "For a while there I stopped believing in fate."

A lazy smile stretched across his face. "And now?"

I reached over and grasped his hand in mine. "And now I know that when two people are meant to be together, they will always find their way back to one another, no matter how far apart they might be."

My heart surged with happiness and I could almost hear Mags's voice whispering in my ear. *"Life is funny that way, Addy. The road to happiness isn't always straight and narrow. Sometimes there are bumps along the way that throw you off track. But one thing is certain. Fate is*

stronger than we are, and in the end things always have
a way of working out."

After we said good-bye to our family and friends, Jake scooped me up in his arms and carried me to his truck. He opened the passenger door so I could slide inside, then helped pile my dress in around me. Sitting in the center of the front seat was his cowboy hat, the one I had grown so used to seeing him wear. Reaching for it, I placed it on top of his head. His dark waves poked out from underneath the rim and I felt my breath catch, my thoughts racing back to the first time I had seen him, pulling up in that old pickup toward my grandparents' farm.

"Are you all right?" he asked, stepping forward so his face was inches from mine.

I nodded. "I'm fine. I just can't help but think about how long it took us to get here. How much time we wasted being apart."

Jake stepped even closer and gently brushed his lips to mine. "Life started the day you stepped onto my porch." The whisper of his words tickled my mouth. "Whatever happened before that doesn't matter. It's all about the present and the future. No looking back."

My heart spilling over, I leaned in and kissed him again, letting my fingers slide through the waves of his hair. When we separated, I swallowed the lump of emotion that was stuck in my throat.

"I love you, Mrs. Grady." Jake's blue eyes pierced through mine as he stroked my cheek with the back of his fingers. "Thank you for being my wife."

I counted my blessings and smiled through the tears. "I love you, too, Mr. Grady. Thank you for waiting for me." Before my emotions and hormones got the best of me,

I pulled at the lapels of his jacket. "Come on, husband. Let's get outta here."

"I thought you'd never ask." Jake kissed my forehead before hopping into the truck.

Leaning back in my seat, I smiled as he slid in beside me, squeezing my hand before pulling away . . . the boy I'd fallen in love with the first time we met and the man I had waited my entire life to find. The wedding aisle that brought us together was unlike the long, winding road we had traveled to get there. But in the end it brought us here, to this very moment.

And that is everything.

Books by Bestselling Author
Fern Michaels

___The Jury	0-8217-7878-1	$6.99US/$9.99CAN
___Sweet Revenge	0-8217-7879-X	$6.99US/$9.99CAN
___Lethal Justice	0-8217-7880-3	$6.99US/$9.99CAN
___Free Fall	0-8217-7881-1	$6.99US/$9.99CAN
___Fool Me Once	0-8217-8071-9	$7.99US/$10.99CAN
___Vegas Rich	0-8217-8112-X	$7.99US/$10.99CAN
___Hide and Seek	1-4201-0184-6	$6.99US/$9.99CAN
___Hokus Pokus	1-4201-0185-4	$6.99US/$9.99CAN
___Fast Track	1-4201-0186-2	$6.99US/$9.99CAN
___Collateral Damage	1-4201-0187-0	$6.99US/$9.99CAN
___Final Justice	1-4201-0188-9	$6.99US/$9.99CAN
___Up Close and Personal	0-8217-7956-7	$7.99US/$9.99CAN
___Under the Radar	1-4201-0683-X	$6.99US/$9.99CAN
___Razor Sharp	1-4201-0684-8	$7.99US/$10.99CAN
___Yesterday	1-4201-1494-8	$5.99US/$6.99CAN
___Vanishing Act	1-4201-0685-6	$7.99US/$10.99CAN
___Sara's Song	1-4201-1493-X	$5.99US/$6.99CAN
___Deadly Deals	1-4201-0686-4	$7.99US/$10.99CAN
___Game Over	1-4201-0687-2	$7.99US/$10.99CAN
___Sins of Omission	1-4201-1153-1	$7.99US/$10.99CAN
___Sins of the Flesh	1-4201-1154-X	$7.99US/$10.99CAN
___Cross Roads	1-4201-1192-2	$7.99US/$10.99CAN

Available Wherever Books Are Sold!
Check out our website at www.kensingtonbooks.com